Arming the Future:
A Defense Industry
for the
21st Century

ANN R. MARKUSEN AND SEAN S. COSTIGAN
Editors

COUNCIL ON FOREIGN RELATIONS PRESS
NEW YORK

The Council on Foreign Relations, Inc., a nonprofit, nonpartisan national membership organization founded in 1921, is dedicated to promoting understanding of international affairs through the free and civil exchange of ideas. The Council's members are dedicated to the belief that America's peace and prosperity are firmly linked to that of the world. From this flows the mission of the Council: to foster America's understanding of its fellow members of the international community, near and far, their peoples, cultures, histories, hopes, quarrels, and ambitions; and thus to serve, protect, and advance America's own global interests through study and debate, private and public.

From time to time books, monographs, and reports written by members of the Council's research staff or others are published as a "Council on Foreign Relations Book." Any work bearing that designation is, in the judgment of the Committee on Studies of the Council's Board of Directors, a responsible treatment of a significant international topic.

Council on Foreign Relations Books are distributed by Brookings Institution Press (1-800-275-1447). For further information on Council publications, please write the Council on Foreign Relations, 58 East 68th Street, New York, NY 10021, or call the Director of Communications at (212) 434-9400. Or visit our website at www.foreignrelations.org.

Library of Congress Cataloging-in-Publication Data

Arming the Future / edited by Ann S. Markusen and Sean S. Costigan
    p.   cm.
Includes bibliographical references and index.
ISBN 0-87609-246-6

Contents

Tables and Figures   v

Foreword   ix

Preface   xi

Acknowledgments   xiii

Part I. Introduction

1. The Military Industrial Challenge   3
   Ann R. Markusen and Sean S. Costigan

Part II. Transformation in the Post–Cold War Decade

2. Contending Security Doctrines and the Military
   Industrial Base   37
   Greg Bischak

3. Cashing In, Cashing Out, and Converting: Restructuring
   of the Defense Industrial Base in the 1990s   74
   Michael Oden

4. The History and Politics of the Pentagon's Dual-Use Strategy   106
   Jay Stowsky

5. Redefining National Defense: The Challenge of Cold War
   Politics and Economics on Capitol Hill   158
   Paul F. Walker

Part III. The Consequences of Defense
Industry Consolidation

6. Private Arsenals: America's Post–Cold War Burden   191
   Harvey M. Sapolsky and Eugene Gholz

7. Defense Mergers: Weapons Cost, Innovation, and
   International Arms Industry Cooperation   207
   Erik Pages

8. Redesigning the Defense Industrial Base   224
   Kenneth Flamm

Part IV. The Push to Export

9. The Changing Economics of the Arms Trade   249
   David Gold

10. Dual-Use Technology: Back to the Future?   269
    Judith Reppy

11. A Framework for Limiting the Negative Consequences of
    Surplus U.S. Arms Production and Trading   285
    Lora Lumpe

Part V. Defense Industry Globalization

12. Globalization in the Post–Cold War Defense Industry:
    Challenges and Opportunities   305
    Richard A. Bitzinger

13. Which Way to Turn? The European Defense Industry
    After the Cold War   334
    John Lovering

14. The Changing Civil-Military Production Mix in Western
    Europe's Defense Industry   371
    Michael Brzoska, Peter Wilke, and Herbert Wulf

Part VI. An Industry for the Future

15. Policy Choices in Arming the Future   409
    Ann R. Markusen and Sean S. Costigan

Contributors   425

Index   431

Tables and Figures

Chapter 1

Table 1.1   Major Defense Contractors by Nation,
             Sales 1995

Table 1.2   Arms Exports: Britain, France, United States,
             1989–96

Table 1.3   Military Expenditures: 1985, 1990, 1994

Table 1.4   Defense Employment Reduction

Table 1.5   Defense-Related Employment: 1987–99

Figure 1.1   U.S. Defense Mergers in the 1990s

Figure 1.2   Military Procurement: Pay, 1970 to 2000

Chapter 2

Table 2.1   Comparison of Alternative Military Force Structure
             and Spending Plans

Table 2.2   Prime Contract Awards

Table 2.3   Selected Weapons Procurement by Sector

Chapter 3

Table 3.1   Merger and Acquisition Activity in the
             Defense Industry, 1989–96

Table 3.2   Twenty-Five Top Defense Contractors: Sales,
             Employment, Defense Dependence, 1989–94

Table 3.3   Major Markets for Diversification

Table 3.4   Performance Measures of Consolidating and
             Diversifying Firms

Table 3.5   Sales and Employment Changes in
             Consolidating and Diversifying Firms

—v—

Table 3.6   Performance Measures of 41 Small and
                   Medium-Sized Defense-Related Companies

Chapter 6

Table 6.1   Defense Drawdowns, Gross Domestic
                   Product, and Constant 1996 $U.S.

Table 6.2   U.S. Defense Employment by Sector

Chapter 7

Figure 7.1   The Consolidation of U.S. Military Aircraft
                   Manufacturers, 1945–96

Figure 7.2   Total Value of Recent U.S. Aerospace
                   Mergers and Acquisitions, 1989–97

Chapter 8

Table 8.1   Prime Contractors in the Tactical Missile
                   Industrial Base

Table 8.2   Major Subcontractors in the Tactical Missile
                   Industrial Base, 1993

Figure 8.1   Distribution of NATO Procurement, 1994

Figure 8.2   Distribution of NATO R&D, 1994

Chapter 9

Table 9.1   Major Changes in the Arms Trade, 1985–90 to
                   1991–95

Figure 9.1   Arms Exports as a Share of Military
                   Spending, Worldwide Totals, 1987–95

Chapter 11

Table 11.1   Value of Worldwide Arms Shipments, 1991–96

Table 11.2   Arms Flow to Greece and Turkey, 1992–95

Chapter 12

Table 12.1   The Globalization of Arms Production: A Typology

Table 12.2　　　Recent Major U.S. Arms Sales Involving
　　　　　　　　Coproduction Offsets

Figure 12.1　　International Arms Cooperation, 1961–95

Figure 12.2　　International Arms Cooperation with the
　　　　　　　　Developing World, 1961–95

Figure 12.3　　Defense Industry Joint Venture Companies, 1986–95:
　　　　　　　　Transatlantic vs. Intra-European

Figure 12.4　　Defense Industry M&As, 1986–95:
　　　　　　　　Transatlantic vs. Intra-European

Figure 12.5　　Transatlantic vs. Intra-European Arms
　　　　　　　　Cooperation, 1961–95

Chapter 13

Table 13.1　　Defense Spending in Europe, 1995

Table 13.2　　Trends in Defense Spending in Western Europe

Table 13.3　　Changes in Defense Spending, 1985–94

Table 13.4　　Changes in Total Defense Spending and Major
　　　　　　　Weapons Purchase, United States and Europe

Table 13.5　　Employment in the European Defense
　　　　　　　Industry

Table 13.6　　European Arms Imports as Percent of Total Defense
　　　　　　　Spending

Table 13.7　　European Defense Companies Ranked by Value of
　　　　　　　Defense Sales, 1993

Table 13.8　　Collaborative Defense Projects Involving the United
　　　　　　　Kingdom

Chapter 14

Table 14.1　　Expenditures on Procurement of Heavy Equipment

Table 14.2　　Exports of Newly Produced Major Weapons

Table 14.3　　Employment in Arms Production in West
　　　　　　　European Countries

Table 14.4　　Performance of West European
　　　　　　　Arms-Producing Companies

Table A14.1   Performance of European Arms Producers:
                The "Expanders"

Table A14.2   Performance of European Arms Producers:
                The "Converters"

Table A14.3   Performance of European Arms Producers:
                The "Downsizers"

Table A14.4   Performance of European Arms Producers:
                The "Terminators"

Foreword

THE VICTORY of the United States and its allies in the Cold War was also a triumph for the American defense industry. Its designs, weapons, platforms, and guidance systems outperformed those of its adversaries. Buyers worldwide have acknowledged the quality of American weapons: In the decade since the collapse of the Berlin Wall, the U.S. share of world arms exports rose from 30 percent to 45 percent.

Yet the end of the superpower rivalry presents a number of questions and challenges for the defense industry and its Pentagon overseers. Although defense spending has fallen in real terms, have Americans reaped the full "peace dividend" that was promised to them? Can the U.S. defense industry preserve its technological lead in an era of budget constraints and corporate restructuring? Should Washington liberalize arms exports as a way of maintaining the viability of military industrial firms? Would transnational mergers help reduce excess capacity? What defense industry restructuring decisions are likely to enhance (or hinder) U.S. competitiveness in the nonmilitary arena? More broadly, as the threats to international stability are vague and evolving, what level of international arms expenditure will best sustain a secure peace in the international system?

Ann Markusen and Sean Costigan have assembled expert authors to explain why the 1990s have been a watershed for the arms trade and offer prescriptions for achieving a rational and efficient U.S. defense industry. Almost universally, the authors favor a more competitive and diversified, dual-use industry. But they do not make the mistake of treating this business like any other: They make the case for strong conventional arms export controls and for cooperation with U.S. allies on issues of military industrial restructuring and security arrangements.

Policymakers cannot afford to stand idle as the defense industry and market forces determine global supply and demand for the instruments of warfare. This book has already helped to hone Pentagon policy and should considerably sharpen the debate over the future defense industrial base.

Lawrence J. Korb
Maurice R. Greenberg Chair, Director of Studies
Council on Foreign Relations

Preface

A FUNNY thing happened to me one day. After years of being an interested but relatively passive participant in the activities at the Council on Foreign Relations, I was asked to chair a study group on defense demobilization and its implications for the U.S. economy and world arms trade. I responded to the invitation by proclaiming my relative ignorance on the subject and was advised by Les Gelb that that was an immense virtue, since I was likely to pay attention to the discourse. I signed on.

Let me state what the study group was not about. There was no breast-beating about why we hadn't demobilized it sooner or why we don't do it faster. There was no attempt to suggest that we had committed some moral lapse by not transferring the money saved in the defense budget to compelling domestic needs. There was no effort to second-guess the Pentagon as to what the state of military preparedness should be in the years ahead.

There was instead a fascinating dialogue among a group of highly informed and intelligent people stretched out over two years. It was led by an extraordinarily able scholar, Ann Markusen, who has an encyclopedic knowledge of the subject matter and an open mind regarding solutions to tough questions about conflicting public imperatives in this field.

The guts of this monthly dialogue was a series of papers prepared by scholars on various of these public policy conundrums. Although the study group was not charged with reaching a consensus on future policy, it became clear that the issues tackled in these discussions were of critical importance to the safety of the world and the economy of the United States. Because these matters are rarely the subject of reporting in the daily press and don't have the visual characteristics (such as shuttered military bases) that might make for good television, it has to be difficult for an otherwise informed citizenry to understand the major issues that we dealt with in our study group.

Hundreds of thousands of jobs were eliminated as a result of cutbacks in defense expenditure. What were the effects on unemployment? What kind of effort was made to retrain or provide alternative employment opportunities for those involved?

How does the United States maintain its superiority in military technology as research and development expenditures are reduced and the number of contractors with the capacity to develop and build the necessary hardware has shrunk? What are the implications for the proliferation of dangerous weapons around the world given that rapidly declining military spending puts enormous pressure on manufacturers and their employees in this country to sell more sophisticated weaponry abroad?

This is not an exclusive list but merely an indication of the gravity of the issues with which the task force contended. This book makes these data and analyses available to the general reader. This is done with a seriousness of purpose and a sincere hope that we will be prepared for all the consequences of our demobilization process, not just the ones we have intended.

Richard Ravitch
New York
September 1998

Acknowledgments

THIS BOOK is the product of two Council on Foreign Relations study groups conducted from 1995 to 1998 on issues of the changing defense industrial base in the United States and abroad. The ambitious scope of these groups was to evaluate the ongoing process of military industrial downsizing and conversion, with an eye toward both economic and security consequences, and to anticipate the policy challenges of the coming decade. Original research was commissioned from a broad range of scholars and policymakers, and their papers were read and debated in group sessions in New York and Washington. Speakers ranged from Wall Street investment bankers to labor union leaders to industry chief executive officers—all presented their views on how the industry ought to restructure. From these papers and sessions, we have crafted this book.

The analyses found in this book already have made a difference to the policy debate. For instance, the study groups' intensive scrutiny of large defense contractor mergers helped to alert the Pentagon to dangers inherent in this tendency and to reverse the relatively permissive policy that prevailed from 1993 to 1997.

We are grateful to the John D. and Catherine T. MacArthur Foundation and our program officer, Mary Page, for funding the study group over the period from 1996 to 1998. At the Council, we enjoyed the active encouragement and participation of our directors of studies, Ken Keller, Ken Maxwell, Gary Hufbauer, and Larry Korb, and the adept administrative steering of Carol Rath. Our advisory committee—Denis Bovin, Rodney Nichols, and David Robinson—helped us focus our efforts and were stalwart and often probing participants in study group sessions. Al Fishlow, who leads the International Economics group at the Council, has been both a promoter and a solid critic.

A special thanks to our chair, Richard Ravitch, who brought to our study group sessions not only his skills as a presider and arbitrator but also his often blunt and sobering questions that brought us back from technical quibbling to fundamental matters of American foreign and economic policy. Thanks also to Jack Gansler, David Robinson, and Rodney Nichols for pinch-hitting as sessions chairs.

In addition to the authors whose chapters appear in this book, the study group heard a number of superb presentations on special issues on the defense industrial base and conversion prospects. On how Wall Street views the defense industry and mergers: Peter Aseritis, Denis Bovin,

Byron Callan, Wolfgang Demische, Ken Flamm, and Dennis Smallwood. On the future of the nuclear weapons laboratories: Sydney Drell, Richard Garwin, Greg Mello, and Bill Spencer. On defense workers: Domenick Bertelli, Bruce Olson, Cynthia Ward, and Joel Yudken. On military base closings: Nicholas Karvonides and Robert Meyer. On the global arms trade: Bill Keller and Andrew Pierre. In 1997–98 the group also read and debated papers on defense industry conversion in selected key countries: Peter Batchelor on South Africa; John Frankenstein on China; Ksenia Gonchar on Russia; and Claude Serfati on France. Thanks also to Peter Almquist for serving as a discussant in the China session.

The dozens of Council members, policymakers, and experts who joined us in our New York and Washington sessions considerably sharpened the debate and improved the analysis. A number of angles we had not originally contemplated emerged in the heat of friendly but often emphatic debate. Those economists and political scientists among us learned a great deal from the participation of our Council military fellows, especially George Flynn, Craig Hackett, Frank Klotz, and Ronald Route.

For engaging with us beyond study group sessions and especially for taking the time and energy to read and respond to chapter drafts, we are particularly grateful to the following: Bénédicte Callan, Domenick Bertelli, David Berteau, Greg Bischak, Joe Cartright, Ken Flamm, Jack Gansler, David Gold, Bill Hartung, Michael Oden, Erik Pages, Michael Renner, Judith Reppy, Jim Shinn, and Lee Sigal. Our arguments and those of our contributing authors were strengthened considerably by the acute observations of three anonymous reviewers. We are delighted to say that every one of our authors graciously and energetically revised their papers, sometimes multiple times, to respond to criticisms and suggestions from the group, the reviewers, and ourselves as editors.

To those who made this all work, Research Associates Nomi Colton-Max and Harpreet K. Mann, we owe an enormous debt. They presided over everything with efficiency and aplomb, from proposal preparation, to orchestrating study group sessions, to manuscript production. And thanks to our Web-savvy and data whiz research assistants David Lewis, Laura Powers, Jim Raffel, and Barbara Brunialti.

Above all, we want to thank Les Gelb, whose vision early on led to the Council's precocious interest in the ways that economics and security concerns are increasingly intertwined in American defense policy. The book has greatly benefited from his strong and thoughtful support.

Ann R. Markusen   *Sean S. Costigan*
New York   New York
October 1998   October 1998

I

Introduction

1

The Military
Industrial Challenge

ANN R. MARKUSEN AND SEAN S. COSTIGAN

EVEN as world leaders struggle to comprehend security in the post–Cold War era, they must consider pressing matters of defense industrial policy: the way nations go about deciding what kinds of weapons to develop or discontinue, and how best to produce or dismantle them. The stakes are high, because it is unlikely that world military spending will be increased appreciably in the foreseeable future. The expenditure of each dollar thus becomes just that much more important. The choices made, in turn, reverberate back on national security and economic competitiveness.

The challenges in developing a sound and workable military industrial policy are intellectually tough and politically eye-crossing. Should nations continue to keep existing production lines "hot," at considerable cost, ensuring their availability in the future? Should resources be conserved by designing new weapons but delaying their production until needed? Should the United States and the European Union pursue innovation at all, given their impressive lead in military technology and the absence of credible adversaries? Should the Pentagon and its advanced weapons-making allies speed the dismantling of factories and facilities no longer needed, and if so, are mergers among large contractors the best way to achieve this? Should nations continue to buy domestic, or, facing fewer competitors, permit foreign firms to bid on major weapons systems? Should nations welcome foreign ownership of domestic military capability? Should they further privatize security-related supply and service functions? Should arms exports be encouraged as a way to achieve economies of scale and lower weapons costs, even if this speeds conventional arms proliferation? Should dual-use firms and production facilities be encouraged or discouraged?

In this book, we examine the American response to these challenges in the 1990s and on into the 21st century, with some attention to the European experience as well. The Bush and Clinton administrations have jumped all over the lot trying to answer these questions. Bush's administration opposed mergers among large defense contractors and repudiated special programs for defense industry conversion. Rivalry between candidates Bush and Clinton in 1992 led to the sale of American fighter jets to Taiwan, angering the Chinese and sabotaging conventional arms control talks then under way. The Clinton administration encouraged conversion and diversification from the outset, but subsequently undercut these initiatives by liberalizing arms exports and welcoming "pure play" defense mergers. In 1997, it shifted gears again—Defense Secretary William Cohen's adamant opposition drove Lockheed Martin to abandon its bid for Northrop Grumman in the summer of 1998, some five years after Secretary William Perry had jawboned the industry into a frantic search for partners. Similarly, policy toward foreign ownership has been muddled—in June of 1998, the Clinton administration agreed to the British firm GEC's purchase of the American contractor Tracor, the largest foreign acquisition since the Bush administration scuttled the buyout of LTV's defense business by French giant Thomson-CSF in 1992. Furthermore, there is the privatization bind: within a month of privatizing the government's uranium-processing operation, alarms sounded as the new private owner began to accelerate the sell-off of uranium stocks, endangering a U.S./Russian agreement to prevent the latter's nuclear materials from falling into the wrong hands.

Much of this drama arises from the clash between economic and security pressures. Policymakers are charged with maintaining an innovative edge in military technology while facing severe budget constraints and a vastly altered and somewhat opaque security environment. For a period in the 1990s, American administration leaders acted as if market-driven solutions to defense industrial base downsizing and reconfiguration would suffice. But more recently, the weaknesses in this strategy have become apparent. In 1997 incoming Acquisitions Chief Jacques Gansler put in place a much improved policy regime that opposes competition-eroding mergers, encourages new firms to enter the market, proposes to buy commercial where possible, anticipates designing but not building new weapons systems, and considers the possibility, previously unthinkable, of buying foreign. Nevertheless, for reasons that we explore in this book, these reforms do not yet comprise a fully coherent defense industrial strategy.

Here, succinctly, are the major policy problems and trade-offs and our prescriptions, tailored to the American case but applicable to the European case as well. First, how can the Pentagon ensure truly innovative designs and appropriately priced weapons? This is more difficult than before as a result of dramatic reduction in the number of large American prime contractors, from more than 15 to 4. The Pentagon either must intensify its regulatory oversight or must seek to expand the pool of competitors. The latter is preferable, but new domestic competitors are unlikely, and buying from foreign suppliers is problematic on both security and political grounds. Further mergers among large contractors, either domestic or transatlantic, should be discouraged, new entrants encouraged, and selectively buying foreign explored. But the Pentagon, in our view, has no alternative to improving the economic savvy of its staff and the efficacy of its industry oversight.

Second, how can the Pentagon have access to commercial technologies, which have surpassed their military counterparts, without risking accelerated proliferation and erosion of America's technological edge? Efforts to buy "off-the-shelf" commercial components and encourage the integration of civilian and military research and development (R&D) and production activities, right down to the shop floor, have two great payoffs: better electronic, communications, and guidance capabilities for the armed forces, and a defense industrial base that is less dependent on government contracts, ameliorating pork-barreling activities that distort military priorities. But the inclusion of more commercial components raises the potential for more rapid diffusion of the sophisticated weapons that are at the heart of America's security strategy. Here again there is no acceptable alternative to vigilant oversight of arms transfers and components trade.

Third, is it advisable for the U.S. military to have access to a wider array of weapons at lower cost by permitting the export of sophisticated weapons more quickly and to a larger number of countries? Liberalizing and promoting arms exports for economic reasons increases the risk of conflict elsewhere in the world, possibly drawing in the United States. It also accelerates pressures for costly next-generation weapons investments. We conclude, echoing the Report of the Presidential Advisory Board on Arms Proliferation Policy, that economic factors have no place in arms sales policy. Despite the intensification of arms export competition among allies in the 1990s, it is never too late to begin talking seriously about restraint.

Finally, from whom should the Pentagon buy weapons? This is not just a matter of soliciting winning bids. The Pentagon has considerable power to shape the size and global breadth of the industry through its role in antitrust approval, procurement awards, and privatization decisions. American policy must balance short-term gains in weapons cost against longer-term assurances that weapons design and production skills survive and provide choice for the armed forces in the future. It also must balance sovereignty issues against powerful market forces pressing for transnational defense firm mergers. Fortress America is no longer an option. American-designed arms will be bought and used by more nations in the future, and we may rely more heavily on foreign suppliers for components if not entire weapons systems. Our leaders have no alternative but to explore with our allies international agreements and machinery to streamline the defense industrial base, share its output, and control access globally. Otherwise, large private-sector corporations will be shaping our security strategy.

As the century draws to an end, the United States and its allies are enjoying a period of markedly diminished threat and relative stability in international relations. Indeed, for the foreseeable future, economic problems loom larger and are more likely to dominate foreign policy than is military confrontation. This affords us a period in which our leaders could take stock, slow new weapons innovation, and restrain arms exports while exploring a world in which weapons design and production, like so many other modern commodities, assume a more global character. The United States will continue to be the leader in this process, as it has been in the dramatic restructuring of global trade and finance. The new realities—an altered security challenge, confronting the escalating cost of high-tech weaponry and fiscal austerity—can be met best by cooperating more closely with our allies. Coordination must include a process for deciding how and where transnational mergers should be encouraged (or forbidden) and how arms-producing countries can share the jobs and economic activity attendant on arms design and production.

Four Post–Cold War Developments

What has happened since the end of the Cold War? Four developments, mostly unanticipated, stand out in what President Dwight D. Eisenhower once and enduringly dubbed the American military industrial complex. At the Cold War's end, industry watchers forecast rapid contract cuts of as much as 50 percent. They expected defense contractors to reinvest their earnings, skilled workforce, and technologies in new nondefense products and markets, becoming smaller and less defense dependent. Large-scale mergers were not anticipated.[1] The more innovative thinkers were prescribing civil/military integration and dual-use technology development to enhance the quality of military equipment and quicken the pace of civilian technology spin-offs.[2] Both the Bush and Clinton administrations appeared to embrace these prescriptions as the decade commenced. Peace and economic development advocates pressed for active conversion policies that would help firms, workers, and communities adjust to downsizing quickly.[3]

In practice, however, four quite different developments came to dominate post–Cold War restructuring in the 1990s. For one, after 50 years of relative stasis in the ranks of the largest defense contractors, a rash of defense mergers reduced the major competitors to a small number of relatively heavily defense-dedicated companies: Lockheed Martin, Boeing, Raytheon, and Northrop Grumman. (See Figure 1–1.) The mergers have enhanced the size gap between U.S. and European firms. (See Table 1–1.) The latter, fearing market dominance of American firms, have become increasingly preoccupied with finding partners themselves; the 1999 merger of British Aerospace and GEC is an outstanding example. Such merger activity may continue, absorbing smaller firms into these same giants. Defense contractors also are becoming increasingly international in orientation, selling larger shares of their output to foreign governments and engaging in strategic alliances, joint ventures, and even mergers with overseas counterparts. In consequence, new controversies about defense industrial base adequacy, character, and control are erupting around the globe.

In a second development, firms and governments in leading arms-producing countries have become more rather than less rivalrous in arms export markets, hampering progress toward controlling conventional arms proliferation. The U.S. share of world arms exports has risen dramatically, even in a shrinking world market. While American exports have fallen by more than 10 percent in real terms since 1989, the U.S. share has increased from 30 percent to 45 percent. (See Table 1–2.)

Traditionally viewed as a foreign policy tool, new weapons sales now are frequently approved and defended for economic reasons: to keep production lines "hot" and lower the cost of weapons to the American armed forces by achieving economies of scale. As highly sophisticated weapons are more freely shipped to problematic governments in politically unstable regions, calls have arisen for expensive new weapons research, especially in the United States. To some critics, this process amounts to America engaged in an arms race with itself.

In a third development, the composition of the defense budgets has been shifting in favor of private-sector procurement and services over

Figure 1-1 U.S. Defense Mergers in the 1990s

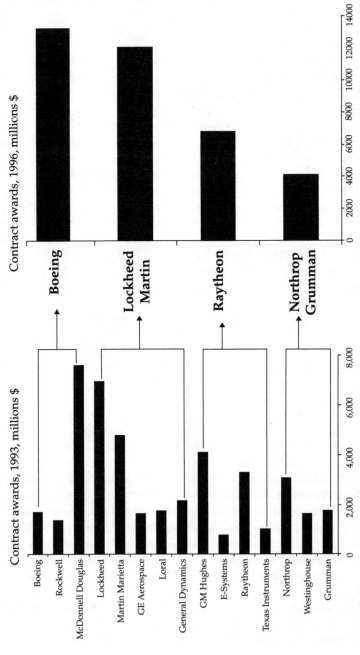

Source: All data are from the Department of Defense publication (P01), *100 Companies Receiving the Largest Dollar Volume of Prime Contract Awards from the Fiscal Years of 1993 and 1996.*

Table 1–1   Major Defense Contractors by Nation, Sales 1995

Company	Country	Defense Revenues $U.S. billion
Lockheed Martin	United States	19.39
Boeing McDonnell Douglas	United States	17.90
Raytheon/Hughes/Texas Instruments	United States	11.67
British Aerospace	Britain	6.47
Northrop Grumman	United States	5.70
Thomson	France	4.68
Aérospatiale/Dassault	France	4.15
GEC	Britain	4.12
United Technologies	United States	3.65
Lagardere Groupe	France	3.29
Daimler-Benz Aerospace	Germany	3.25
Direction des Constructions Navales	France	3.07
General Dynamics	United States	2.90
Finmeccanica	Italy	2.59
Litton Industries	United States	2.40
Mitsubishi Heavy Industries	Japan	2.22
General Electric	United States	2.15
Tenneco	United States	1.80
TRW	United States	1.71
ITT Industries	United States	1.56

Source: Economist, "A Survey of the Global Defense Industry," June 14, 1997.

public-sector provision. This is the joint product of a longer-term shift toward greater capital intensification of warfare—the substitution of sophisticated weaponry for manpower—and a more recent trend toward privatization of defense research, services, and depots, both of which are expected to continue. Over time equipment and services purchased from the private sector (procurement) have grown more rapidly than payrolls for military and civilian Department of Defense (DoD) employees' (pay), the former rising from about 45 percent of defense commitments to 54 percent. (See Figure 1–2.) Within procurement, the mix has favored continued production of several Cold War weapons, such as the B-2 bomber, despite analysts favoring more R&D and prototype development over production and despite forceful arguments from within the military and by independent analysts advocating less expensive and more effective weaponry.[4] American privatization and capital-intensive warfare is paralleled by developments in most countries around the globe, although governments in some countries, such as France and China, are reluctant

Table 1-2 Arms Exports: Britain, France, United States (Millions of 1990 $U.S.), 1989–96

Nation	Arms Exports			Share of World Market			Exports/Procurement		
	1989	1996	% Change	1989	1996	% Change	1989	1996	% Change
Britain	2,541	1,773	–30.2	6.8	7.7	14.2	28.32	25.49	–10.0
France	2,788	2,101	–24.6	7.4	9.1	23.4	15.26	15.80	3.5
United States	11,366	10,228	–10.0	30.2	44.5	47.3	14.02	17.44	24.4

Sources: SIPRI Yearbook 1997, *Armaments, Disarmament and International Security* (Stockholm: SIPRI, 1997); SIPRI Yearbook 1994, *Armaments, Disarmament and International Security* (Stockholm: SIPRI, 1994); 1996 Arms Exports and World Share from 1997 Yearbook, Table 9.1, p. 268; 1989 and 1996 Exports/Procurements from 1997 Yearbook, Table 13.8, p. 484, 1989 and 1996 Exports/Procurements from 1997 Yearbook, Table 9.1, p. 268, and Table 6A.1 and Table 6A.2, pp. 186–88.

Figure 1–2 Military Procurement: Pay, 1970 to 2000 (Millions of 1995 $U.S.)

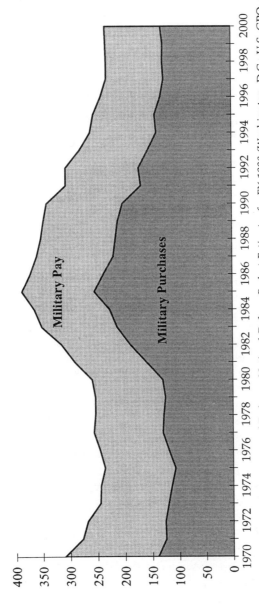

Source: Office of the Undersecretary of Defense, *National Defense Budget Estimates for FY 1998* (Washington, D.C.: U.S. GPO, 1997), see Tables 6–8.

Table 1–3   Military Expenditures: 1985, 1990, 1994
             Selected Countries (Index, 1994 = 100)

Region	1985	1990	1994
Britain	115	106	100
China	95	93	100
France	94	98	100
Germany	165	147	100
Soviet Union/Russia	361	317	100
United States	118	117	100
Developing Countries	121	126	100
Industrialized Countries	164	152	100
World Total	155	146	100

Source: Bonn International Center for Conversion, *Conversion Survey 1996* (New York: Oxford University Press, 1996), pp. 259–62, see Appendix A1.

to divest themselves fully of substantial public ownership and control of military industrial capacity.

Finally, progress on securing a post–Cold War peace dividend has been modest at best. At the macroeconomic level, despite substantial cuts in defense spending (see Table 1–3), the United States and most western countries have weathered the abrupt decline in defense spending rather well as vibrant economies absorbed people, facilities, and technologies released from the defense sector.[5]

The transition has been more difficult in Russia and some developing countries, such as Egypt. Yet even in the United States, military spending cuts have merely reversed the effects of the 1980s buildup and have not fallen below average real Cold War spending levels of the 1970s. (See Figure 1–2.) Remarkably few production lines have been closed down. Success in conversion, diversification, and new start-ups—all methods for the successful transfer of people and technologies into civilian activities—has been mixed. Civil-military integration, championed as a way to lower weapons costs, improve weapons quality, and ameliorate displacement, has been slow to materialize. Promising "dual-use" initiatives have been undermined by cross-cutting government incentives encouraging the creation of "pure-play" defense companies and promoting arms exports. When transformation occurs, and there are quite a few success stories, often it takes longer and is riskier than it need be, in large part because a forceful conversion strategy has not evolved.

What do we know about these developments? Which forces caused and shaped them? What do they mean for future defense industrial pol-

Table 1–4   Defense Employment Reduction
Selected Countries (Index, 1994 = 100)

Region	1985	1990	1994
Britain	152	142	100
China	114	114	100
France	131	115	100
Germany	148	171	100
Soviet Union/Russia	192	205	100
United States	129	125	100
Developing Countries	117	114	100
Industrialized Countries	155	150	100
World Total	141	137	100

Source: Bonn International Center for Conversion, *Conversion Survey 1996*, pp. 272–74.

icy? These are the subjects of the studies in this book.[6] All are original research papers commissioned by the Council on Foreign Relations Study Group on Defense Consolidation, Downsizing, and Conversion in the U.S. Military Industrial Base. Many of them offer new data and original interpretations of the changing defense industry and its capabilities. Each was debated in depth at the Council by a broad-based study group. Some have been published in abbreviated form, and several already have had a considerable impact on the policy debate.

Together, the authors examine the post–Cold War defense industry challenge: How can the United States and its allies shepherd their defense industries in a period of abrupt and deep cuts in defense demand while simultaneously repositioning to meet new and unusual threats that are not yet well defined?

Changes in defense-related arms production worldwide and in the United States demonstrate just how formidable a challenge this has been. Worldwide, employment in arms production fell by 29 percent between 1985 and 1994 (see Table 1–4), by more than 4.8 million jobs. In the United States, private defense industry employment fell by 45 percent from 1987 to 1999, or by 1.6 million workers. Another 1.1 million jobs were eliminated in the U.S. armed services and Department of Defense. (See Table 1–5.)

Confounding the adjustment process, future defense requirements have been difficult for defense contractors to anticipate. Uncertainty about the location and magnitude of future security threats have led to remarkably divergent proposals for defense strategy and budgets, ranging from in excess of $300 billion to as low as $90 billion for the United States.[7] Shifts in policy attendant on presidential, parliamentary, and

Table 1–5   Defense-related Employment: 1987–99
(Millions of Employees)

	1987	1999	Percent Change 1987–99	Percent Change 1987–99
Uniformed DoD	2.24	1.49	−0.76	−34
Nonuniformed DoD	1.13	0.75	−0.38	−34
Private Defense Industry				
Employment (direct & indirect)	3.67	2.03	−1.64	−45
Total	7.04	4.26	−2.78	−39

Source: Office of the Under Secretary of Defense, *National Defense Budget Estimates for FY 1998*, Table 7–5 (Washington, D.C.: U.S. Government Printing Office, 1997).

congressional turnover have muddied the waters in most of the largest arms-producing nations. Many countries, including the United States and France, plan modernization programs whose price tag is inconsistent with deficit reduction goals, and projects like the Eurofighter are kept alive despite grave reservations about the quality of the resulting craft and the existence of a market for them.[8]

Most chapters that follow focus on the United States. As the world's emerging hegemon, largest defense spender, uncontested defense technology leader, and host of the world's leading defense firms, the United States can be seen as a laboratory for experiments in defense industry adjustment. Many of the developments emerging in the American case were swiftly adopted elsewhere, as the chapters on Europe demonstrate. As a group, the authors cast light on the "why" of mergers, arms exports, privatization, and conversion and speculate on the role that the restructured industry is playing in the twin dramas of American security and American economic competitiveness. Each addresses policy issues that are posed by new developments, and not all of them come to the same conclusions. In the final chapter, we sort through the often-conflicting recommendations. Here we briefly summarize the major contributions of each author, with passing reference to other recent writing on each theme.

The Post–Cold War Security Environment: Pentagon, Congressional, and Contractor Responses

In an otherwise lively and contentious arena of debate, few analysts would disagree with the proposition that the size, composition, and output of the defense industry should be driven by American security strategy and not vice versa.[9] Yet in the wake of the collapse of the Soviet threat, no clear, coherent defense policy has emerged.[10] The two-theater, go-it-alone official American posture, reaffirmed in the 1996 Quadrennial Defense Review, anticipates U.S. ability to fight two Persian Gulf War–scale conflicts simultaneously without major allied support.[11]

The policy is controversial, for several reasons. First, the likelihood of two regional conflagrations erupting at once is very small.[12] Second, collaborative efforts with allies are becoming more common, potentially diminishing the demands on American forces.[13] Third, terrorism and weapons of mass destruction, especially chemical and biological weapons, constitute increasingly likely sources of threat that cannot be countered easily with conventional weapons.[14] Fourth, fiscal austerity and competing priorities in the industrialized countries constrain the public-sector resources available for defense spending.[15] Fifth, peacekeeping missions are coming to assume a greater share of defense resources. Peacekeeping is a relatively labor-intensive activity, in contrast to the power projection employed in situations like the Gulf War. Despite these epochal changes, defense policy remains heavily dominated by Cold War–era thinking. The absence of a clear vision of future security challenges tends to grandfather in obsolete weapons systems, a phenomenon that is increasingly indefensible on both security and affordability grounds.

As a consequence of these changes, a number of quite radically different visions of U.S. security strategy have been proposed by experts and analysts outside of the Pentagon. These range from the "two-theater" strategy of the Bush and Clinton administrations to the cooperative security scenarios of William Kaufmann and John Steinbruner at Brookings, to the "defense-only" proposals of Randall Forsberg at the Institute for Defense and Disarmament Studies.[16] In Chapter 2 Greg Bischak evaluates five of these for their implications for the American defense budget and defense industrial base. In an analysis unavailable anywhere else, he shows a stunning range of disparity in budgetary requirements, from $260 billion currently to $180 billion for the cooperative security scenario and $87 billion for a defense-only posture. Bischak also concludes that these different security scenarios have markedly different implications for the defense industrial base. A cooperative security strategy, for instance, would place greater emphasis on civil-military integration and interoperability with allies, resulting in lower procurement and a somewhat slower rate of technological innovation and weapons modernization. The purely defensive strategy would deemphasize new weapons research and development, changing the composition of defense spending and enhancing opportunities for civil-military integration. It also would cut back severely on arms exports, resulting in a smaller defense industry. Strategies that emphasize peacekeeping, prevention, and the strengthening of international institutions also would imply a smaller arms industry, as nations increasingly pursue nonmilitary and nontechnological means of resolving differences.

Bischak concludes that the United States must choose between a go-it-alone security policy committed to power projection and American technological leadership and one based on cooperative security initiatives with greater emphasis on negotiation, peacekeeping, and partnership. The latter, which he favors, is compatible with the new efficient, dual-use emphasis at the Pentagon, while the former is not.

The next three chapters document the major decisions that were made by defense contractors, the Pentagon, and Congress over the tumultuous years immediately following the end of the Cold War. The period from 1989 to 1997 provided an unusual window of opportunity for the industry to reshape itself and for the Pentagon to shepherd this process and revamp its procurement system. In the American case, Michael Oden demonstrates, in Chapter 3, that the largest defense firms, flush with cash but facing deep cuts in long-term orders, initially undertook quite disparate strategies. Some—Lockheed Martin, Northrop Grumman, General Dynamics—concentrated on downsizing, merging with competitors, and increasing sales to overseas markets. Others—TRW, Hughes, Rockwell, Texas Instruments—invested internally in moving people and technologies into new product lines in civilian markets, often building on conglomerate strengths. Oden's analysis shows that up through 1994, firms in the latter group reinvested more of their earnings in R&D, achieved lower defense dependency ratios, and did as well or better in terms of profitability than those who sought to consolidate or expand their defense specialization.

During this period, Oden shows, the U.S. government relayed mixed signals to defense firms. On the one hand, new dual-use incentives, such as the Technology Reinvestment Program (TRP) and procurement reform encouraged diversification into civilian fields and civil-military integration.[17] On the other hand, increased permissiveness toward mergers and arms exports, and expanded subsidies for both, encouraged corporations to consolidate and focus on defense markets.[18] Oden contests John Dowdy's favorable assessment of the outcome of the merger strategy and offers support for concerns raised both inside and outside the Pentagon.[19]

Oden also shows that smaller firms have been more successful than is generally understood in surviving post–Cold War budget cuts. Many have downsized, but most have reduced their defense dependency and expanded nondefense sales. Oden contests other research that suggests defense firms are not specialized.[20] They must overcome formidable handicaps, he argues, and several factors are key to their ability to do so: management commitment, often following a "shock" of recognition; radical reform of management, marketing, and production practices; and successful collaboration with other companies and/or public institutions, often facilitated by regionally based economic development efforts. Oden's work confirms the cautiously optimistic view of industry insiders such as Richard Minnich and counters the pessimism of others.[21] Oden argues that firms' success with dual-use and conversion initiatives is evidence for the feasibility of civil-military integration and more rapid technology transfer but that countervailing Pentagon policies on exports and consolidation threaten to undermine their achievement.

In concluding, Oden recommends drastic changes in American defense policy. The nation could maintain its ability to meet all conceivable security challenges and spend one-third less doing so by relying on vigorous arms control and nonproliferation policies, smaller and more mobile armed forces, and a more diversified and less defense-dependent industry. The savings as well as the benefits of dual-use technology, he argues, would enhance American economic strength and usher in a period of sustained prosperity.

Why did the Bush/Clinton dual-use initiatives fall short? In Chapter 4, a close-up analysis of the TRP, Jay Stowsky examines the construction and subsequent dismantling of this major initiative. The TRP offered several billions of dollars in competitively allocated grants to encourage defense firms to team with others to move promising technologies back and forth between the civilian and military sectors. He shows that the program was carefully and deliberately structured to maximize long-term payoffs and to avoid pork-barreling, with ironic consequences. Few members of Congress felt invested in the program, since it indeed was well insulated from pork-barreling pressures. Furthermore, the competitive process ensured that there would be scores of disgruntled losers, undermining defense industry support. The largest, best-positioned contractors, moreover, were hostile to the program's potential for creating competitors and new technologies that might undermine their own market positions. Trade unions were disappointed at the weak links between the TRP and demonstrable job creation, especially since it was the single largest conversion initiative in dollar terms.

When control of Congress changed hands in 1994, Republicans earmarked the TRP for total elimination, reflecting their antipathy toward technology programs in general and the search for budget savings, partly spent on weapons purchases beyond the president's request, which critics hailed as pork. In retrospect, Stowsky argues, the TRP might have fared better had it been embedded in broader public missions (environment, transportation) and provided demonstrable results more quickly.[22] Furthermore, while the TRP was designed to be an interagency initiative, the lead role played by the DoD led to the reassertion of military priorities and an emphasis on "spin-on" rather than spin-off. Thus, he argues, its broad base of support was undermined even before the Republican congressional attack that all but eliminated it by 1996.

Stowsky concludes that there remains great potential for American technology policy in the coming decades. The Pentagon has no choice, he argues, but to pursue dual-use technologies, although their prospects are better via the slow and more prosaic procurement reforms than in flashy new programs like the TRP, which may become lightning rods for criticism. And, he argues, American economic leadership in the world will be contingent on replicating the Cold War experience in other mission areas—in communications, biotechnology, and transportation, for instance. Public investment in basic R&D and in pioneering applications will be fundamental to such American leadership. The lessons from the political blunders of the 1990s are that our leaders must become more savvy on selling new missions to the public and on working gingerly with the American Congress on matters of public support for science and technology policy.

Congress is indeed, and perhaps increasingly, a major player in determining the level of the defense budget and its composition, although its sway over arms sales appears to have diminished.[23] Options for future weapons research and force structure are first contemplated deep within the Pentagon in consultation with the armed forces and defense contractors.[24] And presidents, through their foreign policy agenda and their control over the budgetary process, especially in making trade-offs between domestic and military spending, also play a powerful role. But in the post–Cold War period, pork-barreling pressures increasingly managed to insert themselves into the final drama in Congress. Large, platform-building projects—Seawolf submarines, aircraft carriers, fighter jets—often support whole communities (Groton, CT; Newport News, VA; St. Louis, MO). Similarly, the $30 billion the United States spends annually on the nuclear weapons complex has created constituencies (Hanford, WA; Los Alamos, NM; Savannah River, GA) whose livelihoods are dependent on continued nuclear weapons research, stockpiling, and cleanup.

In Chapter 5, a fascinating account of the first two years of the Clinton administration, the first post–Cold War opportunity for a Democratic

Congress and president to work together on a downsizing and conversion agenda, Paul Walker, then senior policy adviser to the House Armed Services Committee, illustrates the corrosive pressures that special interests, bankrolled by industrialists but often supported by unions and community groups, exert on rational decision-making about defense. Initial Clinton proposals for deeper spending cuts and a vigorous conversion program were stymied in a Democratic Congress by the inertia and vested interests in existing procurement programs. The long-awaited Bottom-Up Review ended up grandfathering in most Cold War weapons systems, and the Nuclear Posture Review yielded a disappointingly status quo document. Efforts to rein in the arms trade were similarly thwarted, as were efforts to fund conversion programs adequately.

Walker argues that Congress is more important in this process than is generally understood. Political scientists generally depict defense planning and budgets as fundamentally set in place by the executive branch and then merely tinkered with, give or take $10 billion, in Congress. But Walker shows that both the Pentagon and the president continually consult with Congress and second-guess what may be palatable. Thus much of what they propose to Congress is already qualified by sensitivity to constituent demands and political muscle.

Walker warns that much of what dominates congressional/White House scuffles over the defense budget remains tied to Cold War mentalities. He advocates serious threat assessment and concomitant force sizing and procurement strategies, akin to what Secretary Les Aspin initiated while still in Congress but failed to follow through in the Bottom-Up Review process. He predicts that procurement expenditures will fall even without a well-thought-out strategy overhaul, the victim of deficit hawks, public indifference, and other pressing public priorities. He sees this as an ideal time to rethink national defense strategy and calls on the president to lead in this effort.

WAS THERE A PEACE DIVIDEND OVER THE DECADE OF POST–COLD WAR DEMOBILIZATION?

The answer is yes, at least at the macroeconomic level.[25] Savings from defense budget cuts were applied principally to deficit reduction, however, rather than to public-sector initiatives that might constitute new markets for defense contractors. In a recounting of $81 billion in defense cuts from 1993 to 1997, Greg Bischak concludes that 80 percent of it went to reduce the federal deficit, with the balance going to broadly construed conversion programs. Involuntarily retired members of the armed services have received on the whole quite good benefits and readjustment assistance ($3.4 billion); defense workers fared less well. New initiatives to stimulate defense technology received $16.5 billion, but only a fraction of these—Bischak estimates 12 percent—had any real conversion component. Less than $5 billion, under $1 billion per year, went to fund new missions in environment, energy, transportation, and infrastructure. Government investments in alternative-fuel vehicles, urban traffic management systems, "smart" cars, and communications technologies have provided attractive new markets for defense contractors, however, as have new opportunities on the social services side of the budget. Lockheed Martin has, for instance, expanded its business into the administration of welfare systems.

The Consequences of Defense Industry Consolidation

In this post–Cold War decade, just how has the defense industrial base changed and what do these changes mean for the future? In Part III, three chapters present evidence and arguments about the pace and character of defense industry transformation. Writing from concern over defense industrial base performance, Erik Pages argues in Chapter 7 that rapid consolidation in the industry overrides incentives to integrate and diversify across market and international boundaries.[26] Seeing the Pentagon as increasingly dependent on an emerging set of large defense conglomerations, he argues that several negative consequences may follow: a rise in the cost of defense equipment, diminished technological innovation, and a chilling effect on international defense cooperation.[27] Pages concludes that a market dominated by large conglomerates may require a more activist government tightly regulating production and steering contracts to nurture the industrial base rather than to reflect purely market demands. He also advocates the use of various proxy tools to help further stimulate competition in the defense sector. These ideas include design bureaus, more aggressive use of prototyping, and a further expansion of dual-use research and development.

Pages recommends that policymakers aggressively pursue acquisition reform, actively regulate defense-unique firms, and search for proxies to enhance competition among suppliers. He argues for a Pentagon less acquiescent and reliant on market forces and more willing to build new institutions and explore new regulatory arrangements. It might, for instance, want to create independent design teams where it faces monopolization, or buy foreign where politically feasible.

Harvey Sapolsky and Eugene Gholz demonstrate in Chapter 6 that despite large budget cuts and mergers, very few large-scale weapons production lines actually have been shut down. Many are operating at far below capacity, and large numbers of workers have been laid off. Nevertheless, duplicative shipyards, aircraft plants, and other production facilities are kept going in a variant of the famous Kurth "follow-on" imperative.[28] In other words, the causal link between mergers and capacity elimination, a major rationale for Pentagon encouragement of mergers, has not been borne out in recent experience. Mergers have not relieved the Pentagon of the difficult job of eliminating capacity, and the persistence of such capacity generates intense pressures for pork-barreling.

Sapolsky and Gholz also document a secular trend toward greater privatization of military activity. They show that over the past two decades, the ranks of people working directly for the armed services or as DoD civilians have fallen while those working for defense contractors have risen, a counterpart to the shift in the composition of spending shown in Figure 1–2. Privatization of depots, research laboratories, and other civilian DoD functions has become a major Pentagon priority.[29] This trend, combined with the shrinking number of defense contractors, is creating what Sapolsky and Gholz call the "private arsenal" problem in the United States. They consider a number of policy responses, ranging from public takeover, to the introduction of greater competition by requiring the armed services to compete with one another for missions.

Sapolsky and Gholz conclude that even belatedly, we need a plan to demobilize industrially from the Cold War. They counsel getting rid of unneeded production capacity while protecting vital design teams and facilities. They recommend "paying the bill" for the closures—an exit strategy that would effectively eliminate capacity while doing as well by defense workers and their host communities as the Pentagon does routinely for military personnel and communities that host bases. They also, provocatively, call for the construction of a public arsenal system even while defense firms remain nominally private. They would replace our current acquisition system, in which companies lose money on R&D and gain it back on long production runs, by one that pays handsomely for R&D but renders large-scale production contracts the exception rather than the expectation.

The consequences of defense industrial restructuring through mergers, increased exports, and privatization are surprisingly under-researched. In Chapter 8 Ken Flamm argues that the industry has played a lead role in initiating these changes and that the Pentagon did not have a well-worked-out strategy. Although a few studies have been done of the adequacy of defense industrial capacity in a number of sub-sectors, no overall assessment of the projected size and competitiveness of the American defense industrial base was available to guide the Pentagon in responding to the proposed defense mergers.[30] Flamm demonstrates that such an assessment can be done and argues for the importance of building this capability in the Pentagon. Nor did Pentagon officials choose to follow the advice of a number of commissioned studies suggesting that rivalry in design and development capacity could be maintained if the Pentagon paid careful attention to mergers.[31]

The arguments favoring the mergers were made on the basis of economies of scale and scope.[32] Since the demand for weapons systems is way down, the logic goes, it is inefficient and costly to taxpayers to maintain two or more producers of fighter planes or submarines when one would suffice. Scale economies are an issue, as most thoroughly analyzed in the case of fighter aircraft.[33] However, the elimination of competitors creates the potential for monopolistic pricing, especially problematic in this industry where cost-plus contracts are the rule and where the seller often knows more about the performance of the product than does the government buyer. In addition, economists worry (and history offers some evidence) that without competition, designs will be less innovative. Flamm shows how to model these trade-offs and illustrates his approach with the case of tactical missiles. His framework goes considerably further than other efforts to date.

The Push to Export

Because excess capacity, expanded greatly in the unprecedented peacetime buildup of the 1980s, poses such a problem in a period of rather rapid defense budget cuts, military industrial firms and their trade associations have pressed hard for relaxation in arms export controls in the post–Cold War period. They have argued, quite successfully in the U.S. case, that production lines can be kept "hot," and thus available for future unknown demand, only by producing for overseas markets. They point out that such sales potentially lower the cost of weapons for Americans, because without them the government would have to purchase unneeded systems or pay for the costs of mothballing and maintaining "stables" of skilled workers.

The successful push to export sophisticated weapons has been facilitated by relaxed government restrictions both on types of exportable systems and on recipient countries. It also has been underwritten by generous new government subsidies, estimated to amount to as much as $6 billion to $7 billion a year.[34] For the first time economic considerations are acknowledged formally in review of arms exports permits.[35] The rationale for these changes centers on lowering costs to the American taxpayer. The argument goes that if the overhead costs of keeping the F-16 line open, for instance, can be spread across many more customers, then the cost of current and future units to the Pentagon will be just that much lower. Flamm is critical of this argument for its failure to assess the increased threat associated with these sales or to include the costs of further weapons R&D necessitated by the proliferation of such weapons to not entirely reliable regimes. Flamm suggests that before further contractor marriages are blessed or weapons sales approved, a rigorous modeling of the multiple costs and benefits of each action be undertaken by the Pentagon. There is considerable debate about whether lines need to be kept in service at all. One group of analysts and strategists—Flamm and Jacques Gansler among them—argue that countries like the United States would be better off investing in R&D and prototype development, while upgrading the existing, ample stockpile of weapons.

The nature of the economic pressures to export are the subject of Chapter 9 by David Gold. On the macroeconomic side, Gold notes that generous offset agreements undercut the economic payoff to arms exports, making it difficult to determine the net benefits for the U.S. economy in terms of jobs and spending flows. To the extent offsets increase import competition, there is a shift of resources to arms-exporting industries from firms and workers in industries whose output must compete with foreign nondefense goods marketed by defense firms. Where offsets take the form of overseas production of whole weapons or components, they are a conduit for technology transfer that may have adverse security and economic consequences in the future. As for the industrial base maintenance issue, Gold shows that the government's promotion costs add up to more than half of the proceeds of arms export sales and two-thirds of the value of new orders. He finds it difficult to believe that unit-cost savings from spreading fixed costs over a large production run could possibly justify such an extraordinary level of subsidies (over $7.7 billion in 1995). Moreover, the government, which bears the bulk of the fixed costs of capital investment and R&D, has bowed to industry pressure and removed recoupment fees from most arms sales, meaning that exporting firms and buying nations are the beneficiaries of whatever cost savings are derived from larger production runs. The socialization of costs and privatization of benefits that characterize the arms trade for the United States appear to have reinforced incentives to expand arms sales.

The proliferation of conventional weapons via the arms trade, Lora Lumpe argues in Chapter 11, poses central security concerns. Lumpe shows that arms makers and governments are exporting top-of-the-line systems previously not for sale, dramatically raising the standards of weaponry in regions such as the Middle East. In addition, some buyers are now demanding, and getting, the technology to make weapons themselves rather than buying them off the shelf. Exporting has also become less discriminating, with weapons sold to nondemocratic or unstable governments and into sensitive regions without even the effort to influence buyers' behavior that once accompanied such sales. Despite concern about the security consequences from a broad spectrum of critics inside and outside of government, the Bush and Clinton administrations have continually liberalized arms exports, most recently to Latin America, for reasons that are more economic than strategic.[36]

Lumpe proposes a two-pronged toughening of export policy, screening on the basis of buyer and weapons system. Sales would be made to a country only if it meets standards of conduct in human rights, democratic governance, and nonaggression—reasonable correlatives with peace and stability. Sales of the most dangerous weapons also would be barred under Lumpe's regime, adding to current bans on ballistic/cruise missiles and land mines items such as diesel attack submarines, advanced bombers, cluster bombs, and fuel air explosives on either proliferation or humanitarian grounds. Lumpe argues that lead producing countries, such as the United States, should unilaterally pursue such a strategy while simultaneously seeking multilateral agreements.

The increasing importance of commercial computing, electronics, and communications technologies to leading-edge weaponry throws a potential wrench into the arms control works. To the extent that technologies are genuinely "dual use," it is difficult to control their spread around the globe. As Judith Reppy explains in Chapter 10, historical research shows that the term "dual use" was coined first in the late 1940s during the formation of the Coordinating Committee for Multilateral Export Controls (COCOM) regime. Then it was employed strictly in the interests of national security and used as a screen to bar exports, including civilian commodities, which might be incorporated into problematic weapons. Over the decades and especially in the 1980s, Reppy demonstrates, the term came to connote a strategy for enhancing economic competitiveness through military spin-off and cross-fertilization of contemporary dual-use initiatives, especially when combined with relaxation in arms export oversight.

Reppy addresses the downside of dual-use technology initiatives: their potential contribution to proliferation. She analyzes the factors that impede or facilitate technology transfer and asks whether it is possible to encourage civilian and military integration in an increasingly globalized defense industry without also encouraging undesirable technology transfer to other countries. Persistent problems in negotiating international agreements for control of dual-use technologies suggest that it may not be. Taking issue with most of the other chapters, Reppy concludes by suggesting that, because of the danger of proliferation, it may be preferable to retain a separate defense industrial base, reconsider our dual-use strategy, and even consider restricting access to university-based training of foreign nationals in defense-sensitive areas.

Defense Industry Globalization

As the century draws to a close, the defense business is becoming less and less a predominantly domestic activity. Exports are increasingly important as a percent of sales, as Table 1–2 shows for the United States and France. Although governments have not cooperated very successfully in integrating and rationalizing their procurement strategies, the private sector has been exploring ways to globalize capacity through mergers, coproduction agreements, and offset arrangements. In Chapter 12 Richard Bitzinger, using a longitudinal database constructed while at the Defense Budget Project, documents the extent of these alliances. He reiterates the warning that the private sector is well ahead of the government in this process and that globalization without oversight poses dangers of increased conventional arms proliferation. But Bitzinger also examines the resistance to a truly international industry.[37] He senses a trend toward continental consolidation in which a North American complex goes head-to-head with a European complex, exacerbating inefficiency and creating the potential for further proliferation, as each tries to utilize capacity by selling to the developing world.

European nations led by Britain, Germany, and France are attempting to cooperate on security strategy and armament policy.[38] But they are hamstrung by historical and institutional differences and by corporate and community fear of displacement. In Chapter 13, a survey of post–Cold War European security and procurement policy, John Lovering notes that the Community is lurching toward a collective security strategy, especially in the formation of the Western European Union, but that defense sectors are exempt from the integrative processes and market discipline imposed on other industries. Even on the security front, tensions over sovereignty are far from resolved, and domestic regime changes can sabotage progress. In the defense sector, a preference for creating and defending national champion firms places roadblocks on the path to an efficient, integrated European military industrial complex. Lovering raises the interesting prospect that disarray in the European market might result in transatlantic mergers instead.

Europe offers a window into alternative configurations for a defense industry and varying strategies for post–Cold War downsizing. Lovering notes that German industry always has been more "dual use" in character, facilitating the rapid downsizing of the past few years. France, on the other hand, has supported a large, specialized, and quasi-nationalized sector, relatively dependent on exports. French nationalism and vulnerability to displacement, a function of both the size and specialization in the sector, has resulted until recently in maintenance of relatively high defense budgets, reticence to buy internationally, and greater efforts to export arms as a solution to excess capacity. Britain, Lovering shows, pursued a strategy of vigorous downsizing and outsourcing under Prime Minister Margaret Thatcher, for whom free-market ideology prevailed over national interests. Britain thus became more willing to import weapons if superior to or less costly than domestically produced ones and was less concerned with American buyouts of defense companies. However, since 1996 British policy has backtracked, and the new labor government may restore "Buy British" practices.

When the Berlin Wall fell and the Soviet Union democratized without bloodshed, many expected the West to reap a huge peace dividend, the payoff from decades of an expensive Cold War arms race. The realization of this dividend was pressing, because the protagonist countries were becoming increasingly challenged by economic competition from emerging Asian countries, whose blend of low-wage labor and increasing technological sophistication was fueling growing American and European trade deficits. President Clinton in particular envisioned the transfer of workers and technologies into commercial aircraft, electronics, communications, transportation, and shipbuilding expertise. American and European governments designed and funded, albeit modestly, new initiatives in conversion to facilitate rapid transition of people, plants, and equipment from military to civilian activities.

How much conversion actually has taken place, and how much of it can be credited to government programs? In both the American and the European cases, rather remarkable progress in conversion and diversification has been achieved, more than is acknowledged by certain academic and corporate naysayers. Many military bases have been converted into civilian uses, although the process is taking longer than it should. Many firms, large and small, have successfully lowered their defense dependency by developing new products and expanding civilian sales. However, government programs have played a relatively minor role in this drama, chiefly because they are underfunded and, in the U.S. case, under ideological attack.

Surveying the European case, in Chapter 14 Michael Brzoska, Peter Wilke, and Herbert Wulf relate a post–Cold War scenario quite similar to that of the United States. In the leading European arms-producing nations—Britain, France, Germany—the excess capacity problem is exacerbated by the relatively small size of national markets. By and large consolidation has taken place on a national rather than Europe-wide basis, because intense industry lobbying and other, overriding political problems with European integration have thwarted attempts at creating a pan-European sector. A common West European or European Union foreign and security policy concept does not exist yet. Additionally, since time schedules for procurement of weapon systems are not synchronized among West European countries, unilateral decisions are still likely in the future. These trends, in combination with the continued political will to favor national champions, will hinder the process of forming a competitive West European defense industry.

In general, the largest European nations have officially left adjustment in the hands of private sector companies, which have been modestly successful at conversion, especially in the sense of moving people and technologies into commercial product lines. National governments, facing tight budget constraints and other competing societal demands, have been unwilling to commit resources to conversion, although Brzoska, Wilke, and Wulf note that conversion nevertheless takes place within a labyrinth of historically evolved incentives and institutions that help support industries and workers. In addition, the European Parliament, despite opposition from most member states, created and funds a relatively generous program, KONVER, which offers assistance to regions and firms faced with base closings and contract losses.

Variations across the four countries in post–Cold War industry restructuring are instructive. Germany has been able to lower its defense budget fastest, chiefly because of unification and associated investment and social spending priorities. Because of its historically delimited shape and relatively strong dual-use character, German industry has had a relatively easier time adjusting. France has been least successful to date in lowering its defense budget and reshaping its military industrial base. With large defense-dedicated and quasi-public farms, change has come slowly. In the mid-1990s, however, French leaders finally decided that an autarkic military industrial strategy was simply too expensive and, under Jacques Chirac, are moving toward a dramatic downsizing and privatization of their industry. French strategy, however, probably will continue to promote "national champions."

An Industry for the Future

The original research and insights of our authors suggests that what we have elsewhere called "supply-side resistance" has been the major impediment to achieving both an appropriate 21st-century defense industry and a peace dividend.[39] Profit, technology, and job considerations are driving defense policy in ways that were inconceivable up through World War II. Although the Bush and Clinton administrations did undertake defense cuts, these were modest compared with potential savings, and their allocation was ill-suited to new realities. The Clinton dual-use and conversion initiatives were cross-cut with powerful new signals to large defense contractors to remain "pure-play" providers, both via arms export policy and via a historically unprecedented permissiveness toward mergers, as well as billions in new subsidies for both.

In Chapter 15 we sum up the policy issues facing the United States and its major defense industrial allies as we enter the 21st century. First, the absence of consensus on what constitutes the contemporary threat makes intelligent defense planning and budgeting very difficult. Second, solid research evidence on the appropriate size and composition of the defense industrial base is alarmingly lacking. We propose a thorough review of competing industrial base configurations, linked to a set of potential force structure scenarios. Flamm's work demonstrates that this can be done without much difficulty. Given recent evidence from the General Accounting Office that actual savings from mergers are amounting to only a fraction of those promised, we recommend the elimination of reimbursements for consolidation costs and their allocation instead to dual-use and conversion initiatives.[40] Similarly, the rush to privatize America's arsenal also is based on inadequate evidence and should be approached with great caution and better analysis.

On arms exports, the same dearth of solid research makes it impossible to evaluate the claims of companies that they must export in order to preserve capacity and ensure future capabilities. Because economically driven exports pose serious security and humanitarian problems as well as undermine an agenda of democratization, the United States, Russia, China, and the European Community should play a lead role in capping exports. They should follow the lead of the World Bank and International Monetary Fund in encouraging developing countries to spend on domestic rather than military investment and to forgo military production and convert existing capability where possible.

None of the major western weapons-producing countries have achieved conversion on anything near the scale anticipated when the Berlin Wall fell. Private sector firms have diversified quite substantially, but with very little help from their host governments. We conclude that it is not too late. From the success and failure of private-sector efforts and those modest public programs that have been put in place, important lessons can be learned. For firms, management commitment, willingness to change firm culture and resort to outside expertise, and access to bridging finance are crucial. Government programs, often at the regional rather than national level, have made the difference between bankruptcy and survival for many firms by providing technical assistance and finance to weather the two years or more it takes to shift to civilian markets. Worker readjustment, whether for members of the armed forces, civilian personnel, defense industry engineers, or blue-collar workers, could be improved dramatically in terms of counseling, providing worker transition centers, and enabling many to return to school or receive long-term retraining.[41] Base reuse, often blocked by incomplete withdrawal of the military or the presence of environmental contamination, could be facilitated by expedited property turnover and effective cleanup.[42]

The size and shape of the defense industry are pressing issues for both Americans and the international community as we approach the 21st century. It is an agenda that will not go away, despite the inattention to date. The West could end up with a small set of very large, very powerful, and not very competitive defense firms, favoring the maintenance of Cold War thinking and technologies. If these remain "national champions," without cooperating internationally, elimination of excess capacity will become just that much more difficult. The industry may rely increasingly on exports to problematic nations and worse, on weapons technology transfer, exacerbating arms proliferation and setting off another arms race, ironically among allies.

Or we could be moving into a world with a few large, specialized transnational defense corporations with considerably greater muscle in the world arms market. American orders would comprise a smaller share of the sales of any one of these giants, with negative implications for American security and access. Nevertheless, the United States probably will continue to fund most of the world's leading-edge R&D, even as its ability to control diffusion of sophisticated weapons wanes.

The preferable alternative, in our view, is a move toward an integrated military-civilian sector, with more firms competing to serve the military and fewer of them dependent on defense contracts. Because such a sector also might be more international in scope, it must be accompanied by a military industrial base policy and arms export control regime coordinated among allied nations. Such industry integration and governmental cooperation would lessen supply-side resistance to an appropriate military procurement strategy. It would enable defense dollars, which are likely to shrink in number, to be spent optimally on defending citizens in a very new security world. With lively and diverse civilian markets, firms might feel less compelled to export, making the world a safer place. Reflecting on Walker's account of defense industrial politics, we conclude that leadership for such a strategy is most likely to come from the American president, the Pentagon, and the armed forces. We recommend that President Clinton and his successors vigorously pursue this mix of policies.

Notes

1. William Miller, "After Desert Storm: What Next for Defense?" *Industry Week* 24 (July 1, 1991): 48–53; Eric Schine, "Defenseless Against Cutbacks," *Business Week,* January 14, 1991, p. 69; Anthony Velocci, "Ill-Defined U.S. Defense Priorities Making Industry a 'Gambler's Paradise,'" *Aviation Week & Space Technology,* June 17, 1991, pp. 141–42.

2. For civilian-military integration, see Jacques Gansler, *Defense Conversion: Transforming the Arsenal of Democracy* (Cambridge, Mass: The MIT Press, 1995). John Alic et al., *Beyond Spin-off: Military and Commercial Technologies in a Changing World* (Cambridge, Mass.: Harvard Business School Press, 1992); David Mowery and Nathan Rosenberg, *Technology and the Pursuit of Economic Growth* (Cambridge: Cambridge University Press, 1989).

3. Gregory Bischak, ed., *Towards a Peace Economy in the United States: Essays on Military Industry, Disarmament and Economic Conversion* (New York: St. Martin's Press, 1991); Lloyd Dumas and Marek Thee, eds., *Making Peace Possible: The Promise of Economic Conversion* (Oxford: Pergamon Press, 1989); Seymour Melman, *The Demilitarized Society, Disarmament & Conversion* (Montreal: Harvest House, 1988).

4. William Cohen, *Report of the Quadrennial Defense Review* (Washington, D.C.: Department of Defense, May 1997); National Defense Panel, *Transforming Defense: National Security in the 21st Century* (Washington, D.C.: Department of Defense, December 1997).

5. Robert Coen and Bert Hickman, "Macroeconomic Impacts of Disarmament and the Peace Dividend in the U.S. Economy," in Nils Gleditsch et al., eds., *The Peace Dividend* (Amsterdam: Elsevier, 1996) pp. 27–61.

6. *Boston Review* (February 1992): 5–9; Randall Forsberg, "Cooperative Security: Reconciling the Competing Paradigms of Non-offensive Defense and Collective Security in a Global Approach to Post-Cold War Security Needs," Paper presented at the 89th Annual Convention of the American Political Science Association, Washington, D.C., September, 1993.

7. This book is not about how much or what kind of defense we need. These are topics well researched and hotly debated by other scholars and policy

analysts. The determination of actual spending levels and their distribution among weapons systems, across the armed services, and among research, equipment, maintenance, and personnel bids is the work of individuals and agencies within an elaborate system of foreign policymaking, military strategizing, DoD civilian oversight, presidential priority setting and budgeting, and congressional scrutiny.

8. Werner Voss and Michael Brzoska, *Eurofighter 2000: Consequences and Alternatives* (Bonn: Bonn International Center for Conversion, 1996).

9. See, for instance, Richard K. Betts, *Military Readiness: Concepts, Choices, Consequences* (Washington, D.C.: Brookings Institution, 1995).

10. John Steinbruner, "Reluctant Strategic Realignment: The Need for a New View of National Security," *Brookings Review* 13, no. 1 (1997): 4–9.

11. Cohen, *Report of the Quadrennial Defense Review.*

12. National Defense Panel, *Transforming Defense.*

13. Forsberg, "Defense Cuts and Cooperative Security"; Kaufmann and Steinbruner, *Decisions for Defense;* Janne Nolan, "The Imperatives for Cooperation," in Janne E. Nolan, ed., *Global Engagement: Cooperation and Security in the 21st Century* (Washington, D.C.: Brookings Institution, 1994).

14. National Defense Panel, *Transforming Defense.*

15. Gregory Bischak, "Cooperative Security, Disarmament, and the Construction of International Peacekeeping Institutions," in Kevin Cassidy and Gregory Bischak, eds., *Real Security: Converting the Defense Economy and Building Peace* (Albany: State University of New York Press, 1993) pp. 11–40.

16. Kaufmann and Steinbruner, *Decisions for Defense;* Forsberg, "Defense Cuts and Cooperative Security."

17. On dual-use incentives, see Jacques Gansler, *Defense Conversion: Transforming the Arsenal of Democracy* (Cambridge, Mass.: MIT Press, 1995); William J. Perry, "Three Barriers to Major Defense Acquisition Reform," *Defense Issues,* no. 65, p. 1 (1993); William J. Perry, "Specifications & Standards—A New Way of Doing Business"; Memorandum for Secretaries of the Military Departments, Chairman of the Joint Chiefs of Staff, Undersecretaries of Defense, June 29, 1994; William Rogerson, "Economic Incentives and the Defense Procurement Process," *Journal of Economic Perspectives* 8, no. 4 (1994): 65–90; on diversification and integration, see: Michael Oden, Gregory Bischak, and Christine Evans-Klock, *The Technology Reinvestment Project: The Limits of Dual-Use Technology Policy* (New Brunswick, N.J.: Rutgers University, Project on Regional and Industrial Economics, 1995).

18. Defense Science Board Task Force, *Antitrust Aspects of Defense Industry Consolidation* (Washington, D.C.: Office of the Undersecretary of Defense for Acquisition and Technology, 1994); William Hartung, *And Weapons for All* (New York: HarperCollins, 1994); Ann Markusen, "The Post–Cold War Per-

sistence of Defense Specialized Firms," in Gerald Susman, ed., *Post-War Progress in Dual-Use Technologies,* forthcoming; White House, Office of the Press Secretary, "Conventional Arms Transfer Policy" and "Criteria for Decision Making on U.S. Arms Exports," Fact Sheets, February 17, 1995.

19. John Dowdy, "Winners and Losers in the Arms Industry Downturn," *Foreign Policy* (Summer 1997): 88–101. Kenneth Flamm, "U.S. Defense Industry Consolidation in the 1990s." In Gerald I. Susman and Sean O'Keefe, eds., *The Defense Industry in the Post–Cold War Era: Corporate Strategies and Public Policy Perspectives* (Oxford: Elsevier Science) pp. 45–69; William Kovacic and Dennis Smallwood, "Competition Policy, Rivalries, and Defense Industry Consolidation," *Journal of Economic Perspectives* 8, no. 4 (1994): 91–110; Ann Markusen, "The Economics of Defense Industry Mergers and Divestiture," *Economic Affairs* 17, no. 4 (1997): 28–32; Office of the Secretary of Defense, *Defense Science Board's Task Force on Vertical Integration and Supplier Decisions* (Washington, D.C.: Department of Defense, May 1997); Aaron Zitner, "Mergers Could Endanger Defense," *Boston Globe,* December 23, 1996, p. A1.

20. Mary Ellen Kelley and Todd Watkins, "The Myth of the Specialized Military Contractor," *Journal of Economic Perspectives* 98, no. 3 (April 1995): 52–58.

21. Richard Minnich, "Defense Downsizing and Economic Conversion: An Industry Perspective," in Ethan Kapstein, ed., *Downsizing Defense,* pp. 111–28 (Washington, D.C.: *Congressional Quarterly,* 1993); Murray Weidenbaum, *Small Wars, Big Defense: Paying for the Military after the Cold War* (New York: Oxford University Press, 1992).

22. Ann Markusen and Joel Yudkin, *Dismantling the Cold War Economy* (New York: Basic Books, 1992).

23. Kenneth Mayer, *The Political Economy of Defense Contracting* (New Haven, Conn.: Yale University Press, 1991).

24. Gordon Adams, *The Politics of Defense Contracting: The Iron Triangle* (New Brunswick, N.J.: Transaction Books, 1982).

25. Coen and Hickman, "Macroeconomic Impacts of Disarmament."

26. Erik Pages, *Responding to Defense Dependence* (Westport, Conn.: Praeger, 1996).

27. William B. Burnett and Frederic M. Scherer, "The Weapons Industry." In Walter Adams, ed., *The Structure of American Industry,* pp. 289–317 (New York: Macmillan, 1990); Todd Sandler and Keith Hartley, *The Economics of Defense* (Cambridge: Cambridge University Press, 1995).

28. James Kurth, "The Follow-on Imperative in American Weapons Procurement, 1960–1990, in Jurgen Brauer and Manas Chatterji, eds., *Economic Issues of Disarmament,* pp. 304–21 (New York: Macmillan, 1993).

29. Business Executives for National Security, *The Revolution in Military Business Affairs* (Washington, D.C.: BENS, October 1997).

30. Jeffrey Drezner et al., *Maintaining Future Military Aircraft Design Capability* (Santa Monica: RAND Corporation, RAND/R-41990AF, 1992); TASC, *Bomber Industrial Capabilities Study* (Alexandria, Va: TASC, June 1995); U.S.

Department of Commerce, Bureau of Export Administration, *National Security Assessment of the Domestic and Foreign Contractor Base: A Study of Three U.S. Navy Systems* (Washington, D.C.: Department of Commerce, March 1992); U.S. Department of Defense, *Industrial Assessment for Torpedoes* (Washington, D.C.: Undersecretary of Defense, Acquisition and Technology, DoD, August 1995).

31. William Kovacic, "Merger Policy in a Declining Defense Industry," *Antitrust Bulletin* 36 (1991): 544–53; Kovacic and Smallwood, "Competition Policy."

32. Markusen, "Economics of Defense Industry Mergers."

33. Randall Forsberg, ed., *The Arms Production Dilemma* (Cambridge, Mass.: The MIT Press, 1994); Kenneth Mayer, "Combat Aircraft Production in the United States 1950–2000: Maintaining Industry Capability in an Era of Shrinking Budgets," *Defense Analysis* 9, no. 2 (1993): 159–69.

34. Hartung, *And Weapons for All;* William Hartung, *Welfare for Weapons Dealers: The Hidden Costs of the Arms Trade* (New York: World Policy Institute, June 1996).

35. White House, Office of the Press Secretary, "Conventional Arms Transfer Policy" and "Criteria for Decision Making."

36. Jeffrey Boutwell, Michale Klare, and Laura Reed, eds., *Lethal Commerce: The Global Trade in Small Arms and Light Weapons* (Cambridge, Mass.: Committee on International Security Studies, American Academy of Arts and Sciences, 1995); Natalie Goldring, "Toward Restraint: Controlling the International Arms Trade," *Harvard International Review* 17, no. 1 (1994): 34–37, 78–79; William Keller, *Arm in Arm: The Political Economy of the Global Arms Trade* (New York: Basic Books, 1995); Edward Laurance, *The International Arms Trade* (New York: Lexington Books, 1992); Kevin O'Prey, *The Arms Export Challenge: Cooperative Approaches to Export Management and Defense Conversion* (Washington, D.C.: Brookings Institution, 1995).

37. T. H. Moran, "Foreign Acquisition of Critical U.S. Industries: Where Should the United States Draw the Lines?" *Washington Quarterly* (Spring 1993): 61–74; Defense Forecasts, Inc., *Foreign Investment in the U.S. Defense Industrial Base: A Sound National Strategy for America's Future* (Washington, D.C.: Department of Defense, May 1992).

38. Michael Brzoska and Peter Lock, *Restructuring of Arms Production in Western Europe* (Oxford: Oxford University Press, 1992); Jane Davis Drown, Clifford Drown, and Kelly Campbell, eds., *A Single European Arms Industry?* (London: Brassey's, 1990).

39. Ann Markusen, "Why We Lost the Peace Dividend," *The American Prospect* (July/August 1997): 86–95.

40. U.S. General Accounting Office, *Defense Downsizing: Selective Contractors Business Unit Reactions*, GAO/NSIAD-95-144 (Washington, D.C.: Government Printing Office, May 1995).

41. Laura Powers and Ann Markusen, *A First Transition? Lessons from Defense Worker Adjustment in the 1990s* (Washington, D.C.: Economic Policy Institute, 1999).

42. Catherine Hill, *The Political Economy of Military Base Redevelopment: An Evaluation of Four Converted Naval Bases* (Ph.D. Dissertation, Rutgers University, 1998).

II

Transformation in the Post–Cold War Decade

2

Contending Security Doctrines and the Military Industrial Base

GREG BISCHAK

S INCE 1990 the seriously diminished threat of a catastrophic war of global proportions has led to a major restructuring and downsizing of the Cold War military posture of the United States. The lessening of international threats also accelerated the elimination of redundancies in the military base structure. Several years after the formal end of the Cold War, however, there is still contentious debate about what constitutes the most effective and least expensive security policy for the United States and its allies, with this debate reflecting the fact that such downsizing carries with it far-reaching military and economic effects for the armed services and the military-serving industries.

From its Cold War peak in 1989, military spending for 1995 has been reduced by one-third and weapons procurement by two-thirds, while all defense-related employment has fallen by 2.2 million workers since its 1987 high point. In January 1996 the forecast for future budgets, even after taking into account congressional increases in the Clinton administration's future-years defense plan, implied further reductions in real terms, with budget authority falling from 1995 levels by perhaps 11 percent by the year 2002.[1]

Despite these changes, however, the nation still plans to spend, in real terms, over 80 percent of the Cold War average annual military budget through the end of this decade. In an era of severe budgetary austerity, it is difficult to accept the need for such high levels of military spending, let alone countenance the most egregious examples of pork-barrel procurement programs. In this context the challenge of charting a path to the most effective and least expensive security policy comes into sharp relief. Yet there has been remarkably little debate over the doctrines that shape our current configuration of military forces to meet the most probable and dangerous security threats and the economic implications of these security doctrines for the nation's science, technology, and industrial policies.

Post–Cold War defense planners have assumed that the nation's security is best protected by maintaining the U.S. military's qualitative superiority over all potential foes—especially by developing more flexible and discriminant means of projecting military power throughout the world. Little consideration has been given to how alternative security approaches might meet the security requirements of the post–Cold War environment without requiring continuous modernization of weapons and forces. Nor has there been much discussion of how strengthening and building international institutions could enhance national security and address the new threats to international security through nonmilitary, nontechnological means. Such considerations could yield substantially different approaches to national security planning for scientific, technological, and industrial investments and lessen the drive to develop a faster, more flexible, and more mobile military force equipped with the most advanced weapon systems.

In this chapter I compare the budgetary requirements of current long-range defense plans with alternative defense plans proposed by several defense analysts and examine the security doctrines that underpin each plan and their implications for research, development, and procurement policy. These alternative policies are then counterposed with the economic and industrial requirements implied by the strategic-military assumptions, force levels, and technology of each framework. In the final section, I examine the implications for the industrial organization and management of such alternative defense policies.

Alternative Defense Budget Plans

With the lowering of the Soviet flag over the Kremlin at the close of 1991, the Bush administration revised its national defense plan that called for phased reductions in military spending and lower force levels that would establish a "base force" to meet major regional contingencies and permit continued power projection.[2] These changes called for a 21 percent real reduction in military spending by 1997 and required substantial cuts in major Cold War weapons modernization programs. The Gulf War, however, compounded the problem of restructuring the military and complicated the debate over post–Cold War security requirements. Indeed, the force requirements of the Gulf War became a widely accepted benchmark for sizing military forces to meet regional major contingencies.

Under the Clinton administration, the Desert Storm–equivalent force became codified in the Bottom-Up Review (BUR) that calibrated U.S. forces to simultaneously wage and win two major regional conflicts without any assistance from its allies. The review also called for the capacity to meet other contingencies, such as humanitarian relief operations and international peacekeeping operations.

These geostrategic requirements differ from the Cold War military posture that was geared to fighting two and one-half conventional wars simultaneously, while still fielding a large and diverse strategic and tactical nuclear force. By contrast, a post–Cold War military force geared to a more selective set of geostrategic objectives requires a somewhat smaller navy, a smaller, highly mobile ground force, a tactical air force capable of delivering precision-guided conventional munitions, and a larger air and sea-lift capability to rapidly move troops and materiel. Moreover, meeting these objectives does not require a large strategic or tactical nuclear force. Nor is a huge standing force for a conventional standoff with the Soviet Union in Central Europe required.

The principal differences between the Clinton and Bush plans (see Table 2–1) lie in a slightly smaller navy but larger marine force and a somewhat smaller army and air force under the Clinton plan. Strategic nuclear forces remain basically the same in both plans because each assumes the forces laid out in the START I and II agreements. According to the Congressional Research Service, the Clinton plan will cost $118 billion less in budget authority (current dollars) than the force that former Defense Secretary Richard Cheney had planned to field by 1999.[3]

While the Bottom-Up Review plan initially galvanized thinking within the defense establishment about post–Cold War defense requirements, this loose consensus has begun to unravel both because of substantial questions about the realism and affordability of the plan, and continued pressures to reduce the deficit.[4] In addition, partisan criticism from defense hawks has whipsawed the administration, first by arguing that there was a readiness crisis and then by arguing that there was not enough money in the plan to modernize adequately the force needed for the contingencies outlined in the plan.[5] These factors have generated some debate within and outside of the defense establishment over the need for a new basis to plan for post–Cold War security. Within

Table 2–1 Comparison of Alternative Military Force Structure and Spending Plans

	Bush/ Cheney	Clinton/ Perry	O'Hanlon Proposal	Wiesner et al.	Forsberg Proposal
Army					
Active Divisions	12	10	8	5	5
Reserve Divisions	8	5	8	10	2
Navy					
Carrier Groups/ Air Wings	12/11	11/10	8/7	5/5	3/3
Training Carriers	—	1	—	—	—
Attack Subs	45–55	45–55	35	40	20
Total Battleforce Ships	430	346	300	160	124
Marines					
Active Duty	159,000	174,000	100,000	50,000	42,000
Reserve Divisions	1	1	1	1	1
Air Wings	5	5	2	1	1
Air Force					
Fighter Wings	14	13	11	6	5
Reserve Wings	10	7	7	6	3
Strategic Nuclear Platforms					
Ballistic Missile Subs	18	18	9	10	10
B-2 Bombers	20	20	—	0	0
B-1 Bombers	96	0	—	0	0
B-52H Bombers	95	94	—	60	0
Minuteman III	500	500	100	300	0
Warheads	5,000	5,000	1,000–3,000	<1,000	240
Ballistic Missile Defense					
Theater	Y	Y	Y	Research	Research
Continental	Y	Limited	Research	Research	Research
Projected Year Budget Authority (billions of current $U.S.)	$293	$266	$246	$163	$87

Sources: Department of Defense, Office of the Secretary of Defense and Joint Chiefs of Staff, Report on the Bottom-Up Review, September 1, 1993, Washington D.C.; Michael O'Hanlon, *Defense Planning for the Late 1990s: Beyond the Desert Storm Framework* (Washington D.C.: Brookings Institution, 1995); Jerome Wiesner, Philip Morrison, Kosta Tsipis, *Beyond the Looking Glass: The United States Military in 2000 and Later* (Boston, Mass.: MIT, 1993); Randall Forsberg, "Defense Cuts and Cooperative Security in the Post-Cold War World," *Boston Review* 17, nos. 3–4 (May–July 1992); National Priorities Project, *Creating a Common Agenda* (Amherst, Mass.: National Priorities Project 1995), p. 64.

the Pentagon there is a push for a postelection reassessment of the Bottom-Up Review. Elsewhere various proposals have been advanced, with defense hawks generally calling for more money for defense, while others have proposed a scaled-back, less ambitious basis for defense planning.

Kaufmann and Steinbruner's Collective and Cooperative Security Proposals

Prior to the development of the Bottom-Up Review Plan, several prominent defense analysts put forth alternative defense budgets that suggested that the defense spending levels at the start of the 1990s could be nearly halved by the end of the 1990s and still provide a robust defense posture for the United States. Most prominent were William Kaufmann and John Steinbruner of the Brookings Institution, who made the case for scaling back dramatically the forward-based presence of the U.S. military, terminating many major Cold War weapons programs, and reducing weapons research budgets. In addition, they argued for eliminating many of the redundancies within the force structure for air and ground forces and deep reductions in nuclear forces.

More significantly, they outlined operational principles for a cooperative security framework that would fundamentally revamp security policy for the world's major military powers. They proposed systematically to limit the offensive capabilities of the air and ground forces of the major powers, agree to prior announcement of military maneuvers, increase transparency for new weapons research programs, and establish an integrated weapons export regime. Finally, they made a case for eliminating tactical nuclear weapons and deeper reductions in strategic nuclear weapons. Such a nuclear force policy also would provide encouragement for wider nonproliferation efforts.

They argued that such changes would generate real security benefits in the post–Cold War world by reducing risk and demonstrating the commitment of the leading powers to cooperative approaches for security. If these changes in force structure had been fully adopted by the year 2002, they would have yielded cumulative budget savings of $670 billion as measured in 1996 dollars. This force structure is not depicted in Table 2–1 because too much water has gone over the dam since it was first advanced. Nonetheless, these proposals have spawned wider discussions and variants of cooperative security.

While the Kaufmann and Steinbruner proposals were not influential in determining the Bush administration's base force structure, they did provide some impetus for trying to terminate a few Cold War weapons systems and in implementing the stand-down of tactical nuclear forces. Nor did the Kaufmann and Steinbruner proposals have a discernible impact on the formation of the Bottom-Up Review, although they probably had some influence on the Clinton administration's position in negotiating the Wassenaar Arrangement for conventional and dual-use arms export policy. In budgetary terms, the Clinton administration's defense plan may yield only 18 percent of the defense budget savings outlined by Kaufmann and Steinbruner.

Ironically, today the Bottom-Up Review force assumptions have become the basis for pressing for increases in defense spending to maintain readiness and modernize forces. For these reasons alone, it seems worthwhile to enlarge the circle of debate by considering alternative security frameworks that could provide guidance for defense planning. In addition, the pressures to reduce the budget deficit, coupled with the need for a more realistic and affordable security policy, make this exercise relevant. Several other contemporary approaches have been advanced, but I choose to focus on those that examine key issues of doctrine and that pose challenging institutional questions about post–Cold War security policy. In the interest of enlarging the debate, I consider not only a new variant from the Brookings Institution but also a proposal from respected scientists and another from the peace and security community.

O'Hanlon's Proposal

Michael O'Hanlon of the Brookings Institution has advanced a force plan that rationalizes the two-war model upon which the Bottom-Up Review was built. He argues that there is little likelihood in the foreseeable future of needing a dual Desert Storm–equivalent force. Instead of planning for a force that addresses two simultaneous major regional contingencies, O'Hanlon argues for a more credible planning scenario demanding a Desert Shield–style force plus a Desert Storm–equivalent force. Such a force would rely on air power and precision-strike munitions and greater prepositioning of supplies in regions of vital national interest. In addition, it would boost the air and sealift capabilities of the military to enhance logistical and military capabilities.

Force reductions beyond those currently envisioned by the BUR are feasible. In particular, O'Hanlon calls into question the need for continuous forward presence of naval aircraft carrier battlegroups throughout the world, suggesting that this force could be cut by a third and still provide more than adequate power projection capabilities. In addition, he argues for further rationalization of ground and air forces that were left virtually untouched by the Roles and Missions Commission. But there is some need for buttressing training and support for U.S. participation in United Nations and other peacekeeping and humanitarian operations. He also counsels against an aggressive extension of the North Atlantic Treaty Organization (NATO) eastward because of its potential for engendering antagonism with Russia.

O'Hanlon eschews much of the modernization currently in the procurement pipeline, especially for next-generation systems that originally were conceived to meet the Soviet threat. In particular he proposes terminating the F-22 fighter, the V-22 tilt rotor aircraft, the new attack submarines, and the Trident missile program, and making procurement cuts associated with modernizing additional aircraft carrier battlegroups. He does, however, propose more air and sealift procurement, although he substitutes reconfigured 747s for additional C-17 aircargo jet transports. In addition, more F-15s combat aircraft and CH-46 and CH-53 helicopters are recommended instead of new systems.

Finally, O'Hanlon argues that the nation should move beyond START II nuclear weapons limits by negotiating bilateral agreements with Russia to further reduce the number of strategic delivery systems and warheads. He also rejects calls for continental ballistic missile defense as destabilizing and dangerously provocative. In addition, he proposes modest cuts in communications and intelligence budgets and a less ambitious and less costly nuclear stockpile stewardship program. Like his predecessors at Brookings, he sees tangible security gains coming from the reduced nuclear-related risks and enhanced potential for nonproliferation. Furthermore, given the emphasis on acquiring more precision-guided munitions and a more mobile and lethal conventional military force, O'Hanlon argues that we no longer need large nuclear forces for a credible deterrent.

Taken together, by 2001 these changes in force structure will yield modest cumulative savings as compared to the Clinton administration's 1995 defense budget of about $80 billion as measured in 1995 dollars. But the reductions in procurement will yield further savings in the next decade, adding several billion annually to the steady-state annual savings of $27 billion by 2005.

The virtue of the O'Hanlon plan is that it seeks to check some of the Cold War baggage, particularly the assumptions about needing a continuous forward presence and the overwrought need for a two–Desert Storm contingency force. Perhaps more important, the push for further reductions in nuclear forces, as well as cuts in nuclear weapons research budgets, is a salutary step toward lowering the nuclear-related risks and advances nonproliferation. In addition, the critique of proposals for a continental ballistic missile defense puts into stark relief the risks associated with launching a new phase of the arms race. Numerous aspects of this set of proposals will be examined in more detail in the next part of this chapter. But in general, O'Hanlon's security framework postulates a more austere power projection capability that begins to decouple from the Cold War military-strategic conception that relied on continuous modernization of weaponry. Finally, these proposals imply substantial changes in the defense industrial base, a point that will be addressed in the last part of this chapter.

Morrison, Tsipis, and Wiesner Proposals

Members of the scientific community have had questions of national security since the beginning of the nuclear age, but few have been so bold as to sketch out a whole framework for national security planning as three scientists from the Massachusetts Institute of Technology (MIT): Philip Morrison, Kosta Tsipis, and the late Jerome Wiesner. Early in 1993 these scientists sought to open new lines of debate over national security issues. While they generally tried to outline how the nation could be secure for far less money, they also set forth a few broad principles for thinking through post–Cold War security needs and phasing in these planned reductions by the year 2000.

Starting with normative assumptions, they see the need for the United States to retain a strong but minimum nuclear deterrent and to keep enough of a conventional military force for it to prevail in any potential theater with or without allies. On nuclear deterrence issues, they underscored the need for only a few hundred nuclear weapons, since anything beyond that level has marginal deterrence value and only increases the risks of accident or proliferation. Under their proposals, nuclear force levels would be reduced to fewer than 1,000 total warheads, with a scaled-back tirade of strategic subs, land-based missiles, and strategic bombers capable of delivering 780 strategic nuclear warheads. All nuclear delivery vehicles would be limited to single warheads, including the missiles on Ohio-class submarines. They propose to retain 250 tactical nuclear weapons pending the negotiation of a multilateral treaty to eliminate these altogether. They reject any need for continental ballistic missile defense as unnecessary and counterproductive to implementing deep reductions in strategic nuclear weaponry and argue for only limited research. Elsewhere in the nuclear weapons complex they call for deep reductions in the nuclear weapons research and testing budgets and for the consolidation of the weapons design labs. Nonproliferation efforts would be enhanced greatly by deep reductions in the great powers arsenals because, in the views of the authors, such initiatives would reduce the political incentives for other nations to emulate the great powers.

Conventional force restructuring would be guided by the dramatically reduced threat and the need to eliminate the armed services' current redundant force structure. These principles lead the authors to conclude that the military could be reorganized based on operational security missions. Major mission planning requirements would focus on functional deployment of forces for air-land battles, control of the seas, land-sea operations, intelligence and space operations, nuclear deterrence, and research and development. According to the authors' calculations, fairly dramatic reductions would result from this approach that would roughly halve the active duty forces of the army, air force, and navy. In a similar fashion they recommend that military-related space and intelligence operations could be downsized radically by eliminating the redundancy and the Cold War–oriented missions, leading to roughly half the outlays as compared to 1990 levels.

While these proposals are very general, the virtue of this approach is that it refocuses discussions on the basic issues of security doctrines and institutions. The doctrine of minimum deterrence is advanced to fundamentally reconfigure nuclear forces and strategy to reflect the new realities. In addition, they argue for the need for aggressive demand-side initiatives to stem nuclear proliferation. Their proposal to break up the traditional armed services structure offers new organizational principles for eliminating the redundancies in the current force. Finally, the authors acknowledge that adopting these changes will have a heavy impact on the defense industries and military-related employment, but they offer no specific policies to address these problems.

Forsberg's Cooperative Security Proposals

Randall Forsberg, the director of the Institute for Defense and Disarmament Studies, has advanced a framework that goes well beyond the assumptions and force requirements of other cooperative security proposals to outline the steps for a more demilitarized world. Forsberg argues for the phased development of a cooperative security scheme based on confidence-building measures, the adoption of nonoffensive defense posture, a very low minimum nuclear deterrent, and the buildup of multilateral security capabilities both within and outside of the United Nations system. While Forsberg concedes that such proposals are nowhere near being considered seriously by defense planners, the risks and costs of conducting business as usual should compel policymakers and citizens to consider such an approach.

A first step toward developing such a process would require the implementation of a series of confidence-building measures to establish guidelines for multilateral actions to intervene in cases of international aggression or genocide. In addition, guidelines would limit the use of force in ending or preventing further conflict. Reforms in the United Nations Security Council decision-making process would be needed to implement such guidelines as well as to ensure that the great powers do not dominate the whole process. Finally, standards for defining non-offensive defense forces would have to be developed to adjudicate a multilateral process for reducing and restructuring conventional military forces as well as strategic nuclear capabilities.

Leadership from the principal participants in the Cold War is essential for launching the next phase, which involves mutual reductions by the major powers of their air, ground, and naval forces and a reconfiguration of the remaining forces into a nonoffensive conventional defense geared to territorial defense. Thus air and naval weaponry used for deep strikes and interdiction would be eliminated from such forces. A parallel process of multilateral strategic nuclear arms reductions would be initiated to establish a small minimum deterrent level for the nuclear powers. Limitations on the production and export of all conventional defense systems and dual-use components also would be imposed under this multilateral process. This phase would further encourage other nations of the world to adopt similar strategies for their own security postures.

The eventual objective of the next phase would be to entirely eliminate a single great power's military capacity for unilateral intervention, although each major power probably would retain the capacity to be militarily superior within its region. The challenge during this phase would be to develop a true multilateral capacity to intervene into major regional conflicts since no one power would retain the capacity to go it alone. Each major power would retain some dedicated capacity to supply multilateral peacekeeping efforts with peace-enforcement and peacekeeping forces. Furthermore, each major power would have to retain the air and sealift capability to deliver these forces to a given theater. Another challenge would be to foster the further adoption of nonoffensive defense postures by the lesser military powers and of regional security arrangements that would lessen the risk of conflict.

Forsberg calculates that full implementation of this cooperative security process would leave the United States with the need for a much smaller military, costing perhaps only $87 billion annually. As Table 2–1 illustrates, based on Forsberg's estimates, such a force would cost about one-third of that planned by the Clinton administration. Active-duty army divisions would be cut by half from currently planned levels and reserves by 60 percent. Naval forces would retain roughly one-third of their planned levels, but aircraft carrier battlegroups would retain only 3 of the 11 battlegroups envisioned by the administration with the effective capacity essentially geared to humanitarian operations. Active-duty U.S. Marine Corps would be cut to one-quarter their current size. The air force active and reserve air wings would retain approximately 40 percent of levels projected for the end of the century.

The most distinguishing difference from other security proposals is the adoption of a very small minimum deterrent of 240 strategic nuclear warheads. Little is explicitly mentioned regarding the size or composition of the military's research budget, but some of the projected savings of this proposal would have to come from dramatic cuts in procurement and research and development funding since the overall force level is not reduced commensurately with the budget.

Clearly, Forsberg's proposal goes far beyond the current security framework, including the complete elimination of unilateral power projection capabilities. Moreover, Forsberg argues for breaking the cycle of continuous modernization of military forces and research in pursuit of military technological superiority. The deep reductions in weapons procurement and research implied by these force structure changes would effectively scrap much of the current defense research and industrial base for both conventional and nuclear weapons.

However, as with the other analysts, Forsberg does not examine the implications for the science, technology, and industrial base of adopting any of these changes. Moreover, given the lack of detailed treatment on remaining research and production capabilities required for any of these proposed force postures, some baseline of comparison must be constructed to examine the implications of these alternatives. However, even in the case of the Clinton administration's defense plan, there has been little integrated analysis of the effects of changes in security doctrines and force structure on the science, technology, and industrial base.[6] For these reasons it is important to trace out the doctrinal implications of these alternative security models in order to analyze their implications for the defense science, technology, and industrial base.

Security Doctrines: The Military-Strategic Model vs. Alternatives

Throughout the Cold War the military-strategic rivalry between the United States and the Soviet Union led to the pursuit of breakthrough technological advances in weaponry, continuous improvements in weapons-related technologies, and strategic research to prevent techno-logical surprises from the other side's military innovations. At the heart of this rivalry was the threat of mass destruction that enforced the search for military innovation. This technological dynamic helped fuel the arms race and generated an inherent instability in the military-strategic con-frontation as each side sought to compensate for any perceived or actual technological advantages held by the other side with corresponding quantitative or qualitative advances in weaponry. Military-oriented research and development absorbed large shares of each nation's total science and technology resources and put into place increasingly lethal weapons of mass destruction that reached global proportions at the apex of the nuclear arms race. But the risk, instability, and uncertainty of the strategic arms race, coupled with its mounting economic costs and social resistance to the nuclear arms race, gave rise to various arms control efforts to ensure a "stable deterrence" relationship between the super-powers. Deterrence and arms control, however, did not put an end to the technological arms race; it continued after the formal end of the Cold War.

The legacy of this arms race goes beyond the vast stores of the means of mass destruction to the central assumptions that still guide both mil-itary planning and federal science and technology policy. Today many national security planners argue that the strategy was successful: deter-rence prevented nuclear war while the technological leadership pro-vided by the market economy supplied ultimate victory. These same planners argue for an extension of deterrence doctrines to the post–Cold War military posture and for the continued pursuit of U.S. military tech-nological superiority, especially through the integration of commercial technological advances in military weapons.

But for such a military deterrent to be credible, it requires the contin-uous development of all types of weaponry in order to ensure that U.S. forces possess an absolute advantage for all contingencies. In essence, this approach assumes a global gradient of power projection, not to police the world, but to intervene selectively to advance vital U.S. inter-ests with maximum effect and minimum casualties for U.S. forces. Such a gradient of power, however, requires a technological push across all fronts relevant to multiplying the military effectiveness of U.S. forces. Accordingly, the post–Cold War military requires fewer troops but rela-tively more technological investment. Moreover, the basic doctrines of deterrence must be revised since the effectiveness of the deterrent pre-sumably depends on maintaining technological superiority for a wide range of contingencies.

The implications of this military strategy for U.S. science, technology, and policies are far-reaching. Such a strategy ensures that military-oriented research and development will continue to command substantial shares of total federal R&D investments. Moreover, the influence of military objectives on the selection of so-called dual-use research and development projects raises questions about how the pace and direction of technological change might be affected. But in order to assess these issues, we must first examine more closely the nature and implications of the post–Cold War doctrines of deterrence for military research and development priorities. Only then can we make a critical appraisal of these doctrines and examine the opportunity costs raised by alternative approaches to security and to science and technology policy in the post–Cold War environment.

DETERRENCE AND GLOBAL POWER PROJECTION IN THE POST–COLD WAR ERA

Few within the military establishment would argue that the United States should literally police the world—although continuous forward presence amounts to being the cop on the world beat. Rather, the military doctrines that have evolved over the last decade are based on the observation that the U.S. military has developed a capacity to apply power selectively, with varying degrees of force, to match the objective. Such power projection, however, is to be applied only in those areas of the world where vital economic or political interests of the United States are threatened. The systematic development of increasingly lethal and precision-guided high-tech weaponry supports the trend toward selective intervention. Moreover, the development of advanced conventional weapons permits large-scale military action without the political and radioactive fallout that would follow from the use of even tactical nuclear weapons. Furthermore, such technology ensures maximum military effectiveness with the minimum likelihood of the loss of U.S. troops. Finally, the development of a global capacity to project military power selectively should exert a deterrent effect on most types of potential threats to U.S. interests.

Military plans for selective global power projection in the post–Cold War era are founded on a revision of the old strategic concepts that have guided military planners for decades. The Cold War conception of deterrence holds that threat of massive retaliation against a potential adversary's aggression should deter it from such actions. In the nuclear era, however, this threat carried with it the prospect of mutual nuclear annihilation, making the threat of escalation from a conventional war to a strategic nuclear war a deadly game of potentially catastrophic dimensions. Indeed, despite elaborate war-making plans by strategic planners, political and military leaders came to realize that they were at an impasse with the strategic nuclear arms race: they could threaten but they dared not use their most powerful weapons. As a result, the nuclear threat had become less credible.

Out of this dilemma came the recognition by military planners that the combination of increasingly lethal conventional munitions with precision-guided delivery systems could yield a measure of deterrence against potential adversaries. In the late 1980s this idea of a more flexible, nonnuclear deterrence had come to be dubbed a "discriminate deterrent." Meanwhile, some strategic planners began to conclude that a smaller arsenal of nuclear weapons might be less risky and still capable of accomplishing its alleged mission of deterring the use of nuclear weapons. This latter notion, called "minimum deterrence," has become particularly attractive to many planners since the demise of the Soviet Union. And while the idea of minimum deterrence actually had its origins on the eve of the strategic missile buildup, it has really begun to be considered only in the post–Cold War era—even though it has not affected strategic nuclear policy yet.

Today these two notions of deterrence are increasingly shaping the mainstream debate within the national security establishment about the nature of the U.S. role in the post–Cold War security order. In one sense the discriminate deterrence concept is a more comprehensive doctrine, which presupposes the adoption of a minimum deterrent nuclear force as part and parcel of an overall strategy to preserve U.S. military superiority. Yet, while there has been clear movement toward operationalizing the more general conception of discriminate deterrence, there has been no movement toward adopting a minimum deterrent policy.

THE DISCRIMINATE DETERRENCE DOCTRINE

The lineage of this new concept of deterrence can be traced to a report of the Commission on Integrated Long-Term Strategy entitled *Discriminate Deterrence,* which was published in January 1988. This report, authored by several prominent veterans of the national security state, recommended that the United States integrate its strategies "for a wide range of conflicts: from the most confined, lowest intensity and highest probability to the most widespread, apocalyptic and least likely." It further asserted that the credibility of the policy depends on assuring potential adversaries that "military aggression at any level of violence against our important interests will be opposed by military force."[7] While this doctrine was conceived during the late stages of the Cold

War with the Soviet Union still in the strategic equation, the main thrust of the analysis was to recast the military's strategy to address a wider range of more likely scenarios.

The war with Iraq was a demonstration of the discriminate deterrence doctrine. The Gulf War demonstrated the precision and lethality of high-tech conventional weaponry and how the possession of such weaponry acts as a "force multiplier" that permits the fielding of a relatively smaller military force while maintaining a decisive military advantage. These force multipliers mean that the U.S. military can deploy smaller forces more rapidly, thereby making possible a wider range of global military contingencies.

IMPLICATIONS FOR RESEARCH, DEVELOPMENT, AND TECHNOLOGY

Such a configuration of forces was identified by the Pentagon's Bottom-Up Review geared to a range of probable threats against vital U.S. interests. However, while the review called for the maintenance of a robust research and development budget capable of ensuring a technologically superior force, it did not specify a research agenda to attain these ends. The critical defense technologies necessary to field such a force were spelled out in several technology planning documents in the early 1990s that identified defense research priorities.

The *DoD's Key Technologies Plan for 1992*, authored under the Bush administration, was mandated by Congress to ascertain how the specific military objectives for maintaining air, sea, and land superiority would define the parameters of advanced military R&D priorities over the next several years. The 1994 *Defense Technology Plan*, authored by the Clinton administration, determined R&D priorities for defense technologies that met the war-fighting needs identified by the Joint Chiefs of Staff in the *Defense Science and Technology Strategy*. The Joint Chiefs' top five war-fighting capabilities were to:

1. Maintain near real-time surveillance and communications;

2. Engage regional forces on a global scale;

3. Achieve military objectives with the minimum of force and minimum casualties and collateral damage;

4. Control the use of space;

5. Counter the threat of weapons of mass destruction and ballistic and cruise missiles.

Accordingly, the most critical defense technologies were for sensors for global surveillance, precision strike, air superiority and defense, sea control, and advanced land combat. Communications networks ranked next most critical, especially for global surveillance, precision strike, and advanced land combat. Software and design automation ranked next, with computers and electronic devices following closely in their priorities.

Electronics, computing, and information technologies are deemed essential by war-fighting commanders for multiplying the effectiveness of military forces, increasing the precision and lethality of weapon systems, and avoiding surprise. Such force multipliers permit the fielding of more effective and smaller military forces. Many transportation and materials research projects are geared to increase the range and capabilities of the military to meet worldwide contingencies with lighter and more mobile forces.

This configuration of technology and forces reflects a more comprehensive and less stylized conception of military-strategic needs. It does not presuppose the two-regional-war scenario of the Bottom-Up Review. For these reasons the review is likely to be eclipsed in the near future as a planning document by a successor plan that more clearly reflects the global power projection model. Furthermore, the BUR force seems saddled with Cold War artifacts such as the need for continuous forward presence and the START II nuclear force.

Nuclear Deterrence: Strategic Arms Reduction Treaty II vs. Minimum Deterrence Doctrine

With the demise of the Soviet Union, the Cold War rationale for maintaining large strategic nuclear forces expired, leading some policymakers to consider ways to reduce dramatically U.S. dependence on large nuclear forces. Two studies published by the National Academy of Sciences and the Congressional Budget Office suggest that the international environment has changed so fundamentally that it is now possible to consider a policy of "minimum nuclear deterrence."[8] Minimum deterrence is a strategy that seeks to maintain the minimum number of strategic nuclear weapons required to inflict unacceptably large damage on an adversary after a nation has suffered a nuclear attack.

This idea was last seriously considered in the early 1960s when Jerome Wiesner, the science adviser to President John F. Kennedy, argued that a few hundred survivable nuclear weapons would be sufficient to deter nuclear attack. Yet this incisive insight into the logic of deterrence theory was lost in the strategic rivalry that unfolded between the Soviets and the United States following the Cuban missile crisis of October 1962. The asymmetries in the nuclear balance and guided missile technology revealed before and after the Cuban missile crisis led both sides to a massive buildup of strategic missile forces and the acceleration of military strategic research in order to assure the development of the most advanced strategic weaponry. However, this technological dynamic introduced new instabilities into the deterrence relationship. These problems in turn led to the adoption of various arms control regimes to restrain the strategic buildup and curb the onset of a new arms race in strategic missile defenses through the Antiballistic Missile Defense (ABM) Treaty. Nonetheless, even a restrained arms race led to the buildup of huge strategic nuclear forces that are only slowly being brought down.

Decades later the idea of minimum deterrence is being revived by some as a means to reduce the tremendous strategic nuclear arsenals to levels that would not threaten the survival of the planet if a nuclear exchange were to take place. The National Academy of Sciences has postulated a post–START II Treaty framework for further reductions in strategic forces, although this scenario envisions retaining 1,000 to 2,000 nuclear weapons.[9] Others have gone further to suggest a nuclear force of 100 strategic warheads.[10]

The emphasis is on developing nuclear forces that are reliable, available, and survivable, and therefore capable of ensuring a "stable deterrent." Nonetheless, even a minimum deterrent of this size holds potential adversaries at risk of near-total catastrophe. Indeed, one study notes that just 600 missiles would be adequate to functionally destroy Russia.[11] Thus even a minimum deterrent would leave in place a terrifying potential for mass destruction. In addition, the retention of a minimum deterrent by each of the nuclear powers could make nuclear proliferation more difficult to control as aspiring nations might seek to emulate the nuclear powers by building a small nuclear arsenal.

Despite numerous studies, the minimum deterrence idea has yet to play a significant role in shaping current policy. Neither the Bottom-Up Review nor the Nuclear Posture Review went beyond the nuclear force limits set forth by the START II Treaty. This failure to consider changes in strategic forces is at odds with the implicit assessment of current force planning that nuclear weapons have little military value in most likely conflicts. The failure to revise nuclear force assumptions in the BUR may be largely a result of the inertial forces of the Cold War. It also may reflect the influence of a more hegemonic view of military power. Another factor undermining the consideration of the minimum deterrence doctrine is that some in the national security establishment favor rapid development and deployment of a robust antimissile defense, including space- and ground-based missiles, and continued research on directed-energy weapons.

Strategic and Theater Missile Defense
While the Clinton administration has refocused antimissile defense programs on so-called theater missile defenses to protect U.S. and allied forces in conventional battles on foreign lands, there is still in place a significant national strategic missile defense research program. However, the current debate between the administration and Congress is over whether the deployment of a multiple-site national missile defense threatens to undermine continued adherence to the 1972 ABM Treaty. The call to weaken the interpretation of that treaty has been advanced by Republican congressional leaders, defense contractors, and domestic and international lobbies.[12] While there is debate over how much to spend on theater and national ballistic missile defenses and what to deploy, there are few differences over which technologies to fund, with both the administration and defense hawks calling for the best available technologies. The major concern, however, among adherents to the treaty is that a concerted push to weaken the ABM Treaty and rapidly deploy both theater and continental ballistic missile defenses may halt the implementation of major cuts by Russia in strategic nuclear arsenals as mandated under the START II Treaty. Furthermore, pursuit of national missile defense could undermine compliance with the Nuclear Nonproliferation Treaty (NPT) by the nonnuclear nations.[13]

Force Plans and Doctrines
Force plans outlined in Table 2–1 make abundantly clear that each of the alternative security proposals either accepts the minimum deterrence doctrine for strategic nuclear forces or makes substantial progress toward it. Moreover, each set of proposals rejects anything other than research for the development of national ballistic missile defense. O'Hanlon sees merit in theater missile defense but is cautious in limiting the technology to a type that does not threaten to become so robust as to be a virtual continental ballistic missile defense system. He is willing to consider only a very limited national missile defense if it is accompanied by parallel progress toward a minimum deterrent. Wiesner and associates argue for strict limits on research and believe that the best way to reduce risk is to eliminate large nuclear arsenals. Similarly, Forsberg sees deep cuts in nuclear arsenals and adoption of minimum deterrence doctrines as the key to risk reduction and supports only very low levels of research for missile defense.

Power projection capabilities are retained under the O'Hanlon proposal, but they are downsized relative to current capabilities, especially with the elimination of continuous forward presence. Conventional force modernization would continue, but at a slower pace, given a smaller research and procurement budget and the reduced emphasis on technological gains in military capabilities.

Wiesner and associates retain a much smaller, but still capable, power projection capacity and recommend a smaller research budget focused on "ample funding for communications, electronic countermeasures and surveillance-and-attack systems that will keep American arms immune to obsolescence." Moreover, they focus exclusively on the unilateral military capabilities of the United States and do not attempt to make recommendations for enhanced multilateral capacity.

Forsberg's framework is the only one that openly questions and rejects the power projection model and the objective of technological supremacy that underpins it. As noted, Forsberg's security doctrine is founded on principles of cooperation that require institution building rather than technological investments. While Forsberg labels this approach a cooperative security framework, it owes much to the doctrine of "common security" that evolved in western Europe during the late stages of the Cold War. This common security doctrine holds that in an interdependent world, a nation's security increasingly depends on recognizing the security requirements of its neighboring nations in order to maintain and guarantee the political, economic, and environmental conditions of international stability.[14]

Under such a common security approach, the United States would require a far more limited military force geared more to territorial defense, one that is noninterventionary, nonprovocative, and far less nuclear dependent, moving first to a minimum deterrent and then perhaps to zero nuclear weapons. The reduction in military expenditures implied by this framework would be substantial but would require a corresponding increase in other expenditures to improve political, economic, and environmental conditions that currently threaten international security.

According to Forsberg, most of the resources necessary for these security structures are provided as in-kind contributions from the major military powers. These contributions include sharing of assets for global communications and surveillance, airlift and sealift, aircraft carrier battlegroups, and military forces. Yet Forsberg does not treat explicitly the extent of additional investment requirements needed to further build up these structures of cooperation. Clearly, in-kind contributions would not be enough; multilateral and international organizations would have to enhance their own capabilities greatly in order to coordinate such global and regional operations.

O'Hanlon sees the need to treat cooperative security investments as an essential ingredient of his security proposals, although the details are not fully spelled out. Nonetheless, he does account for the dedication of forces to peacekeeping, crisis response, and humanitarian operations. In particular, he argues for redirecting much of routine forward naval presence to support for peacekeeping, crisis operations, or other such missions. In addition, the marine expeditionary force, in his view, would be better used for backing up forces or resolutions of the United Nations. Furthermore, O'Hanlon suggests the need to add more civil and public affairs units to active duty and reserve units in support of peacekeeping requirements.

Beyond these changes in U.S. force posture, O'Hanlon argues for multilateral force planning to establish a clearer international division of labor for peace operations as well as additional commitments for training centers, standardized equipment, logistics, and stocks. Of course, none of this is in the cards without financial reforms to address the persistent arrears in U.N. dues and peacekeeping funding. A more ambitious agenda for multilateral operations would require funding on the order of several billion dollars annually from all member states.

Complementing all of these multilateral security measures are other cooperative investments suggested by these analysts, including wider-ranging efforts for cooperative threat reductions and nonproliferation and greater economic engagement to enhance political and economic stability.

In essence, none of these alternative security proposals relies exclusively on the power projection model to ensure U.S. security into the next century. Both O'Hanlon and Forsberg look to other institutions and doctrines to address a varying range of security problems.

Restructuring the Defense Science, Technology, and Industrial Base

Given the complexity of the defense science, technology, and industrial base, this discussion is broken into two parts. The first deals with the overall trends within the private and governmental defense industrial sectors and the potential effects of changes in security doctrines on the industry's market structure within each major segment of the industry. In addition, this part also evaluates briefly the potential effects of the civil-military integration strategy that has been developed in the early 1990s to cope with the downsizing of military-specific requirements.

Table 2–2   Prime Contract Awards (Millions of 1996 $U.S.)

Fiscal Year	1989	1990	1991	1992	1993
Aircraft	$29,594	$28,289	$27,020	$26,818	$24,959
Missiles	$22,887	$20,204	$18,692	$14,599	$13,194
Ships	$11,723	$12,148	$10,647	$9,199	$9,794
Tanks	$4,668	$3,918	$4,942	$3,036	$2,560
Weapons	$1,855	$2,172	$1,963	$1,581	$1,316
Ammunition	$4,764	$4,754	$4,075	$3,617	$2,910
Communications & Electronics	$22,136	$21,797	$17,398	$15,861	$15,455
Total	$97,627	$93,280	$84,736	$74,710	$70,188

Sources: National Defense Budget Estimates for FY 1996 (Washington, D.C.: Department of Defense, 1996), Table 5–7; and *100 Companies Receiving the Largest Dollar Volume of Prime Contract Awards, Fiscal Year 1990 and Fiscal Year 1995 edition* (Washington, D.C.:, Department of Defense, 1995), Exhibit A, page 2.

Most of this discussion focuses on private sector impacts rather than on the government-owned and operated depot system.

The second part of this section is devoted to looking at the defense science and technology base, which is rather extensive in scope and structure. The impacts of alternative security doctrines are less clear for much of this part of the defense sector except for the nuclear weapons complex, which would be drastically reduced.

TRENDS AND IMPACTS ON THE DEFENSE INDUSTRY

Downsizing and the adoption of doctrinal changes due to the Base Force and Bottom-Up Review have had significant and widely analyzed effects on the structure of the defense science and industrial base. Large-scale layoffs in the private sector of the defense industry have totaled 1.3 million jobs since the peak of Cold War procurement in 1987, and consolidation has led to a more concentrated structure for each segment of the defense industry.

Each major segment of that industry has been impacted heavily by cuts in defense procurement, but the decline in missile and space systems procurement has been most dramatic both in terms of inflation-adjusted cuts and in overall procurement share. As Table 2–2 shows based on prime contract award data, missile contracts fell by over 42 percent between 1989 and 1993, while aircraft and shipbuilding and

**Table 2–3   Selected Weapons Procurement by Sector
(Budget Authority, Millions of 1996 $)**

Fiscal Year	1996	1997	1998	1999	2000
Aircraft	6,656	8,860	10,319	12,251	13,370
Missiles	4,319	4,184	4639	5,169	5,539
Ships	5,382	4,138	8,722	4,409	6,589
Tanks	907	980	959	1,203	1,380
Communications & Electronics	1,424	1,538	1,372	1,358	1,199
Ammunition	185	212	271	257	248
Subtotal	18,873	19,912	26,281	24,648	28,324
Unallocated Procurement	23,427	18,391	17,618	23,567	25,821
Total Planned Procurement	42,300	38,302	43,899	48,215	54,145
Percent of Procurement Allocated	0.45	0.53	0.61	0.53	0.55

Source: "Selected Weapons Costs from the Administration's 1996 Program," (Washington, D.C.: CBO, 1995).

repair contracts fell by only 16 percent. Communications and electronics contracts also took a big hit, with a 30 percent reduction over the same period. Tanks and combat vehicles experienced a severe decline, with a 45 percent cut. More recent 1995 data compiled by the Bureau of Economic Analysis confirm that the basic pattern of these reductions remains the same among defense sectors.[15]

Reliable data for forecasting future trends in defense procurement are not readily available since the Future Years Defense Plan is classified. However, we can ascertain the broad trends, as depicted in Table 2–3, by drawing on the Congressional Budget Office's data on Selected Weapons Costs from the administration's 1996 program. These data should be treated with caution, however, since they tend to understate the dollar trends in all procurement categories and distort the segment shares for certain categories, such as Communications and Electronics and Ammunition. Nevertheless, the overall pattern in inflation-adjusted terms is upward, as the procurement budget is projected to grow after 1997.

What is remarkable about these historical and forecast data is the relative stability of the shipbuilding accounts throughout this cycle from 1989 to 2000. Clearly, the requirements for a continuous forward presence and the power projection capabilities of the naval aircraft carrier battlegroups commands a relatively steady share of the procurement budgets. Given that the U.S. military possesses the equivalent of three air forces, the trends in aircraft procurement are less surprising. The other segments of the procurement budget seem to reflect the modernization and replacement cycles that would be expected for missiles, ammunition, and tanks. It is quite clear that the industry for tank and combat vehicle production is sustained largely by exports rather than by domestic requirements.

Impact of Alternative Security Scenarios

What would obviously change with the adoption of even the O'Hanlon scenario is the huge reduction in spending for the shipbuilding and aircraft industries. Indeed, the cuts in naval procurement would lead to a dramatic squeeze on an industry that has largely resisted any significant change since the end of the Cold War.[16] Most likely, the current duopoly structure for surface combatant ships and attack submarines would be unsustainable and the overhaul and repair cycle for aircraft carriers would have to be stretched out for the monopoly supplier. The whole industry might be reduced to three major shipyards.[17] There is little doubt that adopting any of the other force structure scenarios would essentially reduce the industry to a monopoly supplier for three general classes of ships, with these yards being largely dependent on overhaul work.

Combat aircraft production currently depends on upgrades of existing systems, exports, and the start-up of the next generation of aircraft. The F-22 Advanced Tactical Fighter and the Joint Advanced Strike Aircraft will determine the future of the existing aircraft supplier base. Since Lockheed Martin has secured the F-22 contract, the contract for the Joint Advanced Strike Aircraft likely will determine which of the current military-serving firms remains into the next century. O'Hanlon's scenario definitely would make the competition stiffer, as he argues for the termination of the F-22 with greater reliance on the F-15. Meanwhile, the Forsberg scenario calls for a complete halt to combat fighter production and modernization and a mothballing of capacity.

In the case of military jet transports, the C-17 is the moneymaker for McDonnell Douglas Corporation, but under the O'Hanlon, the buys for further C-17 would be reduced in favor of reconfigured 747s. Similarly, the V-22 tilt-rotor aircraft would be terminated in favor of CH-46/53 helicopters. Deeper cuts in aircraft procurement of all types likely would reduce the industry to three and perhaps only two major systems integration firms.

Production of tanks and combat vehicles already has entered the terminal phase of the product cycle, with the whole system already virtually ready to be mothballed once foreign orders are exhausted.[18]

Missile production might not be significantly affected by the adoption of the O'Hanlon approach since precision-guided munitions would be key weapons in the remaining arsenal. Indeed, it is unclear whether missile production would be affected as dramatically by even the Forsberg approach since defensive missiles would seem to be permissible under this scheme. Offensive missiles, such as the advanced cruise missile and other such surface-to-surface and air-to-surface standoff weaponry, would not be permissible.

One potential impact of the most dramatic reductions in defense requirements is the fostering of greater civil-military integration of the nation's industrial production base, a policy that generated many hopes at the beginning of the 1990s for lowering costs in the defense industry in general.

Civil-Military Integration Policies

With the end of the Cold War, the idea of integrating the defense industry with the commercial industrial base was advanced to solve several important challenges. First, in the view of the Department of Defense (DoD) maintaining the U.S. military's technological superiority depended increasingly on the continuous introduction of leading-edge commercial technologies into defense systems. Second, reduced defense budgets meant that, where possible, costly military specification would have to be eliminated so that defense requirements could be increasingly supplied by commercially oriented producers that were flexible enough to meet defense needs. Third, economies of scale could be achieved by spinning off defense technology to relevant commercial applications and promoting dual-use production. Finally, the government-run, government-owned depot maintenance system should be privatized as much as possible.

Despite these cost-reduction efforts, the active promotion of defense industry consolidation through mergers and acquisitions, coupled with the continued pursuit of risky, military high technologies, undoubtedly will undercut the savings promised by this strategy. In particular, the pursuit of technological superiority in all weapons systems likely will force technological frontiers and lead to the classic cost-escalation problems. In addition, the DoD's policy of promoting defense industry consolidation in the name of increased efficiency and reduced excess capacity has the contradictory effect of creating even less competitive and cost-control pressure within the various segments of the defense industry.

Only by moving away from the view that requires continuous modernization and the investment in breakthrough technologies to guarantee decisive military advantages can the idea of civil-military integration even have a chance to work. Thus, relaxing the military-strategic assumption is the key to breaking out of business as usual in the defense sector. Once this step is taken away from the old doctrinal point of view, then the economic requirements also are relaxed and the potential supplier base is expanded.

TRENDS AND IMPACTS ON THE DEFENSE LABORATORIES

During the Cold War a vast array of scientific research laboratories was developed to serve the military's objectives and maintain U.S. technological superiority. These laboratories include the principal nuclear weapons design facilities as well as those other multimission laboratories managed by the Department of Energy (DoE) that serve both defense and nondefense objectives, the DoD's laboratories managed by the individual armed services, and the Federally Funded Research and Development Centers (FFRDCs) that are run by private contractors, nonprofits, or universities. Taken together, these laboratories and related test facilities command about one-third of the total federal R&D annual budgets.[19] While the total number of federal research-related facilities and laboratories has been estimated at over 700, the core of the defense-serving federal laboratory system is dominated by about 100 laboratories controlled by the DoE, the DoD, and the FFRDCs.

Perhaps the best known of these laboratories are the nuclear weapons design laboratories run by the DoE, especially Lawrence Livermore, Los Alamos, and Sandia; however, the DoE runs nearly 100 other laboratory-related facilities, including 6 multipurpose laboratories: Brookhaven, Argonne, Oak Ridge, Idaho National Lab, Pacific Northwest Lab, Lawrence-Berkeley, and the National Renewable Energy Laboratory. The DoD laboratories are relatively less known, but include 81 dedicated research, development, and test facilities that serve the technological needs of each of the armed services. All FFRDCs conduct or manage research for the federal government or one of its agencies and receive 70 percent or more of their funding from the federal government. The defense work of the 10 defense-serving FFRDCs is perhaps best known by the research of the MITRE Corporation, Lincoln Laboratory at MIT, and RAND Corporation.

With the end of the Cold War, the Clinton administration undertook a major reassessment of the missions and functions of these laboratories to evaluate their conversion potential and the need for consolidation, reorientation, or closure. In May 1994 President Clinton issued a Presidential Review Directive that established the Interagency Review of Federal Laboratories, which mandated that executive agencies evaluate the potential of the laboratories to serve other national science and technology needs and options to cut costs and improve productivity. Broadly speaking, the options considered were:

- Shrinking the laboratories to free up money for other public objectives
- Improving the process of technology transfer from the laboratories to serve industrial purposes and to enhance national competitiveness
- Reorienting the laboratories to new national missions in other fields, such as environmental technologies, alternative energy research, transportation, or other areas closely related to the laboratories' core scientific competency
- Downsizing and focusing on new national security objectives, such as nonproliferation, verification, dismantlement
- Retaining the full range of nuclear weapons design and remanufacture capabilities for maintaining a nuclear deterrent

Given the diversity of the defense-related laboratories, not one of these options necessarily would apply to all these facilities, but all have been examined in general by congressionally requested studies.[20] In response to the Presidential Review Directive, the agency studies were completed in 1995 by the Department of Defense, the Department of Energy (DoE), and the National Aeronautics and Space Administration (NASA). The Department of Energy's study fell short of its mandated goal of identifying the costs and benefits of alternative future scenarios for the laboratories. NASA's study recommended large-scale closures and consolidations of many of its facilities. Meanwhile, the Department of Defense made modest recommendations for consolidation and closures that were actually scaled back by the Base Closure and Realignment Commission before being turned over for congressional and presidential ratification.

In September 1995 President Clinton issued his initial set of directives for laboratory consolidation based on these agencies' studies. Virtually no hard decisions were made for eliminating or consolidating any of these three defense-related laboratory systems.[21] The guidelines are so vague that they offer little practical information on how to reshape the Cold War orientation of these laboratories.

Department of Defense Laboratories
Most of the DoD's 81 labs and research and test facilities are completely dedicated to enhancing the military's war-fighting capabilities. Accord-

ing to the DoD, the defense labs act as interpreters and integrators of science and technology into the military's war-fighting needs. They also act to connect these war-fighting priorities with the acquisition managers and to work with private sector contractors to ensure that the latest commercial technological advances are incorporated into new weapons systems and defense technologies.

The areas of research and testing are related to the following general categories of work:

- Human factors engineering
- Aerospace engineering and propulsion
- Weapon platforms testing for land, air, undersea, and surface vessels
- Ordnance, missiles, and lasers
- Environmental conditions and survivability
- Various fields of military medical research
- Operational research on weapons systems
- Surveillance; communications, command, and control

So dedicated are these facilities to their respective service's missions that the director of defense research and engineering, Dr. Anita Jones, reports that "[t]hey can reorganize, reengineer, modernize and outsource, but cannot privatize or otherwise compromise their fundamental stewardship responsibilities to their services and to the U.S. citizens."[22]

The DoD began to downsize the armed services laboratory system by putting 19 facilities on the Base Closure and Realignment Commission 1995 list for possible closure or realignment. However, the commission chose to recommend closure of only 14 of these facilities. Moreover, despite the need for further closures, the commission did not add a single laboratory to the list before passing it on to Congress and the executive branches for further action. This lacuna is particularly curious because of the obvious redundancies within the military's laboratory system. For instance, does the army really need an aeromedical research facility, especially given that the air force and NASA possess far more scientifically complex aeromedical facilities? These shortcomings highlight the drag of Cold War thinking, especially as each of the armed services seeks to maintain its respective control over the existing assets.

The other dedicated defense laboratories are the Federally Funded Research and Development centers, such as MITRE Corporation, the

Aerospace Corporation, and Lincoln Laboratory, that are operated by private nonprofit and university-affiliated organizations. These laboratories have been oriented to provide specialized research for each of the armed services. To date no plan has been developed about how to downsize the 10 defense-dedicated FFRDCs. Indeed, the 1996 House National Security Committee Defense Authorization Bill Report indicates that the principal FFRDCs have not suffered any serious budget cuts or attrition to date and recommends a serious consideration of these budgets.[23] Other sources indicate a modest reduction in funding since 1993.[24] Nevertheless, private defense contractors are beginning to call for the privatization of these laboratories so that they can bid for this work. The armed services have countered that the nonprofits can do the work more cheaply.

At least one military analyst, Lieutenant General William Odom, has argued that the current situation is untenable for the DoD and that it ought to completely eliminate all of the DoD laboratories and privatize their functions.[25] A contest is clearly shaping up between the armed services that wish to maintain their own science and technology capabilities and the private-sector contractors that are seeking new sources of government contracts to make up for the deep cuts that have occurred in defense R&D and procurement funding. Regardless of which security doctrines are invoked, it is clear that Odom is correct: something has got to give. The FFRDCs simply cannot be justified and should be phased out entirely. Meanwhile, the DoD laboratory system overlaps in many key areas that should be consolidated on an interservice basis. These two actions would save more money directly than all the efforts of civil-military integration.

Department of Energy Laboratories
Since the end of the Cold War, the U.S. Department of Energy's budget for Atomic Energy Defense Activities has remained relatively stable as compared to other defense-related budgets. However, the reduction in strategic weapons procurement stemming from both actual arms treaties and reduced tensions has had a substantial impact on the U.S. nuclear weapons complex. DoE spending for the research and production of nuclear materials and warheads has been scaled back dramatically. In contrast, the massive environmental damage from the 45-year nuclear arms race has required significant new spending to begin the daunting task of cleaning up the nuclear weapons design and production facilities. Until very recently estimates suggested that the cleanup costs of the entire weapons production complex could range from $300 billion to $1 trillion.[26] As DoE officials have noted, these environmental

cleanup activities have given them a "new mission" that will last into the middle of the 21st century. But in 1995 the DoE scaled back its commitment to total cleanup costs by setting a ceiling at $230 billion to stabilize, rather than clean up, the environmental problems at the DoE complex.[27]

Recent political changes in the 1995 Congress are altering the trends evident since the end of the Cold War: halting the growth in environmental restoration work, cutting back funding for conversion and technology transfer to relevant commercial work, and increasing nuclear weapons–related research.

On another front, the administration's nuclear posture review of the future requirements for nuclear weaponry in the post–Cold War era has essentially left unaltered the strategic nuclear forces agreed to under the START II Treaty, thereby delaying further decisions about future disarmament. Nonetheless, the extension of the NPT and the commitment to negotiate a comprehensive test ban treaty does raise the prospect of further restructuring the nation's nuclear weapons complex. Meanwhile, the administration is developing a "nuclear weapons stewardship" program that places a premium on laboratory research work in advancing nuclear weapons physics as well as maintaining and monitoring the existing nuclear arsenal. Despite possible consolidation of nuclear weapons design and a halt to nuclear testing at the Nevada Nuclear Test Site, the administration's currently proposed nuclear stewardship program likely will require an expansion of the DoE's nuclear weapons research, development, and testing budget.[28]

In February 1995 the DoE released its much-anticipated study of what the nation should do with its nuclear weapons and other laboratories after the Cold War. The Galvin Commission report was supposed to identify costs and benefits of alternative future scenarios for the laboratories, including possible closure and consolidation of some and the redirection and restructuring of the remainder. Most of the report's recommendations, however, offered little in the way of dramatic change in the size, structure, or mission of the laboratories that would serve public needs in civilian fields. Instead, the recommendations support new investments in nuclear testing–related infrastructure, continued dominance of the basic energy research agenda by nuclear science, and a proposal to "corporatize" the national laboratories.

President Clinton's interim decision to maintain the current structure of the nuclear weapons laboratories essentially commits the nation to the Stockpile Stewardship plan, replete with its nuclear weapons test–related investments.[29] It remains to be seen if these investments will reinforce the perception among the world's nonnuclear nations that the United States desires to ensure for itself a permanent and overwhelming advantage in nuclear weapons. Such criticisms were lodged against the U.S. delegation to the NPT conference in the spring of 1995 and reemerged in negotiations for a comprehensive test ban treaty in 1996.

Economic Implications of Alternative Security Policies

As this analysis shows, current policies for restructuring the nation's security framework and its defense industrial base have not moved substantially from the trajectories set during the Cold War. At this stage, procurement and R&D budgets will not move much lower than the previous Cold War lows established in the mid-1970s. Under these circumstances, most of the discussion of defense-industrial base policy has focused on how to generate cost savings to maintain the current military structure while ensuring U.S. military technological superiority. By ignoring the far-reaching implications of security policy, the result is to fall back inevitably to the status quo.

By contrast, even reforms like O'Hanlon's will imply major restructuring of industry, especially if investments in international institutions permit further scaling back of national defense postures over time. Implementation of O'Hanlon-type proposals probably will increase the incidence of monopoly supplier situations and deepen the duopoly structure for other segments. However, if the power projection model gives way to more dependence on international peace and security institutions, the chances for a more commercially based industry increase.

Radical restructuring of the defense industry envisioned by Forsberg might imply at least two outcomes. First, the curtailment of continuous modernization of weaponry increases the potential for a more purely commercial supply base to fill the needs of any remaining domestic military requirements. Second, for the segments that are more defense unique, there is the prospect of maintaining the industrial base either through a cold shutdown, with capacity preserved under some arsenal system, or as a warm arsenal system geared to maintain the equipment either as government-owned, contractor-operated or government-owned, government-operated systems. In between these extremes there lies a range of options.

COMMERCIAL-MILITARY INTEGRATION

Commercial-military integration opens up the number of potential suppliers by accepting far fewer military-specific requirements. Such a strategy is supposed to generate economies of scale and scope and permit defense procurement at lower cost. Such projected economies are most likely to come from subcontractors and suppliers that adopt these flexible techniques rather than from larger prime contractors that act as designers and systems integrators. Potential gains for buying more strictly commercial products would seem to be the greatest in the electronics, communications, computers and software products, and components applications. However, the DoD's stated objective of achieving flexible manufacturing processes capable of producing lot sizes of one for specialized military components with near-perfect quality seems extremely unlikely, as even some dual-use advocates admit.[30]

Studies by the Congressional Office of Technology Assessment (OTA) indicated, however, that even under the most optimistic assumptions for adopting these practices through procurement reform, greater dual-use production, and increased use of state-of-the-art and off-the-shelf commercial technologies, the upper limit of cost reductions would yield savings only on the order of 17 percent of total privately supplied procurement costs.[31] The OTA study, however, failed to examine what happens when the requirement for technological superiority is relaxed. Indeed, the critical question is whether civil-military integration is possible only once the power projection model is dropped as the paradigm. Thus the model of civil-military integration may depend more on the assumptions of security doctrines than on the institutional practices of military procurement.

OLIGOPOLISTIC COMPETITION

The bias cultivated during the long Cold War by the military for surplus capacity would seem to make oligopoly markets attractive to the Pentagon since they imply more excess capacity. Oligopolistic competition yields the alleged benefits of increased technological competition among suppliers, which might also be attractive to the military.

But these potential benefits do not help solve one of the most vexing problems for developing new complex weapons systems by the large systems integration firms in the defense sector, namely, persistent cost escalation. Many of the cost escalation problems have come from the process of integrating new, complex technologies into a weapons system while trying to meet the military's performance requirements. Two problems have developed over time.

First, the military often has set performance requirements that exceed the capabilities of the available technologies, leading to cost escalation as new technological horizons are explored. Procurement reform was supposed to solve some of these problems by encouraging military acquisition officers to relax performance in favor of lower costs. However, at this stage the system of procurement reform has offered only the stick of austere procurement budgets and few carrots to encourage this practice. Moreover, as we have already seen, many military-strategic considerations still set rather demanding performance requirements, and these norms still dictate the terms of most development and procurement contracts.

A second, and even more intractable, set of problems arises from the strategy of major defense contracting firms and the structure of the defense industry. Within any given segment of the defense market for combat aircraft, bombers, rockets, missiles, tanks, and various types of ships, the market tends to be dominated by a few large firms. These markets typically are characterized as oligopoly markets where competition and rivalry usually is played out more in terms of the qualitative advantages of a particular technology than a singular focus on price. In the defense sector, the nature of this technological competition is amplified by the military's specification of performance requirements that can meet the tactical and strategic needs of the armed forces. Meanwhile considerations of price competition are correspondingly deemphasized.

These conditions create certain direct incentives for firms to concentrate on developing leading-edge technological capabilities, since performance criteria are especially important to the military. On the other hand, firms face a high degree of technological risk and uncertainty in such projects, which creates a large margin for error. Thus the military must leave room for renegotiating the development contract to accommodate this uncertainty in the management of technological risk (hence the shift away from fixed-price development contracts). These development cost problems are compounded by the practice of testing and evaluating the weapon simultaneously with the start-up of production runs. This trend toward concurrency was largely a product of Cold War strategic competition to field the latest technology quickly so as to gain a military advantage. Together these practices have led to chronic problems of cost escalation and schedule slippage. Solutions usually involve renegotiation of the contract for fewer buys, stretch-outs, and downgrading of performance requirements. Thus there are few incentives to control costs and few penalties for underbidding on both development and procurement contracts.

To combat this set of dynamics, Congress began requiring competitive bidding on procurement contracts as well as of dual-sourcing contracts. Competitive bidding yielded only marginal improvements, but dual sourcing was found to have some impact on the production cost of mature weapons technologies.[32] Nevertheless, the technological risk and cost problems of new technologies have persisted, leading to the dual-use strategy as a way to control costs. The continued pursuit of technological superiority in all weapons systems likely will force technological frontiers and lead to the classic cost-escalation problems. Meanwhile, as a result of extensive corporate consolidations among the top defense prime contractors over the last few years, the systems integration process has become more highly concentrated in the upper tiers of defense contracting among several firms.

The question for the public is whether this costly strategy really yields any benefit. There is little need for oligopolistic technological competition in the post–Cold War environment, and, once a technology is mature, it is doubtful that the benefits of dual sourcing outweigh the costs of the excess capacity for the industry as a whole.

REGULATED MONOPOLY

Some segments of the defense industry are moving toward a natural monopoly situation where production runs are so small that only one supplier could possibly supply the technology in question. This is particularly the case for "defense-unique" systems, such as an additional Seawolf submarine or nuclear-powered aircraft carrier, or tanks. In an era of reduced need for rapid technological change, the revenue that will sustain the firm is going to come largely from routine maintenance and repair work. From the point of view of the public's welfare, such a bilateral monopoly leaves price and profits indeterminate. We must consider whether such an industry should be regulated as a natural monopoly.

ARSENALS: WARM LINES VS. COLD SHUTDOWN

One variant of the natural monopoly is the arsenal system, which was once larger. This idea might be relevant in those cases where there is a need to keep intact a "warm" industrial capacity and workforce to build and maintain complex, defense-unique systems. By contrast, while the depot system might maintain the weapon in question, the arsenal might be kept mothballed or in cold shutdown. If a depot system or contractors could manage the maintenance work and realize some economies of scope for maintaining a variety of equipment, then the cold shutdown option would be economical.

COMMERCIALIZED VIRTUAL FIRM/INDUSTRY

One view of the future defense industry reduces the military-specific content to its minimal level and opts to have a virtual firm undertake systems integration work on new defense equipment. This virtual firm and its network of suppliers then would build from scratch any new weapons system. Whether such an outcome is commercially feasible, or whether it depends on dramatic relaxation of demanding military requirements, is largely conjectural.

Toward a Post–Cold War Technology and Industrial Policy

As the foregoing analysis has shown, changing the assumptions about security doctrines has wide-ranging implications for restructuring the post–Cold War military-industrial base. To date, most of the discussions of defense-industrial base policy have sought to find ways to generate cost savings while maintaining the current military structure and ensuring military technological superiority. Virtually none of the current debate has examined how alternative security doctrines might change the unique requirements for the defense industry; nor has there been much effort to analyze how a relaxation of military requirements for leading-edge technologies might affect the potential for civil-military integration. Relaxing these assumptions and changing doctrinal approaches opens up a whole menu of options for restructuring the defense industry.

As this comparison of alternative security models has shown, a restructuring of our national security policy would lead to a real commercial-military integration policy only if there were serious reductions in the power projection capability of the United States. Marginal adjustments in power projection capabilities such as those proposed by O'Hanlon probably would increase the incidence of monopoly supplier situations and deepen the duopoly structure in other segments of the defense industry. However, if power projection capacities are reduced in favor of more security capabilities delivered through international peace and security institutions, the chances for a more commercially based industry increase, as these military requirements would not be predicated on maintaining continuous technological advance.

By contrast, the radical restructuring of the defense policy advanced by Forsberg would curtail continuous modernization of weaponry and thereby increase the potential for a more purely commercial supply base to fill the needs of any remaining domestic military requirements. Even in the case of the more defense-unique industry segments, the industrial base could be maintained either through a cold shutdown under an arsenal system or as a warm arsenal system geared to maintain the equipment. The interests of the private sector in this area would determine who maintains the industrial base, the government or industry.

This analysis indicates that the experiment in dual-use technology policy has been fundamentally flawed. Defense technologies cannot be made more affordable while the military services and doctrines are still dedicated to forcing technological frontiers to satisfy military-strategic requirements. Civil-military integration requires the establishment of specific criteria and incentives for relaxing technological requirements so that military requirements can be satisfied substantially through commercial technologies.

Current military-industrial policy virtually guarantees that most of the defense industry will be dominated by oligopoly suppliers, although the staying power of such a two- or three-firm market structure will depend on the potential future size of the procurement budget. If the budget continues to shrink, then the industry structure will devolve to a monopoly supplier situation. Under these conditions, the public will continue to face chronic problems of cost escalation in building new weapons systems.

Notes

1. Computations are based on Office of Management and Budget, *Historical Tables, Budget of the United States Government, FY 1996* (Washington, D.C.: U.S. General Accounting Office, 1995), Table 3.2. Deflators for 1996 dollars are taken from Department of Defense, Office of the Undersecretary of Defense, Comptroller, *National Defense Budget Estimates for FY 1996* (Washington, D.C.: Department of Defense, 1995), Tables 5–8; and from Conference Report, *Concurrent Resolution on the Budget for Fiscal Year 1996*, June 26, 1995, Report 104–159, p. 47.

2. Lorna S. Jaffee, *The Development of the Base Force, 1989–92* (Washington, D.C.: Joint History Office, Office of the Joint Chiefs of Staff, July 1992).

3. Stephan Daggett, "A Comparison of Clinton Administration and Bush Administration Long-term Defense Budget Plans for FY 1994–99," Congressional Research Service, December 20, 1994.

4. General Accounting Office, *Future Years Defense Program, Optimistic Estimates Lead to Billions in Overprogramming* (Washington, D.C.: GAO/NSIAD-94-210, July 1994); General Accounting Office, *Bottom-Up Review, Analysis of Key DoD Assumptions* (Washington, D.C.: GAO/NSIAD-95-96, January 1995).

5. Charles A. Gabriel et al., "A Report on Military Capabilities and Readiness," Paper prepared for U.S. Senator John S. McCain, February 7, 1995.

6. The now-defunct Office of Technology Assessment produced what was probably the best set of analyses that addresses these complex questions, although only one of these studies made even a passing mention of the relationship of security doctrine to science and technology requirements. See Office of Technology Assessment, *Defense Conversion: Redirecting R & D* (Washington, D.C.: U.S. Government Printing Office, May 1993), and Office of Technology Assessment, *Assessing the Potential for Civil-Military Integration: Technologies, Processes and Practices* (Washington, D.C.: U.S. Government Printing Office, September 1994). Various defense science and technology plans developed by the Bush and Clinton administrations identified specific science and research capabilities needed to implement their respective defense plans, yet the security doctrines often were deeply embedded in the assumptions of these documents rather than being treated explicitly.

7. Long-Term Commission on Integrated Strategy, *Discriminate Deterrence* (Washington D.C.: Department of Defense, January 1988), p. 64.

8. National Academy of Sciences, *The Future of the U.S.-Soviet Nuclear Relationship* (Washington D.C.: National Academy Press, August 1991); Congressional Budget Office, *The START Treaty and Beyond* (Washington, D.C.: CBO, October 1991).

9. National Academy of Sciences, *Future of the U.S.-Soviet Nuclear Relationship*, p. 58.

10. Herbert F. York, "Remark about Minimum Deterrence," Lawrence Livermore National Laboratory, University of California, January 25, 1991.

11. Congressional Budget Office, *The START Treaty and Beyond* (Washington, D.C.: CBO, October 1991).

12. Pat Towell, "GOP Tries to Heat Up Debate on Anti-Missile Program" (Washington, D.C.: Congressional Quarterly, April 1, 1995), vol. 53, no. 13, pp. 949–55.

13. John Steinbruner, "Unrealized Promise, Avoidable Trouble," *Brookings Review* (Washington, D.C.: Brookings Institution, Fall 1995), vol. 13, no. 4, pp. 8–13.

14. Stockholm International Peace Research Institute, *Policies for Common Security* (London: Taylor & Francis, 1985), pp. 219–35.

15. See *Survey of Current Business* (January/February/March 1996): Table 3.11.

16. Office of Technology Assessment, *Assessing the Potential for Civil-Military Integration: Selected Case Studies* (Washington, D.C.: U.S. Government Printing Office, September 1995), chap. 3, pp. 58–59.

17. Ibid.

18. See "Alternatives for the U.S. Tank Industrial Base," *CBO Papers* (February 1993): 37.

19. Office of Technology Assessment, *Defense Conversion*, p. 8.

20. Ibid.

21. White House, Office of the Press Secretary, "Statement by the President, Future of Major Federal Laboratories," September 25, 1995.

22. Department of Defense, Director, Defense Research and Engineering, Memorandum for Assistant to the President for Science and Technology, Department of Defense Response to NSTC/PRD #1, Presidential Review Directive on an Interagency Review of Federal Laboratories, February 24, 1995, p. 5.

23. House National Security Committee Report, *Defense Authorization Act Fiscal Year 1996* (Washington, D.C.: House of Representatives, September, 1995), p. 81.

24. Jeff Erlich and Warren Ferster, "R&D Centers: Dynamos or Dinosaurs?" *Defense News*, September 18–24, 1995, pp. 1, 50.

25. William E. Odom, *America's Military Revolution* (Washington, D.C.: American University Press, 1993), p. 159.

26. U.S. Environmental Protection Agency, Office of Federal Facilities Enforcement, *Interim Report of the Federal Facilities Environmental Restoration Dialogue Committee* (Washington, D.C.: U.S. Government Printing Office, February 1993); Department of Energy, *Alternative Futures for the Department of Energy's National Laboratories* (Washington, D.C.: U.S. Government Printing Office, April 1995).

27. Department of Energy, Press Release (Washington, D.C.: Department of Energy, April 3, 1995).

28. Congressional Budget Office, "The Bomb's Custodians," *CBO Papers* (Washington, D.C.: CBO, July 1994).

29. Hisham Zerriffi, and Arjun Makhijani, "The Stewardship Smokescreen," *Bulletin of the Atomic Scientists* (September/October 1996): 22–42.

30. John A. Alic et al., *Beyond Spinoff* (Boston, Mass.: Harvard Business School Press, 1993), p. 332; Director, Defense Research and Engineering, *Defense Science and Technology Strategy* (Washington, D.C.: Department of Defense, September 1994).

31. Office of Technology Assessment, *Assessing the Potential for Civil-Military Integration: Technologies, Processes and Practices* (Washington, D.C.: U.S. Government Printing Office, September 1994).

32. Jacques S. Gansler, *The Defense Industry* (Cambridge, Mass.: MIT Press, 1982) and *Affording Defense* (Cambridge, Mass.: MIT Press, 1991).

3

Cashing In, Cashing Out, and Converting: Restructuring of the Defense Industrial Base in the 1990s

MICHAEL ODEN

MAJOR transitions from periods of high to low military spending historically have generated fundamental organizational and technological advances greatly benefiting the U.S. economy. In the years following the Civil War, World War I, and World War II, major new industries and technologies, new infrastructures, and new forms of firm organization flowered out of massive war investments. The current era is potentially such a major transition period, with industry facing a secular rather than cyclical downturn in overall defense demand. Will this transition benefit the economy by speeding technical and organizational change, creating new products and jobs, and freeing resources for more beneficial investments? Or will the rendering down of the military research and industrial base simply lead to a further deterioration in U.S. technological and industrial performance? The answers to these questions depend in large part on the interaction between government defense transition policies and strategies defense firms employ to adjust to declining military markets.

The post–Cold War transition obviously presents challenges not present in previous demobilization periods. The long duration and special requirements of the Cold War created a large group of highly specialized private and public establishments with limited exposure to non-defense markets. Creating an efficient transition path for these specialized institutions is a daunting challenge. It first requires shedding significant defense capacity while preserving a research and industrial base capable of meeting remaining defense requirements. Second, our huge 45-year investment in defense must be leveraged, as much as possible, into growth-enhancing activities.

The first section of the chapter examines how the new direction in security policy outlined in the 1993 Bottom-Up Review (BUR) shaped Department of Defense (DoD) policies toward the acquisition system and the reshaping of the defense industry. The industrial base inherited from the Cold War era included significant excess capacity that was purposely maintained to meet national security requirements. With the diminution of the rivalry with the Soviet Union, this excess capacity needed to be rationalized. Yet the extensive requirements embedded in the Bottom-Up Review in an era of reduced threats and federal budget austerity forced the DoD into a challenging juggling act. The new policy required high levels of force readiness and extensive production and development capacity within a constrained overall budget. It is argued that the particular policies chosen by the DoD encouraged particular types of defense industry mergers more related to preserving outdated capacity than in reducing costs or encouraging a more diversified, integrated defense industry base.

The second section shows that major prime contractors have reacted to market opportunities and new defense policies by consolidating and downsizing their operations. However, consolidating into defense markets is not the only strategy contractors have used. Results of survey work done at the Project on Regional and Industrial Economics (PRIE) show that a number of large defense companies are bucking the consolidation trend. It is quite clear that the familiar story told by some industry executives about the futility of diversification is wrong. In a very difficult environment, a number of large defense companies are committing resources to internal product development and registering real success moving into non-DoD markets. However, the strong incentives offered for merger and defense consolidation are slowing the diversification process.

The next section of the chapter briefly analyzes the restructuring process among small- and medium-size defense contractors. Defense policymakers were concerned that major procurement cutbacks would eliminate a significant number of smaller contracting firms, some of which supplied critical components or subsystems. Surveys by the RAND Corporation and our own surveys at PRIE indicate that small and medium-size companies have adapted to defense losses with surprising success. There has been considerable downsizing among more specialized companies, but no wave of bankruptcies or closings. The majority have reduced defense dependence significantly and expanded non-DoD sales, but they continue to participate in each market. Research also shows that very modest public assistance has aided smaller defense companies in their conversion efforts.

The concluding section offers a provisional critique of the status quo security and defense industry policy. The DoD has not clearly established the need for the current force structure, and there is recognition that the Bottom-Up Review needs to be revised dramatically. Since political support for the status quo may be based more on inertia and a lack of alternatives than on a strong consensus about real national defense needs, we may be restructuring the defense industrial base in the wrong way. Following the current path risks reconstituting a defense industry that is even more isolated, technologically sluggish, and exceedingly expensive to maintain. The somewhat surprising success of defense diversification suggests that an alternative path exists that transfers more technology and know-how into rapidly growing non-DoD markets.

The Rationalization of the Cold War Defense Industry Base

THE INHERITED SYSTEM

Prior to the Cold War, the United States relied on a concept that Richard Samuels coined in his analysis of the Japanese approach to national security, "rich nation, strong army."[1] Mobilizing its diverse, advanced industrial base and its huge resource and manpower endowment, the United States could outproduce and wear down any adversary in a large-scale war of attrition. At the conclusion of each conflict, military spending was slashed. Companies drawn into war production moved back into new or preexisting commercial markets, taking with them government-supplied capital equipment, technical advances, and knowledge gained in war production.

Once the United States assumed a global leadership role in deterring and containing the Soviet Union and China, this basic national defense strategy changed. The defense establishment believed that size and industrial capacity could no longer be relied on to ensure superiority against these huge nation-states capable of commanding resources with few domestic counterpressures. In the 1950s the U.S. security establishment coalesced around a strategy that relied on a sophisticated nuclear deterrent and technological superiority to "multiply" the capability of conventional forces significantly.[2] This approach created a powerful technological imperative for high performance from weapons producers. At the same time, a defense industry base was needed that could rapidly ramp up in response to the outbreak of major regional or superpower conflicts or unanticipated technical challenges.

This core security strategy made demand highly unstable, technical requirements extremely demanding, with large economies of scale and long product cycles for builders of weapons platforms and other defense systems. To sustain a relatively stable group of firms committed to weapons research and production required a peculiar system of negotiated prices, contract allocation, dense and rigid product specification, and other regulatory practices. The system of regulation that evolved provided the Pentagon with the means to secure equipment and deal with security risks, while allowing most military firms or divisions at least average returns across acquisition cycles.

Sustaining constant technological advance in weaponry and swing capacity for the unexpected required a particular bargain between the DoD and the major prime contractors. In major military systems development, the procurement cycle was managed through a system of "prizes for innovation."[3] Major firms or groups would compete vigorously in the design and early development stages of new projects, investing at least some internal funds in the competition. The DoD then awarded a sole-source contract that gave the winner high returns (economic profits) on the production franchise. Through this process, major prime contractors were given adequate revenues to maintain research and production teams and idle capacity. And they also had an incentive to hoard research and design (R&D) team personnel in order to compete for future prizes. These overheads, necessary to compete as a major weapons prime contractor, generally had to be segregated from a company's commercial operations. Doing so typically necessitated setting up separate divisional organizations and facilities to serve the defense market.

As the Cold War sputtered out, the United States therefore inherited a group of large prime and subcontractors who had become highly specialized in defense. As a matter of normal business practice, this group maintained excess capacity to compete for future development and production contacts and respond to unexpected contingencies. The end of intense military and technological rivalry with the Soviets reduced the need to maintain two specific types of excess capacity: the excess plant, equipment, labor, and overhead no longer necessary to deal with the outbreak of a major conflict in Europe; and the specific excess R&D personnel, development teams, and production capacity carried to ensure technological leadership and meet unexpected technical breakouts by adversaries. As will be argued later, new post–Cold War defense policies have been, at best, only partially successful at shaping a more efficient defense base appropriate to the new era.

STRATEGY DETERMINES STRUCTURE: THE BOTTOM-UP REVIEW AND THE RATIONALIZATION OF THE DEFENSE INDUSTRY BASE

The foundation upon which security policy, defense allocations, and defense industry structures were built crumbled between 1989 and 1991 with the disintegration of the Warsaw Pact and subsequent unraveling of the Soviet Union. The Persian Gulf War offered temporary respite, but it was recognized that a more comprehensive and coherent strategy was needed to guide security and defense policy.

There was considerable debate about the appropriate direction of post–Cold War security strategy, with different approaches implying radically different transition paths for the defense industry. Advocates in various camps generally agreed that two central security challenges remained: numerous regional conflicts could expand into larger, more dangerous wars; and a residual danger of renewed conflict with Russia or China existed. There was strong disagreement, however, on the specific policies that would address these challenges most effectively.

Early on, the Clinton administration eschewed bolder demilitarization options that called for more dramatic military cuts, more emphasis on disarmament and nonproliferation, and a more systematic conversion of the defense industry. The new framing strategy that emerged was detailed in the Pentagon's 1993 Bottom-Up Review. This document called for the retention of large, heavy forces for two major interventions, increased mobility, the building-in of advanced information and communications technologies to current generation platforms, and the maintenance of capability to build next-generation systems in each major product segment (ships, submarines, carriers, aircraft, tanks, missiles, command, control, communication, and intelligence [C³I] systems, etc.).

The relationships among threat, doctrine, force structure, and budget embodied in the BUR were questioned immediately by congressional and outside critics. Yet despite widespread skepticism, this document has had two very important influences on defense restructuring. First, it established an interim floor under the defense budget. The Bush administration, in its last fiscal year (FY) 1993 budget, programmed a reduction in total defense outlays of about 4 percent per year over the period from 1993 to 1998. The first Clinton budget added another $69 billion in cuts over this period.[4] What the BUR provided was a doctrine and explicit rationale for sustaining spending at relatively high levels in the late 1990s, after initial post–Cold War reductions. Downsizing of operations by large defense companies was already well under way by late 1992. The spending levels proposed for the late 1990s allowed corporate planners at least to gear their restructuring strategies to some estimate of the overall scale of the longer-term market.

Second, the priorities in the plan provided the only readable signals about overall R&D and procurement spending and specific program funding. Admittedly, these signals were crude because the BUR was never fully embraced by the main institutional players; actual choices would be strongly influenced by intra- and interservice rivalry and congressional negotiation. Nevertheless, the BUR defined some essential parameters. In calling for the retention of large, heavy forces for two major interventions, the plan revealed that manpower and operations and maintenance costs would squeeze overall procurement spending. The plan further signaled that the need for increased mobility would be met by already developed platforms, such as carriers and heavy air transports. Given the two-war scenario, hot production capacity had to be maintained in current-generation systems to replace possible losses in major conflicts. Force modernization would focus on steadily building in advanced information, communications, and sensor technologies to current-generation platforms, weapons, and C^3I systems. By subtraction, the number of large development programs for next-generation weapons would be extremely limited in the 1990s.

The ambitious BUR priorities forced the DoD to finesse a daunting set of objectives and constraints. Although defense budgets would remain high, they would still equal 15 to 20 percent less than the Cold War average over the 1990s. A greater share would go to personnel and O&M categories, squeezing R&D and procurement. Particularly difficult to manage under these tighter budget constraints was the need to maintain hot production capacity and develop next-generation systems in all major weapons categories simultaneously. Since there would be few new weapons development projects to serve as prizes to keep company research and development teams intact, how would the capacity to develop next-generation technologies be secured? Essentially two ways were open to sustain the considerable capacity required by the BUR: massively reduce unit costs in ongoing O&M and procurement; or assume that planned DoD budget levels were soft and that budget increases could be secured later in the decade to fund more development programs.

After the new plan was released, DoD leadership unsurprisingly argued that it could meet BUR requirements through major efficiency gains. Unit acquisitions costs could be significantly reduced by stimulating vigorous downsizing of nonessential defense company operations and by putting a strong emphasis on procurement reform and dual use. The latter elements promised to yield savings by incorporating better and cheaper commercial components into defense systems and generating economies of scale by allowing a greater combination of commercial and military production.

But the most powerful DoD actions by far were directed at supporting and subsidizing merger and consolidation in the defense industry. The DoD saw this as the most direct route to maintaining capacity at a lower cost. Production rates for the remaining capacity would be kept high with continued domestic purchases and major arms sales abroad. While procurement reform and dual use should be pursued where appropriate, the big savings come from having fewer defense companies producing current-generation weapons systems at higher utilization rates. Presumably, in the process the companies could afford to better sustain R&D capacities. Yet this last objective would be met only if more stable revenue streams and higher profitability could be generated in the newly merged defense units—which would inherently dampen overall procurement cost savings.

Large defense companies react to market opportunities and shareholder desires as well as new defense policy signals. Reduced procurement budgets and Wall Street's recognition that "pure-play" defense combinations could yield high short-term profits stimulated considerable merger activity. The defense industry was already engaged in major merger deals in 1992, before the BUR and explicit policies supporting and subsidizing merger were formulated. However, this merger movement, involving predominantly defense versus commercial acquisitions, did accelerate through 1993 and culminated in a series of megamergers in 1994, 1995, and 1996.

A number of strategies besides mergers are available to large defense companies to deal with falling contract revenue. These include consolidating into remaining defense markets, diversifying into non-DoD markets through internal product development or acquisition; or exiting defense altogether. If a large prime contractor chooses to stay focused in defense, often it can deal with excess capacity without merging. The firm simply can shed labor and capital assets to become profitable at a lower overall volume of sales. McDonnell Douglas has executed this strategy successfully and has seen the profitability of its defense operations soar.[5] Why, then, did the sale and acquisition of defense units become so prevalent as a means to deal with defense reductions, and why were mergers so favored by the DoD?

The strongest rationale for merger on efficiency grounds is if sufficient economies of scale cannot be achieved as a single operation. If the efficient scale for producing fighters for a similar mission is 100, and there are two contractors each producing 50, combining operations reduces unit costs. The remaining reasons for merger are to reduce the cost or improve the quality of supply by acquiring a producer of a major input (vertical merger) or to diversify into other markets to stabilize and expand company revenues (market extension merger).

The real savings accrue in horizontal mergers, as when Hughes purchased General Dynamics' missile division, where several production lines were combined to achieve economies of scale. In the many merger deals profiled in Table 3–1, offices and facilities have been combined.

In many of the biggest mergers, however, the primary motivation was market extension, not horizontal combination, as Table 3–1 shows. These combinations of large primes with diverse portfolios of production and development contracts reduce the total number of major contractors. But the surviving firms could be active in more segments of the defense market. Having fewer major companies more diversified across programs might reduce the R&D and overheads associated with keeping reserve R&D and development capacity. But this would occur only if the company managed to integrate and consolidate management and research functions across business segments—an uncertain and time-consuming process.

Given the type of mergers that have occurred, the decision by the DoD to directly subsidize the merger process becomes harder to understand on cost-saving grounds. Contractors argue that in the case of development or fixed-price production contracts, companies would not reap the rewards of merger efficiencies, since profit margins would remain the same.[6] On this basis, the DoD offered significant direct and indirect subsidies to merging companies, an action that accelerated the merger and consolidation movement over the period from 1993 to 1996.

The extent of subsidies that have been given to merging companies is hard to pin down in the public record. Presumably the DoD allows restructuring costs including severance pay, plant closure costs, and unemployment payments to be added to allowable costs on a firm's contracts.[7] Reports vary on the extent to which the financial costs of the merger deal are reimbursed.[8] In return for these subsidies, defense companies promise to pass on future savings in the form of lower prices. However, as the General Accounting Office (GAO) notes, if the DoD pays for restructuring costs up to the amount of projected savings, it

Table 3–1 Merger and Acquisition Activity in the Defense Industry, 1989–96

Year	Buyer	Unit Acquired	Seller	Buyer Motivation	Seller Motivation
1990	Loral	Ford Aerospace	Ford Motor Corp.	Market extension—defense	Cash-in/exit
	Northrop	LTV Aircraft	LTV	Commercial diversification	Cash-in/exit aerospace
1991	Textron	GD-Cessna	General Dynamics	Commercial diversification	Cash-in/exit commercial
1992	Hughes	GD-Missiles Systems	General Dynamics	Horizontal merger/consolidation	Cash-in
	Loral	LTV Missiles Division	LTV	Market extension—defense	Cash-in/exit aerospace
	Martin Marietta	GE-Aerospace	General Electric	Market extension—defense horizontal Merger/consolidation	Exit defense electronics
1994	Lockheed	GD-Military Aircraft	General Dynamics	Market extension—defense	Cash-in
	Northrop	Grumman	Grumman	Market extension—defense	Hostile takeover
	Loral	IBM-Federal Systems	IBM	Market extension—defense/commercial	Cash-in/exit defense

Year					
1995	Martin Marietta	GD-Space Systems	General Dynamics	Horizontal merger/consolidation	Cash in/exit segment
	Martin Marietta	Lockheed	Lockheed	Market extension—defense horizontal Merger/consolidation	Friendly takeover
1996	Loral	Unisys-Defense	Unisys	Market extension—defense	Cash-in/exit defense
	Litton	Teledyne-Electronics	Teledyne	Horizontal merger/consolidation	Exit defense electronics
	Raytheon	E-Systems	E-Systems	Market extension—defense	Friendly takeover
	Hughes	Magnavox Electronic Systems	Carlyle Group	Vertical merger—space Global Positioning Systems	Cash-in/by investment group
	Northrop Grumman	Westinghouse-Defense Electronics	Westinghouse	Market extension—defense	Exit to buy TV network
	Lockheed Martin	Loral-Defense	Loral	Market extension—defense horizontal Merger/consolidation	Exit to commercial space

Source: Defense News, January 8–14, 1996; Aviation Week, September 15, 1995.

receives no net benefit.[9] Moreover, the DoD, in its own report to Congress entitled *Payment of Restructuring Costs Under Defense Contracts,* acknowledges that "it is not feasible to completely isolate the effect of restructuring from other complex determinants of the difference between projected and actual costs over a long period of time."[10] No comprehensive estimate of overall subsidies to large defense companies for merger and consolidation exists. However, Lockheed Martin alone expects to receive $1 billion to complete its various mergers.[11] If this amount is representative, the overall merger bill could be in the neighborhood of $3 to $5 billion.

In addition, most newly combined companies reap high margins on their ongoing arms export contracts (which also involve substantial indirect government subsidies in the range of $5 billion to $7 billion per annum). Profits have been boosted, but the actual net savings to the DoD are more ephemeral.[12]

Finally, compare these estimates of subsidies to keep large companies active in defense with the paltry $300 to $500 million in annual assistance offered to companies over the period from 1993 to 1995 to create dual-use development and production capacity and to diversify into non-DoD markets. It is clear that consolidation subsidies have swamped incentives to diversify.

The most obvious interpretation of this murky process is that the DoD's main concern is keeping capacity in weapons production and design. Encouraging market extension mergers has established an amended incentive and reward system to sustain development capacity for new technologies and next-generation weapons. In newly combined and diversified companies, high profits are allowed on production contracts in one weapon area in order to maintain capability to carry out new development programs or keep less profitable production going in other defense segments. In this way the restructured industry base can continue to provide the full capability required by the force structure and long-term missions of the BUR with lower current R&D and procurement spending. The rewards flowing from sole-source production contracts are still present, but now more production profits come from foreign arms sales. Moreover, instead of winning profitable production contracts from design competitions, it is now possible simply to buy profitable production backlog through acquisition.

This process makes sense only in the context of the BUR's overly ambitious objectives. The plan really calls for an immediate capability to produce all major weapons types and to develop new-generation systems. While a more robust conversion policy or a more determined effort to integrate commercial and military suppliers through dual-use production conceivably could have supported a long-term latent capacity to develop next-generation systems, maintaining a "hot" capability in each major weapon segment could not be readily ensured through these means. There are, therefore, strong reasons to believe that maintaining production and development capability was more important than cost savings in prompting the permissive government stance toward mergers. The cynical conclusion is that the DoD and contractor community are hoping that the defense budget plans for the late 1990s and early 2000 years can be pushed up to support a higher volume of new weapon development. If this is the wrong bet and the threat assessment and force requirements in the BUR are significantly downgraded, the recent restructuring of the defense industry will be seen in retrospect to have been a wasteful and costly blunder.

The emphasis on merger and consolidation certainly has slowed the transfer of defense technologies and other assets to the commercial sector. The debt-service pressures and internal disruptions associated with merger and consolidation slow down technology transfer and entry into alternative markets. Diversification out of defense actually has been more typical and successful than is commonly assumed. By tilting the balance toward merger and consolidation into defense, the DoD has limited the migration of technology and know-how into high-growth markets.

In addition, the current path risks reconstituting a defense industry that is even more isolated, technologically sluggish, and exceedingly expensive to maintain. First, competition for upgrading existing systems and developing next-generation products is being reduced dramatically, giving remaining players more power over the projects chosen and the associated costs. If a Northrop Grumman risks bankruptcy through a loss in a major development competition, it is hard to imagine that Congress or the Pentagon would not find other work to sustain the company. Third, while improving defense production practices and increasing the use of lower-cost commercial components is occurring in select cases, the overall result of most market extension mergers is to increase the segregation between defense and nondefense activities. Accessing and designing around leading commercial technologies (spin-on) will become more difficult in the new, more segregated structure. Fourth, because a number of merged defense companies are squeezed by high debt-service pressures, they may use high production contract profits to pay off debt rather than invest company R&D to maintain development capacity.[13] Finally, research has shown that by destroying teams and networks within companies, merger and downsizing slows down the product development process.[14] The range of technical approaches and choices available in defense technology will be reduced with a few, more isolated defense giants dominating new development work.

RESTRUCTURING AMONG THE MAJOR PRIME CONTRACTORS

Research on 25 major prime contractors confirms that merger and consolidation has been a dominant trend over the period from 1989 to 1994. Table 3–2 presents data on these major prime contractors. (All firms on the list were in the top 35 in terms of total defense sales between 1989 and 1994.) It is noteworthy that the estimate of defense sales and defense dependence for each company is based on an annual estimate in *Defense News*, which includes sales (vs. contracts) to the DoD *and* military sales to foreign governments.[15] Hence these defense dependence estimates are different from other published sources and provide a more accurate picture of actual dependence on government defense markets.

Total overall sales among 25 major primes has fallen in real terms by 9.2 percent from nearly $334 billion in 1989, to about $303 billion in 1994. Given the 41 percent decline in real-dollar budget authority for procurement and R&D over the period, these sales losses might appear to be rather modest.[16] However, many of the largest companies on the list, such as GE, GTE, and ITT, are primarily commercial with relatively small defense divisions, which affects the sales-weighted number. Moreover, several defense-oriented firms, such as Martin, Loral, and Northrop Grumman, acquired new defense and commercial business through merger with companies not on this list, reducing aggregate sales declines. Total defense sales for the 25 firms did, however, fall by $33.6 billion. These companies lost 31 percent of their total defense sales since 1989—with arms exports offsetting to some degree falls in domestic purchases. This is a significant decline.

Downsizing is clearly in evidence, as these 25 firms shed 608,000 workers, or nearly one-fourth of their 1989 workforces. Clearly employment reductions far outstripped real sales declines as many companies merged similar operations, achieved other productivity gains, and/or scaled back to serve a smaller market.

The major sales and job losses were registered by General Dynamics, which sold off most of its divisions, and Litton, which divested itself of its commercial operations and consolidated into defense. McDonnell Douglas and Northrop Grumman did not diversify but simply stayed in familiar defense niches and cut employment to serve a declining defense sales base. Three firms, Lockheed, Loral, and Martin Marietta, achieved major sales gains through aggressive acquisition of other defense and commercial companies or divisions. While these defense megamergers have grabbed the headlines, a closer look at these data reveal that company strategies to deal with the new defense environment have been more complex than is sometimes suggested.

A number of companies have chosen to exit from defense or diversify into non-DoD markets. Overall defense dependence in this group has fallen from 33 percent of sales in 1989, to 25 percent by 1994. This decrease was not due entirely to a fall in defense sales: the total loss in real dollar sales over the period was $30.8 billion; defense sales losses were $33.6 billion; gains in commercial sales were $2.8 billion. The group as a whole showed very modest success at offsetting defense cuts with real commercial sales expansion.

Research confirms that diversification has been a real but limited phenomenon among multibillion-dollar major prime contractors. However, even with significant incentives encouraging a different strategy, 12 companies had better-than-average sales performance and also significantly reduced their defense dependence (Hughes, Martin-Marietta, Raytheon, TRW, Allied Signal, Textron, Texas Instruments, United Technologies, FMC Corporation, GTE, ITT, and Computer Sciences). While several companies, such as Martin Marietta, gained commercial sales through acquisition, many have moved into alternative markets primarily through internal product development. It is therefore worth exploring the factors behind the successful diversifiers to determine if a different set of government policies and incentives might have generated substantially more diversification among large contractors.

Bucking the Trend: Diversification and Conversion in Large Defense Companies

DIVERSIFICATION AS AN INNOVATIVE CORPORATE STRATEGY

To examine the contemporary record of diversification and conversion by large defense companies, it is first necessary to dispose of the powerful myth that this strategy, in Martin Marietta head Norm Augustine's language, has "a record unblemished by success." There are ample cases of comical failure by defense companies attempting to enter non-DoD markets. The Boeing-Vertol trolley car, the Grumman Flexible Bus, and the McDonnell Douglas computer services company often are entered into evidence to demonstrate the futility of defense diversification.

Interestingly, examples of major diversification successes can be tabled for these same three companies. Boeing had spectacular success

Table 3–2 Twenty-Five Top Defense Contractors: Sales, Employment, Defense Dependence, 1989–94

	Sales 1994 (in Millions of 1992 $U.S.)	Change in Sales 1989–94	Change in Employment 1989–94	Defense/ Total Sales 1989[a]	Defense/ Total Sales 1994[a]
Company:					
1 McDonnell Douglas	12,549	−16%	−49%	72%	70%
2 Lockheed[b]	12,590	14%	−9%	80%	78%
3 Martin Marietta[c]	9,404	46%	38%	88%	65%
4 Hughes	13,428	6%	−16%	52%	45%
5 Northrop Grumman[d]	6,391	−35%	−39%	81%	81%
6 Boeing	20,937	−7%	−25%	28%	22%
7 Raytheon[e]	9,536	−3%	−22%	54%	38%
8 United Technologies	19,810	−9%	−15%	24%	18%
9 Litton[f]	3,282	−41%	−43%	60%	92%
10 Loral[g]	3,818	189%	155%	79%	78%
11 General Dynamics[h]	2,912	−74%	−79%	90%	93%
12 Westinghouse	8,427	−41%	−31%	24%	28%
13 Rockwell	10,593	−24%	−34%	28%	21%
14 General Electric	57,247	−6%	−24%	16%	4%
15 Tenneco	11,594	−19%	−39%	15%	15%
16 Texas Instruments	9,824	35%	−24%	33%	17%
17 TRW	8,654	6%	−14%	43%	19%
18 ITT	22,448	1%	−8%	8%	6%

19 Allied Signal	12,207	-8%	-18%	20%	11%
20 Unisys	6,990	-38%	-44%	21%	16%
21 FMC Corporation	3,858	1%	-11%	32%	27%
22 Textron	9,222	11%	-9%	23%	10%
23 GTE Corporation	19,007	-7%	-36%	6%	4%
24 Computer Sciences	2,460	65%	32%	41%	28%
25 Honeywell[i]	5,769	-15%	-22%	21%	7%
Total/Weighted Percentage	302,957	-9.2%	-25%	32.8%	25%

[a]Estimates from *Defense News*, "Top 100 Reports," include sales to DOD and estimate of arms export sales. Does not include other government sales such as NASA and DOE.

[b]Includes purchase of General Dynamics Military Aircraft, 1994 numbers based on estimate before Martin Marietta merger.

[c]Includes acquisition of GE aerospace and GD space systems, 1994 numbers based on estimate before Lockheed merger.

[d]Data for Northrop Grumman combined in 1989–93.

[e]Before acquisition of E-Systems by Raytheon.

[f]Litton spun-off its commercial operations in 1993–94.

[g]Includes a series of acquisitions prior to purchase by Lockheed Martin.

[h]Includes a series of major divestitures.

[i]Includes the formal separation with Alliant Techsystems.

Sources: Analysis of company annual reports, GAO, *Defense Contractors: Pay, Benefits, and Restructuring During Defense Downsizing* (Washington, D.C.: GAO/NSAID-96-19BR, October 1995); *Defense News*, "Top 100 Reports," 1990–94.

leveraging defense technology from its early military jet programs to establish a leading position in commercial aerospace. Grumman successfully entered and succeeded in the small commercial jet market with Gulfstream, which was later spun off. Even McDonnell Douglas had success developing a medical testing company, Vitek, which was sold off and grew into a $150 million firm. Other successes include Raytheon's development and marketing of the microwave oven and Hughes Aircraft's enormously successful dual-use commercial satellite business.

However, the list of diversification failures is almost certainly much longer than successes—but this is normal in any industry. Studies of diversification attempts in other industries show that the majority of new market entry drives fail to generate profits over the long term.[17] A 1991 study by the Wainbridge group showed that in a sample of 148 defense-oriented firms, 36 percent of the diversification projects were considered successful by the firm respondents.[18] This success rate may not be substantially lower than what is found in nondefense companies.[19] In short, defense diversification, like most other strategies available to defense firms, involves significant risk.

MATCHING COMPETENCIES TO OPPORTUNITIES

Studies of military conversion have emphasized a number of technical and organizational barriers that impede the entry of military-serving firms into alternative markets.[20] The main factors that seem to influence a company's ability to diversify successfully out of defense include a company's core technologies and product lines, particularly its position in the defense product hierarchy; the risk/return opportunities associated with downsizing vs. diversification strategies; and the degree to which a company has the institutional capacity and leadership to change its market orientation.

Technology and product specialization strongly condition how firms are positioned to enter non-DoD markets. The major primes, dedicated to large-scale systems integration activities, are usually viewed as facing the highest diversification barriers. The producers of major end-use systems tend to be highly specialized and carry substantial defense-specific overhead costs. Of course, there are differences related to a firm's specific systems integration specialty. Integrators of weapons and platforms tend to have a more difficult time than companies more specialized in electronics and communications. The technology and systems integration tasks tend to be more similar between military and civilian communications systems and networks than in weapons and platforms.[21] A closer look at large primes suggests that they typically have a number of core competencies and assets that may have value in alternative markets: they have excellent systems integration capabilities; they are adept at bidding for and completing multiyear contracts in a highly regulated environment; they often have unique pockets of technology at the system and subsystem level; and they have a capacity to ensure exceptional standards of durability and reliability.

The key issue is if there are major markets where there is robust demand for these competencies and technologies of defense firms. As Table 3–3 indicates, a number of large markets do offer opportunities for large prime contractors. Focusing attention on the major primes, we find that with the exception of General Dynamics and McDonnell Douglas, defense firms are making significant forays into large non-DoD markets where systems integration capability and specific technologies are in demand.

The common transition is into non-DoD government or highly regulated commercial markets were specific capabilities can be leveraged. The ability of some military firms to design and integrate complex systems over long contract cycles is an asset in markets like commercial aerospace, public transportation, air traffic control systems, commercial space, and shipbuilding. In other areas such as medical imaging and transmission, fiber optics, and environmental sensors, defense companies have unique technologies and design experience.

Non-DoD government markets are providing significant opportunities, but growth remains constrained by relatively stagnant federal government investment spending. Yet a number of large primes are surprisingly active in commercial market segments. Perhaps one of the largest diversification targets is automotive electronics, which mostly includes integrating electronics subsystems into new car models. Defense companies are providing subsystems such as air bags, displays, and sensors as well as new internal navigation and other "intelligent-vehicle" devices. Hughes, Rockwell, and TRW, who already were connected to strong automotive divisions, have been active and successful in this market. The fast-growing commercial space telecommunications market is another area attracting major investments from diversifying companies. The tremendous success of Hughes with Direct-TV has shown that a well-executed plan to transfer defense-based technology can yield attractive returns.

While these major markets offer clear opportunities, a serious commitment to diversification carries high risks and demands an almost religious commitment by management. Any management team will evaluate the risk-return trade-off of a major commitment to diversifica-

Table 3–3 Major Markets for Diversification

Industry/Product Cluster	Type of Market	Annual Size	Growth Prospects	Major Prime Contractors Active
1 Commercial Space Launch/Satellite	Commercial	10 billion +	STRONG	Hughes, Lockheed Martin, Loral, TRW, Rockwell
2 Government Information Systems	Government	5 billion +	MODERATE	Loral, Northrop Grumman
3 Environmental Sensors	Mixed	5 billion +	MODERATE	Raytheon, Hughes, Loral
4 Commercial Aerospace	Commercial	10 billion +	MODERATE	Almost All Major Primes
5 Telecommunications	Commercial	50 billion +	STRONG	Hughes, Raytheon, Loral, Northrop Grumman, Lockheed Martin
6 Fiber-Optics Systems	Commercial	10 billion +	STRONG	Raytheon, Litton
7 Automotive Electronics/IV Systems	Commercial	10 billion +	STRONG	Hughes, TRW, Rockwell
8 Alternative Transportation Vehicles	Mixed	1 billion +	WEAK	Hughes, Northrop Grumman, Lockheed Martin
9 Commercial Shipbuilding	Commercial	5 billion +	WEAK	Litton
10 Medical Diagnostic Equipment/Imaging	Mixed	10 billion +	STRONG	Loral, E-Systems
11 Air Traffic Control Systems	Government	5 billion +	MODERATE	Martin Marietta, Loral, Hughes, Raytheon
12 Mass Transportation/Command & Control Equipment	Government	3 billion +	WEAK	Rockwell, Raytheon

Sources: *Defense Contractors: Pay, Benefits and Restructuring During Defense Downsizing* (Washington D.C.: GAO/NSAID-96-19BR, October 1995); Project California, *A Blueprint for Energizing California's Recovery* (Los Angeles, Calif.: Council on Science and Technology, October 1993).

tion against other investment strategies. The policies toward merger and acquisition discussed earlier, which have increased the short-run profits from mergers between sibling defense companies, have likely reduced the pace of diversification among the primes. A number of the market entries described in Table 3–3 are either small niche entries or have not been backed by major investment commitments. Loral's program in medical imaging is quite small, while Litton's interest in double-hull tanker construction has not been backed with major R&D and investment spending. Also, the entry of Northrop and Loral into the non-DoD government information systems market was achieved by the acquisition of Grumman and IBM Federal Systems, respectively. Neither entry involved significant internal product or market development.

THE COMMITMENT TO DIVERSIFICATION

The type of firms pursuing serious diversification lends support to the hypothesis that systems integrators in the communications and electronics segments tend to find more opportunities to diversify than platform or weapons makers. The record suggests that commercialization generally occurs in closely related markets. Platform makers more commonly target civilian aerospace and space launch, while electronics and surveillance companies focus on such markets as telecommunications, environmental sensing, or satellite communications. But large-firm strategies do not seem entirely predictable on the basis of market or industry segment alone. Platform specialists such as FMC and United Technologies are pursuing vigorous diversification, while Loral seems to have gotten little commercial market entrée from its electronics and information technology capabilities.

The decision to pursue commercialization involves intense management devotion to the strategy, creative reorganization of corporate operations, and a major commitment of resources to internal product development. Management commitment is hard to gauge directly, since upper management of most defense companies will tout various diversification projects. Commitment can be assumed if management is actively trying to integrate and reform defense and nondefense units, is pursuing outside funding and partnerships to complement internal product development, and is allocating internal R&D and capital to diversification.

These actions are evident in six diversifying companies on the list (Hughes, TRW, Textron, Texas Instruments, FMC Corp, and Computer Sciences). For example, Hughes has focused for years on integrating its commercial and military satellite operations, creating a real dual-use capacity from design to production. In 1992 company chief executive officer Michael Armstrong set up 50 diversification projects tied closely to corporate R&D laboratories. These exploratory projects involved bringing together personnel from different divisions. Several went forward and have begun to earn a profit.[22] In the bigger automotive electronics segment, Hughes-Delco draws on technology and expertise from across the company to respond to GM and other automobile clients. The division has carried out more than 150 product development projects for GM. To encourage technology transfer from its defense and space segments to automotive applications, TRW set up an Automotive Technology Center at its defense division. Automotive segment personnel, funded by its own business units, come to the center to extract technologies from the defense and space group. Similar examples of intersegment integration and product development also are occurring at Textron and Texas Instruments.

Studies suggest that market diversification through internal product development tends to be more successful than diversification through acquisition.[23] These diversifying firms are relying primarily on internal development in their efforts. However, because of the traditional wall of separation between defense and commercial operations, companies often must develop new sales, distribution, and servicing capabilities through teaming with companies already active in target markets. Raytheon's purchase of Amana in the 1960s was critical to bringing its microwave oven to the mass market. Likewise, Hughes has teamed with the major consumer electronics companies to distribute Direct-TV.

A central hurdle for diversifying companies attempting to transfer technology internally and develop new products is committing internal funds to risky R&D projects. Companies with a strong defense legacy are conditioned to use external funds for development. External assistance may help defense companies develop new products, but a serious attempt to enter or develop a new market requires a significant commitment of company profits.

STRATEGY AND PERFORMANCE AMONG 12 MAJOR PRIME CONTRACTORS

To get a tangible measure of company's commitment to diversification, Table 3–4 presents a provisional comparison of productivity, R&D, investment commitment, and profitability. These performance measures were derived for six companies that have followed basically a merger or consolidation strategy and six companies that have pursued a diversification strategy.

Table 3–4 Performance Measures of Consolidating and Diversifying Firms (%)

	Growth in Sales per Employee 1989–94	Company R&D/Sales 1994	Capital Investment/Sales 1994	Profit/Sales[a] 1994	ROI[b] Average 1989–94
Consolidating Companies:					
Northrop Grumman	7.7	2.6	2.0	0.5	4.1
Litton	2.5	1.7	2.3	1.9	7.2
General Dynamics	23.6	1.0	1.2	7.3	5.8
McDonnell Douglas	63.5	2.3	0.9	4.5	7.4
Loral	13.1	4.3	2.5	5.7	10.2
Lockheed Martin	12.6	2.9	2.3	4.4	7.8
Average—Consolidators	20.5	2.5	1.9	4.1	7.1
Diversifying Companies:					
Hughes	26.2	5.0	5.3	6.6	7.3
TRW	22.4	6.1	5.6	3.7	8.5
Textron	21.7	1.9	3.1	4.5	7.4
Texas Instruments	77.1	6.7	10.4	6.7	6.1
FMC Corporation	13.7	4.1	8.8	4.3	10.9
Computer Sciences Corp.	24.4	na	4.6	3.5	11.4
Average-Diversifiers	30.9	4.8	6.3	4.9	8.6

[a] Calculated as real 1992$ net earnings over sales.
[b] Calculated as net operating income (before interest payments and taxes) over total assets.
Sources: Analysis of company annual reports, GAO; *Defense Contractors: Pay, Benefits, and Restructuring During Defense Downsizing* (Washington, D.C.: GAO/NSAID-96-19BR, October 1995).

The data in Table 3–4 strongly suggest that diversifying companies are more committed to the internal development of their business lines. They commit a significantly larger share of company resources to R&D and capital expenditures than the consolidating firms. The diversifying companies appear more focused on using their defense technology and skill base to build a foundation for growth in new high-growth markets.

The consolidating defense companies, in contrast, seem to be relatively dormant in terms of their commitment to future markets, with anemic levels of R&D and capital investment. When their backlogs and sales begin to stagnate, they either shave more labor and capacity or purchase another defense company. It could be argued that this is not a particularly complex or innovative strategy.

These data raise major questions about the DoD policy of encouraging mergers. If the objective is to reduce costs, these figures are not cause for celebration. The diversifying companies on average appear "leaner and meaner" than the consolidating firms, with higher levels of sales growth per employee over the period from 1989 to 1994. Apparently mergers and consolidation have not fully rationalized excess defense overheads. Furthermore, this evidence also undercuts the hope that the high profits of consolidating companies would be allocated to sustain strong research capabilities. Profitability is actually higher in the diversifying companies; R&D/sales and investment ratios are lower among the consolidators (although these figures may be a function of the stronger participation in electronics and communications segments by diversifying firms). The need to service merger-related debt may be a factor in dampening investment and R&D in the consolidating firms.

As shown in Table 3–5, the diversifying companies have had relatively decent sales growth. They successfully offset defense sales losses with commercial sales gains. In the process they have retained significantly greater employment than the merging and consolidating companies as a group. These diversification efforts have not led to disaster but instead have yielded reasonably good results, especially when compared to other military prime contractors.

Among the consolidators, Loral and Lockheed Martin are the only firms that have expanded sales and employment, primarily through acquisition. However, at Lockheed Martin there have been significant internal pushes into new non-DoD government markets, such as air traffic control and information systems; there also has been success in commercial space launch. Now, of course, Loral and Lockheed Martin are happily married.

This evidence suggest that policies encouraging diversification and conversion among large defense companies hold real promise in terms

Table 3–5   Sales and Employment Changes in Consolidating and Diversifying Firms[a]

	Change in Defense Sales 1989–94 (Millions 92 $U.S.)	Change in Non-Defense Sales 1989–94 (Millions 92 $U.S.)	Change in Total Sales 1989–94 (Millions 92 $U.S.)	Change in Employment 1989–94	Percentage Change in Employment 1989–94
Consolidating Companies:					
Northrop Grumman	–1,658	–616	–2,274	–27,500	–39
Litton	–335	–1,983	–2,318	–21,700	–41
General Dynamics	–7,416	–979	–8,395	–80,900	–79
McDonnell Douglas	–2,010	–369	–2,379	–62,166	–49
Loral	1,928	567	2,495	19,700	155
Lockheed Martin	1,400	3,106	4,506	17,300	12
Total/Weighted Percentage	–8,090	–275	–8,365	–155,266	–30.4
Diversifying Companies:					
Hughes	–585	1,349	764	–15,000	–16
TRW	–1,864	2,336	471	–10,100	–14
Textron	–939	1,867	928	–5,000	–9
Texas Instruments	–762	3,315	2,553	–17,521	–24
FMC Corporation	–198	224	26	–2,766	–11
Computer Sciences Corp.	69	897	966	7,000	32
Total/Weighted Percentage	–4,280	9,989	5,709	–43,387	–12.5

[a] All sales figures deflated to real 1992 dollars.
Sources: Analysis of company annual reports, GAO; *Defense Contractors: Pay, Benefits, and Restructuring During Defense Downsizing* (Washington, D.C.: GAO/NSAID-96-19BR, October 1995); *Defense News*, "Top 100 Reports," 1990–94.

of leveraging our decades-long defense investment into higher-growth non-DoD markets. The markets where the systems integration capacity and technologies of defense companies are in demand are significant and growing. Successful entry requires major reforms in the way defense organizations operate and a significant commitment of internal funds. Modest research support and programs that encourage collaboration between defense and nondefense companies may speed technology transfer. The fact that diversifying companies are very active in nondefense public markets indicates that a higher rate of civilian R&D and public investment would increase the rate of conversion and technology transfer among large contractors. Finally, because the diversifiers in this sample have continued to maintain strong defense divisions, it may be possible to maintain truly essential defense capabilities by encouraging diversification instead of subsidizing merger and consolidation.

The predominant policies encouraging merger and consolidation pull companies in opposite directions. Quick payoffs from selling off defense divisions or acquiring defense units discourage companies from making the wrenching changes and investments necessary to move to alternative markets. Several of the successful diversifiers identified, such as TRW, Hughes, and Texas Instruments, are under intense pressure to sell off defense divisions to the larger defense-dedicated contractors.

Downsizing and Diversification Among Small and Medium-Sized Defense Firms

THE OVERALL RECORD

Sitting below the major prime contractors is an enormously heterogeneous group of smaller companies supplying subsystems, assemblies, components, and materials to the Department of Defense and the large contractors. Companies in this category range from suppliers of generic goods and services to highly specialized manufacturers and research service providers. The vulnerability of smaller firms to losses of defense-related sales obviously depends on their defense dependence and their technical specialization. For producers of generic goods and services, the problem is finding other markets, not developing different products.

As defense spending plunged, there was considerable concern that a critical base of specialized second- and third-tier subcontractors would be eaten away by company closures and exit from the defense business. It was also noted that during past periods when defense sales declined, large contractors tended to bring work in-house.[24] A related worry was that as suppliers of critical components dried up, dependence on foreign suppliers would escalate.

Surveys of the broad community of smaller companies with some sales to defense indicate that there has been no major shakeout in the lower tiers of the supply chain. A PRIE survey of 600 defense companies that excluded the top 50 defense contractors was completed by Jonathan Feldman at PRIE. The firms ranged from specialized makers of electronic components totally dependent on defense sales, to construction contractors with less than 5 percent of their sales to the DoD. The survey obtained information for the period from 1989 to 1993. The surprising results of this survey indicate that there has been considerable stability in the universe of smaller defense contracting firms. Real sales and employment changed very little over this period, and defense dependency of the overall sample declined marginally, from 31 percent of total sales to 29 percent by 1993. Since procurement spending plummeted over this period, the survey strongly suggests that major prime contractors were subcontracting more rather than taking work in-house.[25]

Results of surveys of this type might be biased by exclusion of firms that have gone out of business and the possibility that more successful firms are more likely to respond to the questionnaire. However, work done at RAND based on a survey of 465 subcontractors found a failure rate of only 3 percent between 1992 and 1995.[26] Bias introduced by the second factor may be present, but it is unlikely that it would alter the basic results of the PRIE survey dramatically.

ADJUSTMENT IN MORE SPECIALIZED DEFENSE FIRMS

Most small and medium-size companies that are specialized in defense are concentrated in four Standard Industrial Classification (SIC) groups: 366 (communications equipment); 367 (electronic components); 372 (aircraft parts and equipment; and 381 (search and navigation equipment). The author conducted in-depth face-to-face interviews with over 60 smaller companies with high dependence on defense sales in 1989. The interviews included a mix of companies in the industry classification, plus several in other classifications including metalworking, software, and engineering services above. We do not claim to have a statistically representative sample of this universe of companies. The companies provided basic performance data, and in-depth questions were asked about barriers to conversion and actions taken to adjust to defense sales losses. Basic results are reported below on 41 companies whose 1989 sales were less than $200 million.

Table 3–6   **Performance Measures of 41 Small and Medium-Sized Defense-Related Companies**

Change in Sales Revenue 1989–94 (real 1992$)	–26.9%
Change in Employment 1989–94	–36.8%
Defense Dependency—Sales Weighted Average 1989	69.3%
Defense Dependency—Sales Weighted Average 1994	49.6%
Percentage Reporting Sales from New Commercial Product	72 %
N = 41	

Source: Company interviews summer of 1994 and updated fall of 1995.

Overall employment in this group declined by nearly 37 percent and sales by about 26.9 percent in real dollar terms over the period from 1989 to 1994. (See Table 3–6.) These more specialized companies, with an average defense dependency of 69 percent in 1989, obviously encountered a harsher reality than smaller firms in general. For most firms, sales and employment losses occurred between the years 1989 and 1992, with a notable stabilization in sales and employment levels in 1994.

It is encouraging that the average defense dependency in this group fell from over 69 percent of sales in 1989, to about 50 percent by 1994. Reduced defense dependency in this group was primarily a function of lost defense sales, but a number of firms had a real increase in non-DoD sales. Contrary to naysayer accounts of defense conversion, the majority of the companies were conducting product development, and 72 percent actually were making sales from new products or services in non-DoD markets. We also found that many companies had participated and benefited from federal R&D support and technical assistance partnerships with state and local governments.

Buying or merging with other companies as sales fall is generally not an option for smaller defense firms. Therefore, many smaller companies find strenuous conversion efforts less risky than remaining stuck in unstable and declining defense niches. Our data and other research indicate that diversification among small to medium-sized firms has been both common and relatively successful.[27] In explaining this record, certain common barriers and success factors stand out among firms. In addition, the role of modest federal conversion assistance has been significant for a subset of companies.

An important objective of the interview process was to gauge the types of public services defense companies saw as most useful to their diversification efforts. In general, company leaders in firms that successfully diversified tended to be open to outside collaboration and assistance when it could fill a specific gap. In most cases this involved some form of collaboration with other private firms in R&D and marketing activities. However, over half of the companies interviewed were participating in some form of public-sector program to aid their conversion efforts.

The PRIE research program also has included evaluations of public conversion and labor-retraining programs in five defense-oriented regions (St. Louis, Los Angeles, Long Island, Seattle, and northern New Mexico). For the most part, technology does not rank among the most important concerns of smaller companies, but federal conversion programs nevertheless tend to stress technology development and deployment. Manufacturing extension and technical assistance services perform better on this score than Technology Reinvestment Program (TRP)-type technology development programs, but even here research suggests that more modestly funded full-service programs aimed at assessing and addressing financial, management, and marketing needs of firms were more effective than other technology-intensive approaches that assume firms simply need better equipment.[28] As limited as public conversion assistance has been, our research suggests that it has been effective in specific cases in helping small and medium-size firms survive and diversify. Finally, it is noteworthy that most companies of this size continued to serve defense markets even as they sought to expand commercial sales.

Conclusion

Although the Bottom-Up Review has never been viewed as a particularly durable or realistic plan, it has had an important influence on defense industry restructuring. In a period of falling expenditures, it signaled what the broad budget priorities would be and, in general terms, what kinds of weapons, upgrading, and new development would be required. In particular it called for a relatively large force requiring high operations and maintenance (O&M) spending and a capability to resupply major weapons systems. Procurement of next-generation weapons and R&D funding would hence be limited.

The central problem was how to keep contractors active in each key weapons and system area, capable of producing current weapons and developing new ones. Despite some progress with dual-use and procurement reform, merger and consolidation were seen as the best means to cope with capability needs and limited budgets. The evidence presented here raises troubling questions about this approach, even in a world shaped by the Bottom-Up Review. The type of combinations that have occurred and the subsidies that have been offered suggest that this direction has been more successful at maintaining capability than in producing substantial cost savings. The high profits of consolidating firms have not led to healthy levels of company R&D to keep development capacities sharp. Therefore, the DoD may be responsible for funding an even greater share of future R&D if new development programs actually are needed.

Using arms exports as a way to maintain defense industrial capacity is a particularly irrational policy. A Lockheed official recently testified that the United States had to make a multibillion-dollar commitment to the F-22 fighter to counter the widespread proliferation of high-performance combat aircraft such as the U.S.-made F-15 and F-16.[29] This argument suggests that with the fall of the Soviet Union, we are effectively engaging in an arms race with ourselves.

Equally troubling are the permanent effects defense restructuring has wrought on the broader industrial and technology base. As of this writing, the merger movement continues apace, with Wall Street cheering on the efforts of companies to combine operations and milk short-term profits out of mature production contracts. The merger and consolidation policy has put a damper on diversification and technology transfer by large companies from defense into commercial markets, but also from commercial markets into defense. The giant defense firms are agglomerating into segregated islands as healthy diversified companies such as Rockwell, Texas Instruments, and TRW are forced to sell off their defense divisions because of the high stock premiums available.

Since a key argument of this chapter is that defense industry restructuring has been shaped by the requirements of the Bottom-Up Review, the only way to reverse these troubling trends is to change security and defense policies drastically. In effect, we continue to subsidize through different means a research and production reserve that is not needed in the post–Cold War world. A strong strand of independent scholarship, from former Reagan defense official Lawrence Korb, to Brookings Institution defense specialists William Kaufmann and John Sitenbruner, argue that we could spend up to one-third less than currently planned and still retain the world's biggest military, capable of meeting all feasible security challenges.[30] An alternative security policy based on vigorous arms control and nonproliferation, a much smaller, more mobile U.S. force structure, and broad-based conversion of large and small defense companies could achieve key security objectives—and at a much lower price.

The success of diversification shows that a strong technology and defense industry base could be sustained by large companies retaining profitable defense and commercial divisions and achieving some integration between the two markets. Smaller firms, left out of the merger wave, have been relatively successful at expanding commercial sales. Many also continue to produce for defense. This fact also suggests that a strong industrial capacity can be generated through diversification. The alternative approach, linked to more modest security demands, would involve a defense technology base sustained by commercial rather than defense sales. This base would be less capable of producing or developing a full range of new weapons at a moment's notice. However, experts have failed to convincingly isolate a threat that would not allow some amount of response time for relevant segments of the defense industry.

The record of diversification also suggests that the returns on our huge Cold War investment could be increased. A share of the savings from a more realistic security policy could support strong technical assistance and high levels of public investment, allowing large and small defense companies to transfer technology into more productive pursuits. Such a path could make the post–Cold War transition more like previous demobilizations, which led to periods of increased prosperity.

Notes

1. Richard Samuels, *Rich Nation, Strong Army: National Security and the Technological Transformation of Japan* (Ithaca, N.Y.: Cornell University Press, 1994).

2. Warner Schilling et al., *Strategy, Politics and Defense Budgets* (New York: Columbia University Press, 1962).

3. William Rogerson, "Profit Regulation of Defense Contracts and Prizes for Innovation," *Journal of Political Economy*, no. 97 (1989): 1284–1389; William Rogerson, "Economic Incentives and the Defense Procurement Process," Working Paper 93-33, Center for Urban Affairs and Policy Research, Northwestern University, Evanston, IL, 1993.

4. Department of Defense, *Report on the Bottom-up Review*, (Washington, D.C.: Office of the Secretary of Defense and Joint Chiefs of Staff, September 1, 1993).

5. Michael Oden et al., "Changing the Future: Converting the St. Louis Economy," Working Paper 59, Center for Urban Policy Research, Rutgers University, New Brunswick, NJ, 1993.

6. John Mintz, "Pentagon Assailed on Merger Aid," *Washington Post*, July 28, 1994, p. D9.

7. General Accounting Office, "Defense Restructuring Costs: Payment Regulations Are Inconsistent with Legislation" (Washington, D.C.: GAO/NSAID-95-106, August 10, 1995).

8. Mintz, "Pentagon Assailed."

9. General Accounting Office, "Defense Restructuring Costs."

10. Office of the Undersecretary of Defense, Comptroller, Department of Defense, *Defense Budget Estimates for FY 1995* (Washington, D.C.: Department of Defense, March 1995).

11. Lawrence Korb, "Merger Mania," *Brookings Review* (Summer 1996): 22–25.

12. Anthony Velocci, "Defense Firms Show Financial Prowess," *Aviation Week,* May 30, 1994, pp. 40–60.

13. Philip Finnegan, "Soaring Debt May Tether Industry," *Defense News,* January 15–21, 1996, p. 9.

14. Martin Bailey, Eric Bartelsman, and John Haltiwange, "Downsizing and Productivity Growth: Myth or Reality," Working Paper 4741, National Bureau of Economic Research, Cambridge, Mass., 1994; "Corporate Surveys Can't Find Productivity Revolution, Either," *Challenge* (November–December 1995): 31–34; Deborah Dougherty and Edward Bowman, "The Effects of Downsizing on Product Innovation," *California Management Review* 37, no. 4 (Summer 1995): 28–44.

15. Philip Finnegan and Lance Marburger, "Top 100 Worldwide Defense Firms," *Defense News* (July 1989–95).

16. Office of the Undersecretary of Defense, Department of Defense, *Defense Budget Estimates for FY 1995.*

17. Michael Porter, "From Competitive Advantage to Corporate Strategy," *Harvard Business Review,* May–June 1987.

18. The Winbridge Group, Inc., *The Commercialization of Defense Technology: A Survey of Industry Experience* (New York: DRI/McGraw Hill and the Fraser Group, November 1991).

19. Jacques Gansler, *Defense Conversion: Transforming the Arsenal of Democracy* (New York: Twentieth Century Fund, 1995).

20. Ann Markusen, "The Military Industrial Divide," *Environment and Planning: Society and Space* 9 (1991): 391–416; Seymour Melman, "Characteristics of the Industrial Conversion Problem," in Seymour Melman, ed., *The War Economy of the United States.* (New York: St. Martin's Press, 1971), pp. 201–7.

21. Jordi Molas and William Walker, "Military Innovation's Growing Reliance on Civilian Technology: A New Source of Dynamism and Structural Change," in Grin et al., eds., *Military Technological Innovation and Stability in a Changing World* (Amsterdam: VU University Press, 1992).

22. "Mike Armstrong's Leap of Faith," *Business Week,* March 9, 1992, pp. 58–59.

23. Timothy Dunne et al., "Patterns of Firm Entry and Exit in U.S. Manufacturing Industries," *Annual Journal of Economics,* Winter 1988; David

Ravinscroft and Frederick Sherer, *Mergers, Sell-offs, and Economic Efficiency* (Washington, D.C..: Brookings Institution, 1988).

24. Gansler, *Defense Conversion.*

25. Jonathan Feldman, "The Successful Conversion of Defense Serving Firms to Commercial Activity," Ph.D. diss., Rutgers University, 1996.

26. George Vernez et al., "California's Shrinking Defense Contractors: Effects on Small Suppliers," MR-687-OSD (Santa Monica: RAND Corporation, 1995).

27. Michael Oden, "The Microeconomics of Defense Serving Organization," Ms., PRIE, Rutgers University, 1994.

28. Oden et al., "Changing the Future."

29. *Arms Sales Monitor* (Washington, D.C.: Federation of the American Scientists, February 1995).

30. See William Kaufmann and John Steinbruner, *Decision for Defense: Prospects for a New Order* (Washington, D.C.: Brookings Institution, 1991), and Lawrence Korb, "The Readiness Gap: What Gap?" *New York Times Magazine* (February 26, 1996), pp. 40–41.

4

The History and Politics of the Pentagon's Dual-Use Strategy

Jay Stowsky

HE COALITION that elected Bill Clinton president included factions of the Democratic Party with different attitudes toward the economic and social impacts of technological change. The Clinton administration's Technology Reinvestment Program (TRP) became a key policy initiative of one of those factions—the economic nationalists, who advocated tougher federal trade and technology policies during the "competitiveness" debates of the 1980s. The immediate objective of TRP was to propel the commercial development of technologies critical to the military. Paired with defense procurement reforms aimed at reducing military specifications and encouraging greater use of commercially derived components, TRP was intended to leverage low-cost commercial manufacturing practices and economies of scale to make these technologies more affordable for military users. Its secondary purpose was to bolster the performance of U.S.-based high-technology manufacturers in international competition, by helping to neutralize the strategic trade and industrial policies of other countries. Observers inside as well as outside the administration argued that the program had a third objective, namely helping to ease the post–Cold War conversion of the defense industrial base to commercial production. With all these expectations placed on it, the effort won rapid congressional approval toward the end of the Bush administration (which resisted its implementation). The new Clinton administration arrived in Washington eager not only to implement TRP but to expand it, but by then the program already was saddled with the burden of meeting too many objectives it was never designed to achieve. It struggled to gain its footing for roughly two and a half years before being discontinued at the end of fiscal 1996.

Although the Clinton administration greatly expanded the scope of cost-shared partnerships between government and industry, the political shifts of 1992, in terms of party and program, were greater than the actual policy shifts. Conflicts over sectoral and regional targeting had sunk the notion of a national industrial policy by 1984, but federal policymakers continued to experiment with initiatives to promote joint research in industry, more collaboration between industry and universities, and more collaboration between industry and federal laboratories. Thus most of the Clinton administration's technology policy initiatives expanded on precedents established during the Reagan and Bush administrations, notwithstanding the Republicans' rhetorical rejection of government interference in markets.

The policies the Clinton officials designed stemmed from their belief that the establishment by foreign producers of a dominant position in markets for advanced technology could lock in control of a long stream of follow-on product and process innovations, making subsequent market entry much harder for U.S.-based competitors. The temporary reshuffling of global market position in high-technology industries threatened to translate into a more permanent reshuffling of wealth and power in the international political system. The deep recession of 1990–91 underscored for many Americans the paradox of a defense industrial base in apparent decline despite a decade of record spending for new military hardware. A coalition began to form to support increased Pentagon spending for dual-use technology development—development of technologies that could result in viable commercial products as well as military uses. Dual use was thought of as part of a broader strategy to remove structural obstacles—in this case, an isolated, sometimes parasitic military-industrial complex—that were believed to be impeding the nation's long-term economic growth. The Technology Reinvestment Program differed from previous dual-use initiatives of the Department of Defense (DoD) in that its investments were guided not only by the desire to persuade commercial producers to manufacture products that could be adapted by military users but on the likelihood that the dual-use technologies it sponsored could result directly in the introduction of viable commercial products.

The dual-use coalition combined elements of U.S. business bruised by foreign competition, elements of the labor movement concerned about the loss of domestic manufacturing jobs (particularly in the defense sector), members of the defense research establishment concerned about growing dependence on foreign sources for military technology, and neoliberal or "New" Democrats who believed that traditional liberal Democratic economic policies emphasized consumption and distribution too much over investment and growth. However, despite their common interest in removing obstacles to economic growth, the outcomes desired by business groups and the military research establishment did not match the expectations of other social groups that were important to President Clinton's fragile governing coalition. Organized labor worried about the job displacement effects of new commercial technology and wanted to see more of an up-front commitment to job preservation and worker retraining. Liberal public interest groups—including groups of computer professionals allied with the peace movement—worried that the military's habit of secrecy and its preference for defense-dedicated products would skew the range of advanced technologies developed with public funds. Liberals, labor, and conversion activists wanted federal investments in science and technology to be driven by a broader set of civilian social objectives.

To cement a political coalition with which to sustain TRP, the Clinton administration packaged the program as the centerpiece of its defense conversion effort. But TRP focused mainly on technology development, and this made the program a poor vehicle for quickly replacing lost defense jobs. At the same time, TRP's innovative teaming and cost-sharing requirements limited the actual size of the program's cash grants to individual companies, weakening critical business support for the effort, particularly among defense contractors, who did not necessarily welcome the new competition from commercially oriented companies. The programmatic features that minimized opportunities for congressional earmarking and other forms of political pork also reduced the administration's capacity to cultivate powerful interests that might become vested in the continuation of the program.

Finally—ironically—the tone of the competitiveness debate shifted dramatically just as TRP was getting off the ground. Cyclical recovery and deficit reduction in the United States, post–Cold War reconstruction in Germany, and recession in Japan combined with a significant strengthening of American manufacturing quality and productivity in the 1990s to shift public anxieties away from the factors that weaken or enhance corporate competitive performance. The focus turned instead toward the continued stagnation and unequal distribution of American wages and family incomes, despite the disappearing deficit, record highs on Wall Street, and robust corporate profits. In the search for explanations, job-displacing technologies were near the top of every expert analyst's list, and the administration's technology policies appeared to reward only those groups that already were benefiting from the new information economy. At the beginning of fiscal year 1997, TRP was replaced by a new, dual-use technology development program more clearly designed to fulfill military needs.

The Technology Reinvestment Program might have commanded more broad-based political support had it been embedded in a broader set of public purposes and linked to a set of more rapidly demonstrable results. But TRP's dependence on technical experts and dollars earmarked for the military created a fundamental political imperative that its projects be justified in terms of their alleged value to national defense. The increasingly apparent contradictions between TRP's actual objectives and the expectations it had raised narrowed the political constituency for the program even before a resurgent Republican Congress moved to kill it in the early months of 1995.

It is still too early to render final judgments about the economic and technological accomplishments of TRP. Although its life was short, the initiative facilitated new collaborative relationships between military and commercial firms, thereby enhancing the U.S. military's access to best-practice manufacturing and commercially derived technology. It also appears to have encouraged some private- and public-sector actors to overcome the kinds of collective action problems that many times prevent them from exploiting significant potential commercial opportunities—a point underscored by the continuation of some collaborations even after the participants failed to win any TRP awards. Progress toward civil-military integration is still impeded, however, by the slow pace of defense procurement reform and the continued preference of the military services for defense-dedicated products. The public remains ambivalent about the involvement of profit-seeking firms in publicly subsidized projects. And program managers from the Defense Advanced Research Project Agency (DARPA) remain skittish about focusing federal technology investments on regional industry clusters, despite some evidence that geographic proximity facilitates the generation of innovation-based returns.

In the absence of broader public support for federal investments in technology and science, TRP's utility for accelerating the commercialization of innovations—whether for defense or "competitiveness" objectives—was limited. The federal government has remained constrained in its capacity to launch new technologies as a means to promote social goals other than national security and public health. Experience with the short-lived TRP confirms, moreover, that military-sponsored technology policies cannot be depended on to contribute in a consistently positive manner to the nation's economic performance. Commercial technology spin-offs or the creation of viable commercial industries can never be anything more than by-products of a defense technology policy whose ultimate goals are not economic or scientific but political.

Dual-Use Policy and Politics Before Clinton: Evolution of a Coalition for Investment-Led Growth

THE POLITICS OF "INDUSTRIAL POLICY" (1978–84)

Americans began to debate the need for a national industrial policy late in the stagflationary years of the Carter administration. Although the United States already had a vast store of industrial policies, they were uncoordinated and often inconsistent, designed to further the specific missions of various federal agencies. Interest in a national industrial policy—the planned and coordinated use of microeconomic incentives, implemented at the level of the firm or industry, to restore growth and productivity to the national economy—emerged initially from the search by Democratic politicians for an attractive answer to Republican supply-side economics.

The deficiencies of the Democrats' Keynesian macroeconomics seemed evident in the late 1970s, in the face of record wage and price inflation combined with high unemployment. These deficiencies seemed even less tolerable in light of the mounting competitive diffi-culties of the nation's basic manufacturing industries, particularly auto-mobiles and steel, as U.S. integration into the world economy increased. Drawing on the experience of the 1978 Chrysler bailout, President Carter responded to the growing sense of national crisis by creating a set of tripartite committees to devise plans for reviving the nation's struggling manufacturing sector. The elements of industrial policy were already present in these discussions—the use of direct subsidies, loans and loan guarantees, tax incentives, government procurement, research and development grants, import restrictions and export adjustment assistance, worker training and relocation assistance, infrastructure spending, and regulation and deregulation to facilitate the moderniza-tion and rationalization of basic industry and to facilitate the movement of capital and labor to growth industries fueled by new technology.

In the U.S. political environment of the late 1970s, however, it was easy for a revitalized Republican coalition to question the application of "more government" to the nation's economic problems. The experience of stagflation had hardened the public's attitude toward government social spending in general and tax hikes in particular. This was doubly true as long as the specific sectoral problems at hand seemed confined to the nation's "Rust Belt," with conservatives like Ronald Reagan blaming the competitive difficulties of auto and steel producers on Big Government regulations and Big Union contracts, and with many liberals blaming the producers themselves, for being arrogant, oligopolistic, and out of touch with changing consumer tastes. The Carter administration bolstered the arguments of critics on both sides when the package of import relief and tax benefits it offered required no quid pro quo from the steel and auto companies in the form of new investments in manufacturing modernization or advanced technology. This amounted to precisely the sort of protectionism that economists of both parties scorned. It was easily dismissed by conservative opponents as a political payoff to the unions and quickly delegitimized by the behavior of the assisted producers themselves—U.S. Steel, for example, subsequently used its publicly subsidized profits to buy Marathon Oil.

In contrast, the rhetoric of supply-side economics appealed not only to traditionally Republican business interests but also to many traditionally Democratic middle-class and union households. The program's radically redistributionist details were obscured by President Reagan's sunny, populist rhetoric about cutting taxes and cutting government waste. Business groups understood supply side's likely costs—particularly the prospects for ballooning budget and trade deficits—and this created internal tensions that would later help undermine business support for George Bush. But most business groups understandably supported the Reagan economic program in 1981, the most probusiness, antiunion, antiregulation policy package to come out of Washington since the administration of Calvin Coolidge. Pundits portrayed Reagan's victory as a massive rejection of liberal economic, military, and social policies. Even though Jimmy Carter had arguably been the most conservative Democratic president since Grover Cleveland, the new conventional wisdom constrained the domestic policy options of congressional Democrats and aggravated divisions within the party.

By the time the industrial policy idea blossomed briefly in the depths of the 1982 recession, its leading advocates represented a new faction within the party—a group of baby boomer politicians mainly from western and southern states, variously labeled neoliberals, "Atari Democrats" and, later, "New Democrats," who sought to distance themselves from the Democratic party's traditional interest-group politics and Great Society programs. Convinced that traditional Democratic economics favored consumption and redistribution at the expense of investment and growth, the neoliberals advocated new "partnerships" between business and government. They wanted to hasten the movement of labor and capital out of the nation's declining industries and into the high-tech sectors of the future.

There were differences in emphasis. Some New Democrats traced the nation's declining competitiveness to inadequate savings and capital formation and the power of entrenched interest groups to block needed change; others blamed the economy's problems on the misallocation of capital by speculating "paper entrepreneurs" and the inefficient, ad hoc manner in which the federal government channeled research and procurement funds to industry, primarily through the Department of Defense. Some stressed the need to reallocate resources from "sunset" to "sunrise" industries; others advocated the use of advanced technology, particularly "flexible manufacturing systems," to modernize the nation's existing manufacturing base. All of the neoliberal analysts nevertheless agreed on the need for more coordinated industrial policies, including some form of government-subsidized bank to provide high-risk capital for jump-starting new sectors and retooling old ones, more funding for high-risk civilian technology development, and various labor market and regional economic development policies to blunt political opposition to industrial modernization.

These proposals did not sit well with the labor movement, a still-influential remnant of the Democrat's fragmenting New Deal coalition. Labor officials wanted an industrial policy that would focus on revitalizing the fortunes of the existing manufacturing base; they thought the neoliberals were too intent on abandoning the "Frost Belt." Even proposals to introduce flexible manufacturing technologies into older industries appeared to threaten union jobs in existing plants. Consequently the unions began to develop their own industrial policy proposals, which traced the competitive problems of U.S. manufacturers to the growing international mobility of capital, to the intentional "deindustrialization" of America by globalizing U.S. corporations. They criticized the neoliberals' proposals and called instead for the establishment of tripartite reinvestment planning at the national level and within firms, regulatory and tax incentives to discourage U.S. corporations from moving capital and production facilities abroad (including strong plant closure notification laws), tax reforms to achieve a more equitable distribution of income, and a restoration of social welfare spending slashed by Reagan administration budget cuts.

The growing concern within the American labor movement for protecting domestic production and jobs clashed with the increasingly international outlook of American business. The conflict blocked the efforts of Democratic politicians to resuscitate the growth coalition that had emerged out of the New Deal. Still, globalization was leading a growing number of U.S. business executives to experience the competitive impact of other nations' aggressive trade and industrial policies for the first time. A small number of them were becoming convinced that the federal government needed to play a more active role in restructuring the domestic economy. None went so far as to support a full-blown industrial policy in the form of a government-subsidized bank or a tripartite planning agency. But some proposals that began to emerge from business groups in the mid-1980s ventured beyond the Reagan administration's limited menu of tax cuts, deregulation, and lower government spending to embrace slightly more activist measures, including export promotion assistance, tougher trade legislation, and increased spending for the development of economically and militarily "critical" technologies ("technology policy" rather than "industrial policy"), among others.

With public opinion ambivalent about government's role and opposition surging from academic economists, most business groups, and the Reagan administration, the notion of a national industrial policy quickly died. It had become overly identified with the parochial interests of union labor in declining sectors located in the Northeast and the Midwest. Although legislative hearings on the matter continued into the spring of 1984, industrial policy did not play a major role in either the Democratic primaries or the general election, which returned Ronald Reagan to the White House for a second term.

MILITARY REFORMERS, HIGH-TECH PROFESSIONALS, AND THE "DEFENSE INDUSTRIAL BASE"

As previously mentioned, it had not escaped the attention of participants in the industrial policy debate that one prominent agency of the U.S. government already ran an extensive and highly coordinated industrial policy—the U.S. Department of Defense. Concerns about the declining performance of U.S.-based industry in international competition were broached in military circles in a series of research reports released just after Reagan's election. The reports all decried the deteriorating state of the nation's "defense industrial base," the industrial infrastructure that formed, according to the reports, the civilian backbone of the nation's military posture. Emerging as it did in an increasingly conservative political climate, the notion of a defense industrial base provided convenient political cover for a Pentagon-led industrial policy.

By the late 1970s, military technology planners were convinced that technologies developed in the commercial sector were yielding performance capabilities beyond those that characterized much of the technology available in the military sector. Although product applications, such as military and commercial aircraft, had diverged since the 1960s, both sectors increasingly depended on the same supply base of materials, components, information technology, and production equipment. In addition, mass consumer markets had emerged for new products based on highly sophisticated advanced technologies. Some, such as antilock braking systems for cars, had to work rapidly and reliably in hostile operating environments, characteristics previously considered unique to military systems. Pentagon-backed technology development projects in the 1980s, such as the Very High Speed Integrated Circuit (VHSIC) program (begun during the Carter administration) and the artificial intelligence (AI)–based Strategic Computing Program (SCP) (a Reagan-era initiative) sought to upgrade military technology to commercial capabilities, by increasing the pace at which commercially developed technology was fielded in military systems and by yoking further commercial advances to the specific needs of military users.

Among the strongest supporters of the Pentagon's dual-use technology initiatives was a new coalition for military reform that had attracted many of the neoliberal Democrats in Congress. The group hoped to fill the political space that opened up between a revitalized peace movement dedicated to a unilateral nuclear freeze and the reenergized Cold War coalition headed by President Reagan. By stressing the issue of weapons procurement reform, leading neoliberal Democrats, including the future vice president, Albert Gore Jr., were able to champion lower defense spending and a stronger military simultaneously. This was an appealing combination politically, and it helped the neoliberals to gain control of the national security debate within the Democratic party. From this foundation, they would take control of the party's positions on technology policy as well.

During the same period, a new coalition of scientists and other high-tech professionals had been drawn into the established peace movement by their alarm over the Reagan administration's apparent determination to accelerate the nuclear arms race. Ronald Reagan's strident Cold War rhetoric had resuscitated a large, grass-roots nuclear peace movement. U.S. public sentiment shifted anxiously toward support of the peace movement's campaign for a unilateral nuclear freeze, and the freeze proposal, combined with mounting opposition to the president's Strategic

Defense Initiative, became a rallying point for a more general liberal counterattack on the Reagan administration's overall program. Established peace organizations expanded, and new peace groups proliferated, many of them tied to professional and technical occupations, such as Business Executives for National Security (1982) and Computer Professionals for Social Responsibility (1983). Links were forged between these groups and activists representing other constituencies and liberal causes, including environmental and consumer coalitions, civil rights organizations, and elements of the labor movement. With these allies, scientists and technical professionals in the peace movement gained an increasingly influential voice within the liberal wing of the Democratic party and sought to shape the party's response to the Reagan administration's militarized science and technology agenda.

In fact, throughout the 1980s, both groups—the neoliberal advocates of defense procurement reform and high-tech professionals allied with the peace movement—expressed concern about the Reagan administration's remilitarization of federal research and development spending. Both groups condemned the Pentagon's tendency toward "gold-plating" weapons systems with every new advance in electronics, avionics, or armor regardless of prudence or practicality. Finally, both groups decried what they perceived as a growing trend in weapons procurement and the arms industry toward "waste, fraud, and abuse." Despite the similarities in their analyses and in their rhetoric, however, the two groups were ultimately in pursuit of very different political objectives. Whereas the peace groups sought to provoke a national debate over the ends of U.S. military policy, reformers were content to emphasize the means.

With increasing vehemence, high-tech professionals in the peace movement used their newly amplified voices to organize opposition within the Democratic party and the country to the increased militarization of U.S. science and technology research. They publicized and decried the growing dependence of academic computer scientists on grants from the Defense Advanced Research Projects Agency and warned of the growing threat to intellectual autonomy inherent in tying academic research agendas *ex ante* to military performance objectives. They questioned the Pentagon's reliance on computers to achieve qualitative technological superiority over a quantitatively superior Soviet-led force. In particular, they criticized what they saw as the military's imprudent reliance on computer systems to override human decision makers on the battlefield—from the use of computers in the command and control of nuclear weapons, to the reliance on untested computer systems for deploying President Reagan's proposed Star Wars "peace shield," to DARPA's Strategic Computing Program, with its mandate to install artificial intelligence software in everything from tanks to fighter planes to "battle management" systems.

On the other hand, New Democrats were increasingly comfortable with the idea of using the Department of Defense, particularly DARPA, as a stalking horse for civilian industrial policy. Convinced that national security was now as much a matter of economic strength as of military superiority, they supported expanding the use of DARPA and other defense agencies to fund selective research and development (R&D) projects aimed at enhancing the ability of American-owned companies to generate militarily critical but also commercially competitive dual-use technologies. Some New Democrats shared the peace movement's concerns about the remilitarization of publicly supported research but felt the most pragmatic way to shift R&D resources quickly to civilian-oriented projects was to assign DARPA the authority to undertake civilian technology initiatives under the heading of dual use.

By the late 1980s the concept of "competitiveness" provided a convenient framework around which various groups could express their concerns about the country's economic difficulties while avoiding the conflicts over sectoral and regional targeting that had sunk the concept of industrial policy. The basic tenets of the competitiveness concept—emphasizing broad microeconomic initiatives but without any calls for a central coordinating council, a public development bank, or government intervention in specific sectors—were laid out in the report of the President's Commission on Industrial Competitiveness, which was presented to President Reagan early in 1985. The report stressed economy wide measures to improve the rate of growth in U.S. productivity: more federal spending on civilian technology development and more widespread and effective application of advanced flexible production technology to basic manufacturing ("technology policy" instead of "industrial policy"); and pursuit of dramatic improvements in American education and worker training. Nevertheless, the competitiveness advocates' martial rhetoric was troubling to many liberal activists, who suspected that the former were attempting to mobilize political support for their neomercantilist strategies by substituting a new Japanese enemy for the increasingly cooperative Soviets.

"INDUSTRY-LED" POLICY AND
THE HIGH-DEFINITION TV DEBATE

By the time of the presidential campaign of 1988, prominent members of the military research establishment felt increasingly empowered to speak out against the nation's indirect, ad hoc approach toward maintaining the health of the defense industrial base. The Defense Science

Board sounded the alarm in a report it issued early in 1987: 21 critical military systems were built around chips made only in Japan; Japanese producers were more technologically advanced than their U.S. counterparts in 25 key semiconductor technologies and had pulled even in at least 8 more. (Late in 1987 Congress approved the Pentagon's dramatic response—for 5, ultimately 10, years, the federal government would provide 50 percent of the annual funding for the new commercially oriented semiconductor research consortium, Semiconductor Equipment Manufacturing and Technology Consortium [SEMATECH].) A study released by the Defense Science Board in October 1988 pressed the national security justification for technology policy even further and called for putting the Pentagon directly in charge of planning the American economy. A second study, issued by the undersecretary of defense for acquisition the previous July, was more focused but no less ambitious. Overseen by Robert B. Costello, a former executive of General Motors, the study called for restructuring the Pentagon's internal acquisition system to encourage civil-military integration and more widespread use of commercially derived components in weapons systems and other military equipment.

Like the defense industrial base studies issued just after the election of Ronald Reagan, the studies released by the Pentagon on the eve of George Bush's presidency traced the troubles threatening the U.S. defense sector to the competitive erosion of the nation's commercial manufacturing base. Unlike the earlier reports, however, the 1988 reports went on to demand a more formal role for government—the Department of Defense itself, if not some other public entity—in planning the civilian economy. Coming, as they did, from officials of an administration whose proudest boasts were the twin restoration of laissez-faire capitalism and American military might, the proposals foreshadowed mounting tensions within the Republican camp.

The tensions intensified during the first half of the Bush administration. At the Commerce Department, the Pentagon, and the Office of the Special Trade Representative, newly minted Bush appointees seemed at first to be sounding a clarion call to economic nationalists in both political parties. Commerce Secretary Robert Mosbacher asserted that the Commerce Department should assume responsibility for promoting U.S. research and development in commercial technology. Mosbacher declared himself "comfortable" with "industry-led policy." He voiced support for Senator Ernest Hollings's Advanced Technology Program (ATP), to be modeled on DARPA and housed in the Commerce Department's old National Bureau of Standards, now renamed the National Institute of Standards and Technology (NIST). ATP would provide companies with matching grants to develop high-risk commercial technologies.

"Industry-led policy" was also becoming a top priority at the Pentagon, where Craig Fields had been installed as DARPA's director. Following the direction set by Costello, Fields began to experiment with projects aimed at integrating military technology development with commercial market opportunities and technology efforts already under way in the civilian sector. Seed money from DARPA had effectively created the modern computing field in the 1960s; it also had led to commercial successes in the 1970s and 1980s by enabling companies to leverage their government backing to attract private venture capital. The effectiveness of DARPA, like that of Japan's Ministry of International Trade and Industry (MITI), derived not so much from its capacity to award subsidies as from its ability to build consensus and facilitate cooperation among scientists and engineers in universities, government agencies, and industry. The growing presence of foreign corporations in the markets for dual-use technology now drove a subtle shift in DARPA's funding strategy. Following on the heels of SEMATECH, Fields launched a series of attempts through DARPA to invest in commercial companies directly, particularly in sectors that appeared to have both military and commercial applications, such as biotechnology, parallel processing, and supercomputing.

Suddenly plans for government-supported technology development consortia were everywhere, as were lists of "critical" technologies; among them were X-ray lithography, superconductors, and fiber optics. Proposals also circulated to expand existing government-backed consortia, including SEMATECH, the Microelectronics and Computer Consortium (MCC), and the National Center for Manufacturing Sciences (NCMS). Nevertheless, it was the emergence of a critical technology embodied in an easily understandable and seemingly familiar household product—television—that finally focused the public's attention (and the attention of conservatives within the Bush administration) on this unexpected burst of government activism.

The Japanese had launched a project to develop the next generation of consumer television receivers, so-called high-definition television (HDTV). Because HDTV would permit higher-resolution images, with greater clarity, depth, and detail than the current generation of TV receivers could provide, it promised to be an important platform technology for a variety of commercial and military applications, from medical imaging, to computer-aided design and manufacturing, to dashboard monitors on supersonic fighter jets and tanks. With strong backing from the American Electronics Association, Commerce Secretary Mosbacher testified before the Senate Commerce Committee that domestic development and commercialization of high-definition television was his "top priority." During the early part of 1989 Mosbacher toured the country, publicizing his plans for a big American initiative to recapture the domestic television industry from Japan.

The ensuing debate over HDTV revealed a host of new tensions within Republican ranks, most deriving from the increased internationalization of American business. By 1989 many American companies were drawing a significant share of their profits from selling Japanese technology in the United States; Japanese-owned U.S. subsidiaries were increasingly active in the Electronics Industry Association (EIA), a rival trade association to the American Electronics Association (AEA). Moreover, Japanese interests enjoyed considerable and growing political clout. Stanton Anderson, a Washington lawyer, former Nixon administration official, friend, and key fund raiser for George Bush in 1988, now represented the U.S. interests of the Electronic Industry Association of Japan (EIAJ). The new chairman of the Democratic party, Ron Brown, also had recently represented Japanese firms, as did influential former Democratic chairs Robert Strauss and Charles Manatt. These individuals and corporate groups opposed the efforts of Mosbacher and others to launch an American HDTV initiative; at the very least, they demanded that foreign (primarily Japanese) subsidiaries be made eligible to participate in any such U.S. government-funded project.

To most voters, HDTV seemed to offer nothing more significant than an improved television picture. Among the rush of consortia proposals now bombarding Congress, HDTV looked like one more dubious case of special pleading from a struggling consumer electronics industry that had, in any case, almost entirely abandoned domestic production of television sets more than a decade before. The initiative's advocates argued that it was in the nation's long-term interest, nevertheless, to reestablish a domestic supply base for high-end consumer electronics products such as HDTV, because their evolution inevitably would drive the development of several critical dual-use component technologies. Opponents claimed that it would be folly to allow government bureaucrats, not the market, to "pick winners and losers" among competing companies and different approaches to HDTV technology. Analysts on both sides of the debate pointed out, moreover, that it was becoming increasingly difficult to tell which companies the "domestic" industry should be defined to include. Zenith, the only remaining American-owned manufacturer of televisions, actually designed many of its sets in Japan, with components from Japan, South Korea, and Taiwan, for assembly in Mexico. In the end, the successful opponents of a federal

HDTV initiative were able to note that developments in digital HDTV technology ultimately rendered obsolescent most of the Japanese government–driven analog-based approaches; the policy's proponents emphasized the vast infrastructure that Japan's investment nevertheless had successfully put into place to mass-produce HDTV components, even ones invented in the United States.

Throughout the HDTV debate, Bush administration conservatives made clear their growing hostility to the Pentagon's emergent dual-use strategy. As the Cold War rushed toward its end and U.S. defense budgets began to decline, the conservatives argued that it was more important for the Department of Defense to focus its R&D efforts on military-specific technologies that promised significant benefits for defense. Channeling scarce defense dollars into dual-use technologies like HDTV—technologies that likely would be developed without government assistance anyway—would only ensure that critical, defense-dedicated technology remained underfunded. Even when the Department of Defense focused exclusively on developing military technologies, they asserted, the armed services already encountered long delays and other difficulties producing and fielding new weapons systems. A dual-use mission, encompassing commercial technology development, would only make things worse; it would divert the DoD from its central purpose.

During the summer and fall of 1989, conservative Bush administration officials called Commerce Secretary Mosbacher and his cohorts onto the carpet. With the active support of Vice President Dan Quayle, White House Chief of Staff John Sununu demanded that Mosbacher cease his public statements in support of HDTV. Still, despite growing White House opposition as well as internal Pentagon opposition from the armed services, Craig Fields persisted in using DARPA funds to underwrite the commercial development of dual-use technologies.

Fields was increasingly concerned about foreign purchases of such technologies—and of the American firms that had invented them—particularly when their development had been financed, in large part, by DARPA itself. Unable to gain access to domestic venture capital, U.S. start-ups now often turned to foreign investors when they wanted to expand; this was how Japanese companies had been able to purchase 30 of the 151 firms producing sophisticated semiconductor production equipment in the United States. Fields decided that, in some cases, it made sense for the U.S. government to act like a venture capitalist itself, in return for a voice in future decisions concerning prospective purchases of the company or its technology by a foreign firm. Congress authorized Fields's plan for DARPA to invest $25 million over two years in such arrangements. Bush administration conservatives were displeased, to put it mildly. "If he keeps sticking his neck out," Defense Secretary Dick Cheney reportedly said of Fields, "somebody's going to lop it off." In April 1990, after Fields invested $4 million of the government's money in a small gallium arsenide semiconductor business called Gazelle Microcircuits, somebody did: Fields was fired.

After the Cold War: Fighting over the "Peace Dividend"

Just as a worsening recession propelled the nation's economic problems once more to the forefront of U.S. public discussion, the Cold War came to a swift and sudden end. The coincidence of these events in the fall of 1989 underscored for many the paradox of a defense industrial base in apparent decline despite more than a decade of massive spending for new military hardware. Faced with a budget crisis but pledged not to raise taxes, President Bush had entered office touting a "flexible freeze" on domestic discretionary spending. With the fall of the Berlin Wall, it became clear, even to conservatives, that the Pentagon would have to face the budget ax as well.

Whatever their ultimate size, the apparent inevitability of large military spending cuts quickly generated a nationwide debate over what might be done with the anticipated savings, the so-called peace dividend. Liberals seized the moment to renew their across-the-board attack on conservative political priorities. They called on the government to reinvest the peace dividend to address a raft of long-neglected social problems—public education, AIDS, unemployment, health care, homelessness, pollution, urban poverty. Competitiveness advocates focused more narrowly on the paradox of the nation's swollen military budget and its declining industrial base. They also called for a dramatic shift in the government's investment priorities: toward more public investment in the country's telecommunications and transportation infrastructure and more spending, both public and private, for civilian R&D, education, and worker training.

Conservatives called mainly for more tax cuts—"I don't think," said Phil Gramm, Republican senator from Texas, "[that] the benefits from winning the Cold War should go to the Government"—but the monstrous deficit was beginning to hobble the conservative agenda as well. Many conservatives, moderates, and even some disheartened liberals agreed that most of the anticipated savings from defense cuts would have to be applied toward reducing the deficit. In their view, the peace dividend was more like an overdue debt, the true price of the Cold War, much of it owed to foreign banks. To the frustration of some conservatives as well as most liberals, that debt would continue to constrain the range of domestic political choices in the decade to come.

1992: SEARCHING FOR SECURITY

Despite the short-lived shot of adrenaline it provided to the American psyche, the Persian Gulf War in January 1991 only exacerbated growing doubts within the business community about the Bush administration's laissez-faire attitude toward the nation's industrial base. The weaponry that the United States used to contain Saddam Hussein was based on decade-old technology—the Patriot missile, for example, used an outdated microchip that its original manufacturer, Intel, no longer produced. In addition, allied military officers had to turn to diplomats in Paris and Tokyo for help in obtaining critical spare parts—special battery packs for computers, a transponder, parts for flat-panel display terminals. The allies had cooperated fully, but the specter of military dependence on foreign commercial sources was deeply troubling to many U.S. military strategists, defense analysts, and members of Congress.

Proponents of a more activist government technology policy seized the opportunity. New Mexico Senator Jeff Bingaman, a New Democrat and chair of the Senate Armed Services Subcommittee on Defense Industry and Technology, now spearheaded a legislative drive to increase the portion of Pentagon R&D devoted to the development of dual-use technologies. Taking up where Craig Fields had left off, Senator Bingaman proposed that DARPA fund commercial consortia to develop dual-use technologies. He also proposed federal funding for outreach programs to help defense-dependent companies enter commercial markets, manufacturing extension centers to help diffuse existing technologies and best practices to U.S. manufacturers, and "regional technology alliances" to promote the restructuring of defense-dependent regional economies. Passed with many Republican as well as Democratic votes, Senator Bingaman's proposal would later become the core of the Clinton administration's Technology Reinvestment Program. Still leery of anything resembling industrial policy, the Bush administration refused to implement it.

As the recession seemed to persist and the presidential election of 1992 approached, American voters were in a frustrated and surly mood. "The Cold War is over," said the sardonic former senator and presidential candidate Paul Tsongas. "Japan won." A dozen years before, Jimmy

Carter's pinched interest-group liberalism had been rejected decisively in favor of sunny supply-side Reaganomics; now that too appeared to have failed. Core Democratic constituencies, represented by labor leaders and liberal public interest groups, had never supported the conservative counterrevolution—they saw themselves, correctly, as being among its main targets. Neoliberals—self-described New Democrats—considered Reaganomics socially divisive and dangerously indifferent toward the strategic trade and industrial policies of other countries, but they continued to believe that traditional Democratic economic policies favored consumption and redistribution to the detriment of investment and growth. Now, battered by recession and foreign competition, significant elements of George Bush's normally Republican business coalition were also on the lookout for a viable political alternative.

Dual-Use Policy and Politics Under Clinton: The "Competitiveness" Crowd in Power

MATCHING CAPABILITIES TO TASKS:
ARPA COMES OUT ON TOP

During the 1992 campaign, Bill Clinton promised to reinvest funds cut from the post–Cold War defense budget "dollar for dollar" in the domestic economy. Clinton was careful to distinguish his investment-oriented prescription for the sluggish economy from George Bush's tinny tributes to the marketplace but also from billionaire populist Ross Perot's emphasis on cutting government spending quickly and deeply to reduce the massive federal budget deficit. In addition, Clinton made sure to safeguard his own "New Democrat" credentials: although his campaign literature endorsed the creation of a civilian technology agency modeled on DARPA, the Democratic candidate distanced himself from Perot's suggestion that the U.S. economy needed a corporatist national planning agency similar to Japan's Ministry of International Trade and Industry.

With the addition of technology enthusiast Albert Gore Jr. to the Democratic ticket, the Clinton campaign's descriptions of automated highways, clean manufacturing technologies, and computers in the schools began to coalesce into a concrete image of how a 21st-century economy might work. Although middle-class voters could not always locate themselves in the shiny picture, the campaign's sketch of tangible returns to a strategy of public investment provided voters with an attractive alternative to the abstract economic visions of Bush and Perot. It was attractive enough to appeal to blue-collar Reagan Democrats as well as high-tech Republican entrepreneurs, social activists as well as economic nationalists, and millions of middle-class suburbanites who distrusted Perot but nevertheless had come to view President Bush as hopelessly tone deaf to their chorus of economic anxieties.

The coalition that elected Bill Clinton president thus included constituencies with quite disparate attitudes about the likely economic and social impacts of rapid technological change. The campaign had appealed successfully to adherents of different views by stressing the potential complementarities between the use of advanced technology to address long-ignored national needs (education, infrastructure, the environment) and the role that federal support for technological innovation could play in removing obstacles to long-term economic growth. Indeed, by Election Day in 1992, it appeared that the Clinton campaign had discovered the makings of a new growth coalition that could be counted on to support and sustain the president's economic strategy. For a brief moment, a coalition of disparate interests appeared to form around the core notion of expanded public investment to boost the economy.

But the first Democratic administration in 12 years faced a vexing political dilemma: the innovation policies the new administration thought necessary to attack the economy's structural problems would take a long time to work—and might even contribute to job displacement in the short run—while the Tsongas and Perot campaigns had fixed the country's immediate anxieties on the looming federal deficit, in addition to other, shorter-term adjustment problems related to the initially sluggish economic recovery and the end of the Cold War. To cement a growth coalition that would sustain the new president's investment-oriented economic strategy over the long term, the Clinton administration would have to strike a set of political bargains with constituency groups that had only provisionally returned to the Democratic fold. If these constituencies—blue-collar and middle-class suburbanites worried about wage stagnation, violence, and bad schools—were to be expected to support the administration's plans to subsidize high-risk technology development by large corporations, they would have to see some evidence—and soon—that the policies were making things better in their own lives.

At the same time, the Clinton administration would have to hold on to its tenuous business support. Support from normally Republican high-tech executives had helped New Democrat Bill Clinton to win the election, and corporate-sector backing would be essential to stave off ideological attacks on his administration's public investment priorities. Industry backing and involvement would be particularly critical to sustaining the legitimacy of government-industry partnerships for technology development, for only the words of those who had competed successfully in the international marketplace could counter the claims of free-market critics that government had no role to play in strengthening the technical competence of domestic producers. To demonstrate just how business-friendly a presidency dominated by New Democrats could be, the Clinton administration married its technology agenda to the specific priorities of such groups as the National Association of Manufacturers, the Council on Competitiveness, and the Computer Systems Policy Project, and of such industry trade groups as the American Electronics Association and the Aerospace Industries Association. Indeed, most of the individuals who staffed the Clinton administration's technology policy slots were drawn from management positions with computer and electronics companies or lobbyist positions with their industry trade associations; the rest came from various hubs of the Democratic party's "competitiveness" or economic nationalist faction: erstwhile Senate staffers for Vice President Gore and Senator Bingaman, veterans of Congress's Office of Technology Assessment, and Clinton supporters drawn from think tanks and private advocacy groups known for their nationalist or neomercantilist views.

The policies the Clinton technology officials designed stemmed from their shared belief that the global reshuffling of market position in high-technology industries in the 1970s and 1980s was threatening to translate into a more permanent reshuffling of wealth and power in the international political system. In their view, market leaders in high-tech sectors enjoyed superior learning and profit opportunities: they could build an enduring competitive advantage based on after-sales service and follow-on products for complex technical systems. This meant that companies or countries that were first to attain competitive dominance in a new technical field conceivably could be in a position to control a long stream of subsequent product and process innovations. This would make market entry much harder for technological "followers." Because most of the advanced technologies in question now undergirded military as well as commercial systems, a "temporary" loss of market control threatened to translate into a more enduring loss of political sovereignty over time. The coordinated use of trade, technology, and worker retraining policies was therefore essential—to modernize American manufacturing industry, to prepare American workers for the heightened requirements of international competition, and to neutralize the strategic trade and industrial policies of other countries in advanced technology sectors.

Instead of creating a single, dominant civilian technology agency, the Clinton administration chose to rely on the federal government's existing decentralized R&D structure. To make this work, President Clinton established two new mechanisms for strong interagency coordination and cabinet-level support at the White House: the National Economic Council (NEC) and the National Science and Technology Council (NSTC). Changing the structure of the existing R&D agencies would have been difficult and time-consuming and would have run the risk of provoking entrenched political constituencies—the fabled iron triangles of agency staff, congressional subcommittees, and interested constituent groups. The new president nevertheless would have to share control of his executive bureaucracies with Congress, and this ensured that constituencies with different agendas sometimes would be able to impose some part of their own vision on policies designed by the president's staff with their own policy objectives in mind.

Within the Clinton White House, many technology officials championed the expansion of the Pentagon's dual-use R&D strategy and (then-Deputy) Defense Secretary William Perry's vision of civil-military integration for the nation's industrial technology base. Many others continued to criticize the DoD's record of support for commercial technology, however, and argued that overreliance on the dual-use criterion would inevitably limit the types of R&D projects that the administration would be able to support. This group still supported the establishment of a new civilian technology agency, effectively a civilian version of DARPA (which was temporarily renamed ARPA, with the prefix "Defense" removed); their hopes were pinned on the dramatic expansion of the Commerce Department's Advanced Technology Program at NIST, which was now directed by ARPA veteran Arati Prabhakar, a former close associate of Craig Fields. Clinton technology officials agreed that the most pragmatic way to shift federal R&D resources quickly to improve the technical competence of U.S. industry was to assign ARPA the authority to undertake new or expanded civilian technology initiatives under the heading of defense conversion and dual use. ARPA was the executive branch agency best known for its flexibility, its low overhead, and its quick decisions. Clinton officials reasoned that it would be easier politically to change the mission of an agency that already had a strong constituency (ARPA) than it would be to transfer that agency's funding to a different, perhaps more appropriate but less politically popular agency (in this case, Commerce). Thus when President Clinton announced his intention to shift $8 billion of R&D funds from defense to civilian agencies, ATP was slated for rapid expansion over five years, but most of the money for new civilian technology activities was awarded to ARPA. ARPA would enjoy an R&D budget of about $2 billion, more than 30 times the size of the ATP's budget.

The National Science and Technology Council sometimes provided a forum for those who supported a clearer link among the administration's technology development priorities, the public investment priorities of constituent groups other than high-tech business, and the advocates of defense procurement reform—educators, transportation planners, environmentalists, the labor movement, and research scientists. However, the administration's technology policy agenda was articulated and implemented primarily by the traditional front-line technology agencies, NASA, the Energy Department, and the Department of Defense, plus a new lead civilian technology agency, the Department of Commerce. The fact remained, moreover, that ARPA received—by far—most of the new R&D resources and still possessed the most technically expert staff. ARPA thus remained in the dominant position, more "equal" and more influential, with the occasional exception of NIST, than the other civilian technology agencies that were to be coordinated through the NSTC.

Given its history and resources, ARPA was well suited to advance a dual-use technology strategy for defense. Its role always had been to invest in technologies with military potential far in advance of established service requirements. Since the agency existed to explore technologies that were not yet embedded in the military industrial complex, its staff had direct experience with a number of commercial producers. Doubts persisted, however, about whether ARPA was the appropriate lead agency to ease the transition from military to civilian business for the defense industry or to promote the rapid and widespread commercialization of military technologies. ARPA's effectiveness typically was attributed to the flexibility and independence of its program managers, top-notch scientists and engineers with wide latitude to award research contracts. Until the 1980s ARPA had operated largely outside the glare of the public spotlight. Its processes were neither open nor peer reviewed, but its fairness was rarely challenged since it was an agency of the Pentagon, the sole customer for the technologies it sponsored. Many within ARPA worried that assigning the agency responsibility for civilian technology activities—even if they were limited to technologies identified as dual use—would compromise its anonymity and endanger its tradition of flexibility and independence. Thus from the very beginning of the Clinton administration, ARPA's expert technical staff believed that their professional responsibility and authority for commercial investment decisions would have to be justified by a demonstration of their continued commitment to strengthening national defense.

The Technology Reinvestment Project

THE PROJECT AS POLITICS: BATTLING OVER AGENDAS AND PERCEPTIONS

President Clinton christened the expanded Technology Reinvestment Program the centerpiece of his administration's defense conversion effort in a speech to employees at Westinghouse Electronic Corporation in Baltimore, Maryland, on March 11, 1993. Administration officials in charge of TRP acquiesced to the packaging of the program as "defense conversion" because it was quicker to assign ARPA the authority to fund civilian training and technology deployment activities (e.g., manufacturing extension centers) than to await their assignment to the Labor Department and NIST, which would take a full budget cycle. The young administration was still reeling from the unexpected February defeat of President Clinton's modest economic stimulus package, which contained much of what remained of the 1992 campaign's investment agenda after Clinton's more conservative economic advisers prevailed in the internal debate between new spending and deficit reduction. The Technology Reinvestment Program was to be part of the administration's strategy for addressing longer-term structural problems in the economy; most of the administration's other conversion initiatives emphasized shorter-term economic adjustment assistance of the type included in the failed stimulus package. Pairing them in Clinton's speech was part of the administration's political effort to demonstrate that this president, unlike his involuntarily retired predecessor, planned to attack both the longer-term structural problems that had plagued the economy since the early 1970s and the shorter-term adjustment problems created or exacerbated by the recent recession and the end of the Cold War.

In the chaos of the Clinton administration's early months, however, the message was seriously muddled. Most Americans who were aware of TRP were convinced that it was aimed primarily at solving the short-term adjustment problems created by the end of the Cold War. In speeches and public documents describing the program, administration officials reinforced this impression. In a White House press release dated April 12, 1993, TRP was linked inescapably to the president's commitment to help replace lost defense jobs. President Clinton called TRP "a key component of my conversion plan." He emphasized that the program "will play a vital role in helping defense companies adjust and compete." He even claimed, "I've given it another name—Operation Restore Jobs—to signify its ultimate mission, to expand employment opportunities and enhance demonstrably our nation's competitiveness."

DEFENSE CONVERSION VS. CIVIL-MILITARY INTEGRATION

Despite these sorts of statements, the Clinton officials responsible for the design and implementation of TRP never saw it as a defense conversion program. In their view, TRP would support "spin-offs" of defense technology to commercial markets mainly where commercial production was expected to make the technology more affordable to the DoD or where such efforts were deemed necessary to preserve military access to specialized technical capabilities. Most administration officials believed that U.S. defense companies would never be successful at directly converting their high-overhead, cost-plus operations to compete in commercial markets. They believed instead that the defense companies should be encouraged to partner with commercial firms to learn something about marketing and low-cost production; the commercial partner, or perhaps a commercially oriented start-up backed by a defense company parent, might then shepherd a dual-use technology into the civilian sector. The transition of displaced defense scientists, engineers, and production workers to new employment would be accomplished through the labor market as the economy recovered—which meant, primarily, through the out-migration of people from defense-dependent regions to other regions of the country. Thus the bulk of the administration's defense conversion programs were aimed at facilitating relocation and retraining, not job retention in "converted" defense companies.

CONFUSED CONSTITUENCIES: LABOR, CONVERSION ACTIVISTS, AND BUSINESS

Efforts to support job retention and conversion, however, were precisely what many working-class Americans and activists allied with the peace movement thought they had been promised by President Clinton, both during the 1992 campaign and as the result of many of the messages that continued to emanate from the White House whenever the subject was TRP. After the first round of TRP grants had been awarded, representatives of these groups allied in a vigorous campaign to shift TRP's focus away from "technologies deemed critical to military or economic security" and back toward defense conversion. They demanded, and ultimately won with support from liberal Democrats in Congress, a provision that TRP extend eligibility to trade unions for submitting grant proposals. They also argued that TRP grants should explicitly require job retention as a criterion for evaluating TRP proposals. They suggested that TRP provide a bonus match to companies that retained or reemployed laid-off workers and that these workers' wages be counted as part of the companies' matching funds for TRP awards. They pressed again and again for new public investment initiatives keyed to job creation, particularly in areas of neglected social need such as transportation, energy, the environment, and public infrastructure.

Meanwhile, TRP's primary targeted constituency—business—was at first similarly confused about the program's objectives. Even though White House and ARPA officials were widely praised for disseminating a complex solicitation and making awards in record-breaking time, there were many losers in the first round of grant competitions, because many business applicants simply did not understand the various definitions of "dual use" offered in TRP's "red book" proposal solicitation handbook, released in March 1993. Twelve thousand companies submitted proposals, most of them expecting a ride on the government gravy train—this was the first Democratic administration in 12 years, after all, and defense contractors saw TRP as a partial reprieve from drastic military budget cuts. Commercial industry and state governments also viewed TRP as a rare opportunity to tap the federal spigot for research and development dollars. So they lined up and threw $8.5 billion in matching dollars at the much-hyped TRP. Then 10,400 came up empty-handed, and many of the rest were disappointed by the relatively small size of the awards.

Because TRP required partnering—defense and commercial firms with universities, state and local governments, or national laboratories—each TRP grant had to be parceled out to a number of recipients. In the first round 212 projects were selected, which meant $605 million was to be split among roughly 1,600 participants. Thus, once a big TRP winner, such as GM/Hughes, got finished paying off its partners and proposal costs for 16 successful projects valued at $208 million, the company ended up with just $11 million, very small potatoes in the defense contracting world. Aside from that, there was the added burden of negotiating the details regarding intellectual property rights and other complicated matters among "team" members who often had no prior relationship. In a few cases teams succeeded in winning TRP awards only to see a member of the original team drop out of the project entirely. Finally, representatives of small business complained bitterly that the mandatory 50 percent matching costs made TRP inaccessible to innovative but cash-strapped start-ups. In part, this was a reflection of policy; TRP's managers wanted these small entrepreneurial commercial firms to team with large defense contractors.

Project managers responded quickly to the initial complaints by looking for ways to help more small businesses participate—for example, by allowing Small Business Innovation Research (SBIR) grants to be used as matching funds. In addition, to stem the tidal wave that had greeted the first round and to spare companies the expense and frustration of fruitless bidding, ARPA fine-tuned its solicitations. Program officials shifted to a strategy of holding "focused" competitions for TRP grants in defined technical areas, such as high-density data storage and uncooled infrared sensors. This greatly increased the number of successful proposals in successive rounds, but it also reopened TRP to the charge that its government managers were attempting to "pick winners and losers" among competing technology areas. In October 1994 ARPA awarded $200 million to 224 participants for work on 39 more TRP projects. (With the new Republican Congress threatening to pull the plug, a third round of bidding, worth $415 million, was delayed in early 1995; a new, smaller and more military-centered program replaced TRP at the beginning of fiscal year 1997.)

CONFLICTING OBJECTIVES: TECHNOLOGY POLICY VS. TRADE POLICY

Along with the rest of Clinton's technology agenda, TRP suffered from a widespread perception that the administration's technology development objectives conflicted with its equally misunderstood trade objectives. An early conflict involved differences between Clinton trade and technology officials over the proposed language on R&D subsidies in the provisional text of the General Agreement on Tariffs and Trade (GATT). Anxious technology officials argued that new subsidy rules proposed in the provisional text threatened to smother the administration's fledgling technology promotion efforts in the crib. Annoyed trade experts countered that the new subsidy rules—which they themselves had drafted despite much resistance from the Europeans and the Japanese—were essential to prevent foreign governments from unfairly subsidizing companies that intended to compete with U.S. firms for domestic and international business. In their view, the new U.S. technology policies, which would support specific domestic industries with matching grants for R&D, would seriously undermine traditional American arguments against foreign R&D subsidy practices. U.S. complaints about European Airbus subsidies or closed supplier and distribution networks in Japan would ring hollow if Washington began providing its own direct subsidies restricted to American-owned firms. Such an approach would likely set off a round of subsidy wars for which the United States was ill prepared and in which all sides eventually would lose. With less than two weeks to go before negotiations over the global trade pact would have to be either concluded or abandoned, Deputy Defense Secretary John Deutch intervened, arguing forcefully that the existing draft language posed a serious threat to the DoD's entire dual-use strategy. Officials of the Commerce Department's Technology Administration and International Trade Administration, the White House Office of Science and Technology Policy, and the new cabinet-level National Economic Council then met to draft acceptable compromise language. The new constraints on R&D subsidies remained in the GATT text, but the definition of allowable subsidies was changed to protect the bulk of the Clinton technology initiatives.

Another source of continuing friction involved congressionally mandated efforts to restrict the participation of foreign firms in federally funded technology projects. U.S. trade and State and Treasury Department officials (and most high-technology business groups) argued that such restrictions would prevent U.S. companies with foreign business partners from participating in the programs. They also predicted that the expansion of such restrictions eventually would result in foreign retaliation, cutting U.S. companies off from access to important foreign sources of new technology. They cited the views of Labor Secretary Robert Reich, an early proponent of industrial policy who now argued that corporate ownership had become so transnational—and transitory—that it no longer made sense to speak in terms of "U.S." or "foreign" companies. Clinton technology officials tended to be more comfortable with the arguments of the president's chief economist, Laura Tyson, who pointed out that U.S. multinationals still employed their most highly skilled workers and did the lion's share of their advanced research and production in the United States. Thus, in her view, technology policies directed at strengthening these companies in their home base would still redound to the benefit of Americans first.

Nevertheless, the administration's technology officials generally agreed with the Clinton trade, State, and Treasury Department officials that rigid restrictions on foreign firm participation were counterproductive and protectionist—the technology officials desired, instead, the flexibility to strike bargains with foreign companies, which would open the door to their participation in programs such as TRP and ATP in return for their commitment to share proprietary technology with U.S.-based partners. Policy in this area remained frozen, however, while Congress considered passage of the "competitiveness" bill that officially would authorize the Commerce Department's expanded technology development role. Democratic committee barons were, if anything, inclined to place stricter, more protectionist restrictions on foreign firm participation in the programs. In late 1994, largely because the Democratic White House could not resolve this dispute with the Democratic Congress, the

competitiveness bill failed to pass, and the various restrictions on foreign participation remained in force.

In general, the Clinton administration had a difficult time reconciling
its anti-neomercantilist arguments for major new free-trade initiatives—
principally GATT and the North American Free Trade Agreement
(NAFTA)—with its "competitiveness" rationale to justify federal support
for commercial R&D. The competitiveness rationale often was neomercantilist in tone, if not always in substance. Moreover, working-class
Americans, concerned about job retention and suspicious of the job-
displacing effects of new technology, were hardly likely to embrace the
business-centered technology policies of a Democratic administration
whose trade policies seemed unexpectedly hostile to their short-term
economic interests. The unresolved conflict between the administration's
trade and technology policies thus contributed to the fragmentation of
political support for President Clinton's economic program.

ATTACK OF THE KILLER ECONOMISTS (PART 2)

As the Clinton administration battled through its second year—the year
of the national health plan debacle—Democratic economists who had
snuffed out the party's flirtation with industrial policy a decade earlier
returned to the public spotlight to criticize the administration's technology policies. To the consternation of administration technology officials,
these critics often ignored the provisions the administration had put in
place to ensure market relevance and to insulate the new programs from
congressional pork—principally the reliance on peer-reviewed competitions and the requirement that grant recipients share at least half the project costs. Instead, the critics would simply repeat criticisms of famous
government technology boondoggles of the 1970s as if Clinton administration policymakers had learned nothing from past experience. However, the criticisms reached deeper than the usual arguments over how
best to limit the potential inefficiencies a public subsidy can cause in the
market's allocation of scarce resources. The economists mocked what
they saw as the nonsensical core of the administration's competitiveness
and dual-use arguments; they thought it intellectually indefensible to
compare an economic rivalry (say, between the United States and Japan)
to a military rivalry. To most economists, economic rivalry is indisputably
a positive-sum game: economic rivalry actually expands production possibilities and increases global wealth, so both "sides" end up better off.
Military conflict, on the other hand, is often a negative-sum game, in
which both sides can conceivably lose. Thus the federal government
should increase spending for basic research in nondefense areas, but it

should not engage in technology development partnerships with private companies. The U.S. government should not block participation by foreigners in its R&D efforts either, because the economic benefits of that research will diffuse inevitably to foreign competitors anyway; it would be better to induce foreign governments to share research costs. In addition, the economists argued that technological innovation—in addition to deregulation, globalization, and the weakening of unions—was implicated in America's increasingly unequal distribution of wages and family incomes, because it increased the economic returns to education and training. Labor Secretary Reich and his allies used these arguments to push for more funding for President Clinton's education and training initiatives (labor, unlike capital and technology, is relatively immobile with respect to national borders), but this had the effect of simultaneously undercutting the arguments that other administration officials were using to promote the president's technology programs.

Thus, nearly a year before the midterm congressional elections, the fragile coalition for the administration's technology initiatives within Democratic party circles (and within the Clinton administration itself) already had started to break apart. Despite the fact that the economy grew at a brisk rate of 4.1 percent in 1994, leading to a high rate of job creation that offset rising productivity and thus brought down the rate of unemployment, Americans were again deeply skeptical about the capacity of government programs to promote economic growth. In part this was due to the news media's increasingly negative portrayal of the Clinton administration's health plan, the president's key legislative initiative in 1994. In part it was due to the continuing recession in ultra-defense-dependent southern California, where the administration's conversion initiatives, TRP included, seemed ill matched to the scale of the problem. More than any of that, however, the lack of public enthusiasm for the administration's technology policies stemmed from the fact that after-tax real wages for working- and middle-class Americans continued to stagnate, despite the robust recovery and a series of reports that the country's high-tech industries had regained the advantage in international competition. The administration's technology policies—and its trade policies—appeared to reward only groups in American society that were already benefiting in the new economy: corporate executives, wealthy bond traders, and highly educated high-tech professionals.

THE PROJECT AS POLICY: THE DILEMMAS OF DUAL USE

By the time the Technology Reinvestment Program was launched in 1993, its designers were able to draw on two wells of relevant experi-

ence to design an effective and economically efficient dual-use investment program. Because past efforts to provide federal support for commercial technology development sometimes had created unproductive,
high-profile pork barrels (or simply had never gotten off the ground),
the project's designers wanted to ensure that TRP awards provided
government support without dampening market signals. Thus TRP
required grant applicants to compete for cash grants and to cover at
least 50 percent of the project costs. In soliciting TRP projects for fiscal
year 1993, ARPA required applicants to provide evidence that the proposed technology could be commercially sustained within five years,
without further federal funding.

The key difference between TRP and other DoD dual-use initiatives
was the emphasis ARPA placed on the ability of TRP technologies to
result in commercial products. Other dual-use efforts focused mainly
on military applications and left subsequent commercial development
of the technology to the private sector. To achieve its objectives, TRP
supported commercial projects that promised to "spin off" emerging
military technology for civilian use and projects that aimed to "spin-on"
emerging commercial technologies for military use (i.e., broaden the
market for the commercially derived technology to include the Department of Defense). To attract companies that might not otherwise wish
to work with the DoD, ARPA used special, flexible research agreements rather than traditional contracting instruments to fund both
kinds of TRP development projects.

The project got off the ground very quickly by Washington standards. Competitions were conducted by the Defense Technology
Conversion Council, a multiagency group, chaired by ARPA, which
consisted of government employees who already worked for one of
TRP's six sponsoring agencies—ARPA, NASA, the National Science
Foundation, the Department of Energy, the Department of Transportation, and NIST. The council selected broad technology focus areas for
use in soliciting TRP proposals. Within these broad areas, specific topics were identified that were judged by ARPA to meet critical defense
needs and by the entire council as having significant potential to stimulate commercial product development. During the selection process
for 1993 and 1994, the military services participated informally in the
selection of technology focus areas used to solicit TRP proposals, but
they were not formally represented on the Defense Technology Conversion Council. Initially ARPA did not invite retired business executives or venture capitalists to review project proposals either, an
innovation utilized by TRP's commercially oriented counterpart, the
Advanced Technology Program.

LESSONS LEARNED: TRP AND PREVIOUS
DUAL-USE RESEARCH PROJECTS

The project's managers sought to replicate features of past military research efforts that had led successfully to commercial spin-offs. They wanted to avoid features that had led to the creation of expensive, defense-dedicated products. The designers sought specifically to improve on 1980s projects such as the Very High Speed Integrated Circuit (VHSIC) program and the artificial intelligence (AI)–based Strategic Computing Program (SCP), which also had sought to upgrade military technology to commercial capabilities. Both programs had sought to develop military uses for the latest generation of a technology that was already under development (both domestically and abroad) in the commercial sector. But eventually both programs had gravitated toward an emphasis on military-specific forms of their respective technologies, applications that had no obvious commercial potential and were for that very reason not under development by leading commercial firms.

In these cases, the need to develop technical attributes of specific interest to military users came to dominate the original objective of developing dual-use technologies that could be incorporated flexibly and interchangeably into both military and commercial systems. In the case of VHSIC, the emphasis on developing chips for immediate insertion into weapons systems eventually shifted the program's locus of development work from commercial semiconductor companies to defense systems suppliers; a similar shift from university laboratories to the laboratories of large defense contractors occurred during SCP as generic AI technologies were increasingly tailored to the needs of specific military products. In the end, both projects were moderately successful at developing applications that proved useful to the military but were basically unsuccessful at creating new commercial markets or civilian product spin-offs of dual-use technology. The dual-use projects did not handicap companies pursuing already well-established commercial development trajectories; rather, they created separate, defense-dedicated "niche" trajectories attractive only to defense systems houses and the specialized military divisions of otherwise commercially oriented firms.

Designers of TRP wanted to avoid the creation of new defense-dedicated industrial niches. They wanted to promote instead commercial-military integration, the creation (where possible) of a single, unified industrial base for both commercial and military technology development. Thus they preferred to fund projects that would advance the general technological state of the art, rather than merely develop specific military product applications. Where military product development was the main project objective, TRP program managers would attempt to ensure that any military-unique performance specifications complemented the commercial requirements of the involved industry. The requirement that award applicants compete for funding as members of teams (defense contractors with commercial firms, universities, federal laboratories, and/or state and local governments) was similarly designed to discourage technical overspecialization and also to avoid the development of a new reliance by the DoD on sole-source suppliers. The award of grants to subsets of industry rather than to entire industries was meant to encourage competitive product development and discourage the formation of domestic cartels. (Some within ARPA worried, however, that the 50 percent cost-share would dissuade small, cash-strapped, but innovative and entrepreneurial companies from participating in the program.)

Where a technology development trajectory already had been established commercially and confirmed by a pattern of private-sector investment, TRP projects typically were designed to accept the market-driven trajectory, not to reshape the line of technological development to achieve a particular military objective. (Some ARPA managers worried, however, that the use of peer review panels would bias TRP awards toward conservative technical approaches.) The project's mix of development and deployment awards reflected ARPA's desire to balance its efforts to increase the technical competence of domestic producers with efforts to promote technology diffusion, in order to establish scale economies through broad use. Finally, all TRP grants were time-limited as well as cost-shared, meaning that project managers and private-sector participants would be required periodically to evaluate each project's performance and abandon those that were not working.

The Clinton administration's dual-use technology initiatives, including TRP, were part of a more general thrust in the direction of civil-military integration. Another major component of this effort involved removing the legal and regulatory obstacles that prevented Department of Defense procurement officers from buying commercial products "off the shelf." Along with Vice President Gore, Defense Secretary William Perry became the Clinton administration's most forceful advocate for federal procurement reform; within the Pentagon, Perry launched an ambitious initiative to wean DoD procurement officers away from the military specifications that had long been part of the Pentagon's acquisition process.

Finally, in areas where there were no commercial products "on the shelf" yet, the DoD would be willing to try to create them from scratch in order to satisfy future defense needs. This was the part of the Clinton administration's technology agenda that most clearly distinguished its efforts from the dual-use investment efforts of previous administrations. The Clinton administration's most ambitious gambit along these lines was ARPA's flat-panel display initiative, which would provide matching seed money for R&D to companies that pledged to build production facilities in the United States. In general, the administration's aim would be to identify and shrink the military-unique part of the defense base to an absolute minimum, so that it included only things that had no commercial use, such as submarines and torpedoes. Once those specialized pockets were identified and protected, Pentagon officials wanted long-time defense contractors to diversify into the commercial marketplace as a first step toward establishment of an integrated industrial base. To spur the transition, they launched a host of dual-use technology initiatives, one of which was TRP.

THE SPIN-OFF STRATEGY

About half of all TRP projects sought to serve defense needs by moving DoD-funded technologies into new commercial applications. Despite the size and sophistication of the defense technology base, the bulk of defense R&D never has left the military sector to build commercial capabilities. Projects therefore targeted new uses for defense technologies, from the application of amorphous silicon, to medical imaging, to the use of advanced composites for bridge repair. The DoD was expected to benefit primarily from the lower costs achieved through more efficient commercial production and economies of scale.

As previously noted, TRP managers looked for technology development projects where military performance requirements would complement commercial market requirements. Critics contended that TRP projects could not simultaneously leverage commercial capabilities while developing dual-use technology specifically for military use. This was incorrect. A project's focus on developing technological attributes of interest to military users did not necessarily mean that its results would be irrelevant or harmful to commercialization of the technology. At issue was whether military-unique performance requirements *complemented* the requirements of commercial markets, not whether they are identical. For example, TRP funded a project to develop a turboalternator for electric hybrid vehicles. The turboalternator would serve a clear commercial need for small, energy-efficient, low-emission engines that could be used in hybrid-electric city buses. It would simultaneously serve a military-specific need for tank engines that would be harder to detect with infrared sensors, because hybrid-electric engines emit less heat. Similarly, the development of a mechanism to recharge engine batteries on the fly would serve to make battery technology more commercially attractive because it would increase the range and power of electric buses in congested urban centers and on the open road; the same attribute also would serve the uniquely military need for a propulsion system that is stealthy, because the recharge mechanism enhances a tank's ability to run only on batteries, with the main engine turned off.

THE SPIN-ON STRATEGY

The purpose of the TRP "spin-on" development projects was to provide the military with superior technology that would, over time, become affordable because the technology had contributed through its own evolution to the creation of a self-sustaining commercial industry. Thus, for TRP projects seeking to spin on emerging commercial technologies for defense, acceptance of the market-driven development trajectory was key—as was resistance to pressure from the military services to reshape the line of technological development to achieve a particular defense objective. Projects involving flat-panel displays (FPDs) and high-density data storage devices were supposed to fit this pattern. Another example was new technology for the treatment of battlefield casualties, including digital X rays, sensors, and software packages.

Again, contrary to the contentions of some critics, a military-sponsored effort to adapt a technology that is already under development for commercial purposes will not *necessarily* disrupt the technology's commercial development trajectory. At issue here is whether the military-sponsored project is focused on the development of defense-dedicated equipment or generic, flexible, reprogrammable tools whose state of the art can be advanced by trying them out in a variety of similar yet distinct applications. For instance, a TRP project aimed at enabling military surgeons to learn surgical procedures on a computer-simulation–based training system would be based on technologies already developed for commercial purposes. The aim of the TRP project would be to ensure that commercial producers develop these systems further with military needs in mind, addressing the types of injuries, such as shrapnel wounds, found frequently on the battlefield but rarely in civilian life. Yet the software and hardware packages that will be developed for these specific military purposes will be adaptable for use in civilian medical training, civilian disaster response, emergency room medicine, and commercial telemedicine. Indeed, the effort is expected to facilitate the commercial development of many minimally invasive surgical techniques, for which there is now a growing demand among civilian medical professionals.

ENDURING DILEMMAS

The National Flat-Panel Display Initiative

Learning from past experience, TRP managers consciously attempted to fund alternative technical approaches to meeting an identified "critical" need; they worried that too big a commitment to a single approach in the first round of TRP competitions might overprivilege the chances of funding for that approach in subsequent rounds. So, for example, TRP funded two approaches to developing lithium ion batteries; three approaches to developing low-cost manufacturing processes for advanced display technologies; and three approaches to developing uncooled infrared sensors.

It is reasonable to question, however, whether TRP's choices among competitors and their technological solutions at one stage of the competition can be prevented from constraining or channeling its investment choices at subsequent stages. Project managers are investing taxpayer dollars in dynamic technology areas that can follow any one of a number of paths of evolution, and DoD planners will find it difficult to abandon their investments in particular technological alternatives that have been justified specifically in terms of their supposedly "unique" value for national defense.

Along these lines, the Clinton administration's single most controversial effort has been in the area of flat-panel displays, a fast-growing market mostly controlled by Japanese companies. The National Flat Panel Display Initiative is not itself a part of the Technology Reinvestment Program but part of its technology development effort is being run through TRP, and its rationale and TRP's are fundamentally the same. Nothing better distinguishes the divergent approaches of the Bush and Clinton administrations toward dual-use technology than their different attitudes toward the necessity of government involvement for spurring the commercial development of flat-panel displays, a critical component of HDTV.

The strategic focus of Japanese companies in the area of flat-panel displays has been on high-volume commercial markets. However, according to the designers of the National Flat Panel Display Initiative, in which TRP is a participant, the Japanese companies were initially uninterested in providing the American military with early access to leading-edge display technology or in producing nonstandard displays customized for military use—indeed, in private conversations with DoD officials, representatives of the Japanese companies reportedly refused outright to supply the U.S. military with components. In addition, several U.S. companies complained that Japanese FPD suppliers were in other ways already favoring Japanese users, for example, by delaying delivery of the components to their U.S. commercial customers. Although several South Korean firms also were expected to enter the market, the designers of the FPD initiative argued, after extensive consultation with potential U.S. suppliers, that there would be no spontaneous development of a domestic U.S. FPD industry, because of high start-up costs, the preexisting Japanese advantage, and the lack of a domestic base of equipment and component suppliers for American FPD producers. So, through TRP and other programs, the DoD set about trying to construct incentives that would lead private companies to create a domestic FPD industry.

Specifically, the initiative made a portion of the DoD's R&D investment in future display technologies available only to companies that would commit to domestic volume production for current-generation products and that would commit to support the department's specialized display requirements. Proponents of the initiative believed that the DoD's standard approach to guaranteeing access to a military-specific technology—subsidizing a small, defense-dedicated FPD supplier based in the United States—would only create an expensive, technologically backward white elephant. The FPD initiative was supposed to enable the DoD to "piggyback" on commercial production, to benefit from economies of scale, and to keep up with leading-edge technologies that are driven by mushrooming commercial demands. (Responding to a prior congressional earmark, and hedging its bets, the Pentagon has supported such a company. The problem, designers of the FPD initiative contend, is that, even when a U.S.-based company, such as Xerox, creates the highest-resolution flat-panel display yet unveiled, little of this advanced technology makes it off the laboratory bench and onto a production line.)

As with TRP, the aim of this dual-use effort was to leverage U.S.-based commercial capabilities and markets for defense. In this case, however, the goal was to generate a globally competitive American industry in an established sector already dominated by a globally competitive Japanese industry. Nevertheless, the effort had to target military-specific markets initially; after all, it was only the customized military displays that the Pentagon could not already buy from Japanese suppliers. Thus the TRP efforts that were related to the FPD initiative emphasized military-specific product requirements that had no complementary

commercial counterpart: Flat-panel displays that can operate in both
desert and Arctic temperatures and be readable in sunlight as well as in
night combat; offer extremely high resolutions; integrate specialized
information-processing capabilities; and are available in nonstandard
sizes. Each TRP effort was designed specifically to demonstrate new displays in military hardware. One planned to demonstrate active-matrix
electroluminescent (EL) panels in head-mounted displays for helicopter
pilots. Medium-sized EL displays were tested in an army artillery vehicle. Field-emission displays were used in an infrared rifle sight and a
cockpit display. This was similar to ARPA's approach to the Strategic
Computing Program in the 1980s, where AI software was customized
for use in specific weapons systems for each of the military services.

The danger of this approach was that the military-sponsored initiative would create a noncompetitive U.S. source of supply for FPD components, which the DoD would then feel compelled to protect.
Designers of the initiative stressed the rigorous competition among
technical approaches that characterized the first round of awards; they
contended that the initiative should be viewed as an insurance policy
that could be canceled before the premiums got too high. But if the three
or four production plants envisioned by the initiative's designers
resulted in display technology that was ultimately of interest only to
military users, the temptation to protect the American companies willing to produce them would be strong. The companies would produce
their customized FPDs in smaller volumes, and as a result, their operating costs might exceed those of foreign display producers. U.S. users
of FPDs would be left to choose between lower-cost foreign suppliers or
domestic suppliers of high-cost, technically backward displays that
would be of little interest to U.S. producers of nondefense products.

Regardless of its eventual impact on domestic supply sources, the
FPD initiative apparently succeeded in putting political pressure on
Japanese FPD suppliers to supply military-relevant technologies;
Japanese companies quickly became more flexible and forthcoming in
discussions with Pentagon officials. In addition, the DoD attempted to
midwife strategic alliances between U.S. FPD and equipment producers and the well-financed South Korean firms preparing to enter the
FPD market. Given the recent history of the market for dynamic random access memories (DRAMs), in which the entry of South Korean
firms increased supply and depressed prices for Japanese memory
chips, it did seem in the interest of the U.S. military to encourage the
efforts of the South Koreans in markets for FPDs, if only to further pressure the Japanese. If the Koreans entered anyway, and U.S. military
markets therefore began to look more attractive to the Japanese, the

DoD's initiative might no longer be needed to prevent an interruption of supplies from foreign sources.

The point of all this is not that it is necessarily a bad idea for the U.S. government to encourage the creation of a domestic flat-panel display industry but that dependence on a military justification and the DoD to do it creates unnecessary and perhaps insurmountable complications for commercial producers. Indeed, the military-directed initiative could end up creating exactly what the Department of Defense says it wants to avoid: the creation of a specialized defense supplier, an "arsenal" for military FPDs. In the process, the initiative might retard, rather than promote, the adoption by U.S. firms of flat-panel displays. To work, such initiatives should be designed to follow a market-driven technology development trajectory as closely as possible. This could be hard in the near term (which may last as long as 30 years), when newer technologies such as FPDs are being used to retrofit weapons systems that have already been built. In designing and building new systems, however, the military services should be forced to abandon their "defense-unique" requirements as much as possible and rely on what commercial producers are willing to sell them.

The Regional Character of U.S. Growth
As it has for all attempts at national industrial policy, economic geography remained a troublesome subject for TRP. This was true both in terms of politically motivated challenges to the geographical distribution of TRP awards and in terms of impediments placed internally on TRP's efforts to facilitate industrial restructuring in particular defense-dependent regions. The distributional complaints were a red herring; the distribution of TRP awards merely reflected the disproportionate number of defense and dual-use producers and facilities that are located in the South and West, particularly in California. The motive for the internal impediments, however, has roots deep in the American political economy. Recall that it was the regional character of American growth, and the consequent battles about the conflicting needs of declining industry in the North and growing industry in the South and West, that "did in" the Democratic party's industrial policy proposals before 1984. Policies that would have had the effect of fostering development in the South and West were seen as policies likely to accelerate the decline of labor-intensive industries in the Northeast and Midwest; policies to prevent the decline and relocation of these sectors were viewed as policies that would likely retard growth in southern and western states.

The point of TRP's Regional Technology Alliances Assistance program was to help industrial clusters in defense-dependent regions to restructure and retool by building on the unique strengths afforded by geographical proximity. The point was not to try to create new regional industrial clusters, new "Silicon Valleys," but rather to identify and nurture such clusters where they already existed as part of TRP's overall strategy for achieving civil-military integration. There was broad support for this notion among White House staffers from the National Economic Council, the Office of Science and Technology Policy, and the Council of Economic Advisers, but top DoD officials and ARPA's program managers remained reluctant to make awards in this area. They were convinced that any pot of money labeled "regional" would most likely turn into a magnet for congressional pork. Despite economic evidence suggesting that regionally targeted investments can create economic benefits that disproportionately benefit the United States—because certain types of scientific and technical knowledge diffuse more readily and rapidly within geographically confined areas than across national borders—DoD and ARPA officials resisted investments in "centers of innovation" at universities or research parks and concentrated instead on funding discrete technologies that could be incorporated into a specific product or production process for defense.

In terms of their political analysis, the DoD officials may have been right—it is instructive to note that one of the apparent survivors of the Republican congressional attack on the Clinton administration's technology programs was the Manufacturing Extension Partnership (MEP), administered by NIST but funded initially through TRP. This technology deployment effort, which helps spread new technology and best manufacturing practice among small to medium-sized companies, is modeled on the nation's Agricultural Extension Service (which dates back to the Civil War). The partnership placed more than 40 industrial assistance centers in more than 30 states. Plainly, the tangible presence of these centers in so many states and congressional districts translated into a supportive political base in Congress. Even as it was threatening to eliminate TRP, the Republican House actually agreed to raise MEP's budget. For similar reasons, the National Flat Panel Display Initiative survived, downsized but intact, because there was a well-organized, politically connected group of companies armed with an active trade association dedicated to ensuring the initiative's survival.

Still, there is some empirical evidence that innovative firms tend to encourage their competitors and suppliers to innovate at a higher rate, and that this occurs particularly if they are in geographical proximity. Indeed, the economic significance of knowledge spillovers in constrained geographic regions recently has attracted increased attention among academic economists, including some of the leading critics of national industrial policy. It appears that a firm's investment in R&D may promote not only its own competitiveness but also the competitiveness of its neighbors. Companies remain clustered geographically because proximity facilitates the easy exchange of ideas, resources, and people, the argument goes: this reduces the costs of searching out required information and stimulates rapid transfers of technology among companies, thereby accelerating the rate of technological progress. Because certain types of information about technological innovation diffuse more quickly within local economies than outside of them—even in this age of electronic mail and the Internet—the information can be kept "local" for a time and can perhaps be turned into a source of enduring competitive advantage for local producers. Thus some economists conclude that investments in the local or regional infrastructure for research may indeed create disproportionate economic benefits for that region. In any case, this was the intellectual rationale for TRP's Regional Technology Alliances; it may or may not have proven convincing on its own terms, but DoD officials and ARPA's program managers, worried that congressional earmarks would undermine the broader rationale for dual-use investments, never really considered putting the theory to a serious test.

AN EARLY ASSESSMENT: THE ECONOMIC BENEFITS OF COLLECTIVE ACTION AND THE COSTS OF MILITARY SPONSORSHIP

Although TRP ceased to exist officially after barely three years, its key programmatic features persist in the TRP projects that were funded previously and in the more military-oriented dual-use technology program that has succeeded it. These features reflect the desire of TRP's designers to make their grant competitions for dual-use technology development similar to the merit-based, peer-reviewed competitions for basic research grants conducted year after year by the National Science Foundation. These programmatic features appear to have worked as advertised: government-industry cost-sharing, competitive selection, and the requirement that applicants be made up of industry-led teams did render TRP free of political pork. This, ironically, turned into one of the program's greatest political disadvantages. However, to assess whether the effort might have successfully avoided the other pitfalls of previous military-sponsored commercial technology development initiatives, and to judge whether the TRP did, in its short life, accelerate the development of commercial technology and also improve the competitive position of commercial producers, it will have to be examined, project by project, after several more years. There are hundreds of TRP projects; some replicate features that have promoted successful commercial technology development in the past while others replicate features that have led only to unmarketable, defense-dedicated products.

On the positive side, TRP appears in some cases to have facilitated the successful acceleration of technology transfer and innovation by requiring teaming by defense and commercial companies, universities, and national labs. It took some time for participants to work out the internal contractual relationships to make such partnerships go—particularly with respect to the assignment of intellectual property rights. But many recipients of TRP awards reported that the program facilitated institutional connections that would not have been made otherwise. With TRP funds, for example, the defense contractor Aerojet partnered with potential commercial end-users—General Motors, Admiral, Boeing—of a class of new materials called aerogels, which have extremely good heat-insulating properties. Many TRP projects also boosted or accelerated the efforts of organizations that were already working together, often as a consequence of previous government initiatives. For example, TRP made awards to California's CALSTART electric-vehicle consortium, which had been around for several years, with substantial backing from the state government as well as corporate funders such as Lockheed, Allied Signal, and Hughes.

It is important to note, moreover, that similar positive reports came from teams that linked arms originally to apply for TRP grants but that did not, in fact, win any TRP money. That is, the teams reported that they found the partnerships they had created and the joint planning they had done to compete unsuccessfully for TRP so valuable that they decided to stick together anyway and search for funds from alternate sources. This fact suggests that TRP was adding something of significant value to the economy—government involvement appears to have been useful for helping private companies to overcome the collective action problems that often prevent them from exploiting potentially significant economic and technological opportunities. The key policy question is: How much money does the government really have to put on the table to induce such relationships into existence, and is the resulting benefit really worth the cost?

In other cases, however, TRP appears to have replicated certain dilemmas that plagued other recent dual-use technology development initiatives. Many TRP projects clearly targeted technologies that had both military and commercial applications. Yet there remained a political imperative that TRP projects be justified in terms of their value for military purposes. This continuously threatened to channel the more commercially oriented projects in more specialized, defense-dedicated directions.

The project justified the value of its investments to the DoD's defense mission in two ways: (1) the particular TRP investment had to meet the "but-for" test—that is, "but for" federal funding, industry would not undertake the investment on its own, and (2) the TRP investment would either lead to the creation of a viable commercial industry that was also capable of meeting defense needs or would induce leading companies in an emerging commercial sector to emphasize technical or performance attributes that the military services require but that commercially oriented companies would not otherwise develop.

The projects justified using the but-for criterion remain vulnerable to the strongest argument of the dual-use strategy's detractors: that the R&D in question would be conducted by private industry regardless of TRP's involvement. It is nearly impossible to prove that a company would not have made the same investment in the absence of the TRP subsidy, and many TRP awardees volunteered that, in fact, the TRP funds simply accelerated an investment that they were planning to make anyway. Thus, critics would argue, TRP was merely substituting public funds for private, and it was not increasing the total amount of militarily useful research done by commercial firms. Indeed, if the TRP-funded project ultimately is successful, private investors will reap most of the economic rewards; if it is not, the public has been sentenced to bear at least half the cost.

A stronger justification for TRP involvement in such cases thus rests on the notion that the investment would *speed* the development of the technology, enabling U.S. military systems to incorporate it sooner and at lower cost. Recall the argument of technology policy proponents that the initial establishment of a dominant position in markets for an advanced technology—the achievement of a first-mover advantage, as game theorists put it—can lock in control of a long stream of follow-on product and process innovations, making market entry much harder for technology "followers." Planners at the DoD thus may determine that the military risks of enduring technological dependence on foreign sources outweigh the risk that U.S. government intervention in commercial technology markets will alienate allies or significantly raise costs.

Any such determination is bound to be controversial in sectors where sophisticated companies elsewhere in the world already have developed the technology for international commercial markets (some, granted, with prior government assistance). In order to amortize their large R&D investment (not to mention play their role in fulfilling their nations' military commitments as U.S. allies), these companies eventually must sell products and processes incorporating the technology to companies and consumers based in the United States. In such cases, it might actually be to the advantage of U.S. manufacturers—and the American military—to be second rather than first—to accept the slightly slower pace of technological diffusion but still reap the windfall of (subsidized) commercial investments that companies based in other countries have made to move along the technological learning curve. This is a more standard economic argument, but it implies something significant for a program such as TRP: It implies that TRP should have been making more awards for technology deployment and fewer for technology development (exactly the opposite of the direction TRP's successor has taken). It implies that the DoD should focus on helping U.S. industry to upgrade and modernize its manufacturing capabilities, in order to improve the productivity, efficiency, and speed with which both defense and commercial industries in the United States adopt new technologies, whether they are first developed in this country or abroad.

The other justification for TRP's investments in potential spin-on technologies—that they were necessary to emphasize military-specific attributes commercial producers otherwise would have ignored—is more problematic. It replicates the pattern that rendered 1980s efforts such as VHSIC and the Strategic Computing Program irrelevant, although not harmful, to the competitive performance of the companies involved in them. It is possible, it should be granted, that TRP projects that emphasize military-unique performance attributes will succeed in hastening the overall pace of innovation—they may end up providing the military with what it wants and creating a technological breakthrough that enables U.S. companies to leap-frog their most sophisticated foreign-based competitors. Yet we cannot routinely expect revolutionary technological breakthroughs. It is just as likely that the TRP project will result in the creation of a defense-dependent niche industry that is chronically unable to exploit the technology's commercial potential. The DoD might well end up paying higher procurement costs for a military-specific technology when it should have been forced to rely on a lower-cost commercial technology.

Different problems are likely to attend TRP projects that have attempted to spin off technologies from defense to new commercial applications. Program managers justified these investments as necessary in order to broaden demand and thus lower production costs for the dual-use technology or simply to keep defense companies in operation should their specialized skills be needed in a military emergency. If there is clearly already a commercial market for the application, however, then these TRP projects are again vulnerable to the charge that they are spending taxpayer money to subsidize profitable investments that the industry would be making anyway. If it is again a question of being first to market with a technology that has great potential to generate significant follow-on products and processes, TRP's defenders need to show that the government investment has facilitated private-sector actions that clearly accelerated commercial introduction of the technology—and that the competitive benefits of this acceleration justify the costs of the subsidy.

It has already been noted that TRP appears to have been successful at helping companies overcome the collective action problems that sometimes prevent them from exploiting well-known economic and technological opportunities. Where there is already a big untapped market for the results of such efforts, such supply-side policies should be enough to facilitate a successful commercial outcome. In the past, however, the Pentagon's greatest contribution to accelerating technological development and commercial introduction was on the demand side, not the supply side. The DoD's contribution to the successful commercialization of integrated circuits, for example, was based on its provision (and NASA's) of a guaranteed launch market, at premium prices, for the new technology—not on the provision of R&D subsidies before the fact. The political justification for the Pentagon's payment of premium prices was that there was a social benefit—in this case, a national security benefit—that exceeded the private economic benefit that an unsubsidized market would otherwise return to the investing firms.

Project spin-off projects often were said to promote social goals that the Clinton administration views favorably—energy efficiency, job retention, improved public health, environmental remediation, and pollution prevention. But the administration never attempted to construct a full-blown demand-side strategy in which a government customer—a non-defense mission agency, such as the Department of Transportation or the Environmental Protection Agency—guaranteed procurement at premium prices to launch a technology commercially as a means to promote a clearly articulated social goal. Indeed, any attempt to do so would run counter to the administration's ongoing procurement reform efforts, which aimed at removing government-mandated restrictions and inducements and replacing them with market signals. Thus, for TRP-backed technologies, there was no publicly subsidized civilian demand analogous to that provided by the Department of Defense, which was committed to purchase TRP-developed technologies expected to strengthen the nation's defenses. There was no plan, for example, to require or even to encourage the procurement of hybrid electric vehicles by federal, state, or local government agencies, although the DoD was committed to buying them for use on the battlefield.

Nevertheless, it still can be credibly claimed that TRP *contributed* to defense conversion, with technology development projects that attempted to find commercial uses for military technology and with technology deployment projects that attempted to modernize engineering education and promote the diffusion of best-practice manufacturing throughout the American economy. The project's insistence that defense companies team with commercial companies is certainly an essential part of any strategy to teach defense contractors more about how to develop commercial marketing strategies and how to organize for low-cost production. The project also helped to promote economic adjustment in defense-dependent regions, not by funding regional technology alliances but mainly though the geographic distribution of its awards. However, TRP did little to improve access to finance for defense companies wishing to enter commercial markets; to be fair, it was not set up to provide assistance with management reorientation or marketing, both of which appear to be more essential to commercial market entry (and hence defense conversion) than technology assistance. Indeed, TRP was not designed, and so did little, to counteract the dominant adjustment strategies of companies in the shrinking defense sector: mergers, consolidation, and the search for new overseas weapons markets.

Pressure on TRP's program managers to place even more emphasis on military needs increased significantly after the congressional elections of 1994, which brought to power a more conservative and ideologically driven Republican majority. Even before the election, the then Democratic-led Congress mandated that fiscal 1995 TRP funds were not to be obligated until the secretary of defense ensured that representatives of the military services were full members of the Defense Technology Conversion Council and were fully involved in selecting focus areas and evaluating proposals for funding. The new Republican Congress added further restrictions, also aimed at ensuring the military relevance of all TRP projects: the undersecretary of defense for Acquisition and Technology now must certify to Congress that representatives of the military services constitute a *majority* of the membership on TRP project selection panels; before obligating any TRP funds, Congress now must receive a report describing each new TRP project or award and the military needs that the project addresses.

In response to the new political and budgetary climate, ARPA (re-renamed DARPA) has made a number of additional changes. The Technology Reinvestment Project was discontinued at the end of fiscal 1996 and replaced with a similar dual-use technology development program more clearly designed to fulfill military needs. The new program does not solicit technology deployment or manufacturing education and training projects, because these efforts are considered less relevant to defense. Technology development efforts driven primarily by competitiveness concerns are left to the Commerce Department's Advanced Technology Program. DARPA officials have been paired with representatives of the military services to jointly manage previously funded TRP projects. In the end, TRP projects—even if they succeed in generating commercial as well as military applications—will be judged almost entirely on their alleged value for national defense.

For the advocates of technology policy who thought that the Department of Defense, or at least DARPA, could be used to promote the competitive performance or technical competence of commercial producers, the lesson should be clear: the DoD's fundamental goal is to ensure military performance (and its own bureaucratic influence within the government); commercial technology spin-offs or the creation of viable commercial industries can never be anything more than by-products of a defense technology policy whose ultimate goals are not economic or scientific but political. Thus the capacity of TRP or any other DoD-sponsored dual-use initiative to promote defense conversion or commercial-military integration or national industrial performance will remain hostage to its overriding military goals.

Conclusion

SCIENCE AND TECHNOLOGY BEYOND THE MILITARY AND THE MARKETPLACE: BUILDING A BROADER-BASED COALITION FOR INVESTMENT-LED GROWTH

"Remember Clinton's Industrial Policy?" asked *Business Week* soon after the Republicans took control of both houses of Congress for the first time in 40 years. "O.K. Now, Forget It." After the midterm elections of November 1994, business support for sustaining the Clinton administration's technology partnership programs proved to be lukewarm at best. The administration's overall political fortunes began to improve along with the economy and the shrinking federal deficit, but President Clinton's reelection in 1996 was paired with continued Republican control of Congress and thus a continued policy preference for tax reduction and regulatory reform, as opposed to the use of targeted subsidies, for accelerating market-driven technological advances.

The features that had been incorporated into TRP to ensure that its projects remained market driven—and that minimized opportunities for congressional earmarking and other forms of pork—ended up reducing opportunities for administration and congressional supporters to cultivate powerful interests that might then have been vested in the continuation of the program. The relatively small size of TRP awards, a consequence both of the program's teaming requirements and of President Clinton's preinaugural decision to sacrifice the size of his overall public investment package to achieve additional deficit reduction, meant that the tax incentives the Republicans now offered as an alternative approach for promoting technological development were more attractive to many chief executive officers and corporate financial officers than the administration's earnest invitations to compete for direct, albeit cost-shared, aid. The congressionally mandated restrictions on participation in the programs by foreign-owned companies threatened to impinge on the increasingly international scope of corporate strategic alliances for expensive, high-risk technology development. Restrictions rooted in national security concerns often had the same alienating effect, most famously in the case of the Clipper Chip, which the Clinton administration supported as an approach—hated by most companies and many groups of both progressive and libertarian computer professionals—for preserving the U.S. government's access to encrypted information on computer networks. Finally the Clinton administration's fairly activist antitrust stance confounded some in the corporate community, as well as some economists, who felt that the Clinton administration was working overtime to penalize the country's most successful innovators merely because they have grown large.

Support for the technology partnership programs from organized labor, and more important from large numbers of middle-class voters who remain concerned about their economic future, has been even more scarce. Although economists still typically presume that new technology will generate more jobs than it eliminates, as it leads to new products and services, lower prices, and expanded markets, lately some have joined other policy experts and much of the rest of the American public in asking whether the speed with which new technologies are being applied currently is destroying good jobs faster than new good jobs can be created, even though the overall rate of unemployment has continued to decline.

Officials of the Clinton administration argue that, even if this is true, the U.S. response must be to push even harder to develop new technologies and to provide the American workforce with the advanced training it needs to use them. This is the best way, the administration argues, to generate the wealth the nation needs to create new jobs in the long run and to compensate workers for any job losses they may suffer in the short run. Given the reality of tough international competition, a refusal by the federal government to help U.S. industry develop and diffuse new commercial technologies would lead to even more job loss over time.

Others argue, however, that the government should do just the opposite—slow down the promotion of new technology, especially in light of current efforts to reduce social spending, including spending on basic scientific research. They argue that the pace of technological change is eroding the quality of jobs and exacerbating wage and income inequality. They further argue that values and assumptions encouraging job loss are embedded in the technologies themselves. Other than in cases in which TRP has supported commercially oriented projects in order to preserve an existing defense capability for future use, for example, the program's military objectives typically work against the consideration of a technology's impact on civilian job retention or expansion. Indeed, technologies often are valued by the military precisely for their capacity to reduce risk to soldiers in the field, and this often translates into a preference for automation and the creation of technical systems that can be centrally controlled for unmanned operation in distant locations.

The federal government probably could sustain political support for promoting new civilian and dual-use technologies if social policies were put in place to mitigate the social disruptions the technologies might cause. During its first two years, the Clinton administration was open to exploring some alternatives along these lines. Proposals for more worker-oriented approaches to technology development were circulated, including (1) encouraging companies supported by TRP and ATP to include labor unions in joint ventures as a matter of policy; (2) requiring companies to address how their proposals for support would serve clearly articulated social objectives (e.g., protecting the environment, reducing health and safety problems in the workplace, and enhancing worker skills, as opposed to the abstract goal of promoting "economic competitiveness"); and (3) exploring ways in which workers and consumers could be brought into the process of designing new technologies. Such ideas were attractive to some officials at the Labor Department and certain members of the White House staff, but they tended to evoke skepticism among technology officials at the Departments of Commerce and Defense. Program managers at NIST and ARPA ultimately rejected the recommendations as being outside the scope of ATP and TRP; the proposals were viewed as "sociological"— that is, related to labor-management relations—rather than technical in nature. The Republican takeover of Congress, with its promise of less government intervention in business, simply increased the level of discomfort that already existed around such issues within the Clinton administration among the scientists, engineers, and erstwhile lobbyists and executives of high-tech companies who designed and implemented most of the administration's technology development programs.

In the long run, and particularly given the current political environment, the route to higher real living standards for American families will lie in fiscal policies that encourage increased investments in education and basic research and monetary policies that encourage fuller employment and higher rates of economic growth. Given this country's recurrent populist and libertarian impulses, however, it may be easier to construct a broad-based political coalition in support of the latter than the former.

During the Cold War, the political bargain that sustained federal investments in science and technology reflected a broad consensus that the Soviet Union must be contained militarily; research was understood to play a vital role in the containment effort. Scientists paid a price for this in public esteem; images of Dr. Salk sometimes were obscured in the public imagination by images of Dr. Strangelove. As the Cold War consensus faltered, particularly at the height of the Vietnam War, conservative supporters of military research spending sought to enlarge the political support base for science by supporting the expansion of the federal government's R&D effort to include certain nondefense social goals, such as protecting the environment and enhancing public health. Liberals accepted the bargain and began to look for ways to expand the scope of federal science and technology spending to address other social problems and also to shape the direction of national economic development.

Until the 1970s, American industry benefited from this allocation of federal R&D resources, through spillovers from defense and health-related programs, and because technological innovations based on federally sponsored research were relatively slow to diffuse across international boundaries. By the end of the 1970s, however, circumstances had changed. Defense spillovers began to diminish in significance as military product performance requirements diverged more from the needs of commercial users; larger and more dynamic commercial markets for high technology began to dictate the direction of technological innovation worldwide. At the same time, new information and communications technologies were facilitating more rapid exchanges of scientific and technological knowledge across national borders, and the technological capabilities of foreign firms strengthened dramatically relative to firms based in the United States.

In response, well before the end of the Cold War, elements of the military research establishment joined significant segments of the normally Republican business community in believing that government policy could and should help to improve the technical competence—and thus the international competitive performance—of domestic manufacturers. Support for the policy within military circles coalesced around the concept of dual use—larger and more dynamic commercial markets were driving the development of technologies that both military and civilian customers needed to use, at prices even a drastically downsized Department of Defense still could afford.

When the Cold War actually ended, liberals argued that because less defense R&D was now needed to maintain national security, freed federal R&D resources (the peace dividend) should be reallocated to address neglected economic and social needs. New Democrats and moderate Republicans argued that any new public investments should be specifically targeted to restore the rate of growth of U.S. productivity and to overhaul the DoD's research and procurement system in the interests of creating a military that could be mean but also lean. Conservatives, who had been willing to support nondefense R&D efforts mainly to sustain support for a large military research budget, argued that technology development and most basic research should now be entrusted to the private sector, while the military should focus its more limited research dollars squarely on defense needs.

Searching for a way to resuscitate broad-based political support for Cold War levels of public investment in science and technological development, many liberals made common cause in the early 1990s with those elements of the military research establishment and the business community that were advocating federal technology policies to spur economic growth. But this incipient growth coalition began to break apart soon after the 1992 election, as the narrow business and military orientation of the Clinton administration's technology initiatives became more and more clear. To too many Americans, the administration's investments in technology and science appeared to benefit only the multibillion-dollar corporations and the high-tech professionals who were already doing surpassingly well in the new global economy. Most middle-class voters, concerned about the impact of new computer-based technologies on their own jobs, uncertain and impatient about the economic future, saw no evidence in their own lives that these policies actually were working.

So, even though public investment can help the economy to overcome chronic private underinvestment in science and technological development, and even though such improvements are critical to raising long-run living standards, U.S. public support for government investments in basic research (let alone dual-use research or commercial technology development) remains weak. Support persists in just two areas where there seems to be a broad consensus both about national needs and the legitimacy of government's role—national security and public health. (The laboratories of the National Institutes of Health engage primarily in basic research; they also have been successful in stimulating the development of the biotechnology industry, but this is in large part because of the industry's dependence on the professional research community to conduct clinical trials.) It is possible that a set of TRP- or ATP-like partnership programs tied to these and other specific national needs—cleaning up the environment, improving transportation and other infrastructure—might attract broader support. But the necessity of involving profit-seeking firms in the development of commercially sustainable technologies means that the public is always likely to remain ambivalent about government's proper role.

Meanwhile, diminishing military budgets, and the continued shift of technology leadership from defense to commercial industry, will compel the Department of Defense to continue its efforts to integrate the industrial technology base for civilian and defense applications. The most promising route toward this outcome, however, is likely to be found in the continuing efforts to reform the defense acquisition system, not the engagement of commercially oriented companies in cost-shared technology development partnerships. Although the DoD is likely to continue to invest in the development of dual-use technology, likely there will be more pressure in the near future to tailor such development to specific military needs, and this will reduce the DoD's capacity to achieve scale economies by helping defense contractors to diversify into commercial markets. DoD support for commercial diversification may be sustained in isolated cases, however, when it can be shown that such support is necessary to retain the availability of that potential industrial capability for future defense use.

Neither the Clinton administration nor the Republicans—many of whom support tax incentives rather than government-industry partnerships to accelerate technology innovation—have sufficiently addressed the potential contradictions between policies to accelerate technology development to spur long-term growth and the potential this creates for the short-term displacement of jobs. All should take note, however, of the fact that the steady growth of the economy after 1993 has enabled a high rate of job creation to offset rising productivity, thus reducing the overall rate of unemployment. Wall Street may associate slower growth with financial responsibility, but as the U.S. economy becomes less regulated and more global, even mainstream economists are beginning to consider whether it might be able to sustain higher growth rates and fuller employment without sparking inflation. Faster growth might be what is necessary to create the conditions for more equitably distributed prosperity, because fuller employment and fear of worker shortages will induce more companies to upgrade worker skills and to raise wages in line with increases in productivity. The experience of such tangible economic rewards, and the articulation by technology policymakers of broader-based social goals, might create the necessary conditions for a broader-based political coalition in support of technology and science, whatever the performance of U.S.-based corporations in international competition and whatever the rate of technological advance.

5

Redefining National Defense: The Challenge of Cold War Politics and Economics on Capitol Hill

PAUL F. WALKER

PRESIDENT Bill Clinton released his first military budget on March 27, 1993, with much fanfare and a press release entitled "FY 1994 Defense Budget Begins New Era." Newly appointed Secretary of Defense Les Aspin stated that "this is in many ways the first truly post–Cold War budget. . . . It cuts Cold War forces and begins to buy new capabilities we need to meet the new dangers we face."[1]

Secretary Aspin's proposal was indeed a reduction from Cold War spending of prior decades. The president's request to Congress for $250.7 billion in budget authority ($264.2 billion in outlays) for the Department of Defense (DoD) represented a real decline in budget authority of 5 percent below fiscal year (FY) 1993, 24 percent below FY 1990, and 34 percent below FY 1985, the height of former President Ronald Reagan's "peace through strength" buildup. The projected real decline in military spending was programmed to exceed 41 percent by FY 1997.

The newly elected chairman of the House Armed Services Committee, liberal Democratic Congressman Ronald V. Dellums (D-Calif.) asked me to come to Washington in 1993 to serve as a senior policy adviser to him and the full committee as we sought to define our way in the new, post–Cold War world of dissipating Russian and Warsaw

Pact militaries, indeterminate regional threats, growing peacekeeping and peacemaking burdens, a national economy still very dependent on Pentagon spending, and a defense industry in almost total disarray.

My first conversation with Chairman Dellums was telling of the policy battles we would begin to wage and of the considerable obstacles we would face in 1993. Ron Dellums, a member of the 1970 anti–Vietnam War class of congressional freshmen, had long been critical of military spending and boasted of never once having voted for a final military budget in his 23 years in the House. He had organized, for example, ad hoc committee hearings a decade earlier that advocated cuts of 50 percent or more in military spending. (The hearings were "ad hoc" because the Armed Services chairman at the time refused to accept any of Dellums's suggested witnesses for formal committee hearings.[2])

Many observers in both Congress and the press speculated that the new chairman, voted in by the Democratic Caucus as the first African-American chair of the Armed Services Committee, would "slash and burn" the defense budget. But as we sat in his office in June 1993 and joked about "foxes guarding the chicken coop," Dellums stated that he would aim for realistic 1 to 2 percent annual reductions in military spending beyond administration submissions. He was crystal clear in his belief that the Cold War era of large military budgets was over but that the American addiction to defense spending would require time to wind down in ways that were politically palatable to the majority on the committee and not economically harmful to the U.S. economy. As he put it, "I've waited 23 long years to move from being denied a seat, along with [Congresswoman] Pat [Schroeder], in the bottom row of the committee, to occupying the chairman's seat in the top row of the committee, and I can wait another couple of years." We agreed that the 103rd Congress would be a time to quietly build and consolidate political power, not wage it indiscriminately.

Two years later, as Ron Dellums relinquished his chairmanship to the new Republican majority in January 1995 and to a jovial but staunch conservative colleague, Congressman Floyd Spence from South Carolina, he was applauded by fellow members and outside observers as one of the most fair, most gentlemanly, and wisest chairs in the history of the committee. This chapter seeks to describe some of the major issues that were addressed in this historic and interesting period from 1993 to 1995, most still ongoing in policy debate, and draw several more general conclusions concerning defense policy and congressional politics. Much of this information is based on personal recollections, notes, files, and internal memos from that period, so all errors are wholly the author's.

This analysis also touches on the debate over congressional vs. executive branch powers. It advances the thesis that Congress, when it so wishes to exert its authority, can have considerable power in formulating and changing public policy. Congress is by no means a weak sister to the White House and cabinet and, more often than not, engages in an interactive process of budget and policy design with the appropriate executive branch agencies.

What some observers have called the "power pendulum," the balance of power between Pennsylvania Avenue and Capitol Hill, swings back and forth with different presidents and eras.[3] Prior to the New Deal, history shows that Congress was dominant except during the administrations of four presidents—George Washington, Thomas Jefferson, Andrew Jackson, and Abraham Lincoln—all very strong personalities and politicians. Since Franklin Roosevelt's New Deal, however, the White House has exerted more influence. And in the specific field of national defense and foreign policy, where the president is designated commander in chief, the constitutional separation of powers would seem to favor the executive branch.[4]

However, as the American political scholar Richard Neustadt points out: "The constitutional convention of 1787 is supposed to have created a government of 'separated powers.' It did nothing of the sort. Rather, it created a government of separated institutions *sharing* powers."[5] This chapter supports this observation and shows that, should Congress be willing to exert its prerogative of oversight and control of the federal purse strings, it can have considerable influence on the national policy-making process.[6]

Reviewing from the Bottom Up

Secretary Les Aspin's March 1993 announcement of his and the president's first military budget, the first for the Democratic party since the Carter administration's FY 1983 budget, highlighted long-term reductions from prior projections of Presidents Ronald Reagan and George Bush. Four-year projections, for FY 1994 to 1997, were that some $88 billion would be cut from earlier baseline estimates of the Bush administration; these cuts were still larger if put in the context of past Reagan long-term projections that posited Cold War budgets in the $400 billion to $500 billion range by the mid-1990s.

And yet Aspin was quick to point out that at least four new threats were on the horizon: "regional threats to U.S. interests; the growing threat of proliferation of weapons of mass destruction; the failure of democratic reform, especially in the former Soviet world; and continued poor economic performance at home." "This budget," he added, "begins to use resources freed by the end of the Cold War to help at home. The president has made clear that the chief threat we face is failure to revitalize our economy. If we are not strong at home, we cannot defend our interests abroad."[7]

The new administration thus began to introduce the concept of federal budget trade-offs, that is, that domestic economic security was a major part of the national security picture, that some undefined "peace dividend" was critical to strengthening the United States internally, and that conversion and impact assistance would be required to smooth this major transition. Yet almost everyone, including committee members, recognized that the FY 1994 budget submission was, if only out of necessity, very close to the Bush program and that it would take at least another year for the new Clinton administration and the new defense secretary to put their own unique stamp on programs.

With that in mind, the Pentagon announced as part of its FY 1993 budget release that a "Bottom-Up Review of Defense Needs and Programs" (what came to be known as the BUR, or "burr") would be initiated immediately to provide detailed guidance for reshaping defense planning in fiscal year 1995 and for the "Future Years Defense Program" (FYDP, or "fiddup") for FY 1995 to 1999.

Aspin's 1993 program, however, portended the future BUR in emphasizing regional rather than global threats. Two specific initiatives were requests for $398 million in a new account for "peace-keeping, humanitarian and disaster relief operations," and special emphasis on strategic mobility and military power projection. Nuclear weapons–related requests shifted from warhead and missile production to a new $40 million request for "counterproliferation measures," $400 million for so-called Nunn-Lugar programs to cooperatively reduce the threat of weapons of mass destruction from the former Soviet Union, and $3.8 billion for a Strategic Defense Initiative (SDI, or "Star Wars") program refocused on theater (versus national) missile defense.

"Democratic security" and "economic security" also became recurrent themes. For the former initiative, Aspin requested $50 million for "military-to-military" contacts and promised to forge security partnerships with emerging democracies and to demilitarize former Soviet republics and Warsaw Pact members. (The term "Partnership for Peace" would only arise later as NATO [North Atlantic Treaty Organization] policies and rationales evolved.) For the latter initiative, the FY 1994 budget requested $700 million "to assist the transition of people and communities toward a post–Cold War economy" and $1 billion "to advance dual-use technologies, which will facilitate the commercialization of defense research and development."[8]

Also announced were domestic military base closures, based on the 1988 and 1991 Base Realignment and Closure Commission (BRAC) recommendations, which reduced structure by 15 percent; in addition, the overseas base structure was to be reduced by 35 percent, including ongoing drawdowns in U.S. troop strength in Europe (from 304,000 in FY 1990 to 133,700 in FY 1994, eventually to plateau at 100,000 in FY 1996, as mandated by Congress). Perhaps most important were the accelerated military force structure cuts: navy ships from 443 to 413; aircraft carriers from 16 to 12; army active divisions from 14 to 12; and air force fighter wings from 28 to 24. These figures would be further reduced in subsequent years, although this was not announced in 1993.

Many committee members, largely from the Democratic side of the room, were very supportive of this early restructuring. The other side of the committee, however, already nervous from earlier Bush reductions in projected Pentagon spending, was increasingly suspicious. Chairman Dellums was committed to open and full hearings on the changes, convinced that federal budget ceilings and burgeoning deficits would begin to squeeze the military budget still more, whether it was liked or not.

Three months later, in June 1993, Secretary Aspin began to talk publicly about the so-called Bottom-Up Review. In an address before the annual U.S. Air Force Senior Statesman Symposium at Andrews Air Force Base, he described the review as the "heart of our effort to chart the course for national defense for the 1990s." "We've come to the conclusion that our forces must be able to fight and win two major regional conflicts, and do it nearly simultaneously." He argued this on two grounds: if engaged in one major regional war, "we don't want a potential aggressor in a second region to believe that we're vulnerable or cannot respond in full force." And "we want to be prepared in case another adversary emerges on the scene with a larger or more capable force than today's regional powers." Aspin added, almost as an afterthought, that smaller operations, such as peacekeeping and peace enforcement, also would be a goal.[9]

It became increasingly clear to many that tough choices were ahead. If the United States were to maintain sufficient forces for two large, Gulf War–type regional operations and yet not expand a fiscally constrained budget request, trade-offs would have to be made with force size, forward presence (especially of aircraft carrier task forces) abroad, readiness, procurement spending, and research and development (R&D) investment. This would threaten a number of programs and certainly many members' vested interests on the Armed Services Committee. The committee and Chairman Dellums were in for a rocky couple of years in hearings and political dealings.

The policy staff of the Armed Services Committee, in preparation for later hearings, began arranging informal discussions with outside analysts in August 1993. Admiral Eugene Carroll of the Center for Defense Information, for example, argued that the Gulf War scenario and the Iraq-equivalent threat was specious. Many forces, he argued, such as aircraft carrier and amphibious task forces used in the Gulf, were not necessary and would not be appropriate for future regional conflicts. Pierre Sprey, a well-known defense analyst, pointed out that current major weapons platforms would be suboptimal for future regional, "low-intensity" conflict and that new design teams, more R&D investment, and "skunk-works-type" prototype development were necessary.[10]

On September 1, 1993, the Defense Department released its Bottom-Up Review with very mixed results. Supporters applauded Secretary Aspin's effort at downsizing and restructuring, but critics raised many issues, ranging from specific weapons cuts to overall strategy. The Defense Budget Project (DBP), a nongovernmental think tank, alleged there would be industrial "winners and losers" in the restructuring and produced a list of both for press consumption (e.g., Grumman and Lockheed would lose with cancellation of the A/FX aircraft program; General Dynamics would win as prime contractor for the third SSN-21 Seawolf submarine). Two weeks later the DBP raised basic questions over the BUR in a Capitol Hill press conference: How does one support two regional conflict scenarios with $250 billion? How likely are two simultaneous regional wars when such worst-case scenarios have never happened in the post–World War II period? Where does allied support enter the picture when the BUR assumes that U.S. forces must be prepared to operate unilaterally? Is the 1991 Gulf War the appropriate regional scenario for the next century? And are U.S. forces actually equipped for regional conflict?[11]

Members of Congress and outside groups were not pleased. Some alleged that the administration had not gone far enough in providing for a real "peace dividend." Others believed that proposed cuts were endangering national security. And many Armed Services Committee members were simply concerned over their bases and industry back home in their districts.[12]

Chairman Dellums called for hearings on the Bottom-Up Review on February 2, 1994, at which Assistant Secretary of Defense for Strategy and Requirements Edward L. Warner testified. The first four questions to him from both sides of the committee were hostile: Aren't the navy and naval air reductions unfair? Aren't the army force numbers too low? Aren't overall budget figures inadequate? Isn't the BUR over-simplified and rigid? Conservative Republican Congressman Steve Buyer of Indiana accused the administration of orchestrating a "win–nearly win" rather than a "win-win" two-war strategy. (This played into the early Aspin trial balloons of a "win-hold-win" and other bumper-sticker strategies.) When pressed by Republican Congressman Peter Tork-ildsen of Massachusetts as to whether two Major Regional Conflicts (MRCs) were adequate, Warner admitted that the two-MRC scenario was very unlikely but represented a more-than-adequate "flexible instrument" for planning purposes. None of this satisfied or convinced committee members, and it presaged another rough year of defense planning for the Clinton administration.

Many of the representatives were quick to show their constituent interests. Congresswoman Tillie Fowler (R-Fla.) from Jacksonville, Florida, also questioned the size of naval sea and air forces; Congress-man Gene Taylor (D-Miss.), in whose Mississippi district amphibious ships are constructed, warned that increased amphibious warfare capa-bilities would be needed for two regional wars. And Congressman Randy "Duke" Cunningham (R-Calif.) from San Diego, a former navy pilot and never one on the committee to mince words, stated frankly that "I don't accept your figures; even in Bosnia, we'd get our donkeys kicked." The president's promises are in "big print," but where is the "small print"? Right-wing Congressman Robert Dornan (R-Calif.) from Orange County, California, always could be counted on to raise the B-2 strategic bomber issue; Congressman Paul McHale (D-Pa.), a marine veteran, pushed marine force structure (he was key in later transferring M1 Abrams tanks from the army to the U.S. Marine Corps); Congress-woman Jane Harman (D-Calif.) promoted high-tech missile technology (Hughes and other electronics firms are in her district); and Congress-man Ike Skelton (D-Mo.) posed tough questions on army force structure. (Fort Leonard Wood is in his Missouri district.[13])

In the end the president tempered his military reductions and sub-mitted a FY 1995 request $2.8 billion higher than FY 1994; he also added $11.4 billion over five years to cover a military pay raise. Everyone, including Chairman Dellums, realized that change would be slower than even the administration's modest proposals. The new defense secretary at the time, William J. Perry, also began talking about the BUR as a "liv-ing document," promising "changes in it every year, in some cases every quarter," and ensuring Congress that substantial savings would be real-ized from infrastructure and overhead cost-reduction efforts. This was perhaps to be expected in light of the sudden death of Defense Secretary Les Aspin and the opportunity in FY 1995 for the Clinton administration to move beyond the Bush administration program, but by one year into the new Democratic White House it was clear how very difficult it would be to organize, let alone implement, any new defense plan.

The committee remained deeply concerned that the proposed military budget was insufficient to cover the proposed force structure and that the reduced forces would be inadequate to handle two major regional simultaneous or near-simultaneous conflicts. It was a perceived mismatch all around. And then in August 1994 the General Accounting Office (GAO) published a report entitled "Future Years Defense Program: Optimistic Estimates Lead to Billions in Overprogramming," which seemed to confirm these misgivings. The GAO argued that the Clinton BUR force was at least $150 billion short over its five-year plan.

The Department of Defense was quick to respond. Defense Comptroller John Hamre wrote Chairman Ron Dellums on August 16, 1994, that the GAO report was "superficial," "hollow," and "unsupported." In an appended five-page rebuttal, Hamre argued that there could be as much as a $40 billion shortfall in five-year BUR planning but that this was caused primarily by congressionally mandated pay raises for federal employees (the FY 1994 defense budget had proposed a pay freeze) and higher inflation estimates. President Clinton, as a result of these two issues, agreed to increase defense $11.4 billion over five years but, Hamre argued, probably needed another $20 billion, perhaps more, to cover the BUR. The comptroller added to the Perry theme, however, that the FYDP and BUR were only "planning documents," admitting in essence that he could not be more accurate in cost projections.[14]

There continued to be specific instances of efforts to cut defense and specific weapons systems, both in committee and on the House floor, but most met with little success. For example, Chairman Dellums had been successful in reducing the SDI budget by some $500 million in committee, bringing authorizations below $3 billion. But in full committee session, Democratic Congressman John Spratt of South Carolina, chair of the Nuclear Energy Panel, suddenly moved (without having informed the chairman) to add $200 million he had discovered free in his budget; to the chagrin of Dellums and other SDI critics, the motion passed easily.

Another telling case of logrolling on weapons systems came in the Procurement Subcommittee in mid-1994. There had been much debate over priorities for navy shipbuilding, much of it focused on how to retain two nuclear-licensed shipyards in Virginia (Newport News) and Connecticut

(Electric Boat) open for a future submarine industrial base. Two Seawolf attack submarines (SSN-21 and -22) already had been authorized for Electric Boat, and it was likely that a third (SSN-23) would be soon. This left Newport News with little or no new nuclear-powered construction for the foreseeable future. Congressman Norman Sisisky (D-Va.) therefore moved in subcommittee that $1.2 billion be added as a down payment for a new nuclear-powered aircraft carrier, CVN-76, in order "to keep Newport alive." The navy itself much preferred this large request at a later date, assuming that it would impact other shipbuilding funds. Democratic Congressman Gene Taylor of Mississippi, the first to speak, applauded the move but only if his own constituent shipyard could receive $100 million as a down payment for additional amphibious warfare construction. Taylor had even come to the closed hearing armed with charts and graphs to drive home his point.

Subcommittee staff, when questioned by Chairman Dellums, admitted that they could no doubt locate "loose change" of $1 billion to $2 billion in the budget to accommodate both these wishes without increasing the topline procurement figure. Other shipbuilding would not be affected and the navy would have two new heavy-tonnage ships. Immediately after the two programs were voted with only Dellums dissenting, Sisisky asked for a one-minute recess and exited the closed session to the whoops and applause of dozens of lobbyists from Virginia and the shipbuilding industry who had been quietly waiting in the hall outside in the Rayburn House Office Building.[15]

It seemed ironic that the Cold War, as acknowledged by all observers, was over; that many analysts and congressmen recognized the obsolete and inapplicable nature of major Cold War weapon systems; and that the full committee was well aware of the tight fiscal constraints on federal spending and the difficulty of cutting nondefense social programs. Yet the military budget, including many Cold War weapons programs, continued to retain resiliency—what economists might call "inelasticity downward"—that would set the stage for still grander increases of $7.5 billion, $11 billion, and $2.4 billion annually in FY 1996, 1997, and 1998 (above Clinton administration requests) under the new Republican majority in Congress.

The Bottom-Up Review had been called many things in committee, but staff recognized it quickly as "Option-C-plus," a more traditional version of an earlier analysis ("Option C") of Secretary Aspin when he was committee chair. Although total active-duty personnel were set at 1.4 million in both studies, most other force goals rose in the BUR: army active divisions increased from 9 to 10, navy ships from 340 to 346, active air force wings from 10 to 13, and U.S. Marine Corps divisions from 2 to 3

(U.S. Marine Corps active troop numbers rose from 134,000 to 174,000). An internal memo of the Military Acquisition Subcommittee to Armed Services Staff Director Marilyn Elrod commented critically that "after months of anticipation, the Bottom-Up Review that emerged from the E-ring fell substantially short of its advance billing, raising as many questions as it answers. . . . There seems to be a major disconnect between strategy and resources in the BUR results. The force structure that was described as only capable of 'win-hold' in the spring suddenly can support a 'win-win' doctrine by late summer. OSD [Office of the Secretary of Defense] provides no rationale to explain this sudden shift."[16]

The subcommittee memo went on to criticize the BUR as more of a "status quo minus" force structure than a fundamental rethinking of Cold War doctrine and argued that it satisfied "neither fiscal nor doctrinal goals. Such doubts are scarcely allayed by the thin gruel of assorted briefing charts that masquerade as detailed BUR backup. OSD is not stupid—perhaps their omissions are by design, leaving Congress to make the politically difficult choices that would reconcile this forces-resources gap."[17]

All had not been lost, however, in the eyes of Chairman Dellums. He and like-minded colleagues had won some battles, such as a ban on backfit of Trident II warheads on Trident I missiles, a "sense of Congress" resolution for a nuclear test ban, a ban on production of mini-nuclear warheads, and support for the "narrow interpretation" of the Anti-Ballistic Missile (ABM) Treaty regarding theater missile defense, among many other important initiatives. But the battle of the budget, an effort to accelerate the gradual decline in military spending that had begun in 1985 under President Ronald Reagan, had been lost. And while spending was on the upswing, military force numbers were on the downswing, lending credence to widespread and bipartisan perceptions that, indeed, whatever "review" was happening, it was not from the "bottom-up."[18]

Straightening Out Nuclear Posture

In announcing his Bottom-Up Review in the early months of the Clinton administration, Defense Secretary Les Aspin underlined the need to include nuclear weapons policies—R&D, procurement, and strategy—as a key part of the review. It was increasingly obvious that nuclear weapons programs were falling quickly in priority as regional conflicts, terrorism, and peacekeeping supplanted Cold War scenarios and as strategic arms control agreements capped and reduced deployed nuclear arsenals.

Yet nuclear weapons were excluded from the 1993 Bottom-Up Review. Secretary Aspin announced that analysis was proceeding on a "Nuclear Posture Review" (NPR) under the chairmanship of Assistant Secretary for International Security Policy Ashton Carter.

The Armed Services Committee began pressing for informal, off-the-record briefings on nuclear weapons but was stonewalled for months in late 1993 and early 1994 as the Pentagon continued internal debates.

Assistant Secretary Carter, under verbal threat of committee sub-poena, finally appeared before staff in closed meetings in May and June 1994 and discussed the forthcoming NPR. Nuclear weapons were a pressing issue primarily from a financial perspective, accounting for some $30 billion to $40 billion annually, some 15 to 20 percent of an increasingly tight military budget, and in light of the end of the Cold War nuclear standoff. If the former enemy was now an ally, or a soon-to-be ally, why was it necessary to maintain over 10,000 nuclear bombs?

The FY 1995 administration request had included $818.2 million for the B-2 strategic bomber program, $745 million for additional Trident II missiles, and a number of additional expensive "stockpile stewardship" projects at the three nuclear weapons laboratories and the Nevada Test Site. Lobbyists from the laboratories had not been scarce around the committee in both 1993 and 1994. We had also been lobbied by National Security Adviser Anthony Lake for a final series of nine underground nuclear tests before the United States entered into a permanent test moratorium and comprehensive test ban.

We were therefore not surprised by Carter's talking points: the NPR would embrace both the 1991 START I and 1993 START II agreements, supporting gradual, incremental drawdowns to 3,500 strategic war-heads, but would not predict further reductions. Carter described the strategic nuclear force as on a "gradual glide path downward" that could, depending on future turns in relations with our former strategic adversary and on prospects for proliferation, turn upward once again. "We don't want to close options too early," he stated, reflecting a cautious general defense planning guidance we had heard many times before in this immediate post–Cold War period.

Carter also noted that there would be no major changes in the nuclear force structure recommended in the NPR other than to follow the bilaterally negotiated arms control drawdowns. Somewhat discouraged, he did confide that he had sought in internal memos to push the issue of the long-enshrined "triad" of nuclear forces, arguing that land-based missiles could be retired in the post–Cold War period. They were the most vulnerable targets for nuclear first-strike attacks; they could be the most destabilizing offensive weapons in light of their accuracy; and they would require expensive de-MIRVing (removal of multiple warheads) under START counting rules. This suggestion turned out to be a nonstarter, however, particularly in light of the ongoing air force–navy tradition of sharing deterrent forces. The air force wanted to retain both air- and land-based options, the navy its submarines. And the military nuclear bureaucracy was adamant that 1995 was still too early to make any major changes, such as eliminating a 35-year-old tradition that had "deterred world war successfully." In other words, if it ain't broke, don't fix it.

On September 22, 1994, over one year after the release of the Bottom-Up Review, the long-awaited Nuclear Posture Review appeared. Earlier Secretary Aspin had described it with much fanfare as the first such review in over 15 years and the very first to cover the whole array of nuclear-related issues—policy, doctrine, force structure, command and control, operations, supporting infrastructure, safety and security, and arms control. Defense Secretary Perry was more circumspect upon its release: "A fundamental underlying judgment of the Review is that we are at the threshold of a decade of planned reductions [START II cuts would be completed in 2003], and we will continue to assess the opportunities for further reduction or, if necessary, respond to unanticipated challenges as time goes on."

His new strategy, "Mutual Assured Safety," intended to supplant "Mutual Assured Destruction," seemed a bit too facile for most committee members, although it did underline the recommendation to equip all nuclear weapons systems with coded control devices by 1997. The NPR recommended maintenance of a strategic triad of bombers, submarines, and land-based missiles for "selective strike" and possible conventional missions. It also stated that a tactical nuclear force would be maintained with some 450 air-delivered weapons forward deployed in Europe.

The expectation of Chairman Dellums, several colleagues on the committee, and the arms control community that START III negotiations on still deeper cuts and/or a no-first-use policy would be forthcoming was not fulfilled. Perry noted that "we concluded that deeper reductions beyond those we made in the NPR would be imprudent at this time, and, second, we took several actions to ensure that we could reconstitute our forces as the decade went along, if we needed to." Deputy Defense Secretary John Deutch warned in hearings that Russian nuclear reductions had been slower than U.S. reductions, and Assistant to the Secretary for Atomic Energy Harold Smith testified for additional tritium production in order to assure future warhead production capabilities.

Two months later, as the FY 1995 defense bill was finalized, the committee had authorized $125 million for preservation of the B-2 strategic bomber industrial base (against the strong opposition of Chairman Dellums), $4.5 million for an independent bomber cost-effectiveness study, $29 million in unrequested funds for conventional air-launched cruise missiles, $616 million in Trident II procurement (although this was a cut from the $641 million requested), and a cost-effectiveness study of backfitting the Trident II missile onto earlier Trident subs (although the bill prohibited backfitting).

Aside from the Posture Review, some significant changes were in fact accomplished by Congress in nuclear weapons and policy. As mentioned earlier, the FY 1994 authorization bill specifically prohibited "research and development which could lead to the production by the United States of a new low-yield [less than five kilotons] nuclear weapon, including a precision low-yield warhead." In final conference form, this section was conditioned, after considerable lobbying by the nuclear laboratories, so that test devices were not banned, weapons modifications for "safety and reliability" were not restricted, and R&D would be allowed "to address proliferation concerns." (This last point raised considerable concern on the committee with regard to the newly proposed "counterproliferation initiative." Carter later assured committee members that nuclear warheads would not be adapted or developed for such counterproliferation purposes as "bunker-busting" and deep underground counterforce strikes.[19])

Congress, in an effort to limit spending on the submarine force, specifically stated in the FY 1995 authorization bill that the navy "may not modify any Trident I submarine to enable that submarine to be deployed with Trident II (D-5) missiles" unless the defense secretary proves it to be a "significant national security risk." Chairman Dellums also was successful in adding very important restrictions to ballistic missile defense programs in order to ensure that "upper-tier systems" (high-altitude missiles) and tracking systems ("Brilliant Eyes") complied with the 1972 ABM Treaty. These were all perhaps minor and temporary but nevertheless important and symbolic victories for those intent on further nuclear arms control, regardless of what the NPR did and did not propose.[20]

Yet, just as with the Bottom-Up Review, the Nuclear Posture Review had been a fizzle. As Ashton Carter had diplomatically forewarned the committee, expectations had been too high for these first forays of the Clinton administration into defense policymaking. It would take at least another few years, perhaps a second term, for the Democrats truly to undertake fundamental reviews. And especially with nuclear weapons and strategic policy, less amenable to reorientation toward limited, regional conflict, dramatic change ultimately would depend on Russian moves and reciprocity.

Proliferating Arms for National Security

One of the key tenets of the new Bottom-Up Review and the Clinton administration policy was to promote global nonproliferation of weapons and weapons-related technology. Experience in Afghanistan, Somalia, Haiti, Bosnia, Iraq, and elsewhere already had taught the United States that dual-use technology and weapons can easily boomerang back on their original sellers in regional conflicts, subnational terrorism, and civil wars. Therefore, an interagency policy review committee was organized to formulate arms export policy. A review team also tackled the options for successor regimes to the now-obsolete arrangement of the Coordinating Committee for Multilateral Export Controls (COCOM) that had restricted certain trade with communist countries. President Clinton himself had promised immediately after his November 1992 election "to review our arms sales policy and to take it up with the other major sellers of the world as part of a long-term effort to reduce the proliferation of weapons of destruction in the hands of people who might use them in very destructive ways."[21]

On the other hand, procurement of major weapons platforms had fallen dramatically since the mid-1980s, encouraging manufacturers to look abroad for better markets. Over the decade from 1985 to 1995 ship procurement had dropped 80 percent (from 29 ships in 1985 to 6 in 1995) and aircraft 86 percent (from 943 in 1985 to 127 in 1995), while battle tank production had come to a full stop (720 tanks produced in 1985, none in 1995). The production of strategic missiles had fallen 93 percent (from 307 in 1980 to 18 in 1995). While this dramatic fall in weapons purchases was simply a reflection of the high rates of military inventory expansion in the early 1980s, it did not create a hospitable climate for defense corporations in the 1990s.[22]

There was a sizable bipartisan coalition on the Armed Services Committee in favor of nonproliferation policy, including strict arms trade limits, which was led by Chairman Ron Dellums on the Democratic side and Congressman John Kasich from Ohio on the Republican side. It became clear in 1993 that this coalition could inhibit certain worrisome sales. In full committee markup, for example, Congresswoman Jane Harman from southern California proposed allowing an exemption in trade restrictions for the sale of civilian missile technology to China. Many committee members argued that such technology was also applicable to military multiple-warhead (MIRV) packaging; with a polite but stern chiding from the chairman, Harman withdrew her proposed amendment but reserved the right to raise it on the House floor. (She never did.)

One of the clearest signs that the administration had serious plans to promote exports of American weaponry came in late 1993 when the air force hosted a joint closed briefing for staff of the House Armed Services and Foreign Affairs committees. The subject was a new program, "The Coalition Force Enhancement Program," which would market used F-16A/B jet fighter aircraft to allies and friends abroad. This proposal, which eventually became public several months later, met with a very skeptical response from most staff.

The air force proposed marketing some 200 to 300 excess early-model F-16 aircraft with half their lifespan remaining (described by General Michael Carns, the vice chief of the air force, as "some of our best stuff") to foreign countries. The buyers would purchase the aircraft for some $5 million each; be required to have the original manufacturer, Lockheed, renovate and upgrade them for some $8 million each; and finally the air force would invest the original sales price in newer model F-16C/D fighters at a four-to-one ratio. As the briefers explained, everyone was a winner: the foreign buyer obtained a practically new aircraft at a bargain-basement price, less than 50 percent of the cost of a new F-16; the air force upgraded its inventory while contracting its size; and the Dallas-based manufacturer kept its industrial base alive while awaiting production contracts for the forthcoming F-22 fighter.

The Coalition Force Enhancement Program (CFEP) also was described as the first trial of a number of used inventory sales abroad of major weapons systems—battle tanks, armored personnel carriers, helicopters, transport and additional aircraft would be pursued next in order to bolster a sagging industrial base and upgrade many key service inventories.

The Texas delegation, predictably, was quite supportive of this proposal. However, a staff memo written to Chairman Dellums raised several problematic issues with the new program: to whom would the sales be made? (The air force refused to release its list of potential buyers, but it went far beyond what one might call "friends and allies.") How would the profits be handled? (Congress authorizes and appropriates all federal monies; some members perceived this plan as an "end-run" around the congressional purse strings to purchase new weapons never authorized and to add to the top line of the procurement budget.) How would our allies and arms sales competitors—France, Sweden, Israel, Britain, and others—perceive such sales? (The phrase "unfair foreign dumping practices" arose in conversations with foreign military attachés in Washington.) And would it be a good and appropriate investment in the industrial base to push prime contractors into "bridging" gaps in production with foreign sales? (By 1993 the air force seldom requested F-16 aircraft in its annual budget submission, knowing that the strong Texas delegation on the Armed Services Committee would always add a dozen or more as "pork" for Lockheed.)

Administration briefings before the committee and the chairman at the time raised five goals for arms transfer policy: retain technological advantages of U.S. forces; help allies and friends defend themselves; promote regional stability; promote peaceful conflict resolution; and support the U.S. defense industrial base. In theory it was difficult for anyone to disagree with these general principles, but further moves by industry, Hill supporters, and some administration agencies convinced Dellums and others that something had to be done to raise arms sales to a higher level of political debate.

The Senate, with the active support of military industry, proposed in 1993 and 1994 that foreign sales be promoted through an export loan guarantee program. Defense Secretary Aspin, to the surprise of many, publicly opposed this program. Chairman Howard M. Fish of the American League for Exports and Security Assistance (ALESA), the Washington lobby group for most major military corporations, wrote Aspin and Dellums in October 1993 decrying administration and House opposition "to the Senate's attempts to create a $1 billion defense export loan guarantee program." Fish argued that "the defense industry and its workers do not have the luxury of waiting an additional year while the Pentagon studies the 'efficiency and efficacy' of the program," which he believed was "consistent with Administration policy."[23] The Senate section would fail in the FY 1994 bill but would continue to be raised annually thereafter.

Another committee concern was the removal of "recoupment fees" from certain weapons sales. It had been federal government practice to place a fee on all major foreign sales in order to recoup taxpayers' sunk costs for R&D of a weapons system. These fees would range from a few percent to as high as 25 percent at times. Under the Bush administration, recoupment fees had been eliminated for private corporate sales, but they still were retained on government-to-government foreign military sales (FMS). The Clinton administration began to waive these fees in 1994 when competition apparently grew stiffer. One of the first such cases was the sale to Sweden of 100 AIM-120 Advanced Medium Range Air-to-Air Missiles (AMRAAM); the administration agreed to sell the missiles via a direct commercial contract, thus adroitly bypassing recoupment fees, but to be administered by the U.S. Air Force. Removal of the reported $114,000 surcharge per missile (about 25 percent of overall cost) made AMRAAM competitive with the French Mica missile produced by Matra Defense-Espace and also convinced Finland to purchase the missile shortly thereafter. The missile, made by Raytheon in Massachusetts and Hughes Missile Systems in Arizona, also was being marketed under similar cost-cutting measures to Switzerland, Norway, and buyers in the Mideast and Asia. Understandably, this move and others did not help French-American relations.[24]

Another controversial issue that rose to prominence in 1993 and 1994 was the question of "offset agreements," private arrangements of weapons sellers with buyers to counterbalance a weapons export with equal or greater amounts of purchases of other military or, more typically, civilian items from the foreign country. At one point I asked Lockheed to come discuss their offset policy with me and was surprised to discover that most manufacturers had major offset departments led by a corporate vice president. My Lockheed visitors, visibly very nervous discussing offset policy, refused to divulge any specifics about their bilateral arrangements other than to say that the practice was necessary to remain competitive in the world market.

Congress, understandably, was deeply concerned over recoupment fees and offsets; the former, in the minds of many members, meant that taxpayers underwrote foreign military programs and lost their invested tax dollars, while offsets cost jobs back home with the promotion of foreign goods and/or the shift of manufacturing abroad. Ironically, part of almost every offset deal is to license the eventual manufacture and/or assembly of the weapons system abroad, thereby helping the company but not the American worker.

No subcommittee of the Armed Services Committee had been tasked to handle arms sales, and none seemed anxious to tackle the issue in 1993 and 1994. Chairman Dellums therefore proposed forming an ad hoc and bipartisan "Working Group on Conventional Arms Proliferation," which would be chaired by Democratic Congressman Tom Andrews from Maine. Its primary focus would be "to assess the relative weight of export financing as compared to other variables affecting the competitive success of U.S. firms in foreign markets," although Andrews's larger vision was to bring the issue of conventional arms sales "into the light of day for full public participation." Andrews proposed a six-member committee to include Democrats Lane Evans (Ill.), Paul McHale (Penn.), and Elizabeth Furse (Oreg.), and Republicans John Kasich (Ohio) and a nominee of the ranking member, Congressman Floyd Spence (S.C.).[25]

Unfortunately, this task force never materialized owing to Andrews's sudden announcement early in 1994 that he would run for a vacant Senate seat in Maine. While Congressman John Kasich could have taken up the effort, he was made Budget Committee chair late in 1994 by the new majority and Speaker Newt Gingrich.

Chairman Dellums also considered a number of possible amendments to the FY 1995 Defense Authorization bill regarding arms sales: requiring expanded authority for the Armed Services Committees to be notified of sales by the Pentagon; establishing reporting requirements for all coproduction agreements with foreign buyers; creating reporting requirements for all offset deals over $5 million; prohibiting offset agreements for exports funded with U.S. military aid; prohibiting sales of weapons from active inventories; prohibiting the licensing of any Munitions List items by the Commerce Department; prohibiting use of government funds for international arms bazaars; stopping sales to countries that do not participate in the United Nations Arms Trade Register; requesting a study of arms exports and industrial base; reestablishing recoupment fees for government and commercial sales; encouraging President Clinton to follow through on his campaign promises to engage in multilateral negotiations on arms export limits (similar to Jimmy Carter's unsuccessful Conventional Arms Talks [CAT]); and requiring a study of funding U.S. peacekeeping operations out of an arms export fee.[26]

None of these efforts ever moved out of committee and, as of 1998, very few, if any, of the hundreds of annual weapon export notifications to Congress have received any formal scrutiny in either the Foreign Affairs or Armed Services committees. And the review of the arms trade policy of the Clinton administration, after some two years of difficult interagency squabbles, was issued in February 1995 in a six-page document described by industry as "the most positive statement on defense trade that has been enunciated by any administration."[27]

Converting and Diversifying Industry

Considerable efforts were made within Congress in the post–Cold War period to support and encourage industry, workers, and communities to plan for the expected contractions in weapons production, worker layoffs, corporate consolidations and mergers, and, in the worst case, actual factory shutdowns. Defense-dependent states and regions such as Connecticut, southern California, and Texas all faced sizable unemployment in defense. The dramatically falling procurement rates cited earlier illustrate what the military industrial complex faced. At the same time, active military forces were falling from 2.1 million troops in 1985 to a planned 1.4 million by 1999; this final figure has since been further reduced to 1.396 million for FY 1999 and 1.366 million for FY 2003. In 1994 an average of 7,800 troops were discharged monthly.

Reserve forces were no different. Selected reserves are planned to decline 20 percent, from 1.1 million in 1985 to 877,000 by 1999, 837,000 by 2003. And civilians employed directly by the Pentagon are predicted to drop below 747,000 by 1999, 672,000 by 2003, from 1.1 million in 1985. In 1994 an average of 2,750 reserves and 1,165 civilians were discharged monthly by the Department of Defense.[28]

Also having considerable impact on states and local communities was the accelerating rate of military base closures; they averaged one per month in both 1994 and 1995 across the country. Four base closure rounds, all very contentious, were announced in 1988, 1991, 1993, and 1995, with still two more rounds requested in 1998 for 2001 and 2005.

Title XIII of the FY 1994 Defense Authorization bill was entitled "Defense Conversion, Reinvestment, and Transition Assistance" and allocated over $3.5 billion annually for a wide variety of programs: defense technology conversion and reinvestment, personnel transition assistance, community assistance, pilot projects to improve economic adjustment, environmental education opportunities and restoration at closing military facilities, and a national shipbuilding initiative. Most of these FY 1994 programs originated in the House bill; the Senate, with considerable negotiation in conference, agreed to most House provisions but succeeded in reducing funding and restricting a variety of the new and continuing programs.

The Technology Reinvestment Program (TRP) effort, for example, was aimed at encouraging defense companies to diversify and study ways of applying their technologies to the civilian sector. The most famous example by 1994 was the use of strong composite materials from stealth bomber development for light bridge construction. This was one of the favorite programs of Congresswoman Patricia Schroeder (D-Colo.), chair of the Research and Development Subcommittee, where the programs originated. The Senate was concerned that these new technological applications, developed largely with taxpayer support, might benefit foreign corporate partners and therefore required the defense secretary "to ensure that the principal economic benefits . . . accrue to the U.S. economy." The Senate also stipulated that awards be on a "competitive, cost-shared basis."

The TRP was very popular with industry, although the dollar amounts were relatively small, therefore creating stiff competition among numerous competitors. For every award there were some five to ten applicants, and the eventual hope was to expand it far beyond its $600 million allotment.

Another major conversion effort was in personnel retraining focused on perceived national needs. Thus worker adjustment and education programs were begun to encourage discharged troops to become teachers ("troops to teachers"), law enforcement officials ("troops to cops"), health-care providers, and environmental restoration specialists. The final conference report for FY 1994 specified that civilian workers from Defense and Energy Department facilities also would be eligible and provided "environmental education scholarships to . . . servicemembers and employees . . . involuntarily separated, terminated, or laid off as a result of the decline in defense spending or as a result of a closure of a military installation." Language this broad aided in crafting a very inclusive policy, and many workers participated in both FY 1994 and 1995 programs.[29]

Communities benefited greatly from these programs. Defense workers were specifically given priority for employment in environmental cleanup at closing military bases, likely the very ones on which they had worked prior to being laid off. Schools took advantage of highly skilled teachers and police departments hired new, highly qualified recruits, all at federally subsidized salaries. The FY 1995 bill expanded these programs still further by providing retraining for troops and civilians to become fire fighters, initiating a pilot program to place separated individuals into high school teaching positions in bilingual math and science, and demonstration programs to assist terminated defense workers to become small business owners and to enter the recycling field. Worker assistance also was expanded to include those individuals dislocated owing to reductions in weapons exports.[30]

Obviously these diversified programs were intended by supporters, including Chairman Dellums and many other members, to help smooth the transition from Cold War to peacetime military spending, from the weapons procurement peaks of the early 1980s to the troughs of the 1990s, and from the high levels of active-duty forces and military bases to a more civilian-based economy. And yet the skeptics, including many Republicans, criticized the programs for lack of strict evaluation and assessment. Just how many jobs did they really produce? Were the monies absolutely essential to companies and communities for survival? Wouldn't the free market have helped individuals and regions through these tough transitions as well, if not quite as quickly?

In late 1994 the Armed Services Committee began distributing surveys to grant recipients to discover, for example, just how many jobs and products the TRP program had produced nationwide. Credible assessments were difficult to compile, largely owing to the still short-term nature of the programs, which had been initiated largely in 1993 and 1994; some companies began receiving questionnaires only one to two months after they received transition assistance. And many Republicans perceived the conversion programs to be Democratic "pork barrels" for favored districts, political constituencies, and labor unions. Only time will tell, after further analysis, if these allegations are true.

When the Republicans gained the majority in the House and Senate in November 1994, it was too late to save the conversion and re-investment programs. The FY 1996 and subsequent defense bills conspicuously omitted any title on conversion but did include one small section under "other matters" that rescinded most prior programs except for "dual-use critical technology programs" at DoD laboratories. Even this minor provision was eliminated in the FY 1997 authorization bill, thus hammering the final nail into the coffin of well-intended community, industry, and worker transition funds for the post–Cold War world.[31]

Transitioning Defense and Congressional Oversight

The congressional process is complex, very democratic, and very analogous to the story of the blind men and the elephant: depending on which part of the elephant's anatomy they touched, they each obtained a very different picture of the object. Therefore we must be very modest in drawing any overarching stereotypes of Congress, committee processes, or members' motives and behavior. A visiting Russian delegation from the newly formed Duma in Moscow once asked if they could take a copy of the federal and defense budgets back with them. They were astonished to realize that it was not one thin volume but rather thousands of pages of documents, sufficient to fill a few suitcases. They exclaimed: "Is this what democracy is all about?!"

The House Armed Services Committee, in which I worked some two years, for example, had 56 members (34 Democrats and 22 Republicans), each one with his or her own set of beliefs and agendas. Committee responsibilities—essentially defense budget oversight—also often brought members and staff into contact and competition with several other committees, including Foreign Affairs, Judiciary, Commerce, and Intelligence with overlapping legislative jurisdictions. The process, as can be gathered from the preceding analysis, is not simple.

Nevertheless, it seems clear that several important points can be drawn from the past few years of defense planning and congressional oversight and the implications of these for future post–Cold War budgeting and strategies.

THREAT ASSESSMENT REMAINS KEY
TO ALL PLANNING AND BUDGETING

Determining exactly what the foreign threat is to the United States and its interests abroad drives the annual defense budget. Yet the Bottom-Up Review made crystal clear in 1993 how difficult it is to look into the future, if only for five years or less, while turmoil still reigns among former foreign adversaries and regional threats are more opaque to threat analysts.

What was clear in these early post–Cold War years is that the threat is much reduced. No longer must Americans worry about a second super-power; no longer must they face an aggressive enemy in Moscow and eastern Europe; and no longer is any major world war scenario plausible. In fact, recent comparisons of all potential adversaries to current U.S. military capabilities illustrate more a David and Goliath relationship than anything close to a balance of military might. The threats—what James Woolsey, former director of the Central Intelligence Agency, liked to call "snakes in the jungle"—may be more difficult to define, but cumulatively they remain much less than the former Russian bear.[32]

NARROW CONSTITUENT INTERESTS CONTINUE
TO DOMINATE LARGER QUESTIONS OF DEFENSE

The fact that narrow interests continue to dominate larger defense questions is graphically illustrated almost daily in committee and on the floor of the House. One member lobbies for a specific weapons system manufactured in his or her district, even though it is neither requested by the military service nor needed in inventory; another member lobbies to retain a military base open back home although it is no longer part of military force structure plans; a third lobbies for a weapon sale abroad, fully cognizant that the transfer proliferates high technology and eventually may threaten U.S. troops in the region.

Many (maybe even most) members of Congress, partly as a function of the democratic process, have difficulty seeing the forest for the trees. When Senator John Glenn (D-Ohio), for example, remained adamant in closed House-Senate conference meetings in 1994 that the United States needed to bring the high-flying spy plane, SR-71, out of mothballs for several hundred million dollars, most members went along with him; the intelligence and military communities, in pointing out that lower-flying aircraft and higher-altitude satellites more than made up for the SR-71, staunchly argued against wasting money on such duplicative systems.

MAJOR WEAPONS SYSTEMS
HAVE A LIFE OF THEIR OWN

Major weapons systems, once they are funded for full production, obtain a powerful political constituency that is difficult to defeat, a fact that is related to the last point. The strategic bomber program is a very good example. The air force readily admits the limited utility and large expense of the B-1 and B-2 bomber programs, yet both aircraft have absorbed tens of billions of dollars over the past 20 years. Critics of the B-2 bomber program finally were successful at capping it at 20 aircraft for $44.4 billion, but former Senator Sam Nunn (D-Ga.) and several other members continued to seek additional funds to keep the B-2 "industrial base alive." In response to Nunn's support, many members of the southern California delegation, where the B-2 is produced, supported the overly expensive and troubled new C-17 transport aircraft, built primarily in Georgia.

This apparent solidarity among aircraft constituencies also was readily visible within the shipbuilding community. Support for Seawolf submarine production in Connecticut and Rhode Island would win support for Aegis destroyers at Bath Iron Works in Maine, for aircraft carrier construction in Virginia, and for amphibious warfare ships in Mississippi, among other shipbuilding communities. (There are, however, always exceptions to these broad observations. In the early 1990s, when President George Bush sought to kill the Seawolf program, the whole New England delegation, for example, voted to save the obsolete submarine and the Electric Boat shipyard with the exception of Republican Senator William Cohen from Maine, the newly appointed defense secretary.)

THE COLD WAR IS NOT OVER

Although intellectually most members of Congress acknowledge the end of the Cold War, arguments about the Russian threat continue to pop up in committee, on the House floor, and elsewhere. Some of this is understandable owing to the instability that seems to dominate Moscow and beyond. But many congresspeople continue to recognize the high unlikelihood, indeed impossibility according to the intelligence community, of any reconstitution of the Soviet threat in the foreseeable future. It is therefore both surprising and disappointing to see them act and argue otherwise in committee deliberations over Cold War weapons programs.

Forty years or more of Cold War experience, mirrored in Moscow as well, makes political debates very susceptible to arguments, however unsubstantiated, that "the Russians could be coming." This in turn appears in concrete terms with an annual military budget still at Cold War levels: the FY 1999 defense request for budget authority is $270.6 billion with $297.1 billion projected by FY 2003.[33]

NUCLEAR WEAPONS AND DETERRENCE DOCTRINE REMAIN CENTRAL TO DEFENSE

As the Nuclear Posture Review amply illustrated, nuclear weapons, although costly and dangerous to maintain, are judged by the Pentagon as a key, at least for the present and foreseeable future, to stable and robust defense. No doubt this will change over time, assuming a Cold War is not renewed in some fashion, but "stockpile stewardship" is for some congresspeople simply a code word for continuing a very large and unusable nuclear arsenal. Recent plans for large, billion-dollar investments in a National Ignition Facility (NIF), for a new modification of the B61 nuclear gravity bomb as a "bunker-buster," counterforce weapon, for renewed production of tritium as warhead yield boosters, for continued "blue-gold," duplicate crews that alternate sea- and shore-based duty in order to keep Trident missile submarines at sea full-time, and for new "subcritical," underground testing of nuclear warhead designs all underline the continued importance of nuclear deterrence in U.S. military planning.

Several recent signs also, however, point toward more public recognition of the obsolete nature of these weapons: the 1995 renewal of the Non-Proliferation Treaty in which all signatories agreed to abolish nuclear weapons under Article VI; a new Pentagon study of further deep cuts in nuclear arsenals below START II levels; the 1996 decision of the World Court essentially acknowledging that nuclear weapons were illegal except in extreme, last-resort circumstances; the 1996 public call of a former U.S. strategic forces commander, General Lee Butler, and dozens of other retired admirals and generals for abolition; a growing "Abolition 2000" movement aiming at the next Nonproliferation Treaty (NPT) review conference in the year 2000; and the 1998 acknowledgment by the Pentagon that nuclear weapons were not applicable in Iraqi crises.

THERE IS NO CLEAR PLAN FOR DEFENSE CONVERSION AND DIVERSIFICATION

Although all House and Senate members realize the formidable difficulties faced by industry in the current period of falling defense budgets and still-faster falling procurement programs, and they also recognize the need to retain a minimum industrial base, they continue to "muddle through" (as political scientists are wont to say) with deep and partisan suspicions about any federal support for communities, industry, and workers.

As pointed out earlier, the Defense Authorization bill for FY 1994 and 1995 included considerable sums, although still inadequate, to help smooth the transition from a military- to a civilian-based economy. But partisan differences about which constituencies were able to take advantage of these monies; ideological differences about interfering in the free market with federal programs; and concern over the inadequate funding base for a two-regional-war scenario all doomed these programs largely before any serious evaluation could be completed.

THE UNITED STATES WILL NOT BE PREPARED
FOR CONFLICTS OF THE 21ST CENTURY
IF COLD WAR PLANNING CONTINUES

The Cold War programs we continue to invest in—large-deck aircraft carriers, Seawolf and follow-on large attack submarines, heavy battle tanks, gold-plated jet fighters, and nuclear weapons—will absorb most monies in defense for the foreseeable future. Most regional operations will not need such systems, and the challenge will be to provide the equipment, strategies, and training for our troops to function in conflicts very different from past wars, even the 1991 Gulf War.

When deaths and injuries to U.S. forces started to mount, for example, in Somalia in 1993 and 1994, the Armed Services Committee began to examine the training and equipment demands of contemporary peacekeeping missions. It was discovered that army jeeps and trucks were unprepared to protect against sniper fire and land mines. The committee urged that vehicles be retrofitted with bulletproof glass, armored shielding on floorboards, and Kevlar seat covers. Also encouraged was new research and development of land-mine detection and clearance. The Haitian embargo offered still another example of the apparent growing mismatch between military needs and equipment. On a committee visit to the Caribbean, we discovered that our surface ships, highly capable of sinking any ship on the horizon, were not adequately designed and outfitted to board freighters and tankers on the high seas. We began to encourage the Pentagon to address these new needs five years or more ago, but most funding still remains caught in the Cold War mind-set.

CONGRESS REMAINS A POWERFUL POLICYMAKER IF IT WISHES TO EXERT ITS CONSTITUTIONALLY MANDATED AUTHORITY AS OVERSEER OF FEDERAL PROGRAMS AND HOLDER OF FEDERAL PURSESTRINGS

As noted at the start of this analysis, the American system of government was so designed to encourage separation and balance of power in Washington. This balance between the executive and legislative branches varies over time, partly dependent on the personalities in the White House and in House and Senate leadership seats. In the field of national defense, there has been a vehement debate over "war powers"—who has the power to wage war?—for at least two decades now, with most observers recognizing the ultimate authority of the president as commander in chief. President Bill Clinton, after his first foreign policy difficulties in Somalia and Haiti, committed to "consulting" with Congress before deploying American men and women abroad. But he was clear that he would not seek permission in order to retain his flexibility for troop deployment in emergencies.

Foreign and military policy therefore has been judged more the prerogative of the executive branch than of Congress. This analysis illustrates, however, that Congress, especially through the Armed Services and Appropriations committees, can and does exert considerable influence in defense budget and program oversight. It also provides longer-term direction by constant interaction with the executive branch and thereby, through anticipated responses, helps mold proposed federal programs long before they appear annually in January and February in committee hearings. This congressional policymaking process also may be reflective of other budgets and committees, but these are issues for further study.

THE ANNUAL MILITARY BUDGET AND FORCE SIZE WILL CONTRACT, ALBEIT SLOWLY, IN FUTURE YEARS

The Defense Department issued a "Quadrennial Defense Review" (QDR) in May 1997, the stated intention of which was to reexamine all fundamental issues of defense guidance and planning since the 1993 Bottom-Up Review. Early expectations for this review were limited and proven correct, perhaps in recognition of the arrival of a new defense secretary, the continued apparent lack of willingness of the armed services and the Clinton administration for substantive change in military doctrines, and the dominance of Cold War politicians on Capitol Hill. While highlighting new priorities, such as Cooperative

Threat Reduction, Partnership for Peace, Counterdrug Operations, and NATO Enlargement, the QDR advocated only minimal force structure changes. In short, it did not turn a new corner in military and foreign policy planning but turned out to be a "status quo plus" copy of the BUR.

What seems clear, however, is that the FY 1996, 1997, 1998, and 1999 congressional plus-ups of some $30 billion total in military spending, and the relatively high $270 billion defense budget submissions of the Clinton administration, although projected in five-year plans to rise still further, cannot and will not continue for much longer. Deficit hawks, balanced budgeteers, and proponents of nonmilitary discretionary programs are coalescing more every year to dampen any enthusiasms for budget expansion. On the other hand, increasingly optimistic projections of reduced federal budget deficits have shown a balanced budget by as early as FY 1999.[34]

Weapons programs, which normally last several decades from early R&D to final termination and retirement, also will begin to change by the end of the 1990s. Systems designed in the 1970s and 1980s, before the disintegration of Cold War enemies, already have had their production runs cut short or stopped. And no serious enemy has come forth to fill new threat assessment vacuums for the United States.

Congress also has changed considerably, with large numbers of new freshman and sophomore members, most born long after the depths of Cold War confrontations, filling the ranks of retiring senators and representatives.

These factors will all likely conspire to constrain future budgets. Fiscal limits will in turn affect military force sizing and overall strategy. The Aspin-touted "win-win" review likely will give way to a "win-hold" strategy with the realization that the United States can protect both its citizens and its interests abroad with far fewer troops and weapons. This strategy also will encourage more "burden sharing" with allies and friends and a greater focus on non- and counterproliferation, counterterrorism, and peacekeeping missions rather than major regional war options. Back home, even without any coherent conversion and transition programs, the U.S. economy will no doubt wean itself back from its heavy defense dependence; it must, in fact, if it is to remain competitive in the civilian world market.

This final decade of the century is a historic and unique period for American foreign, military, and industrial policies. With sufficient wisdom and planning and courage, the United States just might be able to improve its national and economic security dramatically. The choice is ours.

Notes

1. U.S. Department of Defense, "FY 1994 Defense Budget Begins New Era," Press release, Washington, D.C., March 27, 1993, 10:00 AM EST, p. 1. See also "Annual Report to the President and the Congress," U.S. Dept. of Defense Washington, D.C., January 1994.

2. Ronald V. Dellums et al., eds., *Defense Sense: The Search for a Rational Military Policy* (Cambridge, Mass.: Ballinger, 1983). See also P. F. Walker, "A Post-Bush Military Budget," *Peace Dividend* 3, no. 1 (January 1993): 2–3, 5.

3. See David M. Shribman, "Power Pendulum: It's Swinging Faster Than Ever," *Boston Sunday Globe*, February 9, 1997, pp. D1, D3.

4. This is argued, for example, in Cecil V. Crabb Jr., and Pat M. Holt in *Invitation to Struggle: Congress, the President and Foreign Policy*, 2d ed. (Washington, D.C.: Congressional Quarterly, 1984). "As the presidency of the Great Communicator, Ronald Reagan, illustrated, the chief executive is in a unique position to inform the American people about major diplomatic issues and to elicit their support in behalf of foreign policies and programs advocated by the White House." (p. 245) And Senator Patrick Leahy of Vermont has pointed to the difficulty of making foreign policy on Capitol Hill: "Using the power of the purse to stop an undeclared war is just too difficult." Quoted in Christopher J. Deering, "Congress, the President, and Military Policy," in Roger H. Davidson, ed., *Congress and the Presidency: Invitation to Struggle* (Philadelphia: American Academy of Political and Social Science, 1988), p. 147.

5. Quoted in Louis Fisher, *The Politics of Shared Power: Congress and the Executive*, 2d ed. (Washington, D.C.: Congressional Quarterly, 1987), p. 1.

6. For additional sources on the historic and complex debate over balance of power, see, for example, Nelson W. Polsby, *Congress and the Presidency*, 3d ed. (Englewood Cliffs, N.J.: Prentice-Hall, 1976). Also *Power in Congress: Who Has It; How They Got It; How They Use It* (Washington, D.C.: Congressional Quarterly, 1987).

7. "FY 1994 Defense Budget," p. 1.

8. Ibid., p. 3.

9. Reuter Transcript Report, "Defense Secretary Les Aspin Address at the Annual U.S. Air Force Senior Statesman Symposium," Washington, D.C., June 24, 1993. The week before Aspin spoke of "regional aggressors" during a major address at the National Defense University.

10. Author's notes of August 18 and 19, 1993, meetings.

11. Defense Budget Project, "A Quick Look at the Bottom-Up Review: Analysis and Questions," Washington, D.C., September 1, 1993. Author's notes from press conference, Defense Budget Project, Washington, D.C., September 14, 1993.

12. See, for example, a January 28, 1994, letter of Admiral Eugene J. Carroll Jr., director of the Center for Defense Information, to Chairman Ronald V. Dellums calling for hearings on the BUR in order to expose "the many dangers and excesses of a two-war strategy." Also a January 31, 1994, letter of Congresswoman Elizabeth Furse to President Clinton decrying his proposed $3 billion increase in defense spending for FY 1995.

13. Author's notes, Armed Services Committee hearing, February 2, 1994. See also follow-on hearings on March 10, 1994, before the House Armed Services Committee.

14. Comptroller of the Department of Defense, Letter to Chairman Ronald V. Dellums, August 16, 1994; and appended "Defense Perspectives on the GAO Report Entitled 'Future Years Defense Program: Optimistic Estimates Lead to Billions in Overprogramming.'" Congressional Budget Office, Letter by Robert D. Reischauer, CBO Director, to Alice M. Rivlin, Acting Director, Office of Management and Budget, on "direct spending implications of S. 2182, the National Defense Authorization Act for Fiscal Year 1995," dated September 20, 1994.

    See also Senator Sam Nunn's introductory statement at hearings with John Hamre: "At the same time that some of us are urging the administration to find money for defense and saying we're cutting defense too far too fast, a majority of the Congress is voting to cut the discretionary budget for deficit reduction, to cut the discretionary budget to fund the crime bill, and not to touch the entitlement programs that are the real source of our fiscal problems. So the administration's in a Catch-22. Congress is in a Catch-22. We're all in this defense drawdown together, and in my opinion the budget is underfunded." Transcript, hearing of the Senate Armed Services Committee, "Future Defense Programs," September 20, 1994.

15. See Sections 121, "Nuclear Aircraft Carrier Program," and 127, "Naval Amphibious Ready Groups," in U.S. House of Representatives, "National Defense Authorization Act for Fiscal Year 1995, Conference Report to Accompany S. 2182," Report 103–701, Washington, D.C., August 12, 1994, pp. 21–24.

16. Internal memorandum, "Bottom-Up Review Implications for U.S. Defense Posture," September 10, 1993, p. 1.

17. Ibid.

18. Section 124, "Prohibition on Trident II Backfit"; Section 231, "Compliance of Ballistic Missile Defense Systems and Components with ABM Treaty"; and Section 1509, "Negotiation of Limitations on Nuclear Weapons Testing," U.S. House of Representatives, "National Defense Authorization Act for Fiscal Year 1995," pp. 22, 38–39, and 265–66. Section 3136, "Prohibition on Research and Development of Low-Yield Nuclear Weapons." U.S. House of Representatives, "National Defense Authorization Act for Fiscal Year 1994, Conference Report to Accompany H.R. 2401." Report 103–357.

Washington, D.C., November 10, 1993, p. 408. See also accompanying report language.

The editorial in *Defense News* of September 5–11, 1994, was entitled "Adieu to Bottom-Up."

19. See Section 3136, "Prohibition of Research and Development of Low-Yield Nuclear Weapons," pp. 408, 840–41. This section was primarily the work of Congresswoman Elizabeth Furse and Chairman Ron Dellums.

20. Section 124, "Prohibition on Trident II Backfit," and Section 231, "Compliance of Ballistic Missile Defense Systems and Components with ABM Treaty," pp. 22, 38–40, 627–40. Congressman Peter DeFazio was instrumental in the Trident issue while Chairman Dellums sponsored the ABM restriction.

21. Quoted in Lora Lumpe, "Bill Clinton's America: Arms Merchant to the World," *The Nonviolent Activist* (May–June 1995): 3.

22. Figures are cited in a P. F. Walker keynote address, "Defense in Search of Guidance: From Base Force to Option C to Bottom-Up Review," Annual meeting of the Defense Budget Project, Washington, D.C., April 12, 1994.

23. Letters from Howard M. Fish, chairman of ALESA, to Defense Secretary Les Aspin, October 15, 1993, and to Chairman Ronald V. Dellums, October 18, 1993.

24. Barbara Opall, "Pentagon Uses Loophole to Gain Edge in Foreign Sales," *Defense News*, August 29–September 4, 1994, p. 22.

25. Paul F. Walker, memo on "Arms Transfer Panel," House Armed Services Committee, January 5, 1994. Letter of Congressman Tom Andrews to Chairman Ronald V. Dellums, February 2, 1994. Letter of Ronald V. Dellums to Congressman Tom Andrews, February 16, 1994.

26. Paul F. Walker, Memorandum to Chairman Ronald V. Dellums, "Possible Amendments to DoD FY95 Regarding Arms Trade," April 13, 1994.

27. Joel Johnson, a chief lobbyist for the weapons industry, quoted in Lumpe, "Bill Clinton's America."

28. Most recent figures are taken from congressional testimony, "FY 1999 Defense Budget," William J. Lynn, Undersecretary of Defense (Comptroller), February 1998.

29. See Title XIII in *National Defense Authorization Act for FY 1994*, Conference Report to Accompany H.R. 2401, November 10, 1993.

30. See Title XI, "Defense Conversion, Reinvestment, and Transition Assistance," in *National Defense Authorization Act for FY 1995*, Conference Report to Accompany S. 2182, August 12, 1994, and Title XIII in *National Defense Authorization Act for FY 1994*.

31. See *National Defense Authorization Act for Fiscal Year 1996*, Conference Report to Accompany S.1124, January 22, 1996, esp. Section 1081,

"National Defense Technology and Industrial Base, Defense Reinvestment, and Defense Conversion Programs." See also *National Defense Authorization Act for Fiscal Year 1997,* Conference Report to Accompany H.R. 3230, July 30, 1996.

32. The 1998 Defense Reform Initiative (DRI) reportedly proposes to move the Office of Net Assessment out of the Pentagon to the National Defense University; this move, essentially downgrading a key office of threat evaluation, appears highly questionable.

33. Budget authority requests (billions) for FY 99: $270.6; FY 00: $275.9; FY 01: $283.8; FY 02: $287.1; and FY 03: $297.1. (National Defense Topline, function 050, including Department of Energy and other related spending.) "FY 1999 Defense Budget," February 1998.

34. See, for example, Congressional Budget Office estimates for FY 1999 deficits, which were $204 billion in January 1994, $253 billion in January 1995, $219 billion in January 1996, $147 billion in January 1997, and an amazing $2 billion in January 1998. Cited in Allen Schick, Congressional Research Service, "The Fiscal Year 1999 Budget: Balancing the Federal Budget—Options and Implications," February 3, 1998.

III

The Consequences of Defense Industry Consolidation

6

Private Arsenals: America's Post–Cold War Burden

HARVEY M. SAPOLSKY AND EUGENE GHOLZ

THE UNITED STATES needs to restructure its defense industry. As a nation we have to consider again what part of the defense business is appropriately public and what is appropriately private. We need to find a way to eliminate the excess weapons production capacity that overhangs the defense sector and that distorts defense spending. And we have to plan for the long-term stability of the sector rather than focusing on short-term budget opportunities, imaginary mobilization requirements, and politically expedient campaigns for acquisition reforms. During the course of the Cold War, the balance between public and private facilities in the weapons acquisition process shifted overwhelmingly to favor companies. The post–Cold War reality is such that we need to redesign the system for weapons research, development, and production to give government more control over what weapons are acquired.

The Cold War is over. We just fought and won a war that ran for more than 40 years and that cost in excess of $13 trillion. At the end of wars the United States customarily demobilizes. Civilian contractors, brought in to help produce desperately needed military equipment, shift back to commercial production as the war money dries up.[1] Historically, the nurturing of military-unique technologies, to the extent that it did occur between wars, was done mostly in government-owned arsenals and shipyards. The pattern was short, sharp spikes in funding for wars followed by long periods of minuscule budgets. This is what happened during and after the Civil War and during and after World War I. It also seemed likely to happen during and after World War II— but for the initiation of the Cold War.

The Cold War was different. It was long, not short, and it brought with it a ton of money. To be sure, there were cycles in Cold War budgets for defense—the peaks being the Korean War, the Vietnam War, and the Reagan buildup. But the budget range was narrow, roughly between $400 billion and $250 billion (in fiscal year [FY] 1998 dollars). The contractors found plenty of business. Hardly any wanted to or were compelled to go back to civilian production. Instead, during the cyclic downturns, we closed the arsenals, shifting more business to the contractors, who were politically more influential than were the managers and employees of the public facilities.[2]

A variety of rationales have been offered for the shift of weapons design and production to the private sector. Industry was said to be more responsive to the armed services than were the arsenals; industrial workforces were believed to be more flexible than public workforces; it was possible for the contractors to pay higher salaries than the civil service and thus to attract the really top scientists and engineers to defense work. It is hard to tell which, if any, of these rationales were true, but it is clear that a number of government facilities were closed before the recent rounds of base closures. The Watertown Arsenal that made cannons is now the Arsenal Mall and features 50 of the nation's favorite retailers. Some of the best views of Boston harbor are from the apartments and office buildings at the former Boston Naval Shipyard— once famous for its rope works and as the source of the sailors who roamed Scully Square. In effect, the current debate about government facilities, particularly aircraft repair depots, concerns the fate of only the residual of the government's arsenal system: a few large laboratories, five or six depots, and a handful of public shipyards.[3]

The problem now is that the Cold War is over. It is time to cut back, but unlike the end of previous wars, now we have to deal with a network of private contractors who have taken the place of the arsenals. As Don K. Price so eloquently stated more than 40 years ago when he described the contract state that developed after World War II, there has been a blending of the public and the private in the nation's acquisition of weapons. The government has become the entrepreneur, absorbing the financial risks of technological change normally left to firms in a free-enterprise economy.[4] In turn, government has become dependent on private contractors for most of the military-technical skills that we need to nurture until the next big war. The established acquisition pattern that keeps private contractors willing to maintain our edge in military technology is the large production run of a weapons system. Contractors never have made much money on research and development (R&D) efforts; in fact, they sometimes have lost a great deal—for example, during the 1980s when fixed-price development contracts were in vogue.[5] But even losing money on those contracts in the 1980s did not hurt the majority of firms, because they were making profits on the booming production side of the business.[6]

Now, however, the weapons inventories are bulging. We own 7,500 first-line fighters, but the air force and navy field only about 3,000. We have 8,000 M-1 tanks. The army has six heavy divisions, each with no more than 300 tanks; the marines have the need for another division's worth. Seven times 300 is 2,100 tanks. Without building any new ones, there are obviously plenty of tanks left over for the National Guard, war attrition, and various predeployment options. It makes no strategic sense to support American armored vehicle manufacturers with additional production contracts.

The production capacity overhang is huge. We have eight lines producing military aircraft, six private yards building large warships, five helicopter companies totally dependent on military purchases, and four missile manufacturers. Despite cutbacks, our military's force structure remains large. Leftover Cold War equipment obviates requirements for new weapons production, so new contracts should not absorb the output of the production capacity we have on hand. Once we relied on arsenals to preserve weapons skills in times of low demand. Their technical workforces were paid no matter the production rate—which sometimes was zero. Private enterprise, however, will lobby to maintain multibillion-dollar production contracts—a very expensive way for the government to maintain weapons technologies and skills. This is our defense industry burden.

The Happy Solutions

Some argue that the widely discussed mergers among defense firms already are solving the capacity overhang and that the problem can be left to market forces for a solution.[7] But in actuality, the mergers are not helping. Lockheed, which was a builder of military aircraft and missiles, acquired the military aircraft business of General Dynamics in 1993 and then merged with Martin Marietta, a missile manufacturer, in 1995, forming Lockheed Martin. This firm subsequently acquired Loral, an assembly of a large number of defense electronics companies, and Northrop Grumman, the combination of two famous aircraft manufacturers but also a firm that had acquired significant involvement in defense electronics. Before the mergers, the components of Lockheed Martin independently operated six military aircraft lines (a line being a facility assembling one or more aircraft types—the F-16, the C-130, etc.).

Today, after all the mergers, Lockheed Martin still operates six military aircraft lines. There are fewer defense companies, but the same number of lines.[8] Some of Lockheed Martin's space business has been consolidated—business units that face commercial buyers in addition to the military monopsony and hence have reason to rationalize.[9] But on the defense side, the much-discussed synergies between the electronics and platform components of the new conglomerate are restricted by an antitrust agreement that prevents full communication between the two sides of Lockheed Martin's business.[10] Although there have been some cuts in middle management and consolidation of headquarters, the formation of Lockheed Martin has not significantly improved the efficiency of weapons production.

Another merger offers us an understanding of the likely rationale behind the apparent defense industry consolidation. General Dynamics, which builds submarines at its Electric Boat division in Connecticut, bought another warship maker, the Bath Iron Works in Maine, but neither Bath nor Electric Boat is slated to close. This acquisition was justified on financial grounds: because of the post–Cold War politics of warship production, Bath is essentially guaranteed at least one destroyer contract a year in perpetuity—an assured income stream for General Dynamics.[11] The acquisition price for the Bath yard was less than the present value of that income stream, so investing in the Maine yard was a low-risk, financially profitable venture for General Dynamics. Recently General Dynamics also bought National Steel and Shipbuilding Company, a West Coast builder of naval supply ships, giving the firm three of the six privately held naval shipbuilding yards. Three weak shipyards, each dependent on a political subsidy to stay in business, have joined forces—displaying a clear vision of the post–Cold War defense politics. A consolidation-oriented, capacity-reducing merger would look very different, with a strong company buying a weaker one in order to shutter its competing plant space.[12]

The merger politics shows that James Kurth's theory of the "follow-on imperative" was misapplied to the Cold War. Kurth argued that contractor lobbyists combined with a Pentagon interest in maintaining a reliable stable of weapons suppliers to form a procurement system in which new contracts were allocated to firms just in time to replace old contracts whose production runs were winding down. According to Kurth, the comfortable business-government relationship prevented any military suppliers from closing down.[13] In reality, however, during the Cold War a genuine concern with a strategic threat limited the political ability to allocate contracts; while many firms did receive follow-on contracts, as enumerated by Kurth, many others did not.[14] In fact, it is the post–Cold War era, where politics are not constrained by threat, that is dominated by the follow-on contract.

Many production lines closed during the Cold War. None has closed in the years since its end. For Cold War closures, remember such aircraft producers as Fairchild, Republic, Rockwell, Vought, Martin, and Curtiss-Wright and shipbuilders such as New York Shipyard, General Dynamics' Quincy yard, and Todd Shipyards. None is a prime today, and most have lost their independence. Curtiss, for example, was the second-biggest manufacturing firm in the United States during World War II. It made fighter and transport aircraft, aircraft engines, and propellers. Today it has a few hundred million dollars in sales and makes a limited line of aircraft components. The key to its demise, which occurred during the very busy 1950s when every other weapons producer was going flat out, was that the firm annoyed its principal—essentially only—customers, the air force and the navy.

No matter how it is described, the defense business is not private enterprise, even when direct ownership of the productive capacity is in private hands. The government, specifically the military and Congress, is the market for the defense industries. When the military is politically strong, as when the nation feels a threat to national security, it has the ability to choose which contractors it likes, to reward them, and to squeeze their competitors out of the business. Now, however, after the collapse of the Soviet Union, the political balance within the government customer has shifted to favor Congress, which is concerned with district-level employment economics. Congress buys weapons in response to defense firms' lobbying; unnecessary production facilities receive support in order to prop up district employment.[15] Defense has become a jobs program.

Converting defense plants to commercial production is not the answer either. It is here that an important distinction needs to be made between the big final assembly plants of the prime contractors and the component plants of smaller defense companies. Many Cold War subcontractors, including some sophisticated, first-tier suppliers such as General Electric, always integrated defense with commercial business or at least have redeployed their assets on that model in the past five years.[16] These firms are taking care of themselves, perhaps with the transition smoothed by some of the limited government funding support provided for defense conversion.[17] Too small and too weak politically to try a nonmarket strategy, small defense companies already have moved into the post–Cold War era.

The prime contractors, on the other hand, followed a different Cold War business model, which has led them to a different post–Cold War response to reduced international tension. They dealt directly with the government on big projects that are long lived and very visible politically. Their influence is compounded by the concentration of employment in final assembly operations, often with 10,000 or more workers in a single facility. In Russia, large defense facilities faced pent-up demand for consumer goods and have in some cases successfully converted to production of milking machines or diapers; however, there are no comparable areas of shortage in the American economy. But because of their political visibility, prime contractors have an attractive alternative to desperation efforts to convert to commercial production—lobbying for continuing contracts.[18]

Today, with very few exceptions, commercial market potential for the largest defense companies looks truly bleak.[19] As an example sector, it was once the case that conversion opportunities were considered relatively good in the shipbuilding industry.[20] In the military market that defense firms are used to, unit prices are extremely high. Nearly every combatant costs $1 billion. Many are more expensive. American yards did not build large commercial ships after subsidies were withdrawn in the early 1980s. Instead, they constructed the 600-ship navy. Today there is a market for commercial ships, but not of the billion-dollar variety. The world needs product tankers that sell for only $40 million each; Newport News Shipbuilders is making some with a purchase loan subsidy, but not nearly enough to replace the two $4 billion plus aircraft carriers they now have in the yard.[21] Not surprisingly, then, Newport News continues to lobby hard for new aircraft carrier contracts—and recently has been blessed by Congress, over the navy's objections, with a new contract to build a new class of nuclear attack submarine.

Acquisition reform is the Clinton administration's favorite alternative to restructuring the defense sector. However, such reform will not help, and in fact it is likely to hurt. Some acquisition changes, of course, are desirable. During the 1980s the Democratic-controlled Congress could not confront President Reagan directly over his popular but very expensive defense buildup. Instead, it attempted to hobble the buildup through regulation. Democrats argued that they were not opposed to defense spending per se but that they did oppose waste, fraud, and abuse in defense contracting. Even some Republicans joined this bandwagon so that they could point out that they did not vote blindly for defense. Protection against waste, fraud, and abuse became the justification for literally dozens of laws requiring contract reviews, rewards for whistle blowing, social engineering through contracting, audits, and more audits.[22] It is appropriate for a Democratic administration and a Republican Congress to recognize the burden that these laws place on the government and seek their repeal, if only selectively.[23]

But there is another side to acquisition reform. The administration strongly promotes dual-use technology and advocates eliminating unique production standards that make defense purchases costly. It wants to speed up the development cycle so as to make the acquisition process efficient.[24] This defense policy answer is wrong. Cutting cost at the margin is not going to change the overall defense budget situation much, if at all. Implicitly or explicitly, support for acquisition reform from the military services and from defense contractors is premised on the expectation that lower unit weapons costs will lead not to a reduction in the budget but rather to an expansion of demand for weapons— or, at the very least, procurement supporters hope that the budget cutters will split the windfall with them. Yet if new destroyers were to cost 10 percent less, say, $855 million instead of $950 million each, would we buy more of them? If the savings did not go to buy more destroyers, would the money stay in the shipbuilding account, go to other navy purchases, or even remain in the defense budget? Each alternative seems uncertain—if not downright unlikely. With only slim chances to capture the savings, no defense policy actor will be the long-term political advocate for the reforms.

In the shorter term, what the acquisition reform rhetoric allows is for politicians to give the illusion that they are making a cost-effective investment in the nation's future national security. The participation of the F-22 program office in the air force's "Lean Aircraft Initiative," which claims that acquisition reform and new manufacturing techniques will substantially reduce unit costs, is a leading example of the political cover that acquisition reform provides to some very expensive programs.[25] America's F-15s, F-16s, and F-18s are already better than anyone else's fighters, and with the end of the Cold War the doubts about the value added of new systems, such as the F-22 and the proposed Joint Strike Fighter, are growing. Unfortunately for acquisition reform, a standard congressional reaction to political uncertainty is to slow down production rates, which limits real savings from new efficiencies.[26] Meanwhile, there is a risk that the pro-efficiency advocates of acquisition reform will give defense contractors and procurement bureaucrats the political capital and Congress the political will to purchase unneeded, expensive weapons systems—at those uneconomically slow rates. The illusion of a bargain can be powerful incentive to buy.

The other purported benefit of acquisition reform, speeding up the development cycle, makes even less sense. The hopeful belief is that if we move fast, we can overcome the political uncertainty that besets weapons projects.[27] Some think that once politicians show an interest in a new aircraft, we need to build it before they change their minds. Unfortunately, there is no way to beat the political decision cycle. It is physically impossible to build weapons systems faster than politicians can manipulate budget priorities. Worse, by accelerating projects, we increase technological uncertainty. Compressing development times, trimming test schedules, and the like is a formula for guaranteeing performance shortfalls and cost overruns.[28] And the frequent threat—if we do not do a better job of plugging the latest "commercial off-the-shelf" electronics into our weapons, we will field obsolete systems—is a hollow one, because none of our military competitors implements the upgrades any faster than we do. Our weapons system computers do not need to compete in benchmark tests with the latest commercially available models; they compete in combat with the adversary's military computer systems. In fact, a bigger risk than falling technologically behind is that an unexplored incompatibility or another technological difficulty with midproduction or postdeployment tinkering with weapons designs will generate unexpected, dangerous performance failures.

Instead of accelerating development cycles, we need to slow them down. That we can afford to go slow is one of the benefits of the end of the Cold War. Instead of moving faster, we need to do more experimentation and stretch the work. Instead of increasing the technological risks, we ought to reduce them.

From Pork to Spam

If mergers are not helping, if conversion offers little hope, and if acquisition reform will only make matters worse, what are we to do? To begin with, we need to recognize what the contractors are, in fact, doing. They are doing what they do quite well. They are lobbying to keep the lines running, if only slowly. Extended production runs of mature systems are the cash cows of the defense industry, with great profit potential for the companies. Politically, their lobbying efforts resonate, because the lines represent big lumps of employment.[29] Congress has responded by adding money for a few more F-15s and B-2s to the defense budget, not to mention certain ship types.[30]

With the Cold War over, it is easier and easier for representatives and senators, Republicans and Democrats, to ignore service preferences and Department of Defense (DoD) plans.[31] Lines slated to be closed are being kept open. Ships scheduled to be built later are being moved up. And with these quite understandable political maneuvers, the opportunity to do new things, to prepare for the wars of the future, and to keep our technological edge disappears. Production funding threatens to crowd R&D out of the defense budget. Under the DoD's projected budget ceiling, adding up the already-promised spending on major systems production in the next decade leaves no room for an R&D budget.

Lobbying no doubt adds to the defense budget.[32] As Table 6–1 indicates, the recent defense budget cuts have been the gentlest of the drawdowns, industry protestations notwithstanding. Although Congress and the president recently debated what social programs needed to be cut to help balance the federal budget, no one in Washington found the courage to point to the defense budget as a potential significant contributor to the budget-balancing effort. Instead, we are debating increasing the procurement budget to $60 billion.[33]

We need to stop avoiding the full implications of the end of the Cold War. We need a plan. Contractor capacity has to shrink; if the production lines continue to be fed with production contracts, there will be no room in the budget to fund force structure and, more likely, to fund the readiness and research budgets. All that protects readiness today is a religion born of the "hollow military" era of the late 1970s, when we were still directly threatened by the Soviet Union. Prominent columnists already are starting to join industry leaders in questioning readiness funding in the face of a supposed need for equipment modernization.[34] As much as the services desire to be prepared to fight, their readiness beliefs will not be enough to give them the necessary resources unless they advocate an explicit policy to close lines, to pay off workers and communities, and to do away with the fiction that the market will take care of excess capacity. What is needed is the kind of planning that naval historian Gary Weir describes the navy doing in his study of submarine construction after World War I.[35] The submariners built no new boats for seven years, but they kept the technology developing. They forced the closure of the Lake Boat Company in order to keep Electric Boat alive, because Electric Boat had the better facility, if not the better reputation. Then, in order to keep Electric Boat focused, they developed submarine construction capacity at Portsmouth Naval Shipyard in New Hampshire. During the 1920s and early 1930s, submariners brought in foreign component technology and worked on their offensive doctrine and new submarine designs. What came out of this work was the effective fleet boat of World War II and the strategy that helped defeat Japan.[36]

Of course, times are different now. The legal and political obstacles for officers acting to protect the national interest are many, and the political incentives in the absence of a strong overseas threat work against them. But the services have the responsibility for maintaining national

Table 6–1   Defense Drawdowns, Gross Domestic Product (%), and Constant 1996 $ (in Billions)

	Peak		Low Point		Difference	Average Yearly Change
World	1944	39.3%	1948	3.70%	35.6%	−8.90%
War II	1945	$753.50	1948	$57.50	$695.90	−$232.00
Korea	1953	14.5%	1956	10.20%	4.3%	−1.43%
	1953	$316.00	1956	$243.90	$72.10	−$24.00
Vietnam	1968	9.6%	1978	4.80%	4.8%	−0.48%
	1968	$358.00	1976	$231.30	$126.70	−$15.80
Current	1986	6.5%	1997	3.30%	2.9%	−0.26%
	1989	$355.90	1996	$254.30	$101	−$14.50

Source: 1998 Budget of the United States (Washington, D.C.: Government Printing Office, 1997).

security. The new missions being offered the military are not likely to generate support sufficient to sustain vital technologies. The services have to decide what is important for the long haul and work to protect it. Their political capital is not insubstantial. They have to forge the structure that will protect vital technical and production resources.

Cutting the active forces is not likely to be enough. Cutting DoD infrastructure already seems a dead end. The services have to decide on the private and public skills necessary to keep our military edge and fight to keep them healthy. This means getting rid of unneeded production capacity and protecting vital design teams and facilities.[37]

To give perspective on the problem, Table 6–2 lists the employment levels for the military, DoD civilians, and defense contractors for four key fiscal years: 1966, near the peak of the Vietnam War; 1976, the low point of Cold War budgets; 1986, the high point of the Reagan buildup; and 1997, the most recent year with published figures in all categories. As the table indicates, defense employment cuts to date have been focused on the services and public arsenals. Since Vietnam more than 400,000 wage board (arsenal-type) jobs have been eliminated from the government even though overall DoD civilian employment has dropped by only 150,000. What we have done is substituted contract managers for machinists. Nearly 750,000 service personnel slots have been eliminated since the end of the Cold War. But most striking of all has been how little contractor employment has fallen. It is still almost 400,000 over its Cold War low in 1976. This is where most restructuring needs to occur.

Table 6–2   U.S. Defense Employment by Sector (in Thousands)

	FY 66	FY 76	FY 86	FY 97
Military Active Duty	3,094	2,082	2,233	1,450[a]
DoD Civilian	1,093	959	1,027	800[a]
Defense-related				
Private Industry	2,640	1,690	3,315	2,100[b]

[a] "QDR: Shaping the Force of the Future," *Defense*, no. 4 (1997): 21.
[b] Paul Kaminski (undersecretary of defense), letter, *Issues in Science and Technology* (Spring 1997): 13.
Source: Harlan K. Ullman, *In Irons: U.S. Military Might in the New Century* (Washington, D.C.: NDU Press, 1995), pp. 169–70.

We offer a two-step proposal. First, pay the bill. It is time to buy out the excess capacity and get on with the task of preparing for the future. The existing pro-merger policy of the Department of Defense has been only partially effective: it has encouraged corporate mergers without plant-level restructuring or capacity consolidation. The truly bad news is that the merger policy is increasingly hobbled by political opposition.[38] Congress narrowly rejected language attached to the FY 1997 appropriations bill that would have ended the department's ability to pay restructuring costs for merged companies closing plants; the political environment certainly would block a major government restructuring payment. Defense policy is back to the Bush administration mantra: verbally encourage mergers, but "let the market decide" the ultimate configuration of the industry. The trouble with this policy is that the defense industry is not governed by normal, competitive market forces. Plants that would otherwise be forced to close, either via bankruptcy or a postmerger consolidation, can be kept open by aggressive lobbying, circumventing the market mechanism.

A simple, properly designed subsidy to plant-level restructuring would provide a ready solution to this market failure. Somehow, though, the idea of paying an exit subsidy to defense contractors has been politically branded as a cash handout to influential companies—a form of corporate welfare. The real welfare going on, however, is the continuing production contracts, which are much more expensive than an exit subsidy in the long run, because production requires the purchase of material inputs and the sustainment of high overhead on substantial overcapacity.

The flaw that explains the political demise of the Clinton administration's merger policy is its failure to do enough for workers and communities. Payments for restructuring charges mostly went to company coffers, leaving workers and local officials with an incentive to lobby against plant closings and against the merger policy.[39] Congressional hearings were called in the summer of 1994 by Democratic Representative Lynn Schenk, in whose San Diego district the merger policy helped close the General Dynamics missile plant. It was exactly this issue, protection of the defense workers, that she raised—an issue that could be better addressed by an expansion of the restructuring policy than by its termination. The government already pays both military personnel and civil service workers to leave the federal payroll. It is time also to pay the civilian defense workers and their communities compensation to leave the very same payroll.[40]

Fortunately, the size of the bonus payments required to encourage workers need not be too large.[41] We have recent experience in negotiating the value of defense-related property through the base closing process. Private companies offer incentives to encourage voluntary separation of redundant employees in place of mass firings—at affordable costs.[42] Furthermore, even if we had to agree to pay the workers from plants closed by the proposed merger policy their full salaries for a long or indefinite period of time, a true worst-case scenario, savings would accrue to the defense budget owing to reductions in materials, manufacturing, and overhead costs. During the Cold War, we habitually front-loaded procurement spending based on claims about long-term savings. That practice seems to have survived unmodified into post–Cold War defense programming, but a minor modification would allow us to front-load real savings by paying exit subsidies to close excess capacity.[43]

The second major step we propose for defense procurement is to try to build the equivalent of a public arsenal system even while defense firms remain nominally private. Instead of forcing the system to develop big projects, we should arrange for technological experimentation that is financially worthwhile for private firms. There is no need for a continuous re-outfitting of the entire American military, but there is one for continuous research and prototyping. Our present acquisition policies reward long production runs; historically, production contracts have been the only profitable phase of the defense business for private contractors. A new institutional design, appropriate for a "private arsenal system" for the post–Cold War world, would award contracts with fair rates of return on R&D alone. Follow-on, large-scale production contracts would be the exception rather than the expectation.

In summary, the war is over. Budgets are being absorbed in producing wasteful pork. R&D, force structure, and readiness accounts will all suffer as pressure mounts to cut the overall defense budget, because procurement spending remains at Cold War levels owing to political influences. The services have the responsibility, if not the authority, to shape a reasonable long-term industrial policy for defense. A well-designed, broadly inclusive, pro-consolidation merger policy would enable political support for the elimination of defense industry overcapacity, thereby reducing budgetary rigidities. It is time to begin the serious planning for an uncertain future.

Notes

1. Merritt Roe Smith, "Military Arsenals and Industry Before World War I," in Benjamin Franklin Cooling, ed., *War Business and American Society: Historical Perspectives on the Military-Industrial Complex* (Port Washington, N.Y.: Kennikort Press, 1977); 36–37.

2. William B. Burnett and Frederic M. Scherer, "The Weapons Industry," in Walter Adams, ed., *The Structure of American Industry* (New York: Macmillan, 1990).

3. "Perry Touts Kelly Privatization," *San Antonio Express-News,* January 30, 1996, p. 1; Defense Conversion Commission, Dept. of Defense (DoD) Publ. *Adjusting to the Drawdown,* Washington, D.C., December 31, 1992; "Perry Supports End to 60-40 Split for Depot Work," *Defense Daily,* April 28, 1995, p. 137; Congressional Budget Office, *Public and Private Roles in Maintaining Military Equipment at the Depot Level* (Washington, D.C.: July 1995).

4. Don K. Price, *Government and Science* (New York: New York University Press, 1954). Also Don K. Price, *The Scientific Estate* (Cambridge, Mass.: Harvard University Press, 1965).

5. Karen W. Tyson, J. Richard Nelson, Neang I. Om, and Paul R. Palmer, *Acquiring Major Systems: Cost and Schedule Trends and Acquisition Initiative Effectiveness* (Alexandria, Va.: IDA, March 1989).

6. Ellen M. Pint and Rachel Schmidt, *Financial Condition of U.S. Military Aircraft Prime Contractors,* RAND Project, Air Force, 1994 Santa Monica, Calif. (Booklet).

7. See Sandra Meadows, "Defense Acquisition, Merger Players Shift into Overdrive," *National Defense* (February 1996): 37; David Morrison, "Eat or Be Eaten," *National Journal,* March 6, 1993, p. 559; Jon Kutler, "Merger Pace Will Continue," *Defense News,* November 27–December 3, 1995, p. 19. Fears are starting to appear about the consequences of the mergers for innovation and competition. See David A. Fulghum, "Defense Planners Wary of Mergers," *Aviation Week & Space Technology,* September 29, 1997, pp. 31–32.

8. Employment levels did not change either as a result of the merger. Bill Torpy, "Workers Hope the Deal Will Improve the Company," *Atlanta Journal and Constitution,* August 31, 1994, p. E1. Also "Martin-Lockheed Merger Prompts Cautious Optimism," *Denver Post,* August 31, 1994, p. B6.

9. Jeff Cole, "Loral Sets Pact to Sell AT&T New Satellites," *Wall Street Journal,* May 18, 1995, p. A4. Jeff Cole, "Hughes Plans Major Contract for McDonnell" *Wall Street Journal,* May 18, 1995, p. A4.

10. Author interview with anonymous source. Also Jeff Cole, "McDonnell Plans to Shift Its Purchases," *Wall Street Journal,* April 18, 1996, p. A3.

11. Robert George, "Maine Shipyard Faces Uncertainty," *Boston Globe,* January 21, 1996. The uncertainty stems from the announcement of the state senior senator, Bill Cohen, a member of the Senate's Armed Services Committee, of his retirement. See also Byron Callan, "General Dynamics: What Acquisition Risk? BIW Deal a Plus," *Merrill Lynch Report,* August 28, 1995; and Stan Crock, "General Dynamics Sounds the Charge," *Business Week,* May 19, 1997, pp. 136–37.

12. For useful overview of the industry and its plans, see Vincent P. Grimes, "Navy Budget Woes May Force Wave of Industry Downsizing," *National Defense* (December 1996): 20–23.

13. Two recent versions of the "follow-on imperative" thesis have appeared: James R. Kurth, "The Military-Industrial Complex Revisited," in J. Krusel, ed., *American Defense Annual, 1989–1990,* pp. 195–226 (Lexington, Mass.: Lexington Books, 1989), and James Kurth, "The Follow-on Imperative in American Weapons Procurement, 1960–90," in Jurgen Brauer and Manas Chatterji, eds., *Economic Issues of Disarmament,* pp. 304–21 (New York: New York University Press, 1993).

14. Eugene Gholz, "The Pattern of Cold War Defense Procurement: Theory Testing Using the Case of the Curtiss Wright Corporation," in review.

15. Congressional attention to American defense industry employment recently has been apparent in attempts to legislate restrictions on offset agreements by which prime contractors promise to arrange for purchases by American firms (often but not always the primes themselves) from foreign companies as part of arms export sales agreements. Allan Gerson, "Congress Scrutinizes Offsets," *Defense News,* April 8–14, 1996, p. 20.

16. Maryellen R. Kelley and Todd A. Watkins, "In from the Cold: Prospects for Conversion of the Defense Industrial Base," *Science,* April 28, 1995, pp. 525–32.

17. Michael Oden, Ann Markusen, Dan Flaming, and Mark Drayse, Post–Cold War Frontiers: Defense Downsizing and Conversion in Los Angeles, Rutgers Center for Urban Policy Research Working Paper Number 105, 1996.

18. Alex Berenson, "Firms Protected in Defense Cuts," *Denver Post,* September 31, 1994, p. A17.

19. Greg Bischak, *US Conversion after the Cold War, 1990–1997: Lessons for Forging a New Conversion Policy* (Bonn: Bonn International Center for Conversion, July 1997).

20. Conversion was never predicted to be easy, but similarities to the large-scale construction industry were believed to offer hope. William R. Park

and Robert E. Roberts, *Industrial Conversion Potential in the Shipbuilding Industry* (Washington, D.C.: U.S. Arms Control and Disarmament Agency Contract No. ACDA/E-66, March 1966).

21. Author's interview with anonymous source. Also Lisa Huber, "Newport News Shipyard to Start 1st Commercial Contract Since 1979," *Journal of Commerce*, September 14, 1995, p. 1B; and Christopher Dinsmore, "Newport News Shipyard: Building for the Future," *The Virginian-Pilot & The Ledger-Star*, August 28, 1994, p. D1.

22. See Daniel Wirls, *Buildup: The Politics of Defense in the Reagan Era* (Ithaca, N.Y.: Cornell University Press, 1992).

23. United States General Accounting Office, *Acquisition Reform: Implementation of Title V of the Acquisition Reform Act of 1994* (Washington, D.C.: GAO, October 1996); Colin Clark, "DoD: Acquisition Reforms Mixed," *Defense Week*, August 25, 1997, p. 7.

24. William Perry, *Blueprint for Change* (Washington, D.C.: NTIS, 1994). Part of the intellectual base for this action can be found in John A. Alic et al., *Beyond Spinoff: Military and Commercial Technologies in a Changing World* (Boston, Mass.: Harvard Business School Press, 1992).

25. For a description of the Lean Aircraft Initiative, see Stanley W. Kandebo, "Lean Initiative Spurs Industry Transformation," *Aviation Week & Space Technology*, July 28, 1997, pp. 56–63.

26. Harvey M. Sapolsky, Eugene Gholz, and Ethan McKinney, "The Quest for Weapons Acquisition Reform," in review.

27. Interviews. See also Bill Lewandowski, "Acquisition Reform: Picking the Low Hanging Fruit," *Aerospace Industries Association Newsletter* 7, no. 7 (January/February 1995), p. 1.

28. Michael Brown, *Flying Blind: Politics of the U.S. Strategic Bomber Program* (Ithaca, N.Y.: Cornell University Press, 1992).

29. General Robert Gard Jr., USA, ret., explained, "We're not buying some of these major weapons systems because we need them. We're buying them to keep up employment in states with influential members of Congress." Quoted in Katherine Barrett and Richard Greene, "Procurement: 'Once You're Burned, You Shouldn't Be Burned for Life,'" *Financial World*, October 24, 1995, p. 49.

30. James Kitfield, "Ships Galore!" *National Journal*, February 10, 1996, pp. 298–302. John Glashow, "Extra Funds to Boost Black Hawk, F-22, Arsenal Ship," *Defense News*, February 26–March 3, 1996, p. 10.

31. "Plenty of Pork," editorial, *Washington Post*, October 9, 1997, p. 22.

32. Dwight R. Lee, "Public Goods, Politics, and Two Cheers for the Military-Industrial Complex," in R. Higgs, ed., *Arms Politics and the Economy* (New York: Holmes & Meir, 1990), pp. 22–36.

33. "Service Chiefs Split with White House on Modernization Requests," *Defense Daily*, March 14, 1996, p. 392. Sandra I. Meadows and Christopher

T. Heun, "Pentagon Weapon Spending Hits 50-Year Low, Could Exceed $68 Billion by 2002," *National Defense* (April 1997): 19–21.

34. George Melloan, "Military Readiness Borrows from the Future," *Wall Street Journal*, April 1, 1996, p. A15. Don Fuqua, "Once Again, It's Wait 'Til Next Year," *Aerospace Industry Association Newsletter* 8, no. 8 (March 1996): 3.

35. Gary E. Weir, *Building American Submarines, 1914–1940* (Washington, D.C.: Naval Historical Center, 1991). The navy seems to have done this recently for the torpedo business. "U.S. Torpedo Base Confronts No Navy Order for 25 Years," *National Defense* (November 1995): 18–19.

36. For the World War II success, see Carl Boyd and Akihiko Yoshida, *The Japanese Submarine Force and World War II* (Annapolis, Md.: Naval Institute Press, 1995). See also Mark P. Parillo, *The Japanese Merchant Marine in World War II* (Annapolis, Md.: Naval Institute Press, 1993).

37. For an early recognition of this problem, see Kenneth R. Mayer, "Combat Aircraft Production in the United States 1950–2000: Maintaining Industry Capability in an Era of Shrinking Budgets," *Defense Analysis* 9, no. 2 (1993): 159–69.

38. The policy is briefly described in Thomas E. Ricks and Joe Danson, "Defense-Industry Mergers Will Get Pentagon Support," *Wall Street Journal*, September 1, 1993, p. A16. Political opposition is apparent from U.S. General Accounting Office, *Defense Restructuring Costs: Payment Regulations Are Inconsistent with Legislation* (Washington, D.C.: GAO, August 1995).

39. John Mintz, "Union Hits Martin-Lockheed Merger," *Washington Post*, December 7, 1994, p. F3.

40. Suzanne Chapman, "Civilian Drawdown Hard and Fast," *Air Force Magazine* (January 1996): 28–31.

41. Stephen Barr, "Government Trims Downsizing Tool," *Washington Post*, December 30, 1997, p. 11.

42. Nynex is reported to have paid at the high end of severance bonus requirements at $119,000 per worker. Leslie Cauley, "Technology: Nynex, Bowing to Union, Slates Charge of $1.3 Billion for Severance Sweetener," *Wall Street Journal*, March 25, 1994, p. B2. More than 14,000 New York City employees left the payroll for just over $14,000 each in incentives. Vivian S. Toy, "For $125 Million in Case City Cedes Budget Control," *New York Times*, March 30, 1996, p. 27. Civilian DoD personnel are given $25,000; and some officer reductions were achieved with $30,000 bonuses for early separation, according to Suzanne Chapman, "Civilian Drawdown."

43. A recent example is the proposed V-22 buy. Robert Holzer, "U.S. Marines: Buy V-22s Now, Save Billions Later," *Defense News*, April 8–14, 1996, p. 12. Also Robert Holzer, "U.S. Navy Pushes for Speedier Buy of Carrier," *Defense News*, April 29–May 4, 1996, p. 26.

7

Defense Mergers: Weapons Cost, Innovation, and International Arms Industry Cooperation

ERIK PAGES

I F WE wanted to summarize the last decade in the history of the U.S. defense industry in one word, "turmoil" would fit the bill. Descending from the dizzying heights of the Reagan military buildup in 1986, to the lows of the early 1990s, to today's more stable but historically low levels of procurement spending, the American defense industry has been transformed and reshaped.

A comparison of the industry in 1986 and today presents this dramatic contrast in clear detail. In 1986 the top ten U.S. defense firms were General Dynamics, General Electric, McDonnell Douglas, Rockwell, General Motors, Lockheed, Raytheon, Boeing, United Technologies, and Grumman. In the decade since 1986, General Electric and Rockwell have divested their defense businesses, and General Dynamics has sold the core of its 1986 defense business, aircraft and missiles. Grumman was saved from near bankruptcy through a purchase from Northrop, Lockheed merged with Martin Marietta, and Boeing purchased McDonnell Douglas. While Raytheon, Boeing, and United Technologies remain in the defense business, they also have undergone dramatic transformations.

This chapter traces this revolution in the U.S. defense industry and highlights the dominant trends now impacting the industry. It also examines the U.S. government's policy toward the defense industrial base. Reacting to the Bush administration's hands-off attitude toward the defense industry, the Clinton administration assumed a more activist posture toward shaping that industry's future structure.

I argue that, despite the efforts of both industry and government to promote greater internationalization and commercialization in the defense sector, technological and political trends actually are moving in the opposite direction. Rapid consolidation is changing the U.S. defense industrial base dramatically. What will emerge over the next decade is a private "arsenal" system highly dependent on five to ten large defense conglomerates and largely closed to international cooperative efforts.

The implications of this new industry structure and direction remain largely unexamined. Ongoing programs to enhance civil-military integration and to "reinvent government" make sense for those industrial sectors with commercial counterparts. However, these new policy tools are unlikely to offer much utility when applied to large defense conglomerates producing defense-unique goods. Effectively managing these firms may require movement in the opposite direction toward a more activist government role that tightly regulates production and steers contracts based on industrial base needs as opposed to market demands.

Trends in Industry Consolidation

Flush with funds from the Carter and Reagan eras of defense buildups, the American defense industry enjoyed unparalleled "fat years" until the end of the 1980s. At that point, total defense spending was near post–World War II highs. Most important, from the defense industry's perspective, spending on procurement (in fiscal year [FY] 1987) reached its highest levels since the Korean War.

Defense spending declines actually predate the collapse of the Berlin Wall in 1989. Spending on defense began declining in 1987 and picked up speed after 1989. Current Clinton administration budget projections estimate that defense spending will have declined 37 percent between FY 1989 and FY 2000.

Critics contend that these declines in defense budgets are highly overstated.[1] Based on some measures, defense spending does appear to be artificially higher than historical averages. For example, the $260.2 billion in FY 1995 defense spending was about 13 percent higher than spending in FY 1976 and 4 percent higher than FY 1980 spending levels. In fact, overall defense budget cuts in the 1990s are of the same magnitude as those following the Vietnam War.[2]

While debates about overall defense spending levels will continue to rage, analysts generally agree that procurement accounts have faced the most drastic cutbacks and still remain underfunded. While spending on other accounts, such as operations and maintenance and personnel, has remained relatively stable, spending on new weapons systems and other purchases have faced large cuts. In post–World War II history, the period between 1985 and 1995 represents the longest consistent decline in the procurement budget of the Department of Defense (DoD).[3]

Such historically unprecedented declines in procurement spending have rocked the U.S. defense industry. Employment impacts have rightly received the highest levels of public attention. According to DoD estimates, defense-related employment is estimated to drop 39 percent between 1989 and 1997, a rate of approximately 5 percent each year. Similarly, the Bureau of Labor Statistics identified private industry job losses of 600,000 between 1987 and 1992, with another 600,000 jobs expected to disappear by 1997.

In addition to this painful human downsizing, the American defense industry has undergone dramatic structural transformations. Mergers and consolidations have been extensive, and the industry looks dramatically different from how it looked in 1986. Figure 7–1 depicts major transformations in the combat aviation industrial sector; Figure 7–2 depicts the growing value of consolidation activity in the aerospace sector.

The changes identified in Figure 7–1 are not limited to the case of combat aviation. Other major mergers include the consolidation of Northrop, Grumman, and the defense divisions of Westinghouse, and the union of FMC Corporation's Defense Systems Group and Harsco's BMY-Combat Systems Division to form a new firm, United Defense.

As a result of these mergers, the number of major prime contractors involved in various defense industrial sectors has declined precipitously. Between 1946 and 1994, the number of U.S. aircraft contractors declined from 26 to 7. Tank contractors dropped from 16 to 2 and missile contractors dropped from 22 to 9.[4] Firms like Rockwell, Curtiss-Wright, and Westinghouse, once recognized as "household names" in the defense business, have left the defense sector completely.

Consolidation and downsizing have affected smaller contractors similarly. For smaller firms, the impact of defense budget cuts has been worsened by the efforts of larger firms to cut their subcontractor base on efficiency grounds. For example, a recent survey identified cuts in the number of subcontractors on major weapons programs ranging from 50 percent to more than 80 percent.[5]

Figure 7-1 The Consolidation of U.S. Military Aircraft Manufacturers, 1945–96

Prime Contractors for Fixed-wing Fighter, Attack, and Bomber Aircraft Programs

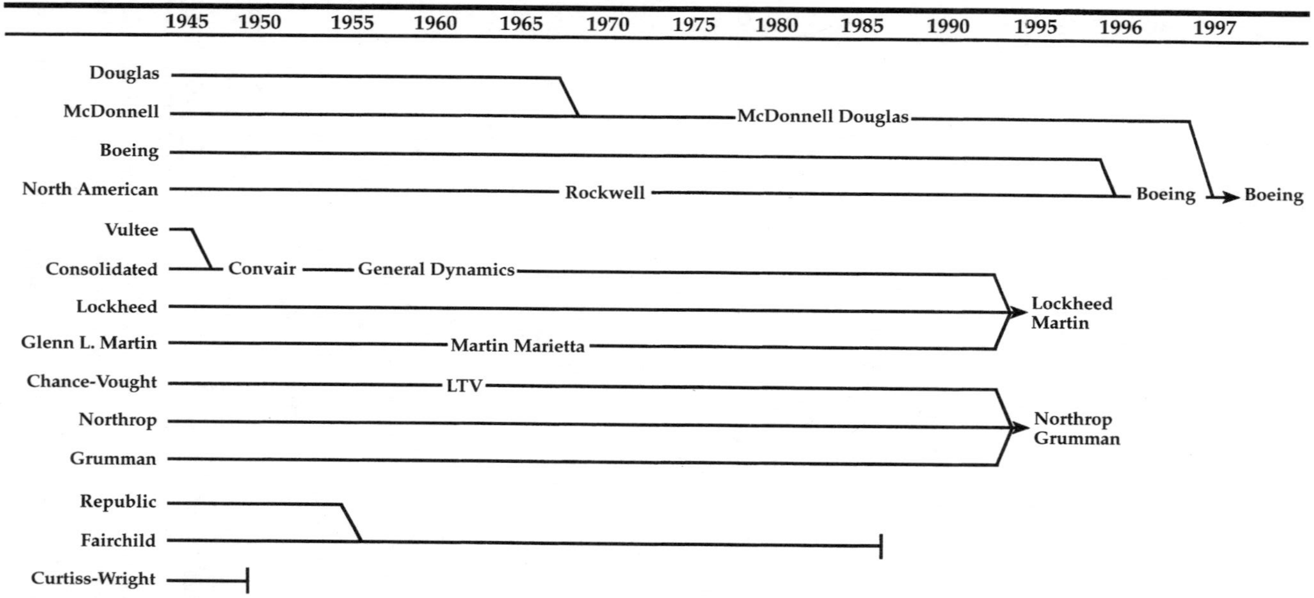

Source: Adapted from charts in Anthony L. Velocci, "Peggy Forges New Shape For Industry," *Aviation Week & Space Technology,* vol. 139, no. 20 (November 15, 1993), p. 52; Randall Forsberg, Andrew Peach, and Judith Reppy, "U.S. Airpower and Aerospace Industries in Transition," Randall Forsberg, ed., *The Arms Production Dilemma* (Cambridge, Mass.: MIT Press, 1994) p. 135.

Figure 7–2   Total Value of Recent U.S. Aerospace Mergers and Aquisitions, 1989–97

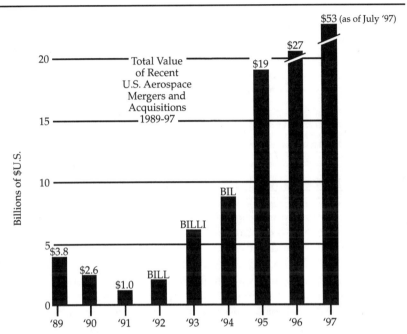

Source: JSA Research, ARDAK, A. T. Kearney. See John Donnelly and Colin Clark, "Merger Mania Hits $53 Billion This Year—So Far," *Defense Week* (July 7, 1997).

Because this supplier base of smaller firms is so heterogeneous, it is difficult to generalize about the present status of these firms. Many firms with high dependence on defense business have exited the military sector, while less-dependent firms continue to offer their services to both military and commercial clients. However, the bottom line remains clear: the number of small firms involved in the defense sector is much smaller than in 1986.

Most analysts expect consolidation to continue and actually accelerate among small and medium-sized defense firms. The appetite for further consolidation remains high. A recent survey of larger contractors found that 83 percent were interested in acquiring other contractors. At the same time, however, only 43 percent of respondents expressed interest in divesting their defense work.[6]

As present U.S. defense firms become more concentrated, obstacles to entering the business remain substantial and could be worsening.

Because of the capital-intensive nature of defense work, the barriers to entry always have been relatively high. The demand for large amounts of capital to prepare proposals, establish high-technology production capabilities, and hire technical talent all serve to deter new firms from entering the defense business. The growing complexity of defense production (e.g., precision guidance, stealth technology) and the decline in new contract opportunities will serve to further lessen the likelihood that new companies will enter the defense market over the next decade.

U.S. Government Responses to Consolidation

This consolidation wave has not occurred in a vacuum. Industry consolidation has been strongly supported by the U.S. government, and the DoD has been aggressive in pushing for mergers and acquisitions (M&As). The most recent Department of Defense report to the Congress noted that the DoD "continues to encourage much-needed rationalization in the defense industry. Since excess capacity in defense firms frequently translates into higher weapons costs, rationalization brings a clear cost savings to the Department and to U.S. taxpayers."[7]

The government's rationale for supporting consolidation is quite simple: present levels of defense spending cannot sustain a Cold War–era defense industrial base. By encouraging consolidation, the DoD hopes to reduce political pressures to maintain higher levels of defense spending and, most important, reduce costs through greater efficiencies.

As defense downsizing began in the 1980s, the Bush administration assumed a hands-off approach to the industry's evolution. While supporting consolidation, the DoD under Dick Cheney argued that market forces alone should determine the ultimate structure of the defense sector. In contrast, the Clinton team, especially Secretary of Defense William Perry and his former Deputy Secretary John Deutch, have actively pressed for and supported M&As among major defense firms. Indeed, Perry noted early in his tenure as defense secretary that "the difference between the previous Administration and ourselves is [that] . . . we're willing to commit to a defense industrial policy."[8] The goal of these policies, according to its proponents, is not simply to subsidize and support American defense firms but to create and maintain a viable defense industry that can support future national security objectives.

In addition to using the "bully pulpit" to tout the benefits of consolidation, the DoD has introduced several new initiatives to back up its rhetoric. These new policies include less stringent antitrust enforcement, subsidies for merging companies, and civil-military integration programs.

ANTITRUST ENFORCEMENT

While the Clinton administration generally has assumed an aggressive stance vis-à-vis antitrust enforcement, regulators have recognized that defense is different. With only one buyer—the Department of Defense—traditional concerns about competition and consumer prices prove less compelling in the defense sector. Thus a less aggressive stance has been used in reviewing defense M&As.

The Clinton team's revised approach to antitrust rules for defense grew out of an extensive debate begun in the last years of the Bush administration. This controversy was triggered by the November 1992 decision of the Federal Trade Commission (FTC) to block Alliant Techsystems, Inc., from acquiring Olin Corporation's Ordnance Division. The FTC justified this action by contending that the new firm would become a monopoly ammunition supplier for the army.

The FTC's decision prompted a huge outcry by the affected industries, resulting in the creation of a special Defense Science Board (DSB) Task Force, headed by the current FTC chairman, Robert Pitofsky, to create new guidelines for regulating defense M&As.[9] Prior to the DSB report, the DoD had little role in reviewing or commenting on industry mergers on military and defense industrial base grounds. As a result of this initiative and pressures from industry, the Clinton administration expanded DoD's voice in reviewing M&As, and antitrust authorities generally assumed a more relaxed posture in reviewing defense M&As. Since the Alliant-Olin case, no other major defense merger has been blocked.

SUBSIDIES FOR CONSOLIDATION

Support for industry consolidation has not been restricted to passive measures like weakened antitrust enforcement. More activist measures are also in place. In July 1993 the DoD issued a new policy that provided reimbursement to defense firms for restructuring costs. Through a very complex procedure, this policy authorizes the DoD to share cost savings that a contractor generates through organizational restructuring and downsizing.[10]

This subsidy policy has proven highly controversial, derided by opponents as "payoffs for layoffs." As expected, the defense industry has applauded these efforts as a rational means to encourage needed consolidation. In fact, industry feels that rationalization might not occur without such subsidies. As James Skaggs, chairman of Tracor, a major defense contractor, noted, efforts to eliminate these subsidies "could dampen the enthusiasm of some [companies] to participate in the consolidation process."[11]

While political opposition to this policy remains quite strong, the program has survived several congressional challenges and may expand as additional M&As proceed. To date, the DoD has paid $302 million to help support restructuring costs for four major defense company mergers. According to DoD figures, the military has saved more than $1.4 billion as a result of these mergers.[12]

CIVILIAN-MILITARY INTEGRATION

In addition to its direct promotion of consolidation, the DoD also indirectly encourages defense industry rationalization through its efforts to promote civilian-military integration. While emphasizing the need for special measures to preserve defense-unique capabilities, the Clinton/Perry approach also acknowledges that few industrial sectors are truly defense unique. In general, it is seeking to transform the current U.S. defense industrial base into a "national industrial base." In other words, the administration hopes to eliminate the current practice whereby many defense firms rarely venture into commercial markets and commercial firms rarely do business with the DoD.[13]

The Clinton administration is promoting integration through two general strategies. First, it is reforming the unwieldy DoD acquisition system by reducing military specifications and making it easier for the DoD to use commercial components in weapons systems and other products. Second, the administration is seeking to promote dual-use research that fosters both commercial and military advances.

The Perry-led acquisition reform effort is driven by the Pentagon's recognition that it can no longer afford to support a defense-only industrial base. Declining budgets have forced the DoD to introduce commercial buying and management practices as a means to save money and streamline the present system. Potential cost savings are considerable; current DoD budget estimates suggest that streamlining could produce annual savings in the range of $10 billion to $20 billion.

In addition to producing efficiency gains, procurement reform also is expected to help encourage innovative commercial businesses to do business with the DoD. Commercial technological advances have begun to outpace defense technological advances at the same time that commercial firms have become reluctant to do business with the DoD.

This reluctance stems in part from onerous reporting and auditing standards required for government work. By eliminating many requirements, the DoD may be able to reduce this problem and better tap the fruits of commercial innovation.

The rapidity of commercial research and development (R&D) advances has created a shift in the U.S. government paradigm for funding R&D. During the Cold War, it was assumed that military R&D would provide "spin-off" benefits for the civilian economy. In the 1990s, military planners anticipate that commercial advances will provide "spin-on" benefits for national defense.[14]

The emergence of the "spin-on" imperative led to the administration's second general strategy of encouraging greater support for dual-use research and development. The Defense Advanced Research and Projects Agency (DARPA) has funded dual-use programs, such as the Sematech semiconductor manufacturing consortium, for several years. More recently, through the DARPA-led Technology Reinvestment Project (TRP), the administration has funded dual-use R&D as part of a larger defense conversion effort. The TRP was further supplemented by R&D programs operated by the Department of Commerce and other agencies.[15]

Fears about declining U.S. competitiveness provided the major impetus for these new R&D programs, but the desire to break down the walls between civilian and defense firms also played a role. Indeed, by stimulating both spin-on and spin-off, these R&D programs were expected to reduce the cost of defense programs and increase the market for new technologies and ideas.[16]

The Arrival of Defense Monopolies: What Does It Mean?

This combination of declining defense budgets, technological constraints, and supportive government policies has created strong pressures toward further industry consolidation. Significant overcapacity still exists. In their chapter, Harvey M. Sapolsky and Eugene Gholz find that the United States still has eight production lines producing military aircraft, five helicopter firms totally dependent on military purchases, six private shipyards assembling large warships, and five military satellite manufacturers.

Despite the fact that historically unprecedented consolidation already has occurred, we can expect even further consolidation over the next decade. As production contracts begun in the 1980s come to a close and additional M&As proceed, more firms will exit (voluntarily and involuntarily) the defense sector. The result will be a much smaller defense industry composed of very large defense conglomerates with high levels of dependence on defense business. In effect, we will have created an arsenal system owned and operated by private contractors.

While government officials have encouraged industry consolidation, they have yet to recognize and prepare for the future implications of these trends. Several challenging issues are likely to emerge: (1) a potential rise in cost of defense goods, (2) a potential loss of technological innovation, and (3) a chilling effect on international defense cooperation.

Despite well-intentioned programs to expand commercial practices and promote civilian-military integration, a significant portion of the defense industrial base—composed of the large prime contractors—will remain defense unique. In addition to the unique nature of the products produced by defense firms, the structure of the industry is also exceptional.[17] Because a single buyer exists and traditional "market prices" do not apply, defense always will be different from other industrial sectors. Costs and prices are based on negotiation, and the relationship between buyer and seller is completely different from that found in traditional consumer markets. Because of this sector's unique structure, crafting effective responses to change poses a difficult challenge.

HOW CAN THE DEFENSE DEPARTMENT ENSURE COMPETITIVE PRICES FOR DEFENSE GOODS?

The DoD currently expects that industry consolidation will save money through increased efficiencies. At the same time, procurement officials recognize that reductions in market competition may make their jobs more difficult. Without the pressures of multiple competitors, contractors may be less inclined to meet stringent cost and schedule objectives.

The DoD traditionally has resorted to a combination of regulation and the use of competition among contractors as the optimal means to maintain fair and competitive prices for the goods and services it procures. Given the DoD's powerful role as a monopsony purchaser of defense goods, such tools could be expected to be quite potent. However, in practice, competition and procurement regulation have not worked as effectively as they should.

In the case of procurement regulations, the DoD's power as the sole customer for defense goods has proven less powerful than would be expected. In many cases, contractors have succeeded in exploiting superior information to negotiate supracompetitive prices or to achieve more favorable terms in negotiated contracts.[18] Thus procurement regulation has proven to be an imperfect tool.

As efforts to reform acquisition regulations move forward, the utility of these regulatory tools further weakens. The reforms are designed to open up contracting opportunities for nondefense businesses, but they also will have the effect of loosening controls on the large prime contractors.

Industry consolidation also will reduce the positive cost effects of contractor competition. With only one or two major suppliers in each market segment, market pressures to reduce costs will prove less powerful. The DoD acknowledged this problem in its 1996 report to Congress, which stated: "Consolidation carries the risk that DoD will no longer benefit from the competition that encourages defense suppliers to reduce costs, improve quality, and stimulate innovation."[19]

The financial effects of this declining competition are likely to pose a severe problem in certain industrial sectors over the next decade. At present, many analysts believe that sufficient competition can be maintained for the near future.[20] However, given the realities of reduced competition and less stringent regulation, major cost savings should not be expected to emerge from the process of industry consolidation.

HOW CAN THE DEFENSE DEPARTMENT MAINTAIN ITS TECHNOLOGICAL EDGE?

While recognizing that cost and price effects of reduced competition are important, defense planners express more concern about industry consolidation's effects on technological innovation. As William E. Kovacic and Dennis E. Smallwood have noted: "The main potential hazard of mergers is the danger that technological competition will diminish, and that specific technologies may become entrenched as the one or two remaining suppliers freeze out innovative design approaches that threaten their vested interests or defy conventional wisdom."[21]

As new weapons starts become increasingly rare, we can expect further losses of technological capability as firms that fail to win new business will exit the industry. A new navy study projects that three of the existing six U.S. shipyards will go out of business within the next ten years.[22]

Because a firm's survival may be at stake, the competitive pressures surrounding new contract opportunities have become quite intense. Take the case of the Joint Strike Fighter program, designed to serve as the next-generation fighter for the U.S. Air Force, Marine Corps, and Navy. Every major aircraft manufacturer is involved in this competition. Firms shut out of this contract, even mega-firms like Boeing and Lockheed Martin, may find it impossible to remain in the fighter aircraft business.

The DoD has clearly indicated its willingness to subsidize remaining suppliers of critical defense-unique items. The decision to purchase a third Seawolf submarine was justified on such grounds. However, the absence of significant market competition may serve to "lock in" old technologies and, over time, to erode the technological edge of the United States.

CAN THE DEFENSE DEPARTMENT CONTINUE MAJOR DEFENSE COOPERATION PROJECTS WITH ITS ALLIES?

One of the more perverse effects of consolidation is its dampening effect on defense industrial cooperation among the United States, Europe, and the United States' Asian allies. While Defense Secretary Perry has designated international defense cooperation as one of his highest priorities, political and economic pressures have made it next to impossible to make much headway toward this goal. Indeed, an international defense "trade war" appears more likely than extensive international cooperation.

This rise in defense protectionism is fostered by industry consolidation on both sides of the Atlantic. With fewer new contract opportunities, pressure to buy domestic is intense. At the same time, lower defense budgets increase demands to reduce the unit costs of new weapons systems through exports. Aggressive export competition further erodes the desire for cooperation among U.S. and European firms.

The July 1996 decision by the United Kingdom to purchase new missiles, maritime patrol aircraft, and antiarmor weapons from British firms signals a period of heightened defense industrial competition among the allies. These contracts, totaling $6.2 billion in new work, had been hotly contested by British, American, and European firms. The United Kingdom traditionally has purchased many of its weapons from U.S. firms, rejecting the buy-domestic policies frequently used in France. Thus the action was taken as a clear signal by U.S. firms. As one industry analyst put it, "this says that fortress Europe is putting the walls up a little."[23] To date, European industry consolidation has lagged behind comparable U.S. efforts, but most analysts believe that the pace of European M&As will quicken.[24] This consolidation will further reduce the opportunities for U.S. business.

What Can Be Done?

Halting these trends of consolidation makes little sense. Defense procurement budgets and, more important, new weapons starts are unlikely to increase dramatically over the next decade. Consolidation can and must occur, as the alternatives require expensive subsidization of unneeded production capacity. What is needed is a series of measures that helps temper the downside of consolidation and avoids the worst-case scenario of an autarkic, expensive, and technologically stagnant industrial base.

Several important steps can help contribute to a smoother transition for U.S. defense firms and create the tools needed to ensure the continued provision of a low-cost, high-quality product for the DoD. Expanded efforts to help workers, communities, and industries respond to downsizing should be supplemented with a variety of management initiatives. Suggested reforms should include continued acquisition reform, activist regulation of defense-unique firms, and proxies for market competition.

CONTINUED ACQUISITION REFORM

The current program of acquisition reform makes sense as a means to deregulate those sectors of the defense business that have clear commercial counterparts. Industries such as food services, personal computers, and clothing should not be subjected to unique military requirements or procedures. In these cases, the military's relationship with its suppliers should be identical to that found in commercial transactions.

Acquisition reform efforts continue to move forward, and significant achievements already have been reached. For instance, the DoD recently has eliminated the vast majority of militarily unique standards and specifications, and also has increased the use of simplified commercial buying practices for all purchases under $100,000 in value.[25] With the passage of the major reform packages in both 1994 and 1995, many of the needed changes in the Federal Acquisition Regulations (FAR) are in place. Future reforms likely will focus on the effective implementation of these legislative and regulatory changes.

ACTIVIST REGULATION OF DEFENSE-UNIQUE FIRMS

While acquisition reform makes sense for DoD purchases with commercial counterparts, much of what we traditionally consider as defense business does not fall into this category. Acquisition reform is unlikely to affect activities that (1) have no commercial counterpart, (2) largely use noncommercial processes, and (3) involve highly classified and controlled technologies or weapons systems. These categories account for a large base of activities. According to a study by the now defunct Office of Technology Assessment (OTA), 40 percent of the value added to defense goods and services is provided in segregated private-sector facilities or operations.[26] OTA further estimated that, even with the most aggressive acquisition reform program, 25 percent of private-sector value added would continue to come from segregated facilities.

As these figures indicate, a large portion of future defense business—including most new weapons programs—will remain segregated from everyday commercial activities. Because of industry consolidation, competitive contracting and other traditional management tools may offer diminishing returns. The need to find new tools is the primary challenge facing defense planners.

As acquisition reform moves forward, defense-unique businesses may fall into the paradoxical state of being more, rather than less, regulated. In other words, the DoD may need to begin treating large U.S. defense conglomerates like a privately owned arsenal. Such a system would require tight controls on pricing and production schedules—akin to current regulation of utility industries. In addition, the DoD should consider providing budget stability to key defense firms, providing them with a regular subsidy even in the absence of new program starts. These subsidies could be used for testing new technological ideas as opposed to initiating major new production contracts.

PROXIES FOR MARKET COMPETITION

Because the DoD will be unable to foster true market competition in defense-unique sectors, defense planners must seek other ways to foster competitive pressures. If acquisition reform efforts help open up some contracting opportunities for new firms, competition on non–defense-unique contracts should be robust. For defense-unique weapons programs, other tools may be necessary. The DoD may want to consider creating independent design teams, requiring increased competition at the subcontract level, or fostering competition among the military services on how to best achieve new missions.[27]

Buying from foreign suppliers offers another means to stimulate competition. Foreign purchases should be utilized when politically feasible—especially at the subcontract level. Nonetheless, domestic political pressures on both sides of the Atlantic may limit the utility of international suppliers as a means to stimulate contract competition.

Conclusion

Addressing the challenge of a restructured U.S. defense industry will require both new and old thinking. Paradoxically, effective management of this new industry may require tools that date back to the era of public military arsenals. While aggressive efforts to reform acquisition rules and reinvent government are designed to make the DoD operate more like a private business, a businesslike approach may run counter to the future needs of U.S. defense planners.

In many cases, a more activist government policy makes sense as the best means to manage a smaller defense industry composed of a handful of large defense-unique contractors. Tighter regulation and guaranteed subsidies may be the only tools available to ensure a cost-effective and technologically savvy defense sector in a world of larger defense companies, fewer new contracts, and reduced opportunities for international cooperation.

Notes

1. See, for example, Lawrence Korb, "The Readiness Gap: What Gap?" *New York Times Magazine*, February 26, 1995, pp. 40–41.

2. U.S. Congress, General Accounting Office, *Defense Downsizing: Selected Contractor Business Unit Reactions* (Washington, D.C.: GAO, May 1995), p. 4.

3. U.S. Congress, General Accounting Office, *Defense Industry: Trends in DOD Spending, Industrial Productivity and Competition,* (Washington, D.C.: GAO, January 1997), p. 10.

4. Ibid., p. 4.

5. Anthony Velocci, "U.S. Shake-out Tests Suppliers' Flexibility," *Aviation Week and Space Technology,* February 14, 1994, pp. 48–51.

6. Philip Finnegan, "Prices, Politics, May Squelch Merger Wave," *Defense News,* July 29–August 4, 1996, p. 14.

7. U.S. Department of Defense, *Annual Report to the President and the Congress* (Washington, D.C.: Department of Defense, March 1996), p. 74.

8. "William Perry: Guarding the Base" (Interview), *Government Executive* (August 1993): 40–43.

9. See U.S. Department of Defense, *Report of the Defense Science Board Task Force on Antitrust Aspects of Defense Industry Consolidation* (Washington, D.C.: Department of Defense, April 1994).

10. For a detailed description of the policy, see U.S. Congress, General Accounting Office, *Defense Contractor Restructuring: First Application of Cost and Savings Regulations* (Washington, D.C.: GAO, April 1996).

11. Quoted in Anthony L. Velocci, "U.S. Industry in Vigorous Fight against Proposed Policy Reversal," *Aviation Week and Space Technology,* July 22, 1996, p. 30.

12. Figures cited in Tony Capaccio, "Moving Fees, Worker Benefits Comprise Bulk of Defense Merger Costs," *Defense Week,* August 12, 1996, pp. 1, 12.

13. For a review of this changed thinking about the defense industrial base, see Lewis M. Branscomb, ed., *Empowering Technology* (Cambridge, Mass.: MIT Press, 1993); Erik R. Pages, *Responding to Defense Dependence: Policy and Ideas and the American Defense Industrial Base* (Westport, Conn.: Praeger, 1996).

14. See John Alic et al., *Beyond Spin-off: Military and Commercial Technologies in a Changing World* (Cambridge, Mass.: Harvard Business School Press, 1992).

15. These R&D initiatives suffered severe budget cuts in the Republican Congress that took over after the November 1994 elections. All of the programs were slashed drastically, but nearly all of these initiatives survived and have been expanded in Clinton's second term.

16. For a flavor of the Clinton administration's perspective, see National Economic Council, *Second to None: Preserving America's Military Advantage through Dual-Use Technology* (Washington, D.C.: National Economic Council, 1995). For a compelling critique, see Michael Oden, Gregory Bischak, and Christine Evans-Klock, *The Technology Reinvestment Project: The Limits of Dual-Use Technology Policy* (Washington, D.C.: National Commission for Economic Conversion and Disarmament, July 1995).

17. For background, see Jacques Gansler, *The Defense Industry* (Cambridge, Mass.: MIT Press, 1980).

18. Jean-Jacque Laffont and Jean Tirole, *A Theory of Incentives in Procurement and Regulation* (Cambridge, Mass.: MIT Press, 1993).

19. U.S. Department of Defense, *Annual Report to the President and the Congress* (Washington, D.C.: Department of Defense, March 1996), p. 74.

20. See, for example, William E. Kovacic and Dennis E. Smallwood, "Competition Policy, Rivalries, and Defense Industry Consolidation," *Journal of Economic Perspectives* 8, no. 4 (Fall 1994): 91–110.

21. Ibid., pp. 102–103.

22. "New Analysis Predicts Tough Times for Shipbuilders," *Inside the Pentagon,* September 26, 1996, p. 9.

23. Giovanni DeBriganti and Phillip Finnegan, "U.K. Contract Could Fuel Trans-Atlantic Consolidation," *Defense News,* July 29–August 4, 1996, p. 1.

24. See, for example, "Building Eurospace Corp," *Economist,* September 7, 1996, pp. 59–61.

25. For a summary of these reforms, see DoD, Annual Report, pp. 111–116; Al Gore, *The Best Kept Secrets in Government: A Report to President Bill Clinton* (Washington, D.C.: National Performance Review, September 1996), pp. 80–83.

26. U.S. Congress, Office of Technology Assessment, *Assessing the Potential for Civil-Military Integration* (Washington, D.C.: U.S. Government Printing Office, September 1994), p. 142. This figure omits the value added by public-sector portions of the defense industrial base, such as repair and maintenance depots. OTA estimated in 1994 that approximately $13 billion was spent on salaries for government employees in these segregated public-sector facilities.

27. For a discussion of this last option, see Harvey M. Sapolsky, "The Interservice Competition Solution," *Breakthroughs* (Spring 1996): 1–4.

8

Redesigning the Defense Industrial Base

KENNETH FLAMM

THE INDUSTRIAL resources of the United States that are dedicated to the national defense effort have not fully adapted to the ending of the Cold War. They have absorbed a cut in procurement appropriations to one-third of the 1987 peak level and have experienced considerable corporate consolidation. But the process of weapons development and production they undertake has not been redesigned to match the needs of the smaller and technologically more agile military force that the United States will have to evolve. Without appropriate restructuring, the current defense industrial infrastructure will generate excessively high procurement costs as it maintains excess capacity and thereby wastes increasingly scarce resources. It will design and produce products that could be better produced in commercial enterprises. It may stimulate unnecessary and potentially destabilizing levels of international arms sales. In an environment of global military downsizing, it may create global resentment and suspicion.

This chapter sketches an approach to analyzing the appropriate size and organizational configuration of the defense industrial establishment under radically altered international circumstances. A study currently underway using this approach develops a method that can be used to establish a coherent relationship between projected force deployments and the industrial establishment that would be needed to support them. The assessment is based on an analytical model that incorporates key economic features of defense systems and the technology procurement process. It applies the model to major defense industries and seeks to determine the industrial configuration required to sustain currently projected force deployments indefinitely. It then compares that configuration to alternatives that would be appropriate for the different force levels that might emerge in the new situation and assesses the relative cost of these alternatives. The approach also is used to assess the potential economic impact of greater procurement cooperation with our allies and mutual restraint in arms exports to third parties.

Motivations

The single largest category of discretionary spending in the federal budget is for national defense. That allocation came about in the course of the Cold War in a context in which rapid technical development and immediate preparedness were considered more important than economic efficiency. Redundant capabilities and inefficient practices were tolerated. The analysis of efficient defense production was not intensively pursued.

In the very different circumstances that now prevail, the industrial infrastructure that currently builds the systems used by the U.S. Department of Defense (DoD; the "defense industrial base") is in the midst of a painful transition. The procurement budget is currently in real terms at roughly one-third of its mid-1980s Cold War peak. A determined push to reform the acquisition process is slowly gaining momentum. If successful, it will lower barriers that have sheltered those willing to invest in mastering the very arcane rules of the defense acquisition process. In technologies once driven by defense, commercial applications now lead the process of technical innovation. In an initial effort to adjust to these developments, the Clinton administration has been attempting to encourage the use of commercial technologies and products in defense systems wherever possible. This initiative promises to erode the boundaries between defense and commercial production even more and to open an already shrinking market to a larger set of commercial competitors.

In this new environment, major investments in systems and technology will be conceived in terms of building and maintaining options available to meet possible future contingencies. State-of-the-art systems and technology will be developed and demonstrated in the form of prototypes. They will have to be produced and deployed on a limited scale to work out operational issues. Even where it is clear that new large-scale weapons platforms must be procured, the production and fielding of such systems may stretch out over years, even decades, into the future.

Figure 8–1   Distribution of NATO Procurement, 1994

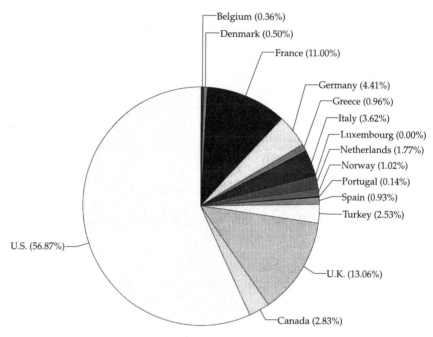

Source: International Institute for Strategic Studies, *The Military Balance 1996/97* (Oxford: Oxford University Press, 1996), p. 40.

The U.S. defense industry has some formidable strengths as it faces these necessary adjustments. It is the premier global producer of a variety of defense systems, the clear world leader in key systems integration skills and specialized technologies. It accounts for roughly half of world exports of military equipment. Its domestic market is by far the largest in the world—more than triple that of Japan, which has the second-largest procurement budget among the western allies. The U.S. weapons procurement budget exceeds the combined total of all its European allies in the North Atlantic Treaty Organization (NATO). (See Figure 8–1.) As a consequence, the formidable volume of U.S. military equipment exports amounts to less than 20 percent of DoD procurement, and in a few cases it is the fundamental viability of a U.S. defense industry critically dependent on success in export markets. Furthermore, despite a continuing decline in military budgets around the globe, U.S. foreign defense sales have remained roughly constant, and U.S. export market share therefore has increased.

The same cannot be said for our allies' defense industries. Japanese companies are prohibited from exporting military equipment, and flat defense budgets—combined with uneconomic volumes and fantastically high costs—have thrust Japan's defense industry into a deepening crisis. In response, both Japan's industry and its promoters within the Ministry of International Trade and Industry (which controls defense procurement) recently have begun to advocate publicly a controversial legalization of military exports.

European governments have long recognized the importance of exports to the survival of their defense industries: in France, for example, exports exceeded 40 percent of arms industry sales in the mid-1980s. Despite aggressive promotion efforts, European export sales have dropped with the continued decline in global defense spending (in France, recently, to 25 percent of a falling industry output), and today European defense industries are in turmoil.

Responses to these developments—championed by France and supported strongly by Germany—have included the formation of a Western European Armaments Group under the political aegis of the Western European Union, the first embryonic steps toward a European defense procurement agency, proposals to restrict European defense procurement to European-only suppliers whenever possible, and a renewed emphasis on export promotion.

For the United States, in contrast, the issue is not industrial survival but how and where to reduce the industrial capability primarily dedicated to defense to a level appropriate to a new, post–Cold War force structure. The United States is a technology powerhouse in defense: it alone accounted for more than 70 percent of research and development (R&D) spending by NATO and Japan in 1994. (See Figure 8–2; in addition to indicating that the United States is a net exporter of military technology to its allies, the figure also reflects that our allies' defense industries are much more reliant on export sales, as opposed to defense ministry funding, to maintain military R&D.) Despite a recent wave of mergers and acquisitions in America's defense industries, existing capacity in the current defense industrial base probably still greatly exceeds the investment requirements of tomorrow's military forces. What those investment requirements are, and what industrial capabilities are needed to meet them, is, unfortunately, a complex set of issues that so far has largely defied a crisp conceptualization or a clear answer.

At one extreme, it may be argued that the manner in which defense goods are contracted and priced today largely guarantees that the costs of maintaining existing industrial capacity—whatever they are—will simply be absorbed into the defense procurement budget. (Indeed, often it is difficult even to know what these costs are: typically some of the initial costs of R&D and engineering funded by a contractor are

Figure 8–2   Distribution of Nato R&D, 1994

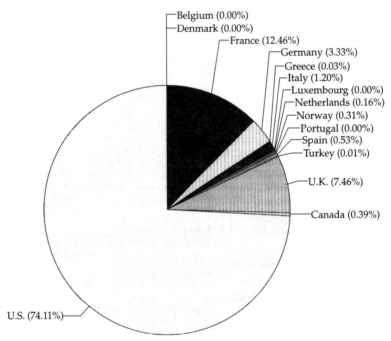

─Belgium (0.00%)
─Denmark (0.00%)
─France (12.46%)
─Germany (3.33%)
─Greece (0.03%)
─Italy (1.20%)
─Luxembourg (0.00%)
─Netherlands (0.16%)
─Norway (0.31%)
─Portugal (0.00%)
─Spain (0.53%)
─Turkey (0.01%)

─U.K. (7.46%)

─Canada (0.39%)

U.S. (74.11%)─

Source: International Institute for Strategic Studies, *The Military Balance 1996/97* (Oxford: Oxford University Press, 1996), p. 40.

recovered as overhead charges during the production phase of a procurement.) Higher overhead folded into smaller output translates into less bang per defense buck and less capability delivered into the field to our forces from some given budget.

There is also the potential for a significant international "feedback" effect. A perception that we maintain a military industrial infrastructure that greatly exceeds our investment needs, in a world in which our military forces are by far the preeminent global presence, may alarm others, leading them to expand their capabilities. That in turn would pose a challenge that drives us to increase our force structure. Force structure, increasingly advanced weapons, and industrial base may interact in a manner that creates a self-fulfilling prophecy of threat.'

The interaction between force structure and industrial base also takes on a political dimension in the United States that further complicates imposition of any simple economic or operational logic. Defense budgets are determined in a highly political environment, with every major program or project scrutinized annually in considerable detail by an activist legislature and an appointed political leadership that extends down into the planning process. The defense industry is actively engaged in the planning and budgeting process, interacting with the political leadership in the DoD, Congress, and the military services. The industry exerts a major influence on the course that is plotted. There is a very real danger that powerful forces arguing for preservation of the incumbent industrial base may determine force structure rather than the force structure driving industrial investments.

It is sometimes argued that the impersonal hand of "the market" can sort out the sizing and organization of the defense industrial base, once military technical planners determine a desired force structure. "Just figure out what we need to field," goes the argument, "and let industry sort out the best way to produce it." The powerful attraction of this view is that the impersonal discipline of competitive market forces would be harnessed in order to generate an efficient industrial configuration. There are, however, three very real problems with this otherwise very attractive view.

First, the defense market is inherently highly imperfect on the demand side. There is effectively a single large customer—the DoD—with enormous monopsony power. Once a program has begun, the power shifts to the producer, who acquires specialized assets and know-how that reduce the government's ability to switch to an alternative supplier. As F. M. Scherer wrote over 30 years ago in his seminal study of the acquisition process, "buyer and seller are locked together in a relationship analogous to bilateral monopoly for the life of the program, and they must deal with each other on a bargaining basis."[1]

Producers do not simply develop a piece of equipment and then try to sell it to the Department of Defense. For defense-unique systems, there is no "market price"—all transaction prices are negotiated before (and frequently, during and after) anything is ever built. The relative bargaining power of the DoD and its potential suppliers determines the price of firm-specific designs that are typically highly imperfect substitutes, not homogeneous commodities. In addition, important informational asymmetries exist. The government, with its internal R&D and intelligence apparatus, knows a great deal about classified technologies, threats, and performance characteristics relevant to the design of a system for its use that are not available to industry. Similarly, industry has proprietary know-how about technological, engineering, and cost issues that the government may not be privy to. The "figuring out" of needs and the mechanics of buying and selling are hopelessly interactive.

The second problem is that the market is equally imperfect on the supply side. Industrial structure is not solely or even primarily determined by independent market forces. Through its contracting rules and behavior, the DoD exercises considerable long-run control over the numbers and capabilities of the firms able to supply it with systems. Historically, the industrial base supplying defense systems developed largely through accretion. The DoD essentially paid the full cost of developing new technologies and industrial capabilities in a constantly expanding set of suppliers. It then maintained the industrial overhead of the supplier base it had created through a cost-plus acquisition system that encouraged its contractors to spread these costs, in an often arbitrary way, across the full life cycle of R&D, low rate production, volume production, and follow-on support.

There are also significant problems of moral hazard. Simply paying a contractor to undertake R&D does not guarantee the development of an innovative, cost-effective, superior new system. In the world of private high technology, innovators typically are given an ownership stake in the outcome of the innovative effort, thus motivating their best effort and tying their personal reward to the outcome of the R&D effort. Rogerson argues that the U.S. military procurement system—by permitting contractors to reap economic profits during a sole-source production phase of systems acquisition, following a competitive R&D phase—has created an imperfect but highly important link between successful innovative performance and material reward.[2] Contractors are even motivated to sink their own resources into producing the very best new designs, driven by the promise of profits to be reaped during their monopoly on production if their design is successful. During the production phase, entirely different agency problems are confronted, as government program managers struggle along with limited information to sequentially negotiate prices for lots of produced systems that successfully balance a "fair" return on a company's investments with "reasonable" expectations about cost reduction over time.

To further complicate matters, there are significant economies of scale—due to fixed engineering costs, indivisibilities in production facilities, and learning economies. Splitting a procurement among multiple suppliers, then, often means trading off lower unit cost against the potential pricing benefits of competitive sourcing. It is clear in many instances that greater competition does not translate into a lower price. The navy, for example, initially had dual competitive sources for its Tomahawk missile but, when volumes declined, was forced to retreat to a single source because of the costly overhead absorbed in maintaining two production lines for the system.

Finally, there are clearly national security issues embedded in the structure of the DoD's supplier industries that are simply not priced out in markets. Vulnerability to disruption of supply in wartime, potential dissemination of militarily sensitive information, and access by potential adversaries are all concerns that are poorly captured in the simple metrics of price and profit on a contract.

In short, no textbook-style, impersonal, perfectly competitive market will generate an efficient defense industrial base. Such an outcome requires an explicit policy, and that policy will involve some hard choices. Without a serious analysis of what industrial capabilities are required to sustain tomorrow's force structure, what portion of those capabilities can be sourced commercially and what must be sustained by the DoD's own investment, and how the discipline of competition can be combined with the benefits of scale in the acquisition process, we are likely to end up with a defense industrial base that is neither efficient nor effective.

Policy Issues

Defense industrial issues already have become a critical hinge on which policy turns in the debate over numerous big-ticket DoD systems. The primary justification in the Clinton administration's plan to build an additional Seawolf submarine was maintenance of critical industrial capabilities, not a traditional service requirement driven by a well-defined military threat. Similar "industrial base" arguments have been mustered by others in support of such diverse causes as procurement of additional B-2s (and maintenance of the "bomber industrial base"), C-17s (the "military transport industrial base"), the F-22 (the "fighter industrial base"), the subsidy of domestic nuclear-capable shipyards and reactor component producers, and restrictions on purchase of space launch services from foreign suppliers.

Discussion of what critical defense industrial capabilities must be subsidized or otherwise maintained necessarily intersects with debates over what capabilities should be obtained from domestic sources, what the nation's allies can be relied on to supply to U.S. forces, and the extent to which U.S. military planners should depend on sales in foreign markets to lower costs or maintain the production base for advanced defense systems. Increasingly, official government support—financial and political—for foreign exports of U.S.-produced defense equipment is being sought, and given, on the grounds that the value of such sales in maintaining the U.S. industrial base for key systems (and in reducing the unit costs) justifies the expenditure of economic and political capital. In fact, the 1995 issuance of presidential directive PDD 34 made this industrial base linkage to support for arms exports crisply explicit for the first time, although it has long been implicit policy in prior administrations.[3]

Obvious examples of such industrial arguments in current U.S. foreign policy include an industry-led push to have Congress create an export loan guarantee facility for foreign defense equipment sales, the waiving of R&D recoupment charges on commercial exports of defense systems (and a current industry campaign to extend this policy to the DoD's official Foreign Military Sales [FMS]), the enormous energy expended by the U.S. government on promotion of U.S. attack helicopter and transport aircraft sales in Europe, and the decision to release advanced, beyond-visual-range air-to-air missiles for sale in the Mideast. Sensitive technology transfer decisions also are decided with increasing frequency based on a primarily industrial calculus—for example, the U.S. Air Force's 1995 decision to offer Japan the source code for the F-15's new flight computer, as part of a package in which the Japanese would purchase the U.S. F-15 radar upgrade from another American manufacturer, along with the flight computer, rather than build their own systems.

International sales of military equipment also create an important indirect linkage between our industrial base policies and those of our allies. As they come under greater pressure to sell advanced equipment and technology to dubious customers in an increasingly competitive, shrinking global armaments market, in order to sustain national defense industrial bases that are much more dependent on exports than ours, our allies are likely to ship systems that will create qualitatively greater threats for our forces in possible future contingencies. (France, for example, reportedly is marketing a new cruise missile with stealth characteristics internationally, and several of our allies are selling quiet, diesel submarines in Third World markets. A recent RAND study argues that although a new Russian threat is increasingly remote, likely future exports of new, advanced European fighters create a potential threat justifying continued funding of our F-22 stealth fighter program.[4])

Such exports by our friends will force us to increase or improve our military capabilities, accelerate procurement of new systems, and increase the scale of investments required for our defense industrial base. As our allies make such decisions, our own industry will observe, correctly, that we are better off selling our own equivalent system to the same potential customer—from both an economic and a security standpoint. In turn, our allies will see our willingness to sell this capability as justifying their sale of the same or a marginally better capability in the next major sales competition, and so on.

Briefly, analysis of the defense industrial base should address three major sets of policy issues:

INDUSTRIAL REQUIREMENTS AND ORGANIZATION

- What industrial capabilities must be sustained by the DoD's investments?
- For a given "steady-state" force structure, what levels of defense-unique capabilities must be maintained?
- How can they be organized in an efficient manner?

With significant economies of scale in many defense industries, possible trade-offs between unit cost and benefits from competition with varying numbers of producers should be explored explicitly. To examine the consequences of different policies toward industrial structure, a number of policy scenarios need to be considered: pure regulated monopoly/oligopoly (cost-plus contracting); competition in R&D followed by negotiated sole-source production contracts; competition in R&D followed by some degree of competition in production from one or more prequalified suppliers; and a separation of procurement into phased R&D and production contracts, with different variants of these scenarios in each phase. Since the government can greatly influence the number of competitors in the defense market through a variety of policies, each of the scenarios may have a "free-entry" variant and a variant with the government choosing the number of competitors sustained within an industry. The extent to which performance incentives can introduce competitive disciplines into sole-source contracts also should be considered.

INTERNATIONAL PROCUREMENT COOPERATION WITH ALLIES

- How significant are the potential resource savings from increased industrial cooperation with our close allies?

International cooperation provides the opportunity to share R&D costs, to lower unit costs by aggregating national demands together to achieve larger production volumes, and, possibly, to support a larger number of competitors in an economic fashion. Supporting those economic considerations are the political benefits of greater industrial cooperation within our alliances and the operational advantages of using the same equipment and logistics train as our allies. International cooperation also may provide a vehicle for agreements with allies to restrain exports of advanced military systems to third parties. Set against these arguments for increased cooperation are increased dependency on foreign sources for important equipment, limits on our independence of action, and the risk that sensitive technology may find its way more easily into third-country export markets through firms not subject to U.S. export control restraints.

One policy scenario in this analysis is an autarkic one, where effectively all major U.S. systems are developed and produced by U.S. suppliers only. These results should be contrasted with a scenario in which at least one European supplier will produce each major category of systems, and where U.S. and European demand will be opened up on a reciprocal basis to suppliers from all European countries. The results of a comparison between these two scenarios may be interpreted as a rough bound on the potential economic benefits from international industrial cooperation with our NATO partners.

FOREIGN ARMS SALES AND PROLIFERATION

- If we were to further restrain armaments exports, what would the cost to our defense industrial base be?

- To what extent would reduced foreign sales drive up DoD investment requirements and procurement costs?

- What would be the economic impact of greater procurement cooperation with that of our allies, coupled with mutual reduction in arms exports to third parties?

Because of the growing linkage between export sales and industrial base concerns, two policy scenarios involving restraint on export sales should be analyzed. In one scenario, the impact of unilateral U.S. restraints on export sales on the U.S. industrial base and defense budget is considered. In a second scenario, linked to the greater international armaments cooperation already discussed, the impact of restraints on export sales to third countries by a combined allied industrial base might be analyzed.

Methodology

The intention of this ongoing study is to construct a framework for defense industrial base policy analysis. The framework is based on an analytical model that starts with a "steady-state" force structure and, under a variety of hypothetical policy scenarios, determines the budgetary costs for the industrial capabilities in which the DoD must invest to maintain that force structure. This analytical framework for defense industrial base analysis should allow policymakers to examine explicitly the effects of alternative technical assumptions used in pricing the investments needed to maintain industrial capabilities and equipment outputs required for a given force structure, and explicitly evaluate alternative defense industrial investment policies. The framework can be thought of as producing an annual budget cost for provisioning some steady-state force structure with the current generation of needed equipment and developing its future-generation replacements. Other elements of the defense budget—personnel costs, logistics, facilities, operations, and maintenance—are associated with the steady-state force structure but are not analyzed in this model.

Five major tasks are being undertaken in the course of doing this research. First, a candidate set of force structures is defined. The basic notion is to start with a "first-principles" projection of what threats will be faced and what forces must be fielded to meet them in the early part of the next century. A reasonable planning goal for the period by which our force structure should be closely aligned with a redefined set of post–Cold War threats to national security is the year 2020.

Several force structures should be considered in this exercise, varying with differing projections of hypothetical conflicts, effectiveness of various systems, regional developments, degree of cooperation with allies, and so on. The 1993 Clinton administration Bottom-Up Review (BUR) force structure and its offspring, the 1997 Quadrennial Defense Review (almost certainly due for overhaul again after the next election regardless of who wins), for example, reflect one set of assumptions that can be translated into a particular menu of needed equipment. The model can be designed to take virtually any force structure assumptions as an input and work through the defense industrial investment implications.

The second step is analysis and taxonomy of defense industrial sectors. In the most parsimonious possible way, we next define roughly 20 defense industrial sectors that capture most of the significant defense-unique systems and technologies critical to a modern military. The level of detail contemplated roughly corresponds to fighters, bombers, transports, helicopters, defensive missiles, strategic missiles, attack missiles, space launch, satellite, C^3I, early-warning systems, radar/sonar, avionics, guidance, ASW (Anti-Submarine Warfare), surface ships, submarines, tanks and vehicles ordnance, turbine engines, and perhaps a few other things.

This task is relatively simple, and depends on the level of aggregation in force structure and specific features of various industrial sectors. The DoD already largely thinks in these terms, although much more detailed work would be needed to address individual procurements.

This model does not aspire to such a level of detail and instead focuses on a top-down model for planning purposes.

Within each of these sectors, three levels of design and production elements will be examined: significant and essential components, major subsystems, and systems integration expertise. For each element within each of these levels of the industrial "food chain," this research will consider what elements are essentially "dual use"—can be provided by commercial industry—and what elements are "defense unique" and require investments or facilities with little or no commercial applicability. Within both the defense-unique and dual-use columns, in turn, different industrial elements will be classified as "commodities" (widely available globally and where our systems are unlikely to differ in major ways from those of both allies and potential adversaries) and as "differentiators" (where access to leading-edge or specialized capabilities may create significant qualitative advantage for U.S. systems).

This research project will focus exclusively on the industrial base for defense-unique differentiators; existence of needed commercial capabilities will be taken as a given in this initial exercise. It is expected that this sectoral analysis will identify areas where inadequate long-term commercial investment, dependence on foreign sources, industrial concentration, and issues related to surge requirements in wartime may create potential vulnerabilities that warrant further analysis.

The industrial sector analysis will serve two important functions. It will be the principal vehicle for defining, discussing, and measuring the defense industrial base as it is currently constituted. (And in doing this job coherently and consistently, the research is expected to provide valuable stand-alone input to future policy analysis.) The sectoral analyses also will develop the empirical data for the cost models used in the analysis of industrial base requirements linked to differing force structures.

The third step will be the construction of a generic cost model for a defense-unique sector that incorporates the major elements that shape industrial base issues. These elements include sustainment, R&D, and production costs.

Typically, it is asserted that there is some fixed cost merely to maintaining a critical mass of people with the unique skills required to design a specialized defense system and providing them with meaningful work that will give them means to exercise and retain their expertise. For example, it has been estimated that the critical mass of design talent for a fighter aircraft requires an annual expenditure of about $500 million.[5] A RAND study has argued that a minimum group of 2,000 to 3,000 skilled designers and engineers (perhaps $300 million to $500 million annually, using average spending typical for industrial R&D) must be maintained and given useful work to exercise their skills on if a nuclear submarine design capability is to be maintained.[6]

R&D costs are approximately fixed in nature, not varying significantly with the volume produced of the final systems design. This area probably should be modeled as fixed costs above and beyond sustainment costs needed to design a new system or system element.

Production costs also are affected by significant economies of scale. The two principal sources of scale economies are probably learning economies, reductions in unit costs that come in a predictable fashion with cumulative production experience, and more conventional scale economies derived from indivisibilities in production facilities size. Other variable costs probably can be approximated as proportional to scale.

A very simple, canonical cost model, encapsulating all these considerations in terms of a very small number of empirical parameters, will be derived. Parameters will be calibrated for each of the sectors based on a review of existing production and industrial base studies:

Sustainment cost	[X$/year to pay for design group]
R&D costs	[Y$/year to design new system every N years]
Learning economies	[unit cost falls Z percent with every doubling of cumulative production volume]
Indivisibilities in production facilities	[cost of minimum scale facility for an aircraft production line capable of M per year]

A priori, we might doubt that such indivisibilities are likely to be highly significant in many sectors.

My intention is to synthesize from an existing literature. A relatively large body of production and industrial studies already can be found at RAND, Institute for Defense Analysis, Logistics Management Institute, Industrial College of the Armed Forces, National Defense University, DoD, and other places. We do not intend to launch any major, original empirical work but instead will synthesize from the existing literature. Where doubts or questions are significant, issues may be posed as different alternatives for parameters in the model, and sensitivity analysis will be used to assess effects on results.

The fourth task is to combine the cost models with the stylized policy scenarios—industry structure (procurement rules, numbers of suppliers, price-cost relationships), degree of international cooperation, degree of arms export restraint—and an exogenously given force structure, and derive the budget and force planning consequences of each of a small number of permutations of these various policy scenarios.

Modeling the price-cost markup—where the scale-competition trade-off comes into play—is likely to be the toughest part of conceptualizing this research. A larger number of producers means diminished scale economies but more competition. Drawing on the existing theoretical literature, we will develop a simple model linking the price-cost markup to the government's contracting mode, the number of producers, and cost model parameters. A single model will be used for all sectors, with sector-specific parameters as arguments in the generic model. A considerable literature exists, but collapsing this into a simple, empirically useful framework will be the trick.

In addition to these broad policy concerns, technical and operational issues serve to further differentiate alternative industrial scenarios. One such issue is the degree of aggressiveness with which a dual-use strategy is pursued and cost-performance trade-offs made in substituting commercial or near-commercial products for defense-unique ones or in integrating production of military systems with commercial products in common facilities. Another such issue is the balance between continuous improvements in the capabilities of existing weapons platforms piecemeal through retrofits and upgrades and the lengthier development of entirely new, optimized platforms using some given generation of all technologies.

The "international" pieces of the analysis are fairly simple follow-ons to the main analysis. Basically, we need to consider the effects of additional volume on unit costs to model the impact of common procurement with allies and the role of exports in affordability. The same model and same data already assembled will be applied to an additional scenario.

Similarly, reductions in the U.S. share of R&D cost can be used to model the economic impact of R&D cooperation with allies. The same model and same data can be used again to consider the effects of alternative scenarios.

An aggressive, dual-use approach to the industrial base, with fixed price competition, dual transatlantic suppliers in each sector, an upgrade/ retrofit strategy, and restraints on third-country exports, for example, might be contrasted with an autarkic, more traditional, cost-plus contracting approach based on new platforms every 15 years, with no export restraints. The steady-state cost of a fixed-force structure, the number of suppliers and amount of capacity sustained, the average technology vintage of systems in the U.S. inventory, and the steady-state shares of research, development, testing, and evaluation (RDT&E), procurement, and other industrial base costs in the overall budget would all be interesting results to be compared in these simulations.

The final element is to perform a sensitivity analysis, to search for the key leverage points in the study, to look for sensitivities to small changes in parameters or assumptions, and to otherwise identify qualitative phenomena that have real impacts on the relationship between a sustainable force structure and the underlying industrial base.

A sensitivity analysis may reveal some vulnerabilities in the industrial base—ways in which small changes in parameters or assumptions, given a fixed-force structure, could have large impacts on industrial requirements. Such an analysis also should lead to refinement of data and parameter estimates, and improvements to both the model and the policy scenarios used as inputs.

Fleshing Out the Issues: The Tactical Missile Industrial Base

One way to get a better sense of these issues is to look at how we might go about dealing with the concrete particulars of a particular sector. I have chosen tactical missiles to illustrate them, for two reasons. First, experiments in dual sourcing of production have been carried out with some frequency for these systems and have been studied by analysts, giving us a bit more empirical insight into the competition-scale economy complexities. Second, the defense-unique elements of the system are a bit cleaner and easier to define.

Table 8–1 shows the firms serving as prime contractors for tactical missiles as of 1993. (It excludes the most recent missiles developed for the army currently approaching initial production: Wide Area Munition [WAM, Textron], and the Sense and Destroy Armor [SADARM Aerojet] and Brilliant Anti Tank [BAT, Northrop-Grumman] submunitions.) The two giants of the sector were Hughes and Raytheon, since merged; with the acquisition of Loral (with ATACMS, Army Tactical Missile System) and ER-MLRS Extended Range-Multiple Launch Rocket System in its current portfolio by Lockheed-Martin, a second large player was formed. Note that TSSAM, Tri-Service Standoff Attack Missile has since been canceled, HARM High-Speed Anti-Radiation Missile is no longer being purchased domestically, and current Hellfire follow-ons are being produced by Lockheed Martin, not Rockwell, so the U.S. prime contractor pool now mainly consists of the two big conglomerates and McDonnell Douglas (now part of Boeing).

Table 8–1   Prime Contractors in the Tactical Missile Industrial Base

COMPANY	PROGRAMS (EXAMPLES)	
BOEING	STINGER	NLOS
		TSSAM
HUGHES	ACM	RAM
	AMRAAM	SEA SPARROW
	CORPS SAM	SPARROW
	GBI	STANDARD
	MAVERICK	STINGER
	NLOS	TOMAHAWK
	PHOENIX	TOW
LOCKHEED	CORPS SAM	THAAD
	GBI	
LORAL	ATACMS	LOSAT
	CHAPARRAL	MLRS
	CORPS SAM	SIDEWINDER
	ERINT	
MARTIN MARIETTA	CORPS SAM	HAVE NAP
	GBI	HELLFIRE
		PATRIOT
McDONNELL DOUGLAS	ACM	HARPOON
	DRAGON-2	SLAM
	GBI	TOMAHAWK
NORTHROP	TSSAM	
RAYTHEON	AMRAAM	PHOENIX
	CORPS SAM	SEA SPARROW
	HAWK	SIDEWINDER
	MAVERICK	SPARROW
	NLOS	STANDARD
	PATRIOT	STINGER
ROCKWELL INTERNATIONAL	AGM-130	HELLFIRE
	GBI	NLOS
TEXAS INSTRUMENTS	HARM	JSOW
	JAVELIN	

Source: Tactical Missiles Working Group, Defense Industrial Base
Subcommittee, Defense Policy Advisory Committee on Trade,
"Preserving a Defense Industrial Base: The Tactical Missiles Sector,"
September 1993.

Building a missile requires expertise in overall systems design and integration and specialized components that basically can be divided into three categories: guidance and control subsystems, propulsion subsystems, and warhead and fuzing subsystems. Table 8–2 shows major U.S. subcontractors producing components in each of these areas as well as other highly specialized subcomponents.

With the ongoing "revolution in military affairs," and its emphasis on stand-off and precision strikes, tactical missiles are increasingly central to U.S. military doctrine. During Desert Storm, for example, missiles fired included about 20,000 ground-to-ground MLRSs, 5,000 air-to-ground Mavericks, 4,000 ground-to-ground tube-launched, optically tracked, wire-guided (TOW) missiles, 3,000 air-to-ground Hellfires, 2,000 air-to-surface HARMS, and 300 Tomahawk cruise missiles. Advanced medium-range air-to-air missile (AMRAAM), now operational and fired in combat in Bosnia, was not used during Desert Storm. A rough estimate of production levels and stocks needed on hand to fight two Desert Storm–size regional contingencies might begin with these numbers and refine them to reflect changes in threats in other theaters.

Understanding how much it costs to develop a missile system, it turns out, can be quite complex. The U.S. acquisition process is basically broken into three major stages. After a preliminary process called concept definition (which nonetheless requires not insignificant R&D resources), the first major stage—serious demonstration and validation of a concept by a contractor, or dem-val—is undertaken. Demonstrated and validated concepts then move forward into full-scale development, the next (and very expensive—10 to 20 percent of total system acquisition cost) stage, which ends as the first prototypes and initial units are built. The third and final phase is full production of the system. U.S. weapons systems, historically, have taken about 3.5 years to go through dem-val, 4.5 years to go through full-scale development, and are in production for about 16 years, on average. They are in service, of course, for many more years.

Competition typically is present during concept definition, then a small number of contractors (usually two) are downselected to participate in dem-val. A sole winner usually is downselected for full-scale development, although sometimes multiple systems have gone to full-scale development and tested against one another (generally in unusual circumstances—a variant of an already developed system being modified, for example, and competed against a system developed from scratch). After testing and evaluation, the developed system is then produced, most often by a sole source. Thus, if we think of procurement as an idealized competitive R&D process followed by a monopoly on pro-

Table 8–2 Major Subcontractors in the Tactical Missile Industrial Base, 1993

SEEKERS	GUIDANCE	FIRE CONTROL	CONTROL ACTUATION	THERMAL BATTERIES	SOLID ROCKET MOTORS	ROCKET MOTOR CASES	SAFM ARM FUZE	LAUNCH TUBES
AEROJET	ALLIED SIGNAL	ALLIANT TECH	ALLIED SIGNAL	EAGLE-PICHER	ATLANTIC RESEARCH	AMFUEL COMPOSITES	ACCUDYNE	ADV. COMP
BALL	E-SYSTEMS	GE	CURTISS WRIGHT		BEI	ATLANTIC RESEARCH	ALLIED SIGNAL	BRUNSWICK
HUGHES	HONEYWELL	HARRIS	ELDEC		GENCORP AEROJET	BRUNSWICK	BOWMAR	CCDI
LORAL	INTERSTATE ELEC.	HUGHES	E-SYSTEMS		HERCULES	HERCULES	BULOVA	EDO
MARTIN MARIETTA	KERRFOTT	LITTON	KOLLMORGEN		THIOKOL	IMCO	EATON-CONSOLIDATED	FIBERTEK
RAYTHEON	LITTON	LORAL	LORAL		UNITED TECH	KAISER ROLLMET	ELECTRO-DYNAMICS	HERCULES
ROCKWELL	MAGNAVOX	MARTIN MARIETTA	LUCAS			NORRI	TRACOR AERO.	KAISER
TEXAS INSTRUMENTS	MOTOROLA	ROCKWELL	MOOG			THIOKOL	HI-SHEAR TECH	TOLO
WESTINGHOUSE	NORTHROP	TELEDYNE	MRC PRODUCTS			SPIN FORGE	KDI PRECISION	
	RAYTHEON	TEXAS INSTRUMENTS	PARKER BENTEA				MAGNAVOX	
	ROCKWELL	UNITED TECH	PLESSEY				MOTOROLA	
	SMITHS		SARGENT CONTROLS				ORDNANCE DEVICES	
			SIMMONDS				PACIFIC SCIENTIFIC	
	TRIMBLE NAVIGATION						QUANTIC IND	
	UNISYS		TEXTRON				RAYMOND ENGR	
			VICKENS				SCOTT, INC.	
							TRACOR AERO.	

Source: Tactical Missiles Working Group, Defense Industrial Base Subcommittee, Defense Policy Advisory Committee on Trade, "Preserving Defense Industrial Base: The Tactical Missiles Sector," September 1993.

duction, the boundary between these two conceptual stages is not easily located within the real-world acquisition process.

The first issue faced in assessing R&D cost is determining where to begin and where to end. Technology R&D projects often are funded to explore new approaches to key subsystems and components before a new systems concept has been formally defined. As the United States begins the formal acquisition process for a new short-range air-to-air missile, for example, U.S. contractors will bring to the table new airframe and seeker technology funded as part of background technology exploration efforts. The fruit of these efforts, which may well be used in the new system, will not show up in the system's R&D cost when a new program is formally set up. In general, R&D efforts prior to selection of a winning concept(s) and establishment of a program office are not going to be counted toward that program's R&D budget. After a formal program office is established, budgets still may provide less than desired detail. A system in development may have both procurement and RDT&E funding associated with it, for example, if procurement funds are used to acquire materials or components used in development. Similarly, after a system enters into production, R&D funds typically continue to flow as improvements and modifications to the system and its manufacturing process, and the next iteration of upgrades to the system are set in motion.

Thus, for example, one accounting of the cost of developing AMRAAM suggests that a system cost roughly $1.9 billion to develop after the concept definition stage, including modifications and improvements after the system entered production. The medium-range air defense missile program (MEADS) now being undertaken with European partners is expected to cost about $2 billion through the end of dem-val and into the very early stages of development (a nonstandard division between phases has been made to accommodate European procurement practices), but this funding excludes the value of R&D on technologies to be used in the system already undertaken by the United States.

Another approach may be had by looking at the DoD's five-year defense plan (FYDP), which counts R&D toward a specific program only until production of the system has been approved (after which further R&D is assigned to a separate R&D "program" category). Recently declassified FYDP figures on development of cruise missiles show the complexities of using this set of boundaries on R&D for a system. A joint cruise missile program office was established in 1977 to oversee development of both a sea-launched cruise missile (SLCM) for the navy and ground-launched cruise missile (GLCM) for the air force version of the Tomahawk cruise missile, as well as a separate air-launched cruise missile (ALCM) for the air force. GLCM carried a nuclear warhead, while SLCM had both nuclear and conventional packages, but except for variations in warheads and guidance systems, they were all essentially the same missile. After 1980 ALCM was severed from the joint missile program and management transferred to the air force. Initial production of Tomahawk was started in FY 1981, and both SLCM and GLCM were first operationally deployed in 1983.

The FYDP shows a "cruise missile" R&D program running in 1972 and 1973, a Tomahawk R&D program from 1973 to 1977 (although a line for Tomahawk in "general-purpose forces" begins in 1978, before the complete system was being assembled), and a GLCM R&D program running from 1978 to 1986. Early cruise missile and Tomahawk R&D amounted to approximately $420 million FY 1995, GLCM R&D to about FY 1995 $630 million, for a grand total of about $1.05 billion. This figure suggests that either Tomahawk was an excellent R&D deal for the taxpayer or that interpretation of the FYDP requires considerable caution, or both.

Tomahawk was also interesting as an example of an experiment with dual-source production. Dissatisfied with both the projected costs and quality assurances forthcoming from General Dynamics/Convair (the original prime, whose missile division later was purchased by Hughes), the program office began discussing dual sourcing with McDonnell, which built the guidance subsystem. Neither side wanted to transfer its technology to the other, and negotiations were stalled until finally the program office threatened to bring in a third party to build the systems. At that point dual-sourcing arrangements were agreed to, with each side guaranteed a minimum buy (30 or 40 percent), with the balance going to the low-cost supplier.

Interestingly, when outside analysts were brought in to study the cost savings and were given access to proprietary cost data, wildly divergent estimates of actual nonrecurring unit costs were produced. The program office's unit cost estimates ranged from 25 percent (in 1984) to 50 percent (in 1981) more than those of the Center for Naval Analyses. Unit costs also fluctuated considerably from year to year, suggesting that varying production volumes and effects on allocation of depreciation and overhead charges had a significant effect on unit cost. Judgments of the effects of competition on costs were similarly divergent (ranging from $20 million to $176 million through fiscal 1987).

Nonetheless, it is clear that sharply divergent factors are at work in assessing the impact of competition. On one hand, competition may be expected to put downward pressure on the costs reported by manufacturers when contracts are negotiated. Analysts typically suggest a one-time shift in the cost/quantity relationship owing to competitive sourcing pressures, along with a downward "rotation" in the curve (a steepening in the learning curve) that persists over time.

On the other hand, there are clearly significant scale economies, both static and dynamic. Industry rule of thumb in missile production is a 15 percent decline in unit cost with a doubling of production volume at any moment in time. Estimates of learning curves in Tomahawk production range from 10 to 20 percent, so 15 percent is a reasonable guess. Taking the production volumes for Tomahawk currently projected over FY 1995 to FY 2010, and dividing those equally between two producers, rather than a sole source, would raise costs by about 18 percent every year owing to static scale economies in production. Given the low procurement rate (about 144 per year, starting from cumulative production of 4,260 units as of 1994), the cost-raising effect of splitting additional cumulative experience would be small—raising unit cost about 4.5 percent above single-source cost by the year 2010.

Thus, these back-of-the-envelope calculations suggest that competitive pressures would have to produce really large effects to compensate for the cost-raising loss of scale and learning economies. The Department of Defense was surely correct in concluding that by "singling up" Tomahawk production it would save resources. (It projects savings of over $500 million on procurement between FY 1994 and 1999.)

Conclusion

This chapter laid out a proposed approach to analyzing the defense industrial base in order to determine how much is needed to sustain our projected force structure and how much it will cost us. A brief dip into the issues indicates there are likely to be two very difficult issues. The first one is conceptual: How can we in relatively simple ways model the likely costs and benefits of maintaining competition in various stages of the acquisition process? At least the costs can be approximated in relatively simple ways, but the benefits are far more subtle and difficult to capture analytically. The second issue, surprisingly, is data. Although the Department of Defense captures huge amounts of data in its reports, none of the public breakouts thus far surveyed seems to lend itself naturally to the kind of conceptual analysis of the procurement process being proposed. More work clearly will be required.

Notes

1. F. M. Scherer, *The Weapons Acquisition Process: Economic Incentives* (Cambridge, Mass.: Harvard University Press, 1964), p. 2.

2. For an insightful review of this argument, see William P. Rogerson, "Economic Incentives and the Defense Procurement Process," *Journal of Economic Perspectives,* no. 4 (Fall 1994).

3. PDD-34 explicitly sets enhancement of the ability of the U.S. defense industrial base to meet U.S. defense requirements at lower costs as a goal of U.S. arms transfer policy. See White House, Office of the Press Secretary, "Fact Sheet: Conventional Arms Transfer Policy," February 17, 1995.

4. See Mark Lorell et al., *The Gray Threat: Assessing the Next Generation European Fighters* (Santa Monica, Calif.: RAND, 1995).

5. See Michael Kennedy et al., "Holding the Lead: Sustaining a Viable U.S. Military Fixed-Wing Aeronautical R&D Industrial Base" (Santa Monica, Calif.: RAND, May 1996).

6. John Birkler et al., *The U.S. Submarine Production Base: An Analysis of Cost, Schedule, and Risk for Selected Force Structures* (Santa Monica, Calif.: RAND, 1994).

IV

The Push to Export

9

The Changing Economics of the Arms Trade

DAVID GOLD

THE VALUE of the worldwide trade in military goods and services has declined dramatically from its peak in the mid-1980s. For the decade ending in 1995, the real value of the international arms trade declined by 11.2 percent per year. The arms trade averaged an estimated $32.3 billion per year between 1991 and 1995, only 45 percent of its 1985 value; the arms trade has not been this low since 1972.[1] The value of arms transfers rose somewhat in the mid-1990s, but remains far below the level of a decade earlier.

The sharp contraction in the arms trade is due primarily to the end of the Cold War and the cessation of superpower rivalry. The trade in many large weapons systems declined substantially after the mid-1980s, and it is not unreasonable to see this change as one of the elements of a global peace dividend emanating from the conclusion of the Cold War. However, an arms trade of some $30 billion to $35 billion per year is still substantial, and that level of spending can purchase a fair amount of lethality. At the same time that trade in large weapons is declining, trade in small arms and light weapons appears to be rising, linked to the large number of regional conflicts and civil wars that have occurred over the last decade.[2] The disposal of surplus weapons by weapons-producing states has been a major contributor to the arms trade in recent years.[3] And black markets in international weapons transfers also appear to have grown in importance, suggesting that the value of the international arms trade exceeds the numbers commonly discussed.[4]

The end of the Cold War certainly did not remove all sources of conflict. It may even have allowed regional and civil tensions to surface more readily and become active conflicts, since the absence of superpower rivalry removed the threat of escalation that was present previously. Without Cold War rivalries, the economic motivations behind the arms trade have become more visible and relatively more important. The demand for arms has fallen far more rapidly than the capacity to produce, as the large, producing countries have struggled with how to rationalize their defense industries. In addition, the number of countries capable of producing weapons for international sales is growing. The result is a classic buyer's market with buying countries able to win substantial concessions from suppliers. The major arms-producing and buying countries have responded with policy initiatives that have contributed to raising the relative importance of economic considerations in the international arms market.

The Changing Arms Market

Table 9–1 presents the major changes in the international arms market. The sharp decline in arms exports is primarily the result of the contraction of the defense sector and the resulting drop in arms sales from the former Soviet Union, the largest supplier at the end of the Cold War. This drop in arms sales, from $25 billion per year between 1986 and 1990 for the Soviet Union to $3.5 billion per year between 1991 and 1995 for Russia, accounted for 56 percent of the decline in the market as a whole. In the absence of political linkages and without extensive government subsidies, it has been difficult for Russian arms producers to be competitive.[5] Substantial sales were made out of inventories; it is only recently, however, that a reorganized Russian industry has begun to make its presence felt in the arms market. Former members of the Warsaw Treaty Organization (WTO), who were main customers for Soviet-made equipment, largely withdrew from the market following the breakup of that alliance. Former WTO members in central and eastern Europe that are seeking to become members of, or ally themselves with, the North Atlantic Treaty Organization (NATO) are expected to become significant arms purchasers as they seek greater compatibility with NATO forces. Companies and governments from NATO arms-producing countries are making major efforts to capture this potentially lucrative market.[6]

The United States now accounts for almost half of worldwide arms exports. The dominance of the United States in the international arms market is not solely the result of the reduced Russian presence. U.S. firms can

Table 9–1   Major Changes in the Arms Trade, 1985–90 to 1991–95
(average annual totals; 1995 U.S. $)

Country or Group	1985–90	% of Total	1991–95	% of Total	% Change in Value
Total Exports	69,618	100	32,302	100	−53.6
United States	18,196	26.1	14,770	45.7	−18.8
NATO Europe	13,958	20	9,555	29.6	−31.5
Soviet Union/Russia	25,192	36.2	3,526	10.1	−86.8
China	2,668	3.8	1,050	3.3	−60.6
Total Imports	69,618	100	32,302	100	−53.6
United States	2,597	3.7	1,683	5.2	−35.2
NATO Europe	8,138	11.7	4,631	14.3	−43.1
Warsaw Pact	5,352	7.7	539	1.7	−89.9
Japan	1,416	2.0	891	2.8	−37.1
China	611	0.9	665	2.1	+8.8
Other East Asia	7,452	10.7	3,906	12.1	−52.4
Saudi Arabia	8,326	12.0	8,160	25.3	−2.0
Other Middle East	15,678	22.5	5,014	15.5	−68.0
South Asia	7,364	10.6	1,499	4.6	−79.6

Source: United States Arms Control and Disarmament Agency, *World Military Expenditures and Arms Transfers 1996* (Washington, D.C.: U.S. Government Printing Office, 1997), table II.

offer a wide variety of equipment with sophisticated weaponry and electronics that was successfully battle-tested in the Gulf War. Indeed, U.S. firms experienced a surge in orders following that war. The United States also can offer a range of ancillary services that is difficult for other countries to match. And with a clear technological lead, U.S. equipment and services are likely to be increasingly desirable as information-based military systems become more prominent in the future.

On the buying side, the Middle East has absorbed 40 percent of arms imports in the 1990s, a larger share, albeit a smaller absolute amount, than in the late 1980s. The removal of Iraq from the market has been offset by continued purchases from Saudi Arabia and other countries in that region, a response to continued tensions and the desire on the part of many countries to upgrade their arsenals after the Gulf War, as well as a reflection of the substantial purchasing power available to many countries there. East Asia, including China and Japan, is the second largest regional market, in part owing to security concerns but also because rapid economic growth there has given countries substantial purchasing power.[7] The 1997 economic crisis and ensuing adjustments in East Asia have led to some reductions in purchases and future orders.[8]

Developing countries in other regions—Africa, Latin America, South Asia—have experienced economic difficulties that have limited their spending on weapons. The International Monetary Fund and the World Bank have informally, but apparently strongly, suggested that countries in financial difficulty should limit both domestic military spending and international arms purchases.[9] Latin American countries have begun considering substantial arms purchases as the adjustments from the 1980s debt crisis have taken hold. In 1997 the Clinton administration removed a two-decades-old ban on sales of high-technology weapons to Latin America, a ban that was imposed by the Carter administration because of human rights violations in that region, and instituted a case-by-case review procedure.[10] Defense firms had sought this change to open up the Latin American market, although the market's size remains in doubt.[11]

In the West, the end of the Cold War and the breakup of the Soviet empire has been accompanied by reductions in military budgets and in arms purchases. Most developed economies have used defense spending cuts as a component of fiscal retrenchments.[12] In western Europe, meeting the Maastricht criteria for budget deficits has contributed to pressures to cut defense spending.[13] As a group, NATO countries have reduced their real annual military expenditures by 22 percent between 1987 and 1995 and cut their arms imports by 58 percent over the same period. This is a pattern similar to that for the market as a whole, where the decline in international arms sales has been much larger, in relative terms, than the decline in military spending (See Figure 9–1.)

In the four largest NATO arms-producing countries, weapons procurement fell by 23 percent (France), 33 percent (the United States), 34 percent (the United Kingdom), and 45 percent (Germany) between 1987 and 1996.[14] However, these countries have not reduced their capacity to produce by anywhere near the same amount. The United States has experienced a major merger wave that has drastically reduced the number of separate producers at the top tier of the industry and is beginning to have similar effects in the middle tiers. It is not clear by how much capacity actually is being reduced; some mergers have sought to combine similar businesses and reduce redundancies, as in the missile business with Raytheon's acquisition of Hughes, while others are creating defense-oriented conglomerates with little product overlap, as in the acquisitions made by Boeing and Lockheed. It is also not clear whether the promised cost savings from production synergies and reductions in administrative overhead will compensate for a reduction in competition, with the number of independent pro-

Figure 9–1   Arms Exports as a Share of Military Spending, Worldwide Totals, 1987–95

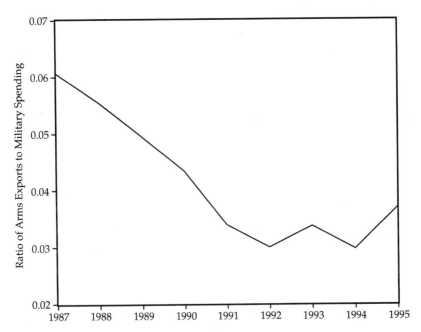

Source: United States Arms Control and Disarmament Agency, *World Military Expenditures and Arms Transfers 1996* (Washington, D.C.: U.S. Government Printing Office, 1997).

ducers being reduced to two or three for many important systems.[15] In Europe, difficulties in formulating Europe-wide strategies have delayed restructuring, and excess capacity in military production remains a serious problem.[16] One result is an intensification of the search for export markets at the very time the size of these markets has been considerably reduced.

Excess capacity among weapons producers and excess supply on international arms markets are not new phenomena. Indeed, excess capacity in defense and aerospace, in the sense of fixed costs being high relative to expected output, has been chronic since the 1950s.[17] Because arms producers contribute to both national security through producing weapons and matériel and domestic economic goals through income and employment creation and technological spin-off, and because arms producers usually have substantial political influence, they often receive considerable subsidies, either directly or through the contracting process. Only gradually are the least competitive weeded out. The number of independent producers in the United States has been declining since the 1950s, albeit in fits and starts, culminating in the merger wave of the 1990s that, in effect, followed the downward drift in defense spending's share of gross domestic product. There has also been increasing concentration in civilian aerospace; with the Boeing–McDonnell Douglas merger, there are only two producers of large passenger aircraft, Boeing and Airbus. In the 1990s, the spread of production technology to smaller developed countries and some developing countries has increased the number of potential competitors, while the disposal of surplus weapons has reinforced the supply overhang and contributed to the current buyer's market.

Policy Shifts

The growing relative importance of economic considerations is evident in the responses of governments to the changing international arms market. Policy in the major supplying nations, while focused largely on reorganizing and reducing capacity, has become more explicit in recognizing economic motives behind expanded arms sales. This has long been the case for France, which is one of the few governments that has explicitly adopted an economic rationale for arms sales, in the form of spreading development costs over a larger output, thereby allowing the procurement of weapons that would not otherwise be possible.[18] The most dramatic change has occurred in Russia, which has shifted from a policy of heavily subsidizing arms sales to allies and client states, to a situation where recently privatized firms are encouraged to export arms in order to earn hard currency.

There also have been changes in the United States, the largest and most visible of the supplying nations. Economic motives and rationales have always been a part of U.S. arms sales. Under the Nixon Doctrine, for example, arms sales to regional powers were motivated at least partly by the desire to recycle petrodollars. Arms sales frequently have been introduced into election campaigns, with candidates trumpeting their ability to obtain foreign business for firms in their districts in order to preserve or expand employment. The Clinton administration, however, has carried an economics focus further than previous U.S. administrations by making preservation of the domestic defense industrial base one of the explicit objectives of arms sales. This is stated in a Presidential Directive on Conventional Arms Transfer Policy (PDD-34), issued on February 17, 1995.[19] According to one knowledgeable observer, "the Clinton Conventional Arms Transfer Policy holds that supporting a strong, sustainable American defense-industrial base is a key national security concern, rather than simply a commercial matter. In doing so, the Clinton policy directive has publicly elevated the significance of domestic economic considerations in the arms transfer decision-making process to a higher degree than has been formally the case in previous Administrations."[20]

In expanding the government's role in promoting arms exports, the Clinton administration has explicitly charged the Commerce and State departments and embassies in potential buying countries with major roles in promoting U.S. arms exports. This is in direct contrast to the policy under President Jimmy Carter, which limited government promotion efforts and explicitly forbade civilian agencies from participating, and even goes beyond the less restrictive policies of the Reagan and Bush administrations. The Clinton policies toward arms sales appear to be linked both to defense industrial base issues and to a strategy of achieving U.S. dominance in global high-technology trade.[21]

The Clinton policy shift was evaluated and criticized by a Presidential Advisory Board on Arms Proliferation Policy, which was formed at the same time the new policy was announced but reported almost a year and a half later.[22] The board argued that industrial base issues should be treated separately from arms exports and that "the best solution to overcapacity . . . is to reduce supply rather than increase demand." The board expressed concern that incorporating economic considerations into arms sales would worsen proliferation problems.[23]

In the primary buying countries, governments have recognized their strengthened market position and have actively sought concessions from sellers in the form of offsets. Direct offsets involve supplying firms entering into agreements with firms in the buying country to subcontract or coproduce elements of the weapon being transferred. Indirect offsets involve supplying firms committing themselves to find markets for products of buying countries other than those linked to the weapon itself, or to obtain investment and technology flows for buying countries. Offsets have grown from an occasional to a central feature of international arms sales.[24] Just about every country involved in purchasing arms has formulated offset requirements, while major arms producers have begun assembling offset networks within buying countries prior to obtaining a weapons contract; offset networks now are seen as part of a firm's efforts to secure future contracts.[25] A major purpose of offsets is for the country buying weapons to obtain a flow of resources that will offset the foreign exchange costs and balance-of-payments effects of the arms purchase. Arms-importing countries also use offsets to gain access to both defense and nondefense markets in selling countries. Selling countries, on the other hand, offer offsets as a means of seeking a competitive edge in weapons deals.

While offsets have become an important means for funding arms purchases at the aggregate level, their significance may lie more as a conduit for transferring aerospace and weapons production technology. Offsets increasingly are used by buying countries to obtain technology that possibly could be applied to stimulate domestic firms in aerospace and other technology-intensive industries.[26] Used in this way, offsets are a form of industrial policy for the weapons-buying country.[27] Japan has long had a policy of using offsets to obtain production technologies as part of a strategy to become more self-sufficient in military production and to speed the entry of Japanese firms into international aerospace markets.[28] The Japanese in particular have employed a dual-use strategy, with research and development (R&D) and production structured to encourage interactions between military and civilian applications.[29] In contrast, the United States has fostered a separation between military and civilian production and R&D. But with civilian technology increasing in sophistication while military technology has become expensive and slow, U.S. policy is attempting to create closer civil-military integration. More recently, South Korea and Taiwan have begun to follow the Japanese pattern and are using offset agreements to obtain dual-use technologies.[30] While the success of these strategies has been mixed, the potential exists for a significant upgrading in the ability of these countries to produce and sell weapons on international markets.[31] Other buying countries demand offsets as a means of retaining purchasing power to compensate for a large arms import. In some instances, offsets have been used to compensate sectors of the economy that lost business when the government decided to import a weapons system rather than produce it domestically.[32] However, in many countries the domestic technology base is not sufficiently advanced to handle much in the way of direct offsets. These countries tend to focus on finding markets for nondefense output or obtaining technology more suited to their needs.[33]

Macroeconomic Issues

Exports of military goods and services have a positive impact on a selling country's balance of payments and stimulate domestic income and employment. The effects are not likely to be large, since weapons exports typically represent a small share of total exports. Only for a few countries—the United States, the United Kingdom, China, Israel, Russia, Bulgaria, and North Korea—do arms exports amount to more than 1 percent of total exports. In many countries arms production tends to be concentrated geographically and in a few industries. Thus the impact of arms exports will be substantial in affected regions and industries.

The growing use of offsets has undermined somewhat the argument that arms exports provide macroeconomic stimulation for the exporting economy. A study by the U.S. Department of Commerce tracked offset agreements whose value represented 47 percent of the value of all weapons export agreements reported by U.S. firms in 1995. The Commerce study found that the value of the offsets in agreements entered into by U.S. companies in 1995 came to 81 percent of the value of the export contracts in question, and that agreements with governments in Europe, which represented the bulk of U.S. offset agreements, came to 104 percent of the related export contracts.[34] The magnitude here reflects the growing importance of indirect offsets, which include a wide variety of both military and civilian activities. With the value of offsets approaching and often exceeding 100 percent of the value of the arms sale for many large sales, the overall balance-of-payments impact becomes ambiguous.

Data on offsets, however, may overstate their macroeconomic impact. In the past, offset agreements have been difficult to enforce, and many offsets have ended up covering less than promised. For indirect offsets, where typically the company undertaking the arms sale assists the buying country's companies in obtaining markets for their products, it is not always possible to judge how many of these sales would have occurred in any event and how many represent new business. Moreover, many arms sales would not be possible without offsets. In many buying countries, offsets are necessary to secure political support for arms purchases. The problem is selecting the appropriate baseline; offsets mean the macroeconomic impact is less than would be the case in their absence, but since it is not possible to dispense with offsets, the selling country must accept a lower level of stimulation. Proponents of arms sales often argue that a small percentage of something is better than 100 percent of nothing. The issue, then, is whether a reduced level of macroeconomic stimulation is worth the costs of obtaining arms exports.

For buying countries, offsets can be seen as a mechanism to break through barriers in imperfect markets. The U.S. defense market is highly protected.[35] Congress and the Department of Defense have substantial legislative authority that favors domestic over foreign suppliers of military goods and services. U.S. military imports, which averaged $1.5 billion per year between 1991 and 1995 (in 1995 dollars), or about

5 percent of the world total, are small relative to the size of the defense budget and include many items, such as fuel, needed to maintain forces stationed out of the country. The few large procurement and research, development, testing, and engineering (RDT&E) contracts given to foreign firms are usually in the context of codevelopment and coproduction arrangements, such as the inclusion of British Aerospace on the Lockheed-led team competing for the Joint Strike Fighter contract, where the United Kingdom is a buyer. The United States also has adopted policies to severely curtail foreign investment in military-industry firms, although such policies have probably not reached into the lower tiers of the subcontracting network or into firms supplying dual-use products.[36]

To the extent that offsets stimulate imports and imports substitute for domestic production, there is a shift of income and employment from the import-competing sector to the sector producing the arms export. In the United States, this has led to some political opposition to offsets from areas that have been impacted by offset-induced imports. Senator Russell Feingold (D-Wis.) became interested in the issue when a Wisconsin firm lost business to an offset-induced import.[37] There also has been opposition to direct offsets on the grounds that subcontracting and coproduction shift employment out of the country. Workers at Boeing and General Dynamics, in a plant producing F-16s that is now owned by Lockheed, have protested the granting of subcontracts to firms in East Asia.[38]

Microeconomic Issues

Military production is characterized by economies of scale, as fixed costs for research and development and capital investment tend to be high relative to output. In addition, weapons production tends to emphasize new, and frequently unproven, product and process technologies, leaving room for substantial learning economies. Modern weapons are complex, involving a melding of a number of different technologies, which increases costs, uncertainties, and learning times. At the same time, budgetary restrictions, made even more severe in the post–Cold War environment, limit output and prevent producers from reaching efficient production levels. The basic microeconomic argument in favor of arms sales is that they enable a producer to spread fixed costs over a larger market, thereby lowering unit costs for both importing and exporting countries. The contracting agency should benefit in the form of lower procurement costs compared to what they would be in the absence of exports.

It also has been argued that exports allow contractors to maintain open assembly lines that otherwise would be closed, giving defense agencies access to replacements for weapons that are lost through accident, normal attrition, or in combat, and retaining the capability for expanding output rapidly to meet a surge in wartime needs. In the absence of active production, high start-up costs and long lead times required for reconstituting production lines make the replacement and surge options less effective from both an economic and military standpoint. However, ongoing R&D programs can maintain the knowledge stock while initial procurement plans can include a significant replacement component. The costs and likelihood of restarting a production line need to be compared to the costs of keeping one open. In addition, the experience of the Gulf War suggests that surge capacity is not likely to be needed, even in the two–Gulf Wars scenarios that underlie current defense planning.

In the typical life cycle for high-technology civilian products, new products have limited markets and relatively high prices. Over time, both scale and learning effects tend to bring unit costs down. Thus, if the product is reasonably successful, an expanding market allows for declining prices. An expanding market, in turn, stimulates improvements in both product and process technology and attracts new entrants. As the product matures, it is transformed from a luxury owned by a few to a common item bought by many. Recent examples include personal computers, cellular telephones, satellite dishes, and the spread of microprocessors into a variety of goods including automobiles; earlier examples are video cassette recorders and television sets, both black and white and color, with high-definition (HDTV) likely to follow this pattern in the future. Even technology-intensive, large products such as civilian airliners and power plants follow this pattern within their own parameters. This type of life cycle forms a virtuous circle—a successful product generates an expanding market, which allows for price declines and stimulates competition, including further R&D, which in turn creates cost-reducing innovations. With market growth, high fixed costs can be spread more widely and lead to falling prices. For example, the unit price of microprocessors has declined rapidly and steadily while their capabilities have grown equally rapidly, despite major growth in the costs of R&D and capital equipment for each new generation.

By contrast, the logic of military production describes a circle far less virtuous. New technology and performance improvements are demanded by the monopsonist buyer, but the combination of high development costs and limited budgets guarantees less than optimal levels of output and rising prices, while rising prices then contribute to further limiting output in the context of budget constraints. The government substitutes for the market in generating incentives for technological change, but the government is unable to deliver sufficient demand to spread the fixed costs and prevent unit cost growth. Governments also tend to demand a high degree of specialization and frequently procure a variety of systems for similar roles, as with combat aircraft and naval vessels, rather than seek fewer separate systems with more generally defined roles, a fact that further spreads budgetary resources.[39] Moreover, the highly politicized procurement process leads contractors and military agencies to overcommit on performance and technological parameters, raising development costs and increasing risks.[40]

Foreign markets are seen as a means of moving out learning curves and reducing unit costs. The reality, however, may be less clear cut. In Chapter 8 of this volume, Kenneth Flamm reports that little is known within the Department of Defense (DoD) about the shape of cost functions; little hard information exists as to how much savings could reasonably be achieved or what level of exports would need to be attained to realize meaningful savings. The typical case for a major export item is that a system initially is purchased for domestic needs and is made available for export as domestic needs recede or as upgraded versions of the system are produced for domestic forces. Most of the fixed costs of weapons production are borne by the government. The DoD either pays for RDT&E through contracts entered into prior to the research phase of a project, or it reimburses contractors through the Independent Research and Development (IR&D) program. Only occasionally do firms bear R&D costs. In addition, the DoD owns a substantial amount of plant and equipment used by military contractors under the Government-Owned Contractor-Operated (GOCO) program; other fixed costs are included in overhead charges in procurement contracts. With the government absorbing the bulk of fixed costs, providing funding or subsidizing loans to some buyers, and engaging in substantial promotion activities, contractors can offer export items at low unit costs, especially when the item already has had a substantial production run and the contractor has incorporated learning economies into the cost structure.

If export markets are utilized to compensate for high fixed costs, the contracting agency that absorbed the costs should receive some of the proceeds from the export sales. Starting in 1967, the United States collected a fee from foreign military sales that was earmarked for recouping R&D outlays; waivers of the fee were allowed on sales to allies—NATO countries, Australia, New Zealand, and Japan—to support equipment standardization and other alliance goals, and waivers were allowed when the buyer utilized U.S. foreign military financing.[41] President George Bush abolished R&D recoupment fees on commercial exports, while Congress has given President Clinton the authority to waive the fees on government-to-government sales on a case-by-case basis, on the grounds that firms from the United States were at a disadvantage vis-à-vis their main competitors in the arms market.[42] With the fees waived, the benefits of lower unit costs accrue to the buying country and the selling company, but not to the government that financed the development costs.

In France, by contrast, export sales are included in the initial projections of market size that are used to determine the expected total and unit costs of a weapons system. As a result, the French government pays a cost that is adjusted for the larger production run generated by the export market. Also, at times, export deliveries have been given primacy over deliveries to the French military, and buyer requirements have led to alterations in weapons at the design stage.[43]

Export markets are costly to obtain. William Hartung of the World Policy Institute has reported that the United States expended $7.7 billion in FY 1995, and an annual average of $7.8 billion in FY 1996 and FY 1997, to finance and promote foreign military sales and manage the governmental apparatus connected with foreign sales.[44] The amounts expended in FY 1996/97 include $3.2 billion per year in aid grants from the Department of Defense to enable countries to purchase arms from the United States, $1 billion in forgiven loans, more than $2 billion from nondefense agencies in the form of aid funds and the costs of loan subsidies for foreign military sales, and more than $400 million in personnel and other support costs for the Departments of Commerce, Defense, and State, including the costs of having weapons at the major international air shows and the arms promotion activities of embassies. Actual arms sales by the United States were $15.6 billion in calendar year 1995 and averaged $14.8 billion per year, in constant dollars, from 1991 to 1995. Arms transfer agreements, which presage future sales, averaged $11.4 billion per year, in constant dollars, from 1994 to 1996.[45] The out-of-pocket costs borne by the government in connection with arms sales amount to half the value of sales and two-thirds the value of new orders.

The Distribution of Costs and Benefits

The large relative cost of carrying out the arms trade can be explained by the difference between the interests of firms and the interests of the relevant governmental bodies. Firms that produce weapons seek exports as a means of generating profits from the assets they control, namely the ability to produce and offer weapons at a competitive price and quality level. There also appears to be a countercyclical component of arms sales. For U.S. firms, exports tend to be a larger share of total military business in periods when domestic procurement is weak, suggesting that firms place a greater emphasis on foreign business during domestic procurement downturns.[46] Firms also seek to develop long-term relationships with buyers and may be willing to accept lower returns on some sales in exchange for the possibility of follow-on business in the form of maintenance and upkeep, upgrading of existing systems, or future orders of new systems.

The motives behind government spending to promote arms exports are mixed. While governments look for economic benefits from military exports in terms of lowering unit costs and stimulating domestic employment and income, they also have political and military objectives in terms of strengthening allies, managing the balance of forces in a region, and supporting interoperability with allies. Thus, many of the expenses undertaken by governments have been justified in terms of these noneconomic objectives. For example, the original justification for direct offsets was to promote the use of U.S. weapons within NATO. Similarly, direct aid and loan guarantees have been used to maintain a balance of forces in tense regions, such as the Middle East. In addition, contractors may exert influence on governments to carry out export-promotion activities. The result is that costs can be socialized while economic benefits remain private.

There is also a separation between costs and benefits in the case of offsets. Offsets may seem less necessary in the U.S. case since most observers give U.S. equipment high marks for quality and consider U.S. firms superior in terms of efficiency.[47] The heavy reliance on offsets by U.S. firms may occur because supplying firms bear a small share of the costs. With indirect offsets, exporting firms incur relatively small extra costs in obtaining outlets for imports from the buying country. The benefits are obtained by the exporter while the lost output is sustained in the import-competing regions and industries.

With direct offsets, the shift of business to buying country subcontractors and coproducers is felt by the domestic firms that are replaced or not offered the business. It is possible that the prime contractor in one offset arrangement is a potential subcontractor in another, so costs and benefits may be internalized to some extent. But since direct offsets appear to be declining in relative importance and indirect offsets rising, most defense firms appear to benefit from the system.[48]

There may, however, be long-term costs that have not been evaluated fully. The transfer of technology to subcontractors and coproducers raises the risk that these firms will become competitors in international markets. This has been at the heart of the debate in the United States over the nature of military technology transfer to Japan, South Korea, and other countries with a high degree of civil-military integration.[49] Companies from these countries are thought to pose a threat to U.S. companies over the long term. That threat has not materialized so far, as even Japan has not attained the required range of skills, particularly in the integration of large, technically sophisticated, and complex systems. Japan, however, has made advances in the international subcontracting of military and civilian systems.[50] At the same time that Asian companies have entered defense and aerospace markets as suppliers, they have become significant buyers. Thus the price of having these countries enlarge the pie is that they want to keep some of the pieces at home.

The fostering of arms sales also may lead to important negative externalities. Arms sales spread weapons and presumably are undertaken by the buyer because they improve that country's military capabilities. Such improvements could have consequences that rebound against the seller. In the Gulf War, the French Air Force was constrained from flying the Mirage F-1 fighter since the French Mirages could not be distinguished on radar from the ones being flown by Iraq.[51] France produces export and domestic models simultaneously.[52] While the United States generally does not export its current top-of-the-line systems, it does so on occasion, and frequently the ones it does export are similar. In combat aircraft, for example, all four of the current top models—the F-14, F-15, F-16, and F-18—have been exported with the differences lying in weapons and electronics capabilities. The proliferation of advanced weapons and ancillary systems raises the baseline against which U.S. forces are measured and contributes to pressures to upgrade domestic forces. Similar considerations may apply with respect to the growing trade in dual-use products and technologies, which are analyzed in Chapter 10. The United States repeatedly has warned against the growth of asymmetric threats, whereby weapons of mass destruction can be created from accessible materials and technologies, many of which originate with U.S. companies.[53] In extreme cases, a country can find itself in an arms race with itself.[54]

Conclusion

The end of the Cold War led to a sharp contraction in the international arms trade. The overlay of Cold War politics has been replaced by a complex mixture of economic, political, and security considerations in the formulation of policies. Economic motives have become more visible and probably would be considered as more important, filling part of the policy void left by the absence of Cold War–related motives. Both the United States and Russia, the major Cold War protagonists that were the dominant arms exporters in that period, have explicitly expanded the importance of economic considerations in their policies and practices with respect to arms sales.

For the United States, however, it remains unclear whether the economic gains from arms sales are sufficient to justify the costs. The macroeconomic benefits have been lessened by the rising importance of offsets, which appear to be approaching half the value of new sales agreements. Not enough is known about the timing, size, and distribution of actual offset arrangements to assess their impact other than in the most general terms. Because the benefits of offsets accrue to the arms-exporting firms while the costs, in terms of lost output, income, and employment, are borne by different firms, there may be a tendency to utilize offsets to a greater extent than is optimal for the economy as a whole.

Similarly, the government absorbs substantial costs in carrying the arms trade while the economic benefits appear to be largely captured by the arms exporters and the governments who are buyers. As in the case of offsets, the separation of costs and benefits may lead to an overstatement of the overall economic benefits of arms exports and an over-reliance on foreign arms sales, a situation that is reinforced by the fact that the government has a powerful set of noneconomic motives to subsidize arms exports.

The long-term effects of the current arms trading system need to be evaluated more fully in terms of the prospects for arms sales and technology transfer leading to proliferation problems. The most important area that needs evidence and analysis is the economic gains that accrue from larger international arms sales. Without better knowledge as to how large they are and where they accrue, it is not possible to evaluate whether the growing importance of economic considerations in the arms trade represents real gains for the economy or a justification for business as usual.

Notes

The views expressed in this chapter are personal and should not be taken to represent the views of the United Nations or any of its subsidiary bodies.

1. All data used in this chapter, unless otherwise indicated, are from United States Arms Control and Disarmament Agency, *World Military Expenditures and Arms Transfers 1996* (Washington, D.C.: U.S. Government Printing Office, 1997), especially figure 6, table I, and table II. Real values are in 1995 prices. The negative growth rate in the value of the global arms trade was derived statistically, p. 192.

2. Jeffrey Boutwell, Michael T. Klare, and Laura W. Reed., eds., *Lethal Commerce: The Global Trade in Small Arms and Light Weapons* (Cambridge, Mass.: American Academy of Arts and Sciences, 1995).

3. Bonn International Center for Conversion, *Conversion Survey 1997: Global Disarmament and Disposal of Surplus Weapons* (Oxford: Oxford University Press, 1997).

4. Aaron Karp, "The Rise of Black and Gray Markets," *The Annals* 535 (September 1994): 175–89; Michael T. Klare, "The Subterranean Arms Trade: Black-Market Sales, Covert Operations and Ethnic Warfare," in Andrew J. Pierre, ed., *Cascade of Arms: Managing Conventional Weapons Proliferation* (Washington, D.C.: Brookings Institution, 1997), pp. 43–71.

5. Clifford G. Gaddy, *The Price of the Past: Russia's Struggle with the Legacy of a Militarized Economy* (Washington, D.C.: Brookings Institution, 1996).

6. Stan Crock et al., "Weapons, Anyone? Western Arms Makers Covet New NATO Members' Business," *Business Week,* June 2, 1997.

7. Desmond Ball, "Arms and Affluence," *International Security* 18, no. 3 (Winter 1993–94): 78–112.

8. Steven Lee Myers, "Thailand Can No Longer Afford to Buy U.S. Jets," *New York Times,* January 17, 1998 (http://archives.nytimes.com); Paul Richter, "Crisis Thwarts pentagon Efforts to Beef Up Asia," *Los Angeles Times,* January 15, 1998 (http://www.latimes.com).

9. Thomas A. Cardamone Jr., ed., "IMF Suggests Southeast Asia Review Defense Budgets," *Arms Trade News* (February 1998) (http://www.clw.org/pub/clw/cat/atn0298.htm).

10. Richard F. Grimmett, "Conventional Arms Transfers to Developing Nations, 1989–1996," CRS Report 97-512F, Congressional Research Service, United States Congress, August 13, 1997.

11. Anthony Boadle, "U.S. Defense Sector Sees no Latin American Bonanza," Reuters (August 27, 1997) (http://biz.yahoo.com/finance/97/08/27/ba_lmt_y0_1.html); Jonathan Friedland, "U.S. Defense Contractors Lick Chops for Latin Market: Washington is Expected to End Carter-Era Ban on Military Sales to Region," *Wall Street Journal* (November 15, 1996) p. A10.

12. United Nations Department for Economic and Social Information and Policy Analysis, "Assessing the Peace Dividend Resulting from the End of the Cold War," *World Economic and Social Survey 1995* (New York: United Nations, 1995), chap. 12.

13. Ronald Tiersky, "French Military Reform and NATO Restructuring," *Joint Forces Quarterly* (Spring 1997): 95–102.

14. Stockholm International Peace Research Institute, *SIPRI Yearbook 1997: Armaments, Disarmament and International Security* (Oxford: Oxford University Press, 1997).

15. United States General Accounting Office, *Defense Industry Consolidation: Competitive Effects of Mergers and Acquisitions,* GAO/NSIAD-98-56 (Washington, D.C., U.S. General Accounting Office, 1998) (http://www.gao.gov).

16. European Commission, "The European Aerospace Industry: Meeting the Global Challenge," Communication from the European Commission, Brussels, September 24, 1997 (http://europa.eu.int/en/comm/dgiii/press/970924.htm).

17. M. S. Hochmuth, "Aerospace," in Raymond Vernon, ed., *Big Business and the State: Changing Relations in Western Europe,* (Cambridge, Mass.: Harvard University Press, 1974), pp. 148–52.

18. William W. Keller, *Arm in Arm: The Political Economy of the Global Arms Trade* (New York: Basic Books, 1995); Edward A. Kolodziej, *Making and Marketing Arms: The French Experience and Its Implications for the International System* (Princeton, N.J.: Princeton University Press, 1987).

19. Andrew J. Pierre, "Toward an International Regime for Conventional Arms Sales," in Pierre, *Cascade of Arms,* pp. 414–19.

20. Richard F. Grimmett, "Conventional Arms Transfers to Latin America: U.S. Policy," CRS Report 97-512F, Congressional Research Service, United States Congress, August 5, 1997, p. 7.

21. Jens Van Scherpenberg, "Transatlantic Competition and European Defense Industries: A New Look at the Trade-Defense Linkage," *International Affairs* 73, no. 1 (1997): 99–122.

22. Janne E. Nolan et al., "Report of the Presidential Board on Arms Proliferation Policy." (http://www.fas.org/asmp/library/white-house/advisory-board.htm).

23. Ibid., chap. 4; Pierre, *Cascade of Arms,* pp. 418–19.

24. Stephen Martin, "Countertrade and Offsets: An Overview of the Theory and Evidence," in Stephen Martin, ed., *The Economics of Offsets: Defence Procurement and Countertrade* (Amsterdam: Harwood Academic Publishers, 1996), pp. 15–48.

25. Glenn W. Goodman Jr., "A Buyer's Market: A Plethora of New Fighter Aircraft Compete for Global Export Sales," *Armed Forces Journal International* (September 1997) (http://www.afji.com/Mags/1997/Sept/feat.html).

26. United States General Accounting Office, *Military Exports: Offset Demands Continue to Grow,* GAO/NSIAD-96-65 (Washington, D.C.: U.S. General Accounting Office, 1996) (http://www.gao.gov).

27. Bernard Udis and Keith E. Maskus, "Offsets as Industrial Policy: Lessons from Aerospace," *Defence Economics* 2, no. 2 (1991): 151–64.

28. Dean Cheng and Micheal W. Chinworth, "The Teeth of the Little Tigers: Offsets, Defense Production and Economic Development in South Korea and Taiwan," in Stephen Martin, ed., *The Economics of Offsets: Defence Procurement and Countertrade* (Amsterdam: Hardwood Academic Publishers,

1996), pp. 245–98; Richard J. Samuels, *"Rich Nation, Strong Army": National Security and the Technological Transformation of Japan* (Ithaca, N.Y: Cornell University Press, 1994).

29.   Reinhard Drifte, *Arms Production in Japan: The Military Applications of Civilian Technology* (Boulder, Colo.: Westview Press, 1986); Masako Ikegami-Anderson, "Japan: A Latent but Large Supplier of Dual-Use Technology," in Herbert Wulf, ed., *Arms Industry Limited* (Oxford: Oxford University Press, 1993), pp. 320–44.

30.   Michael W. Chinworth and Ron Matthews, "Defense Industrialization Through Offsets: The Case of Japan," *The Economics of Offsets*, pp. 177–218.

31.   United Nations, "The Economics of the Arms Trade After the Cold War," *World Economic and Social Survey 1997*, chap. 9 (New York: United Nations, 1997).

32.   Stephen Martin and Keith Hartley, "UK Firms' Experience and Perceptions of Defence Offsets: Survey Results," *Defence and Peace Economics 6*, no. 2 (1995): 123–39.

33.   U.S. General Accounting Office, *Military Exports.*

34.   Bureau of Export Administration, United States Department of Commerce, *Offsets in Defense Trade: Executive Summary* (Washington, D.C.: United States Department of Commerce, 1997) (http://www.bxa.doc.gov/pren/97/off study.htm).

35.   See the remarks attributed to Robert Tice, vice president, Lockheed Martin, in Charles W. Weisner and Alan W. Wolff, eds., *Policy Issues in Aerospace Offsets: Report of a Workshop* (Washington, D.C.: National Academy Press, 1997), pp. 4–5.

36.   David Gold, "The Internationalization of Military Production," *Peace Economics, Peace Science, and Public Policy 1*, no. 3 (Spring 1994): 1–11.

37.   Lora Lumpe, "Economic Costs of Arms Exports: Subsidies and Offsets." Testimony, Subcommittee on Foreign Operations, Committee on Appropriations, United States Senate, May 23, 1995 (http://www.fas.org/asmp/campaigns/subsidies/lora_testimony.htm).

38.   Federation of American Scientists, *Arms Sales Monitor*, no. 31, December 5, 1995 (http://www.fas.org/asmp/asm31.htm).

39.   The United States is attempting to move toward greater commonality of equipment across missions with the Joint Strike Fighter (JSF), currently in development, which is expected to replace the A-10, AV-8B, F-16, and some F-18s for the air force, navy, and Marine Corps, as well as be procured by the United Kingdom. The last major attempt at multiservice commonality in combat aircraft, the TFX, was scaled back by Defense Secretary Robert MacNamara and became the air force's F-111.

40. United States General Accounting Office, *Best Practices: Successful Application to Weapon Acquisitions Required Changes in DoD's Environment*, GAO/NSIAD-98-56 (Washington, D.C.:, U.S. General Accounting Office, 1998) (http://www.gao.gov).

41. United States General Accounting Office, *Military Exports: Recovery of Nonrecurring Research and Development Costs*, GAO/NSIAD-95-147 (Washington, D.C.: U.S. General Accounting Office, 1995) (http://www.gao.gov).

42. Federation of American Scientists, *Arms Sales Monitor*, no. 32, March 5, 1995 (http://www.fas.org/asmp/asm32.htm); Lumpe, "Economic Costs of Arms Exports."

43. Kolodziej, *Making and Marketing Arms.*

44. William D. Hartung, *Welfare for Weapons Dealers: The Hidden Costs of the Arms Trade* (New York: World Policy Institute, 1996); William D. Hartung, *Welfare for Weapons Dealers 1998: The Hidden Costs of NATO Expansion* (New York: World Policy Institute, 1998).

45. Grimmett, "Conventional Arms Transfers to Latin America," table 8A.

46. Ethan B. Kapstein, "Advanced Industrialized Countries," in Pierre, *Cascade of Arms*, pp. 75–88.

47. European Commission, "European Aerospace Industry."

48. Bureau of Export Administration, *Offsets in Defense Trade.*

49. United States General Accounting Office, *U.S.-Japan Fighter Aircraft: Agreement on F-2 Production*, GAO/NSIAD-97-76 (Washington, D.C.: U.S. General Accounting Office, 1997) (http://www.gao.gov).

50. See the comments attributed to Richard Samuel in Weisner and Wolf, *Policy Issues in Aerospace Offsets*, pp. 20–21.

51. Keller, *Arm in Arm*, p. 5.

52. At the time of the Mirage incident, the French defense minister reportedly reminded the armed services that without the export market, they would not have the range of modern weapons they currently deploy. Ibid., p. 6, n. 17.

53. Jacques S. Gansler, "Defense Modernization," Keynote address, Fall meeting, Aerospace Industry Association, November 21, 1997 (http://acq.osd.mil/ousda/speech/modernization.html).

54. Kenneth Flamm makes a similar point in this volume; see Chapter 8. See also Nolan et al., "Report of the Presidential Board on Arms Proliferation Policy," Chapter 4.

10

Dual-Use Technology:
Back to the Future?

JUDITH REPPY

UAL-USE technology lies at the center of current U.S. technology
policy, civil and military. By funding dual-use programs, the
Department of Defense (DoD) hopes to tap the civilian technology base for its most recent advances, especially in the rapidly changing field of information technology. The civilian economy, in turn, can
benefit from military investments in technologies that have applications in both sectors; for example, civilian aircraft and ships can use the
military's Global Positioning Satellite (GPS) system to find their locations. Dual-use policies may even foster economic conversion by
encouraging defense contractors to diversify into civilian markets,
thereby lessening their dependence on defense sales. Little wonder then
that Bill Clinton's administration has enthusiastically promoted dual-
use policies as the solution to its problems of maintaining the defense
industrial base in a time of declining defense budgets and of improving
U.S. economic competitiveness in global markets. (Chapter 12 provides
a history of the politics of industrial policy from the 1980s on.)

These constructions, however, fail to recognize all of the policy
implications of dual-use technology. In particular, they obscure the

Research supported by the Council on Foreign Relations' project on Consolidation, Downsizing, and Conversion in the U.S. Military Industrial Base. The author would like to thank
the members of the study group, especially its leader, Ann Markusen, for thoughtful comments on an earlier version of this chapter. She also wishes to acknowledge helpful discussions with Philip Gummett, Andrew James, Audie Klotz, Dan Plafcan, Alec Shuldiner,
and Rachel Weber.

connection between dual-use technology and technology transfer abroad and so neglect the danger of proliferating military capabilities as an unintended consequence of investments designed to save money in the defense budget while promoting the civilian economy. Dual-use policies increase the number of actors involved in weapons production and the number of legal channels through which technology can flow. Control is both more necessary and more difficult, and the control mechanisms inherited from the Cold War are inappropriate and inadequate. Instead, we need new approaches, rooted in an understanding of dual-use technology and the mechanisms of technology transfer.

History of a Concept

Ironically, given its current construction as the panacea for industrial problems, the dual-use concept originated in proliferation concerns. The phrase first appeared in modern policy discourse around 1948, when the demarcations of the Cold War were hardening. The United States was negotiating with its European allies and with Japan to introduce export controls on transfers of military-relevant goods to the Soviet bloc, which then included China. These negotiations led in 1949 to the establishment of the Coordinating Committee for Multilateral Export Controls (COCOM), an international regime that lasted until April 1994. Negotiating controls on the weapons trade posed no particular problems, but reaching agreement over "dual-utility" goods was another story. The United States was far more interested than its allies in controlling the flow of items of war potential, which at that time were mostly goods for rebuilding the industrial infrastructure of the Soviet Union and China—road and railroad construction materials, sheet metal, and radio communications equipment. Japan, for example, had historical trading relationships with China that it was eager to reestablish, whereas the United States was determined to prevent the export of a long list of industrial goods for which Japan was the natural supplier to mainland China.[1]

The U.S. export control regime in place throughout the Cold War had several parts. Weapons exports were (and are) controlled under the Battle Act of 1954 and its successor, the Arms Export Control Act, while the Export Control Act of 1949 put in place controls on U.S. exports of dual-use goods. At the international level, COCOM was supposed to harmonize export controls among the United States, other countries of the North Atlantic Treaty Organization (NATO), and Japan. Nuclear materials and related technologies have been controlled under provisions of the Atomic Energy Act, the Nuclear Nonproliferation Act of 1978, and the Nuclear Nonproliferation Treaty (NPT), with nuclear dual-use items covered under the Export Control Act.[2] As the Cold War waned, however, this export control regime became increasingly problematic. U.S. firms complained that they were denied export licenses for items that were freely available from other suppliers, while U.S. allies chafed at reexport restrictions on U.S. technology and delays caused by COCOM review procedures. Over the years advisory panels and commissions repeatedly recommended easing export controls and providing expedited licensing procedures.[3]

Within the U.S. government the tension between the economic goal of promoting U.S. exports and security concerns about the spread of high technology to U.S. enemies has played out in enduring bureaucratic rivalries. The State Department oversees the International Trade in Arms Regulations (ITAR), which contains the Munitions List; the Commerce Department is formally charged with drawing up the Export Administration Regulations (EAR), which includes the Commodity Control List of dual-use goods; and the Department of Defense has a consultative responsibility for the contents of the control lists and decisions on individual license applications. At various times—particularly in the early 1980s, when Richard Perle was assistant secretary of defense for international security policy—the DoD perspective, which traditionally has privileged security concerns, dominated interagency policymaking. With the increased concern over U.S. competitiveness and the disappearance of the Soviet military threat, however, economic arguments for expanded trade became more important.

There was a remarkable shift in the discourse on dual use in the mid-1980s. Export control issues faded into the background, and "dual use" was co-opted for the debate over industrial policy and the domestic defense industrial base. Lists of "Critical Technologies," for example, were drawn up not to provide an argument for controlling exports but rather to call attention to the number of technological areas in which Japan might be said to have a leading advantage; predictably dual-use technologies featured prominently in these lists.[4] The prevailing ideology ruled out government involvement in the market, but dual-use programs provided a politically safe way to promote civilian technology under the rubric of national security.

The Clinton administration has pushed dual-use policy still further. It acted early to relax export controls on a range of high technologies, including computers, telecommunication technologies, and space launch technology. (See Chapter 4.) At the same time it launched a set of technology policy initiatives aimed at promoting dual-use technologies, such as the Technology Reinvestment Program (TRP).[5] The DoD has adopted an active policy of encouraging the use of commercial products in military programs. Procurement regulations have been simplified and specialized military specifications relaxed in an effort to transform the culture of military procurement and to make it easier for firms outside the defense industry to sell to the department. At least one observer is unimpressed: "Requests for proposals remain as thick as ever, with no significant reduction in the specifications to which bidders are expected to respond. That tells me the government can do a better job in implementing acquisition reform, because what we're seeing at the operating level doesn't reflect the work that went into the reforms themselves."[6] There is no question, however, that the Department of Defense intends to pursue these reforms and to encourage dual-use technology as much as possible.

At the international level, the end of the Cold War and breakup of the Soviet Union has left the arms control regime for proliferation of dual-use technologies in disarray. With no clear enemy in sight, European NATO countries have been even less interested than the United States in pursuing a stringent export control regime. COCOM was allowed to expire in 1994 with no successor regime in place. By summer 1996 there was a new agreement, the Wassenaar Arrangement, which includes Russia and other former members of the Warsaw Treaty Organization and—like COCOM—covers trade in "sensitive technology" as well as arms transfers, but consensus was not reached easily. For example, the sensitive destination lists put forward early on by Germany, Japan, Britain, and the United States contained a total of 73 countries, but only 28 were on all four lists and 17 countries were on only one list.[7] European countries resisted U. S. pressure to block trade of commercial goods to such countries as Iran, and the Wassenaar Arrangement does not name any proscribed states. It merely calls for cooperation in preventing transfers of armaments or sensitive technology if "the behavior of a state is, or becomes, a cause for serious concern to the Participating States."[8]

There has been convergence, however, on the benefits of dual-use technology for industrial development. Governments from Britain to Russia have embraced the promise of reduced defense costs and enhanced industrial competitiveness and have put dual-use policies at the core of their technology policies. The effect of these dual-use policies on the proliferation of militarily useful technology goes unremarked.

Dual-Use Technology and the Defense Industry

Does dual-use technology present particular problems for proliferation? To answer this question, we need to understand how the context for a technology—whether it is civilian-based, military, or dual use—affects the mechanisms for transfer abroad and the possibility of devising effective controls. That is, we need to look at the institutions and practices that form the environment in which technology is developed and applied, and examine their implications for ease of transfer and potential control points. Controls that were suitable for a world of opposing military blocs and large investments in military technology may not work in the more fluid environment of dual use.

UNDERSTANDING DUAL USE

Dual use has emerged as a central element in current U.S. technology policy in large part because it has been seen as a politically safe way to promote civilian technologies while sheltering under the rubric of national security. Like "spin-off," dual use also promises civilian benefits from military investments, and like spin-off it generally has been considered to be a self-explanatory concept, needing little analysis.[9] Definitions have taken the form of lists of candidate technologies with applications in both the military and civilian sectors or, in more sophisticated treatments, lists of a range of technologies and institutional settings that can be labeled dual use.[10]

The concept rests on making a distinction between civil and military technology, that is, on the idea that there are two technology bases in the United States (and other countries that have invested heavily in military technology); dual-use technologies are those that find application in both sectors. The separation of military from civilian technology has been understood to be the result of:

- Large-scale and long-term Cold War funding that nurtured specialized institutions for performing military research and development (R&D)
- Distinctive characteristics of military institutions for R&D and procurement, especially practices to maintain secrecy, the emphasis on performance over cost, small production runs, and the need to comply with government regulations and accounting requirements, all of which have proved resilient to repeated efforts at reform[11]

- The specialized nature of military applications, which necessarily shapes military technology in ways that diverge from civilian technology

In effect, we are confronted with two cultures, each with its own customs and practices and, importantly, its own technology developed in response to sector-specific requirements.

This two-sector model implies that most technologies can be coded as either military or civilian (i.e., dual-use technologies are a relatively small set of all technologies) and that shifting resources from military to civilian purposes (i.e., conversion) will be difficult for technical and cultural reasons, even if such shifts are feasible from a macropolitical perspective. From the presence of barriers between the two technology bases we can further infer that it matters how we fund research and development, which would not be the case if all technology were freely transferable between uses, and that we can identify those technologies with military applications and control them, through commodity control lists, for example. International technology transfers from the civilian sector, on the other hand, are not an important security issue in this model, although they may pose competitiveness issues.

There is an alternative story, however, one in which military technology is seen as embedded in a larger civilian technology base, with shared roots in a common educational system, shared interest in a range of generic technologies and process technologies, and links into the commercial sector through companies that serve both military and civilian markets. In this story the boundary between military and civilian technology is permeable and open to renegotiation. The policy implications of this model are the reverse of those just listed: dual-use technologies are likely to be numerous and important; if political circumstances allow it, conversion should be technically easy; we can be largely indifferent to where research and development takes place; and international flows of militarily relevant technologies will occur in the commercial sector and be hard to control.

These contrasting narratives illustrate the importance of being explicit about the assumptions under which the term "dual use" is employed in policy discussions. It is precisely because the term can mean such different things to different actors that it was so useful in the 1980s in papering over political differences and providing cover for the shift from policies focused on export controls to the development of a mercantilist policy of promoting competitiveness from within the defense budget. Faced with the two different accounts of the nature of the technology base and their widely divergent policy prescriptions, we must ask: What is the evidence for the competing claims?

RECENT STUDIES OF THE DEFENSE INDUSTRY

For many years the situation in the United States seemed to fit the two-sector model, which went virtually unchallenged. Recent studies of the U.S. defense industry by scholars at the Massachusetts Institute of Technology (M.I.T.) and at the Program on Regional and Industrial Economics (PRIE) at Rutgers University, however, have revealed a more complex picture. In the M.I.T. study of a sample of manufacturing establishments drawn from 21 industries that engage in machining-intensive durable goods (MDG), a sector that includes a little over half of all defense purchases of durable goods, including aircraft, ordnance, and missiles, Maryellen Kelley and Todd Watkins found that 80 percent of the establishments with defense contracts integrated commercial and military production in the same facility.[12] The median defense share of business in 1990 for plants that had defense contracts (approximately 50 percent of the plants in the MDG sector) was a mere 15 percent. In short, the authors conclude, "commercial-military integration is not only feasible but is largely the normal practice at the end of the Cold War." These findings are all the more remarkable because the MDG sector does not include the electronic or computer industries, which usually are seen as the locus of the most important dual-use technologies.

The Kelley and Watkins findings can be criticized for overemphasizing the experience of small and medium-sized enterprises and neglecting the large prime contractors.[13] Almost two-thirds of the plants in their sample were subcontractors or third-tier suppliers with no prime contracts, but these plants accounted for only 22 percent of the defense shipments by value. By contrast, a small number of plants, approximately 10 percent of the sample, were heavily defense-dependent (greater than 80 percent of shipments), and they accounted for 32.7 percent of total defense shipments.[14] In other words, we have here evidence that many defense suppliers are operating integrated production facilities, but a small number of important suppliers fit the conventional description of defense firms as dependent on the DoD, with presumably all the specialized characteristics that status entails.

The work carried out by Ann Markusen and her colleagues at PRIE reached similar conclusions for the small and medium-sized defense firms in their sample. (See Chapter 3.) These companies had lowered their defense dependence since the end of the Cold War, mainly by expanding civilian sales rather than through reduced defense sales. Defense-dependent firms in the sample had experienced greater difficulties, with total sales and employment falling between 1989 and 1994, but they too had increased their civilian sales. By contrast, the prime contractors in the PRIE study have, in general, chosen to concentrate on the defense market and have been engaged in a series of mergers and acquisitions, along with large-scale job cuts, to solidify their position in the declining market. These firms continue to display most of the attributes of the stereotypical military-industrial firm, despite their changing environment.

These empirical studies suggest that to a greater extent than has commonly been realized, production facilities in the defense industry at the level of subcontractors and third-tier vendors can be considered dual use in the sense that the same facilities produce goods for defense and civilian markets. This result is consistent with an understanding that dual-use technologies are most likely to be found at the level of components and manufacturing processes; examples of dual-use end products, such as the Global Positioning System, are relatively rare. It supports the second view outlined earlier, namely, that the boundaries between defense and civilian technologies are fluid rather than sharply drawn, at least in the firms comprising the subcontractor and third-tier level of suppliers. It follows that the defense industrial base can draw support from civilian-oriented plants and that diversification into civilian markets should pose no particular technical difficulties for most defense plants.

To the extent that these findings are typical of the defense industry, we probably will judge the Clinton administration's focus on dual-use technologies as a means to economic conversion to be misplaced. The small and medium-sized firms in the defense sector do not appear to need encouragement from the government to engage in crossover behavior, while the large prime contractors are not interested. Indeed the whole Technology Reinvestment Project with its emphasis on technology push may be misdirected. The missing element in conversion planning may lie on the demand, not the supply, side—for example, with the need for marketing research and finance. These are, of course, areas in which defense firms are notoriously weak, yet they form a crucial part of the complex process of moving a new product to market.[15] Moreover, the administration's dual-use technology policy has implications for other national interests; in particular, it raises problems for the control of international transfers of sensitive technology.

Dual Use and Proliferation

The argument so far has laid out two stages of dual-use policy and considered some recent evidence for the prevalence of dual-use technology. Early concern with controlling technology flows to the Soviet bloc was supplanted in the 1980s by a focus on economic competitiveness on one hand and maintaining the defense industrial base on the other, with both goals leading to a policy prescription to promote dual-use technology. Under the Clinton administration promotion of dual-use technology has become the centerpiece of military industrial policy, which has continued to be the principal locus of industrial policy more generally. The findings of the empirical studies just outlined suggest that intrafirm technology transfer, which is desirable to promote a robust defense industrial base and, potentially, defense conversion, is not a problem for many defense firms. The studies do not, however, tell us anything about interfirm and international technology transfer; that is, they do not address the proliferation issues.

THE DIFFUSION OF TECHNOLOGICAL KNOWLEDGE

To get at the proliferation issue we need a theory of technology diffusion. In standard economic theory knowledge, including technological knowledge, has been held to be a public good, implying that it cannot be appropriated easily by its creators but rather diffuses freely.[16] The patent system and security classification systems are examples of institutions devised to confer appropriability where it does not naturally exist; that is, they impede diffusion without payment or consent. Recent theorizing, however, has challenged the knowledge-as-public-good model, arguing instead that there is a substantial local component to knowledge, especially technological knowledge. This local component is often tacit and cannot be reduced to blueprints or computer code; rather it must be acquired by direct experience with the technology ("learning by doing") or by laboriously retracing the research and development that was necessary in the first place.[17]

Local knowledge is not only a feature of the civil-military sectoral divide but is relevant to all institutions, including civilian firms and universities, engaged in the production of scientific and technical knowledge. We can, for example, see evidence of the importance of site-specific knowledge in the strategies of business firms: acquisition of other firms often is justified as a means of acquiring desired technological competence, a step that would be unnecessary if the knowledge could be acquired through market transactions or the open literature. Similarly, multinational firms invest in production and R&D facilities abroad in part to bring their products into line with local conditions. That these strategies frequently are unsuccessful is further evidence that technology transfer is not easy.

When we bring local knowledge into the analysis, we move toward the model of separate civilian and military sectors. The local knowledge accumulated by a defense contractor cannot be transferred easily to the different culture of the commercial sector, and vice versa. Even though tacit knowledge can diffuse over time, through the codification of practices that were originally informal improvisations and, more important, through people moving to new jobs, there still may be a core of stubbornly local knowledge that depends on its specific environment, whether linked to a particular piece of equipment, to characteristics of the local workforce, or to some other element in the firm's practices.

Local knowledge will be more important for some technologies than for others. For example, consider the systems integration function that prime contractors perform. Military technology is not just a matter of materials, components, and weapons; modern weapons are complex systems, and the ability to design and produce these systems is a specialized skill that has a large component of local knowledge.[18] Moreover, this is a skill the United States pioneered and still retains a considerable comparative advantage. Thus it could be argued that the transfer of U.S. production technology abroad—for example, through licensing agreements or offset arrangements in foreign military sales—does not per se pose a risk to U.S. competitiveness or military security, so long as our competitors do not master the systems skills needed to combine the technologies into final products without assistance. Of course, security risks arise whenever arms are acquired, whether by imports, licensed production, or indigenous development. But from the perspective of dual-use policy, the important point is that systems integration skills are local skills that cannot be acquired easily without direct experience—indeed they may not even transfer within countries between technological domains. Thus where systems integration is important, it constitutes a barrier to proliferation.

IMPLICATIONS FOR PROLIFERATION

The implications for technology transfer—and for technology control—are clear: where local knowledge is important, diffusion is more difficult. Within-firm commonality between military and civilian goods and production processes, as observed by Kelley and Watkins, is no guarantee that technology transfer between firms or countries will take place without considerable effort and investment. We might conclude, then, that policies promoting dual-use technology do not pose the danger of simultaneously promoting proliferation by making it easier for foreign firms or governments to acquire weapons-relevant technologies, because the difficulty in acquiring tacit knowledge, especially in systems integration, provides sufficient protection.

More detailed studies are necessary, however, before we accept such a sanguine conclusion.[19] First, as the case of Iraq (and, earlier, of the Soviet Union) demonstrates, some states are willing to use extraordinary measures to acquire desired technology.[20] We cannot rely on the barriers erected by tacit knowledge in the case of a determined proliferator willing to pay the high costs of technology transfer. When there is time to send nationals abroad for education and training or to recruit scientific and technical personnel internationally, we must assume that tacit knowledge can be acquired across national borders. Second, it is likely that the barriers to technology flows are lower in some cases than in others. Weapons-related work may provide a shared context that facilitates technology transfer; certainly the Soviet Union found it easier to acquire advanced technology from foreign sources to apply in its military sector than to transfer that technology to its own civilian sector.[21] The global culture of the Internet, along with the global spread of chip manufacturing, provides a common (civilian) space for information technologies, which are arguably the most critical dual-use technologies today.[22] Finally, active promotion of dual-use technology could succeed in creating new channels for technology flows, channels that would also be open to foreign actors. The current anxieties about the "cyber threat" suggest the vulnerability inherent in military reliance on commercial information technologies. Even as military planners rhapsodize about the future of Information Warfare, other strategists must concern themselves with a situation in which foreign countries have the same capabilities and access to software as the United States.[23]

Policy Issues

Dual-use technology thus presents a dilemma to policymakers. Far from providing the win-win situation that often is portrayed, dual-use policies that succeed in blurring the lines between military and civil technologies run the risk of creating new channels for proliferation. The problem is to find a way to control undesirable technology flows without stunting commercial trade or consigning the military to inferior technology.

Traditional control regimes have relied on commodity control lists and targeted countries. The New Forum negotiations that resulted in the Wassenaar Arrangement followed that approach, and the arrangement is a good illustration of the problems it faces in a world in which there is no clear-cut enemy and sensitive technologies are widely diffused. Member countries disagree on which countries to target and which technologies to include on the sensitive technology list. Information technologies pose the most difficult problems because of the rapid rate at which the technology is changing and spreading, making it virtually impossible to keep control lists up to date, and yet information technologies are also a primary focus for most dual-use policy.

Beyond the new difficulties of agreeing on targets (whether countries or commodities) lurk the old problems of balancing cooperation on security matters with competition in the economic arena. For example, commercial considerations led Russia to resist rules in the Wassenaar Arrangement that would require prior notification of exports of sensitive technology, and agreement on a set of rules was reached only after months of negotiation.[24] Implementation of the arrangement lies in the future, and there are no provisions for sanctions other than those of friendly persuasion when countries disagree about a particular export. Indeed, the most useful function for the lists of sensitive technologies and reporting rules may be to provide a mechanism for tracking suppliers and destinations of high-technology products. Rather than serving to control sensitive exports, the benefit of the arrangement may come from its provision for a reporting mechanism that, along with other intelligence, can help to identify potential threats and assess motivation.

More is needed. Analysis of the institutions and processes of technology diffusion can suggest alternative ways of thinking about the connection between export controls and national security and about policy instruments that could be employed usefully. One conclusion we might draw from our analysis of dual use is that the emphasis on commercial high technology as the source of U.S. military strength cannot be sustained. If we expect to draw our military technology from a common pool in which civilian technology is dominant, then we must expect that potential enemies will have access to the same capabilities: it is just not practicable to control the flows of technology that are occurring in the context of the globalization of the world economy. It will not be enough to rely on our comparative advantage in systems integration because that capability also can be acquired by potential enemies, albeit with difficulty.

If, on the other hand, we choose to maintain a separate military technology base, we might think of ways to capitalize on its distinctiveness in order to inhibit proliferation. An understanding of the importance of local dimensions of technological knowledge could suggest supplemental policies to the Waasenaar Arrangement. For example, we might restrict access to technical training by foreign nationals in U.S. universities in order to inhibit the transfer of important tacit knowledge. At the international level we should continue efforts to reduce the incentives for nuclear scientists and other weapons specialists in the former Soviet Union to find employment in other countries.

We also might reconsider the policy of promoting commercial technology in the name of expanding the defense industrial base and seek instead to emphasize the special character of military technologies. The costs are obvious—although they may be lessened by new production technologies that remove some of the penalties associated with small-batch production—but they should be weighed against the security gains. By restricting undesirable technology flows we can buy time, the most useful commodity of all in managing national security.

This analysis of current dual-use policy and technology transfer issues has revealed a dilemma for those who advocate dual-use technologies as the solution to problems of the defense industrial base and international competitiveness. Dual use has been an effective slogan in the political rhetoric of the past decade, but the focus on competitiveness has obscured continuing security issues of weapons proliferation. To the extent that the barriers separating military technology from civilian are dismantled, the control of exports for security reasons is made more difficult. In the worst-case scenario, the power to control the transfer of military relevant technology simply disappears in the "tidal wave" of new civilian technology.[25] Consideration of the institutions and processes of technology diffusion, however, may offer alternative ways of thinking about export controls and alternative policy instruments; at the very least it can provide a corrective to the unexamined enthusiasm for dual-use policies.

Dual use also poses a dilemma for the broader political community. Liberal ideology favors international contacts, minimal government controls on trade and travel, and the expansion of civilian society relative to the military sector. Proliferation fears, unfortunately, drive policy in the opposite direction. Control of technology flows requires a trade control regime, controls on international contacts, and—if the arguments about dual-use technology are right—retention of a military core at the heart of our technology base. These are not comfortable conclusions. They suggest that even after the Cold War, there is no easy exit from the dilemmas of the national security state.

Notes

1. Sayuri Shimuzu first called my attention to this early history of dual use. See "The United States, Japan and Export Control Against the PRC, 1949–1958," Mimeo, 1995. For a history of COCOM, see Michael Mastan-

duno, *Economic Containment: COCOM and the Politics of East-West Trade* (Ithaca, N.Y.: Cornell University Press, 1992).

2. See National Academy of Sciences, Panel on the Future Design and Implementation of U.S. National Security Export Controls, Committee on Science, Engineering and Public Policy, *Finding Common Ground: U.S. Export Controls in a Changed Global Environment* (Washington, D.C.: National Academy Press, 1991), chap. 6, for a more detailed description of the U.S. export control regime at the end of the 1980s.

3. The best known of these reports is the 1976 report of a Defense Science Board Task Force, *An Analysis of Export Control of Advanced Technology: A DOD Perspective* (the "Bucy Report"), which argued that the focus of controls should be on know-how rather than on products. Despite the report's call for a pared-down list of controlled items, the Militarily Critical Technologies List grew ever longer. See Mastanduno, *Economic Containment,* p. 215.

4. See, for example, the *Report of the National Critical Technologies Panel* (Washington, D.C.: 1991). For a critical analysis of the assumptions underlying these lists, see Bruce L. R. Smith, "Critical Technologies," *Brookings Review* 10 (Winter 1992): 54.

5. John R. Harvey, Cameron Binkley, Adam Block, and Rich Burke, *A Common-Sense Approach to High-Technology Export Controls,* A Report of the Center for International Security and Arms Control (Stanford, Calif.: Stanford University, March 1995), p. 1.

6. John Kutler, president of Quarterdeck Investment Partners, Inc., quoted in Anthony L. Velocci Jr., "Sea Change Looming for Defense Contracting," *Aviation Week & Space Technology,* August 19, 1996, p. 21.

7. Saferworld, "New Arms Control Regime Risks Being Paper Tiger," *Update* 15 (Spring 1996): 1.

8. International Institute for Security Studies, "The Waasenaar Arrangement," *Strategic Comments* 2 (August 1996).

9. On this point see Ulrich Albrecht, "Spin-Off: A Fundamentalist Approach," in P. Gummett and J. Reppy eds., *The Relations Between Defence and Civil Technologies* (Dordrecht: Kluwer Academic Publishers, 1988), pp 38–57.

10. See, for example, John Alic et al., *Beyond Spin-off: Military and Commercial Technologies in a Changing World* (Boston: Harvard Business School Press, 1992), chap. 3.

11. Some would argue that former Secretary of Defense William Perry was successful in bringing about real changes in the DoD procurement culture; others see continued resistance. See, e.g., Anthony Velloci Jr., "Structural Change Looms as Next Industry Hurdle," *Aviation Week & Space Technology,* February 12, 1996, p. 21. Velloci quotes John Harbison of Booz-Allen & Hamilton, Inc., to the effect that "many companies are paying lip service to the need for wholesale structural changes, but none of the contractors has embraced commercial practices yet."

12. Maryellen Kelley and Todd Watkins, "In from the Cold: Prospects for Conversion of the Defense Industrial Base," *Science* 268 (April 1995): 525–34. Quoted from p. 531.

13. See the letter from Ann Markusen, Michael Oden, and Jonathan Feldman in *Technology Review* 98 (July 1995): 6–7.

14. Kelley and Watkins, "In from the Cold," p. 528. I have estimated the percent of highly defense-dependent firms in the sample from figure 1, p. 527.

15. Recent work at the University of Manchester by Andrew James and his colleagues substantiates this point for British defense firms. "Internal Corporate Venturing: Three Cases from the UK Defence Industry" (internal ms., January 1996).

16. The classic argument is laid out in Kenneth J. Arrow, "Economic Welfare and the Allocation of Resources for Inventions," in Richard R. Nelson, ed., *The Rate and Direction of Inventive Activity: Economic and Social Factors* (Princeton, N.J.: Princeton University Press, 1962), pp. 783–831. For recent discussions, see Partha Dasgupta and Paul A. David, "Toward a New Economics of Science," *Research Policy* 23 (September 1994): 487–521, especially pp. 493–98; and Michel Callon, "Is Science a Public Good?" *Science, Technology & Human Values* 19 (Autumn 1994): 395–424.

17. For an example of this argument applied to nuclear proliferation, see Donald MacKenzie and Graham Spinardi, "Tacit Knowledge, Weapons Design, and the Uninvention of Nuclear Weapons," *American Journal of Sociology* 101 (July 1995): 44–99.

18. This point was put forward in the Council on Foreign Relations study group, where it was argued that systems knowledge is "domain specific." Engineering colleges in the United States, for example, tend to teach systems engineering in the context of specific applications, rather than as an abstract skill, and experience in one kind of system does not transfer easily to another.

19. One such study is Richard A. Bitzinger and Steven M. Kosiak, *Windows of Opportunity: The Potential Application of Japanese Advanced Commercial Technology Transfers to East Asia* (Washington, D.C.: Defense Budget Project, September 1995). Bitzinger and Kosiak find that, although the potential exists in the industrializing East Asian countries for "spin-on" of civilian technology acquired from the United States and Japan to military applications, so far it has not occurred. They attribute this outcome to several factors, including structural and process impediments and the high opportunity cost of devoting resources to defense technology when civilian activities are so lucrative.

20. See the National Academy of Sciences, *Finding Common Ground*, chap. 4, for a description of the measures employed by the Soviet Union to acquire controlled technology from the West.

21. For a counterexample, consider the difficulty the United States had in transferring the technology for the Roland missile from France. See Daniel K. Malone, *Roland: A Case for or against NATO Standardization?* National Defense University Monograph Series 80-5 (Washington, D.C.: National Defense University, May 1990), p. 69.

22. Two articles by Pat Cooper in *Defense News* (May 27–June 2, 1996) exemplify this problem: "U.S. Lawmakers Examine Vulnerabilities of Internet" (p. 3) and "A Senate Panel Adds Funding for 'SAT'" (p. 14). Marcia Smith of the Congressional Research Service is quoted as saying, "There is concern in this Congress over the proliferation of imagery from commercial satellites that can be used for military purposes."

23. See Paul Mann, "Cyber Threat Expands with Unchecked Speed," *Aviation Week & Space Technology*, July 8, 1996, pp. 63–64.

24. "Russia Finally Accepts Curb on Global Arms Sale," *Guardian*, July 13, 1996, p. 15.

25. The metaphor is used by Kenneth Flamm, "Controlling the Uncontrollable," *The Brookings Review* (Winter 1996): 24. We might question what has happened to human agency in this picture of unstoppable technology.

11

A Framework for Limiting the Negative Consequences of Surplus U.S. Arms Production and Trading

LORA LUMPE

HE GLOBAL trade in conventional weaponry has declined dramatically over the past decade, from nearly $80 billion in 1987 (in inflation-adjusted dollars) to $30 billion in 1996.[1] This steep drop is largely attributable to the end of subsidized arms transfers from Russia after the collapse of the Soviet Union and to sharp cuts in procurement by East European governments.[2] Despite this downward trend, the massive arms industrial capacity built up in North America, Europe, and the Soviet Union during the Cold War is resistant to both closure and conversion, and manufacturers are aggressively seeking export markets to offset their own governments' reduced procurement.

Boosted by the powerful advertising of the 1990–91 Gulf War, strong lobbying by the industry, and active government support, American weaponry now overwhelmingly dominates the world arms market. (See Table 11–1.) In 1995 the United States exported over $16 billion of newly manufactured arms, more than all other countries of the world combined.[3] The arms industries of western Europe—in particular, Britain, France, and Germany—are competing fiercely with U.S. industry for sales to the developing world, which accounts for the vast majority of the market (75 percent in 1995, in terms of dollar volume). And in 1995 Russia also reemerged as a major player in the arms bazaar, report-

Table 11–1 Value of Worldwide Arms Shipments, 1991–96

	1991	1992	1993	1994	1995	1996	Total
U.S. government negotiated	$9,557	$10,669	$11,119	$9,943	$12,782	$13,791	$67,861
U.S. industry negotiated	$5,166	$2,667	$3,808	$2,099	$3,620	$706	$18,066
Russia	$6,200	$2,500	$3,200	$1,500	$3,500	$2,900	$19,800
France	$2,200	$1,800	$1,100	$1,300	$2,200	$2,900	$11,500
United Kingdom	$4,900	$4,700	$4,600	$5,200	$5,100	$5,900	$30,400
China	$1,400	$1,000	$1,100	$700	$600	$600	$5,400
Germany	$2,500	$1,100	$1,700	$1,400	$1,200	$500	$8,400
Italy	$300	$300	$400	$200	$100	$0	$1,300
All other Europe	$1,800	$3,300	$1,800	$2,100	$1,500	$1,400	$11,900
All others	$2,000	1,800	2,100	$2,700	$2,500	$2,100	$13,200
Total	$36,023	$29,836	$30,927	$27,142	$33,102	$30,797	$187,827

Note: In millions of current-year dollars. All data based on calendar year except for U.S. industry-negotiated sales, which is on a U.S. fiscal year basis.

Sources: Richard Grimmett, "Conventional Arms Transfers to Developing Nations, 1989–1996" (Washington, D.C.: Congressional Research Service Library of Congress, 1997), and Foreign Military Sales, Foreign Military Constrictions Sales, and Military Assistance Facts as of September 30, 1996.

edly edging out the United States in terms of the value of new sales contracts signed.[4]

The surplus production capacity and diminishing market have rendered the arms bazaar more competitive and commercially driven than ever, resulting in increasing diplomatic tensions as suppliers vie for market share.[5] Several other dangerous trends have emerged from this competition.

First, arms manufacturers and governments are putting top-of-the-line systems previously not for sale—such as American F-15E Strike Eagle and Russian MiG-31 bombers; modern European diesel attack submarines; supersonic, antiship missiles; and advanced air-to-air missiles—on the market. In the past, for security and arms control reasons, the United States generally exported older, less capable systems, a generation removed from those fielded with U.S. forces. Now domestic economic and political considerations increasingly drive modern weapons onto the market, and the existence of a comparable weapons system in another country, whether it has been exported or not, is used as a justification for marketing high-end weapons. The dangers of such exports—stimulation of arms races and possible use in regional or internal conflict—are overlooked to maintain jobs and excess arms-industrial capacity and to maximize corporate profits. In some cases, policymakers use exports to maintain production lines of sophisticated weapons systems that the Pentagon is finished buying.[6] In other cases, policymakers allow contemporaneous sales of new weapons systems abroad to lower per unit procurement costs for U.S. forces.

Recent sales to the Middle East demonstrate U.S. willingness to export higher-technology weapons in order to maintain now-surplus production lines. In September 1992 Congress and the Bush administration approved the export of 48 McDonnell Douglas F-15E Strike Eagle bombers to Saudi Arabia largely on the basis of an aggressive Jobs Now campaign waged by the manufacturer. The air force was finished procuring the jet, and so McDonnell Douglas devised a national campaign to promote the controversial sale explicitly on the number of jobs that it would sustain.[7] The sale became enmeshed in presidential politics, with then-candidate Bill Clinton endorsing the deal while on a campaign stop in St. Louis, where the jet is manufactured. Shortly thereafter President Bush announced his support for the sale while at a campaign-style rally at the McDonnell Douglas factory.

This was the first time the jet—which can deliver 12 tons of bombs 1,000 miles—had been exported to any nation. Only two years previously, the plane was rushed into service with the U.S. Air Force for the Gulf War, where it was used on hundreds of deep-strike bombing raids.

The Saudi planes will be less capable than U.S. F-15E jets: they will carry less ordnance and are not currently slated to carry advanced medium-range air-to-air missiles (AMRAAM) or heat-seeking antiradiation missiles (HARM), and the radar will have a lower resolution. Nevertheless, this sale represented the most sophisticated combat aircraft the United States had ever exported—until a year and a half later, when the Clinton administration and Congress agreed to give Israel 21 F-15E bombers with enhanced capabilities, in order to maintain that nation's qualitative military edge over Saudi Arabia.

Having gained U.S. government approval for two sales of its most advanced fighter-bomber, McDonnell Douglas is eagerly anticipating more: it recently competed (unsuccessfully) for a sale of 20 to 80 long-range attack planes to the United Arab Emirates. Currently still contending for that potentially $8 billion sale is Lockheed Martin, which developed an "enhanced strategic" version of its popular F-16 fighter in the competition for the Israeli sale. This plane sports several improvements over the F-16s flown by the U.S. Air Force: a reduced radar signature, conformal fuel tanks, internal navigation and targeting gear, and an un-refueled combat range of 1,000 miles. In addition, as a condition of the sale, the United Arab Emirates demanded that the jets be equipped with the air force's most advanced AMRAAM, which the Clinton administration agreed to. Previously the U.S. government had declined to export this missile to countries in the region. Whether Lockheed ultimately wins the competition or not, further sales of AMRAAM missiles to U.S. allies in the Middle East can be expected.

Through these sales, Washington has dramatically raised the standard of combat aircraft and munitions in the arsenals of U.S. allies in the Middle East, many of whom are engaged in a "cold peace" with each other. But large-scale transfers of advanced conventional weapons to U.S. Middle Eastern allies play into the threat perceptions of "unfriendly" governments as well—in this case Iran and Iraq, spurring them to seek countervailing weapons. Such sales by the United States also give the green light to other arms exporters to introduce new levels of military technology into this and other tense regions. A 1995 report by the Central Intelligence Agency's nonproliferation center noted that "as countries' reliance on exports to maintain their defense industrial base grows, pressures will increase to export advanced conventional weapons and technologies *to remain competitive with the United States in the world arms market*" (emphasis added).[8] By making multibillion-dollar sales of extremely advanced weaponry to the Middle East, the U.S. government has diminished credibility in pressing other governments to refrain from making sales that it views as dangerous.[9]

At the same time, defense and intelligence officials now routinely cite the spread of advanced and, on occasion, low-end conventional weapons as a security concern.[10] And completing the circle, the military services and industry justify development and production of next-generation weapons on the basis of arms being acquired by developing nations, including previously exported U.S. systems. In lobbying Congress for production funds for its F-22 fighter, Lockheed cites the widespread proliferation of very capable combat aircraft, such as the Russian MiG-29 and the American-made F-15 and F-16.[11]

A second dangerous feature of today's market is that buyers are increasingly demanding the technology to produce weapons instead of buying the weapons off the shelf. Compliant manufacturers and governments grant licenses to recipient countries, usually to produce components or to conduct final assembly of the weapons system being sold.[12] Under pressure to make the sale, U.S. industry and policymakers are willing not only to send manufacturing jobs overseas but also to risk the creation of near-term competition. By contributing to an even greater global surplus of weapons production capacity and—eventually—to more exports, such deals also pose a real security risk.

A prime example of this phenomenon is the $5.2 billion Korean Fighter Program deal of 1991. South Korea contracted to purchase 12 completed F-16C/D fighters and 36 aircraft kits for assembly in Korea. In addition, Korea—which is seeking to develop an indigenous fighter aircraft production capability—purchased the right to manufacture 72 F-16s under license in Seoul. As an offset to the deal, Lockheed is helping South Korea develop an indigenous combat training aircraft. U.S. policymakers will have little control over future Korean exports of fighter jets and trainers, perhaps to destinations of concern to Washington.[13]

A third negative consequence of today's hypercompetitive arms bazaar is the increasing level of public money being expended to generate business. Despite their overwhelming dominance of the market, American arms corporations claim that European competitors receive a higher level of government support.[14] Citing an "unlevel playing field," U.S. industry has sought—and received—many new forms of public assistance to promote and finance weapons exports in the past decade.[15] At the same time, European arms industries seek increased assistance to overcome what they see as unfair competition from American industry. The resulting spiral of initiatives—which make weapons cheaper and easier for customers to finance—calls into question the alleged economic benefits of arms exports. According to one study, the American public paid out an estimated $7.6 billion to underwrite weapons exports in 1995, while new sales contracts signed that year were valued at $8.2 billion.[16]

Fourth and perhaps most dangerous, the competitive market results in indiscriminate exporting by governments. The vast majority of American-made weapons (in terms of dollar volume) are going to non-democratic, repressive, or aggressive governments, often in apparent violation of U.S. law.[17] Diplomatic rationales have long been used to justify arms trading, with proponents claiming that arms sales allow suppliers to gain and maintain "influence" with recipients. Over the years Congress has attempted to exert this leverage by placing conditions on U.S. weapons exports.[18] However, these requirements often have been tepidly enforced or blatantly ignored, as U.S. clients have acted in opposition to American laws or policies largely with impunity.[19]

Today suppliers are shying away from even *attempting* to influence buyers' behavior. As the arms bazaar is increasingly run as a free market, the global oversupply of arms means that buyers call the shots. They threaten to turn elsewhere if they dislike conditions attached to a sale. Thus sales proponents pressure their governments to renounce all conditions that might offend customers.[20]

Elevating Conventional Arms Proliferation to a Core Security Concern

A largely unregulated and highly competitive commerce in conventional weaponry also exacerbates the principal post–Cold War threats to U.S. and global security. According to the Pentagon and White House, the greatest dangers today arise from instability in the developing world (usually engendered by or leading to internal warfare, but also including major regional conflicts) and the proliferation of nuclear, chemical, and biological weapons (weapons of mass destruction) and ballistic missiles.[21] These threats are said to justify the continuation of Cold War–level military spending—$270 billion in 1997. It can reasonably be asserted that the global arms trade contributes to both menaces and, as such, itself should be addressed as a core security concern.

The proliferation of weapons of mass destruction is tied to the spread of conventional arms in two principal ways. First, conventional weapons platforms—bombers, attack helicopters, long-range artillery rockets—are used to deliver chemical, biological, or nuclear payloads. More fundamentally, conventional arms are part of a weapons continuum that can expand and on some occasions has expanded naturally into weapons of mass destruction. Regimes generally do not decide to "go nuclear" (or "chemical") in a vacuum. They usually do so in the context of conventional arms races, often because they face (or perceive) an imbalance of conventional military force.

Careful consideration should be given, then, to the impact that tens of billions of dollars' worth of high-end combat equipment recently sold to the Persian Gulf sheikdoms might have on Iranian calculations about potential nuclear weapons plans. Similarly, South Korea's highly advanced arsenal of imported and locally produced arms must factor in to North Korea's considerations about unconventional weapons and missile development programs. Currently, insofar as U.S. administration policymakers will acknowledge that conventional and weapons of mass destruction proliferation are related, they seem to believe (in select cases) that a shipment of modern conventional arms can effectively dissuade governments from seeking to acquire nuclear weapons.[22]

The accumulation of conventional weapons through the international trade is also integral to the recent internal and regional warfare that has engaged U.S. troops (e.g., Iraq, Somalia, Bosnia, and Liberia). In the more than 30 conflicts currently raging, few combatants produce any, let alone all, of their own munitions. The international arms trade—in both its licit and illicit dimensions—directly enables and sustains fighting.

Throughout the Cold War, the U.S. government used conventional arms transfers to build and maintain military alliances against the spread of Soviet influence. Arms exports also were employed to serve a mix of domestic and foreign policy goals: gaining access to overseas military facilities, attempting to dissuade the proliferation of weapons of mass destruction, maintaining the arms industrial base, promoting "interoperability" of U.S. and foreign military forces, helping friends and allies deter aggression. In its February 1995 policy on conventional arms, the Clinton administration reiterated the legitimacy of using arms exports in all of these ways.[23]

With conflict and weapons proliferation now the central organizing principles of U.S. (and global) military planning, conventional arms proliferation itself should be viewed as a central security concern, rather than principally as an instrument used to advance other goals. Reporting in June 1996, the Presidential Advisory Board on Arms Proliferation Policy said that it was "strongly convinced that control of conventional arms and technology transfers must become a significantly more important and integral element of United States foreign and defense policy if the overall goals of non-proliferation are to succeed."[24] The rationales for arms exporting must be weighed carefully against the negative consequences arising out of the hypercompetitive marketplace and against the potential for contributing to today's central security threats.

Table 11–2   Arms Flow to Greece and Turkey, 1992 to 1995

	Battle Tanks	Armored Combat Vehicles	Large-Caliber Artillery	Combat Aircraft	Attack Helicopters	Warships	Missiles/ Launchers
Greece	940	1,118	493	98	5	18	2,262
Turkey	1,008	703	203	60	32	9	118

Note: 1995 data include only U.S. and British arms transfers.
Sources: U.N. General Assembly Documents, "United Nations Register of Conventional Arms: Report of the Secretary-General," A/48/344 (October 11, 1993), A/49/352 (September 1 1994), A/50/547 (October 13, 1995); 1995 information from the governments of the United States and the United Kingdom.

For example, the pursuit of "interoperability" of weaponry is fast becoming the administration's most prevalent rationale for widespread arms exports. Interoperability—commonality of arms—is considered to be essential for coalition warfare, which the United States built up during the Cold War in order to contain the spread of communism. Both the "National Security Strategy of Engagement and Enlargement" and the Pentagon's "Quadrennial Defense Review" require that U.S. forces be prepared to fight or intervene anywhere in the world, quickly, thus necessitating forward-deployed forces. Arms transfers and joint military training exercises are used to gain access to overseas bases and to establish the infrastructure necessary for U.S. intervention. However, in the absence of discernible enemies, such as the Soviet bloc during the Cold War, U.S.-led coalitions today are arming against such abstract targets as "regional instability" and "uncertainty," according to Pentagon planning documents. What is to prevent the liberal transfers of arms used to cement these alliances from contributing to the regional instability and uncertainty? As a case in point, in February 1996 President Clinton had to intervene personally to head off a military confrontation between NATO partners Greece and Turkey over a disputed Aegean island. Airspace violations are commonplace between the two, and the head of U.S. Naval Intelligence called Turkish-Greek animosity "Among the most worrisome situations developing in Europe, and one of the most dangerous to NATO as an institution."[25] According to the United Nations Register of Conventional Arms, the two countries were the leading arms importers during the mid-1990s, taking delivery of massive quantities of weaponry. (See Table 11–2.)

Given the relative increase in importance of conventional arms proliferation to today's stated security threats, and given the highly competitive nature of today's arms market, rather than presume that arms transfers will advance general foreign and domestic policy goals, security interests would seem to dictate that the burden of proof be shifted, with the presumption toward denial. At a minimum, new policies are needed that ensure, to the greatest extent possible, that only "safe sales" go forward.

Determine Customer Eligibility on a Standard of Conduct

One important screen for determining arms exports should be the character of the recipient government. The Clinton administration's preferred approach has been to isolate a handful of regimes considered to be "rogues"—Iran, Iraq, Libya, and North Korea—acting outside acceptable norms of behavior. The administration has sought to build consensus around cutting off the flow of conventional weaponry and military-related technologies to these countries through bilateral pressure and through the recently established Wassenaar Arrangement while considering most of the rest of the world fair game for weapons sales.[26] In fact, a frequent justification for many arms sales is the need to deter the "rogue" governments.

When asked in 1996 about the criteria for inclusion on the U.S. administration's "rogue" list, then Undersecretary of State Lynn Davis said that United Nations arms embargoes were key in the cases of Iraq, Libya, and North Korea. (Indeed, all U.N. members are committed to follow U.N. Security Council–mandated arms embargoes. However, several other countries or groups under U.N. embargoes have not been singled out for "rogue" status.) Iran is included, according to Davis, because of its nuclear weapons aspirations, support for terrorist groups, and opposition to the Middle East peace process.[27]

The main flaw of such an approach is that it looks backward, selectively targeting for restraint only those governments that already are considered to be outside of the pale. Part of what makes those governments so menacing is weaponry they have already accumulated. Iran and Iraq, of course, used to be American allies, and as such received billions of dollars' worth of American weaponry and advanced military technology, respectively.

Moreover, such an approach ignores signs of instability—repression or even aggression—among governments currently considered to be friends or allies. For instance, in the process of arming Persian Gulf allies against Iran and Iraq, the U.S. administration apparently is willing to overlook many troubling signs. Massive levels of arms sales to Saudi

Arabia have contributed to anti-western (in particular anti-American) sentiment, as these sales undermine the Saudi economy and the regime's ability to maintain subsidies to which Saudi citizens have become accustomed.[28] Similarly, while professing to support movement toward democracy in Bahrain, the U.S. administration has supplied weaponry particularly useful for putting down pro-democracy demonstrations in that country. And high-level U.S. arms transfers continue to Turkey, despite acknowledgment by the State Department, independent groups, and the Turkish government itself of widespread and serious human rights and political abuses in Turkey's prosecution of its 14-year-long war against Kurdish militants and civilians.[29]

A forward-looking framework would seek to ensure that American-supplied weapons do not end up in the hands of a *future* pariah or hostile government. Such a policy would do so by establishing criteria to help determine which governments are responsible and stable allies and which—because they lack popular support or persecute segments of their population—are vulnerable and might lose power in the near term. These criteria would be applied universally—to current friends and foes alike—and only regimes that meet the criteria would be eligible to import U.S. weaponry. Of course, the future cannot be predicted perfectly, but some guidelines can help determine more or less risky transfers.

One effort to do so is embodied in legislation that passed the House of Representatives in 1997, but not the Senate. The "Code of Conduct on Arms Transfers Act" (bill number S.1067) would condition U.S. exports on recipients' adherence to internationally recognized norms of human rights, their participation in the U.N. Register of Conventional Arms, and their embrace of democracy and nonaggression. The code's central premise is that governments that meet these criteria are more likely to be stable allies, better ensuring that U.S. arms do not again outlast U.S. alliances. The law would force heightened scrutiny and—it is hoped—public debate on the very important policy decisions to supply weaponry to particular regimes. And the annual certification process would provide the executive branch with valuable leverage to help move U.S. allies toward acceptance of core American values and stated foreign policy goals. Clinton administration officials have testified that while they support each of the four criteria embodied in the legislation, they do not support the legislation.[30]

As Representative Cynthia McKinney (D-Ga.) said when first introducing the bill in 1993:

> For years we sold weapons to dictators and provided military training for their officers. We armed the Shah of Iran, we armed Iraq, we armed Panama, we armed Somalia and we armed Haiti. We continue to pay for

these sales with American tax dollars and American lives. There are presently some restraints on the arms trade. But the failures of the present regime are all too apparent. In Haiti, the military that has overturned the elected government of President Aristide and scorned the Governor's Island accord is comprised of an officer corps trained in America. At the very least, American arms should not be sold and U.S. military training should not be provided to governments that oppose American principles.[31]

In early 1998 an analogous "code of conduct" was under development in the 15-member European Union, and a similar international "code of conduct" initiative was being promoted by 15 former Nobel Peace laureates with governments around the world.

Bar Transfers of the Most Dangerous Weapons

A second pillar of a responsible arms export policy would bar the export—and in some cases production, deployment, and use—of weapons systems that are particularly destabilizing or that pose an unacceptable humanitarian risk. Only two categories of conventional weaponry currently are subject to multilateral export control: ballistic/cruise missiles (above a certain range) and antipersonnel landmines. Both cases demonstrate that multilateral export controls are possible to achieve once a category of weaponry has been singled out and its export effectively stigmatized through government, media, and public pressure. In both cases the United States first withdrew itself from the market and then worked—successfully—to convince other exporting governments to follow suit. A weapon-specific approach also has the distinct advantage of not challenging the interests of the entire arms industry and its allies in the armed forces, but rather only discrete segments.

Because of the tragic toll they are taking on noncombatants around the world, over 120 governments have signed a treaty completed in December 1997 banning the production, stockpiling, export, and use of antipersonnel land mines. And at the 1995 review conference of the Convention on Conventional Weapons, laser weapons intended to cause blinding were prohibited. Other weapons systems that are by nature indiscriminate, or otherwise violate humanitarian laws of war, should be stigmatized and barred as well. In its 1996 report, the Presidential Advisory Board on Arms Proliferation Policy suggested cluster bombs, fragmentation weapons, and incendiary weapons as candidates for consideration.[32] Cluster munitions, intended to cover a wide area, are inherently indiscriminate. In addition, unexploded ordnance ("duds") from these weapons mirror the dangers to noncombatants posed by antipersonnel land mines. The United States currently exports cluster bombs and fragmentation warheads. Fuel air explosives were used by the allies during the Gulf War, and napalm was used extensively by the United States in Vietnam. U.S. policy currently prohibits exports of napalm. Other weapons that pose widespread danger to civilians, and that should be considered for unilateral and multilateral export control, are handheld antiaircraft missiles, such as the U.S. Stinger. Hundreds of these missiles were provided to guerrillas fighting the Soviet Union in Afghanistan in the 1980s, and their disposition is now unknown.

Western governments decided in the mid-1980s that the spread of ballistic and cruise missiles directly threatened their own military security and that of their allies, and that these weapons were particularly destabilizing. For these reasons, the Group of Seven leading economic powers agreed in 1987 to block such trade through the creation of the Missile Technology Control Regime (MTCR). Now nearly 30 governments have joined the effort, including practically all missile-producing states. While the traffic in missile components and technologies has not been shut down completely, tremendous progress has been made. No government of the world openly sells missiles, an activity that a decade ago was as common as fighter jet sales are today.

Other advanced weapons systems that should be considered for export control owing to their inherently destabilizing/threatening nature are modern diesel attack submarines, advanced bombers, other stealth aircraft, and modern antiship missiles/naval mines.[33] The Presidential Advisory Board on Arms Proliferation suggested that "the combination of high military effectiveness, low substitutability and low opportunity cost could serve as guidelines for selecting candidates for this approach."[34] But, as the example of the MTCR makes clear, it is not necessary or desirable to wait until all potential suppliers agree to stop exports of these most advanced and destabilizing weapons. A stigmatization campaign initiated unilaterally can be built on effectively through bilateral diplomacy and persuasion.

Conclusion

It is, of course, stating the obvious to observe that the Cold War is over. Nevertheless, eight years into this new era, a fundamental reevaluation of the roles and dangers of surplus conventional arms production and trading has yet to occur. New threats have been identified; indeed, they had to be in order to justify continued maintenance of most of the Cold War–era military industry and weapons programs. But connections between the arms market today and the principal new security threats that have been articulated continue to be willfully ignored. Instead, Cold War–era policies of utilizing arms exports to achieve a host of short-term economic, diplomatic, and security policies continue.

Arms supply decisions affect the entire citizenry—through taxes to support the Pentagon and to underwrite occasional wars required to "demilitarize" imported arsenals, and through the lives of soldiers called upon to fight. A visionary policy that allows only the safest sales, by placing respect for human rights, nonaggression, and democracy at the center of arms export decision-making, rather than on the periphery as is currently the case, would appear to better serve the interests of the majority of the American people. Critics will say that such a policy was tried before—during the Carter administration—and failed. The response is, of course, that the Cold War constraints through which that earlier effort was attempted are gone now.

Notes

1. Richard F. Grimmett, "Conventional Arms Transfers to the Third World, 1986–1993" (Washington, D.C.: Congressional Research Service, Library of Congress, 1994), and "Conventional Arms Transfers to Developing Nations, 1989–1996" (Washington, D.C.: Congressional Research Service, Library of Congress (hereafter cited as CRS 1989–1996; Defense Security Assistance Agency, 1997), Foreign Military Sales, Foreign Military Construction Sales and Military Assistance Facts as of September 30, 1996 (hereafter cited as DSAA 1996).

2. U.S. Arms Control and Disarmament Agency, *World Military Expenditures and Arms Transfers 1995*, table II. Washington, D.C.: U.S. Government Printing Office, 1996, pp. 103–52.

3. CRS 1989–1996, p. 81; DSAA 1996, p. 57. According to the CRS report, the U.S. government exported $12.8 billion worth of arms in 1995, but the study omits industry-direct sales from U.S. export totals. The DSAA report shows that in fiscal year 1995, U.S. arms manufacturers exported an additional $3.6 billion of weaponry in deals they negotiated directly with foreign governments. Combined, the United States exported $16.4 billion of arms, out of an estimated world total of $31.8 billion.

4. CRS 1988–1995, p. 5, estimates that Russia made $9.1 billion in new sales agreements and the United States $8.2 billion in new sales in 1995. It is highly likely that U.S. industry contracted for over $1 billion of new sales during 1995, which would mean that the United States remained the leading arms merchant. However, such information is not included in the report, as it is not made public.

5. See, for instance, "Russia: 'Underhand' Arms Trade Moves Criticized," *Nezavisimoye voyennoye obozreniye,* March 15, 1997, as translated in FBIS-SOV-97-057.

6. The following weapons systems are produced solely or principally for export, as no or little further U.S. military procurement is anticipated: F-15E Strike Eagle fighter/ground attack jet, F-16 Falcon multirole jet, M-1A2 Abrams main battle tank, AH-64 Apache attack helicopter, MIM-107 Patriot air defense missile, MIM-23 Hawk air defense missile, M-113 armored vehicles, and Type-209 diesel attack submarines (under license from HDW). See Chapter 6 in this book.

7. See *Arms Sales Monitor,* no. 16, p. 1; *Arms Sales Monitor,* no. 17 (Washington, D.C.: Federation of American Scientists [Newsletter], 1992).

8. Nonproliferation Center, "The Weapons Proliferation Threat," March 1995, p. 6.

9. See *U.S. Nonproliferation Policy,* hearing of the House Foreign Affairs Committee (Washington, D.C.: Government Printing Office, 1994), pp. 27–29, on the difficulty the United States faces in persuading Russia to forgo arms exports to Iran, given high-level U.S. arms transfers to Persian Gulf countries.

10. The director of U.S. Naval Intelligence testified to Congress in 1994 that "the overall technical threat and lethality of arms . . . being exported have never been higher." (Rear Admiral Edward Shaefer, *Director of Naval Intelligence Posture Statement,* 1994, p. 3.)

    Then director of Central Intelligence James Woolsey testified in January 1995 of the CIA's concern about conventional arms proliferation, which he cited as "a growing military threat, as unprecedented numbers of sophisticated weapons systems are offered for sale on the world market." Especially troubling, he said, "is the proliferation of technologies and expertise in areas such as sensors, materials, and propulsion in supporting the development and modernization of weapons systems. Apart from the capability of some advanced conventional weapons to deliver weapons of mass destruction, such weapons have the potential to significantly alter military balances, and disrupt U.S. military operations and cause significant U.S. casualties." (R. James Woolsey, director of Central Intelligence, prepared testimony before the Senate Select Intelligence Committee, January 10, 1995.)

    The Office of Naval Intelligence reiterated in 1997 that "Countries of concern like Iran, Iraq, North Korea, Syria and Libya are purchasing a mixture of Russian, Chinese and, when available, Western air defense systems and are coherently integrating them—all in a manner worrisome to the U.S. and its allies. Ironically, it is likely that systems of Western origin, while costly, will be the most stressing in the future." (*Worldwide Challenges to Strike Warfare 1997,* Office of Naval Intelligence, 1997.)

11. "The F-22 Air Superiority Fighter: Peace Through Conventional Deterrence," March 1994, promotional material prepared by Lockheed, Boeing, and Pratt & Whitney.

12. On the prevalence of coproduction and licensed production of weapons systems, see Office of Technology Assessment, *Global Arms Trade* (Washington, D.C.: U.S. Government Printing Office, 1991).

13. In 1988 the General Accounting Office disclosed that South Korea had violated the terms of a license for the manufacture of M-16A1 assault rifles, producing in excess of the licensed quantities and exporting them without U.S. approval. The State Department classified the names of the third-country recipients, but Representative Larry Hopkins disclosed that they were "hostile" destinations. According to the Pentagon, however, the rifle was a "Koreanized" version of the M-16, outside of U.S. controls.

14. On this, see United States General Accounting Office, "Military Exports: A Comparison of Government Support in the United States and Three Major Competitors," GAO/NSIAD-95-86 (Washington, D.C.: U.S. General Accounting Office, May 1995).

15. These subsidies have included U.S. taxpayer guarantees for up to $15 billion of commercial loans for weapons purchases (in addition to annual grant military aid appropriations); the waiver of a fee previously included in the price of arms sales to recover some portion of taxpayer-financed research and development costs for the weapons system being exported; and appearances by U.S. military personnel and equipment at overseas air shows and arms bazaars. On the latter point, since 1994 the Department of Defense has certified on nearly 10 occasions that Pentagon assistance to the U.S. arms industry at various arms bazaars is "in the national security interests of the United States." The key justification is that "U.S. industry faces formidable competition from other nations which are actively marketing their equipment globally." For reportage on these and other subsidy issues, see various issues of the *Arms Sales Monitor* (Washington, D.C.: Federation of American Scientists, 1991–1996).

16. For the $7.6 billion figure, see William D. Hartung, *Welfare for Weapons Dealers: The Hidden Costs of the Arms Trade* (New York: World Policy Institute, 1996); for the new sales contract figure, see CRS 1988–1995, p. 78. This figure excludes arms sales agreements negotiated directly by U.S. arms industry, as such information is not made public.

17. *Dictators or Democracies? Annual Analysis of U.S. Arms Transfers to Developing Countries, 1991–1994* (Washington, D.C.: Project on Demilitarization and Democracy, August 1995) shows that 85 percent of U.S. arms exports to developing countries from 1991 to 1994 went to unelected governments.

18. U.S. weapons exports are currently subject to the following stipulations of law:
    No retransfer: Section 3(a)(2) of the Arms Export Control Act (AECA) requires that countries obtain approval from the U.S. government before retransferring U.S.-supplied weapons to another country.
    Nonaggression: Section 4 of the AECA authorizes provision of military equipment and services only for internal security, "legitimate self-

defense," participation in U.N. operations or operations consistent with the U.N. Charter.

Respect for human rights: Section 502B of the Foreign Assistance Act (FAA) requires that "no security assistance may be provided to any country the government of which engages in a consistent pattern of gross violations of internationally recognized human rights."

Non-proliferation: Section 620E(e) of the FAA mandates that "no military equipment or technology shall be sold or transferred to Pakistan" unless the president certifies that Pakistan does not have a nuclear weapon.

19. Witness, for example, ongoing widespread human rights abuses by the Turkish military and police, Israel's 1982 invasion of Lebanon and recent use of U.S.-supplied arms in attacks on civilians, and Saudi Arabia's retransfer of American-supplied arms to Iraq in the 1980s.

Human Rights and U.S. Security Assistance (Washington, D.C.: Amnesty International USA, 1996) reports that for fiscal year 1997, the U.S. administration sought military aid for 19 governments that are widespread violators of human rights.

20. Recent events illustrate the reverse conditionality in today's arms market. When several European governments criticized Turkey for human rights abuses in its war against Kurdish militants, the Ankara government announced it would no longer buy arms from those countries. Turkey placed vocal critics Austria, Finland, Sweden, and Switzerland on a prohibited, or "red," list; less critical Norway and the Benelux countries were placed on a "yellow" list, meaning that arms purchases from these countries would be reviewed on a case-by-case basis. (See *Janes Defence Weekly,* April 17, 1993, May 29, 1993, December 11, 1993.)

In 1990, when President Bush certified that Pakistan had a nuclear bomb under development, the United States cut off most arms sales, as required by law. Now many in the United States are working to end this prohibition, claiming that it is ineffective and simply diverting business from U.S. industry. (The close U.S. military relationship with Pakistan prior to 1990 was also supposed, and failed, to dissuade Pakistan from building nuclear weapons.)

21. See the *Report on the Bottom-Up Review,* October 1993; *A National Security Strategy of Engagement and Enlargement,* July 1994 and February 1995; *Annual Report by the Secretary of Defense to the President and the Congress,* March 1996.

22. Joseph Nye, then assistant secretary of defense for International Security Affairs, made this case before the Senate Foreign Relations Committee in March 1995. As required by U.S. law, the United States suspended most arms transfers to Islamabad in 1990 because of Pakistan's nuclear weapons program. Nye criticized the conventional arms embargo and suggested that it actually might strengthen Pakistan's resolve to pursue nuclear weapons. (Prior to the embargo, the United States had supplied Pakistan

with very sophisticated fighter-bombers and a multitude of other conventional arms. These aircraft now provide Pakistan's most likely means of delivery for a nuclear weapon, according to CIA testimony to Congress in 1991.)

The Clinton administration has taken the opposite tack with Iran, working assiduously in this case to persuade Russia and European arms suppliers to cut off conventional arms transfers to that country precisely because it is suspected of seeking to develop nuclear weapons.

23. According to the policy statement, "Transfers of conventional arms [are] a legitimate instrument of U.S. foreign policy—deserving U.S. government support—when they enable us to help friends and allies deter aggression, promote regional stability, and increase interoperability of U.S. forces and allied forces." In addition, the administration policy imbues weapons exports with several unsubstantiated and near-mythical qualities, alleging that U.S. arms exports serve the following goals:

- Prevent the proliferation of weapons of mass destruction and missiles,
- "Promote peaceful conflict resolution and arms control, human rights, democratization,"
- "Enhance the ability of the U.S. defense industrial base to meet U.S. defense requirements and maintain long-term military technological superiority at lower costs."

White House, Office of the Press Secretary, "Fact Sheet: Criteria for Decisionmaking on U.S. Arms Exports," February 17, 1995.

24. Janne Nolan et al., "Report of the Presidential Advisory Board on Arms Proliferation Policy," undated (released June 1996), p. 2.

25. Rear Admiral Edward Shaefer, *Director of Naval Intelligence Posture Statement, 1994*, p. 7.

26. Meeting in Wassenaar, The Netherlands, in December 1995, the United States and 27 other governments agreed to the formation of a new regime on exports of weapons and dual-use military technologies called the Wassenaar Arrangement on Export Controls for Conventional Arms and Dual-Use Goods and Technologies.

According to a State Department fact sheet, the arrangement will primarily be a forum for consultation and transparency, and "where appropriate, multilateral restraint" on weapons and dual-use technology transfers. The regime relies on each participating nation's own laws and policies to monitor and control export of items to be included on the forum's munitions and dual-use technologies lists. The fact sheet says, "A central part of the regime is the commitment by its members to prevent the acquisition of armaments . . . whose behavior today is, or becomes, a cause for serious concern, such as Iran, Iraq, Libya and North Korea."

27. Unpublished. Stated on the record at a seminar hosted by the Carnegie Endowment for International Peace, January 23, 1996.

28. For an overview of political instability in Saudi Arabia, see Milton Viorst, "The Storm and the Citadel," *Foreign Affairs* (January/February 1996).

29. See U.S. Department of State, *"U.S. Military Equipment and Human Rights Violations,"* July 1997; U.S. Department of State, *Country Reports on Human Rights Practices for 1997,* February 1998; Human Rights Watch, *Weapons Transfers and Violations of the Laws of War in Turkey,* November 1995; Kelly Couturier, "Report Ties Turkey to Assassins: Gunmen Allegedly Targeted Kurds," *Washington Post,* January 24, 1998, p. A17.

30. See testimony of Undersecretary of State for Arms Control and International Security Lynn Davis, Assistant Secretary of State for Human Rights John Shattuck, and the Director of the Defense Security Assistance Agency Lieutenant General Thomas Rhame, May 23, 1996, before the Senate Appropriations Committee (published as S.Hrg. 104–222).

31. *Congressional Record,* November 19, 1993, pp. E2939–40.

32. *Report of the Presidential Advisory Board on Arms Proliferation Policy,* p 6.

33. See John Sislin and David Mussington, "Destabilizing Arms Acquisitions," *Jane's Intelligence Review* 7, no. 2 (19): 88–90.

34. *Report of the Presidential Advisory Board on Arms Proliferation Policy,* p. 6.

V

Defense Industry Globalization

12

Globalization in the Post–Cold War Defense Industry: Challenges and Opportunities

RICHARD A. BITZINGER

THE ARMAMENTS industry has long been one of the more protected parts of most countries' economies. Most nations traditionally have preferred, whenever possible, to be "autarkic," or self-sufficient, in arms production, and therefore indigenous defense industries generally have been regarded more as "national assets" critical to a country's defense than simply as one more manufacturing sector. Even in the West, armaments production often was placed outside the bounds of free market economics, and the typical free market standards of open competition, efficiency, and even profitability were considered secondary to guaranteeing that a nation could mobilize internally the material resources it required for its national defense. In most instances arms production was a decidedly national affair, with ownership, design, research and development (R&D), manufacture, and procurement largely kept within a country's borders. Even in many capitalist countries, defense companies were state owned or heavily state controlled, and governments tended to limit or discourage foreign involvement in indigenous defense industries.

Not surprisingly, the end of the Cold War has done much to challenge this once-sacrosanct notion about autarky in arms production. The large defense industrial bases of the United States, western Europe, Russia, and the other industrialized countries, assembled during the period of East-West hostilities, now face excess capacity and redundancy in the post–Cold War era as defense budgets shrink and national arms markets contract. This overcapacity is compounded by the unwillingness or inability of arms producers to convert from military to commercial manufacturing, thus leaving them few options in their struggle to remain profitable in today's global arms marketplace.

Industry is not the only player feeling the pinch. Governments as well are trying to continue to modernize their armed forces in the face of rising R&D and manufacturing costs associated with next-generation weapons systems. Additionally, as arms industries continue to scale down workforces and close factories, public officials are under growing pressure to save manufacturing jobs in the defense sector.

As governments and industry search for solutions to these problems, "going global" in arms production is becoming an increasingly attractive strategy for ensuring the survival and viability of defense industry assets. The globalization of arms production is defined here as the shift away from traditional, single-country patterns of weapons manufacturing in favor of "internationalizing" the development, production, and marketing of arms. Admittedly, certain types of international arms cooperation, such as licensed production, have been around for decades, if not centuries. However, since the mid-1980s, the pace and scope of global arms collaboration have expanded significantly, and such cooperative activities increasingly have become an integral and critical part of defense production in many countries.

While globalization promises many material and technological benefits, it also raises a number of concerns. The emergence of a transnational defense industrial and military technology base is fundamentally affecting the shape and content of much of the global arms market. This changing defense market could, in turn, have profound implications for a variety of national security issues, including defense policy, conventional weapons proliferation and arms control, regional security cooperation, and the future composition and capabilities of national defense industrial bases.

Why Globalize Arms Production? The Growing Economic Driver

Until quite recently international arms collaboration was largely driven by *strategic* rationales. During the Cold War, for example, the North Atlantic Treaty Organization (NATO) supported the idea of intra-alliance arms cooperation as a means of enhancing alliance combat efficiency and effectiveness by eliminating wasteful duplication in arms production while also promoting battlefield rationalization, standardization, and interoperability (RSI). In addition, transfers of arms production capabilities often were used to bolster allies and friends, thereby serving as a substitute for direct military involvement—for example, U.S. military-technical aid to Israel on the Lavi fighter jet, or Taiwan being permitted to license-produce American military equipment. Military technology transfers also have served as a signal to third parties that the recipient was regarded as an important ally or protectorate of the supplier. Finally, many governments attempted to use collaborative arms activities to help foster other types of international cooperation, such as west European political and economic integration or NATO solidarity.

Increasingly, however, *economic* motivations have come to dominate defense industrial globalization and, consequently, kick the process into a higher gear. The recent economic and fiscal pressures facing arms producers are readily apparent; since the late 1980s, defense expenditures have dropped dramatically. Between fiscal year (FY) 1985 and FY 1996, U.S. defense budgets, for example, declined in real terms by nearly 35 percent; procurement budgets have dropped even more precipitously—over 67 percent—during this same period. From 1988 to 1993 Soviet/Russian defense spending fell from $380 billion to $114 billion (in constant 1993 dollars).[1] And while overall west European military expenditures have remained largely static, procurement spending on so-called heavy weapons did decline significantly—approximately 18 percent—from the mid-1980s to the mid-1990s.[2] In addition, European arms producers must contend with skyrocketing R&D and production costs for next-generation weapons systems and a defense industrial base that is far too large for their needs. For example, western Europe still possesses five major combat aircraft producers (vs. two major fighter jet builders in the United States), four major missile manufacturers (compared with two in the United States), and four tank producers (compared with just one in the United States), even though its regional arms market is roughly half the size of that of the United States.[3]

Defense industries around the world are confronted with shrinking national arms markets, compounded by rising weapons costs. In the absence of any offsetting actions, a significant decline in military production—and with it, the accompanying loss of defense jobs—is inevitable. The Bonn International Center for Conversion has estimated that, for the period from 1987 to 1995, 37 percent of the worldwide defense-related workforce, or nearly 6.5 million jobs, already has been made redundant.[4] In western Europe approximately 600,000 jobs have been lost over this period.[5] At least 1 million defense jobs have been shed in the United States since the peak of the Reagan military buildup in 1987, while future job losses in the U.S. defense industry could total as much as 1 million more by the end of the decade.[6]

Defense industries throughout the world face a major restructuring over the next several years. *Diversification* into nonmilitary production is one option, of course, and, in fact, armaments-manufacturing enterprises around the world have been successful in moving into nonmilitary activities.[7] At the same time, for many arms producers—particularly in the United States and western Europe—diversification has turned out more to be a supplement to rather than a substitute for arms production. These firms have chosen to remain heavily or primarily engaged in defense production, and, as a result, *consolidation*—involving both corporate downsizing (through layoffs and the closure of unneeded factories) and the acquisition of other defense-related businesses—has been a critical industrial strategy.[8] Recent consolidation activities in the United States include the merger of defense giants Lockheed and Martin Marietta (and the subsequent purchase of Loral Corporation); Boeing's takeover of McDonnell Douglas; Raytheon's acquisition of E-Systems, Hughes's missile and defense group, and Texas Instruments' defense electronics division; and Northrop's purchase of Grumman Corporation. In western Europe, several countries have witnessed the emergence of "national champions"—monopoly suppliers created through mergers or acquisitions—within many of their defense industrial sectors.

Despite their problems, many overwhelmingly defense-dependent arms producers are choosing to remain in fields where their experience and expertise are strongest. Still, industries that refuse to reduce their dependency on military manufacturing face a daunting future, since national defense markets are likely to shrink below levels at which national defense industrial bases can afford to operate. To remedy this situation, defense enterprises around the world are seeking to offset declines in national demand by expanding into foreign markets. The most obvious and simplest means of accomplishing this is through overseas sales. In fact, arms exports are being sought increasingly as at least a partial solution to their overcapacity problems. Defense firms, particularly in the United States, have been very aggressive in recent years in pursuing overseas arms sales. Between 1992 and 1993, for example, U.S. foreign military sales (FMS) agreements (as opposed to deliveries) jumped from $15 billion to just over $33 billion.[9]

Arms exports have their limitations, however. For one thing, efforts on the part of U.S. and European defense firms to increase their overseas sales have collided with a major contraction in the international arms market. According to the U.S. Arms Control and Disarmament Agency, global arms *deliveries* fell by 72 percent between 1987 and 1994, from $78.8 billion to $22.1 billion (as measured in constant 1994 dollars). Data put out by the Stockholm International Peace Research Institute also note a "precipitous decline" in international arms exports beginning in the late 1980s/early 1990s.[10] By the mid-1990s, U.S. FMS agreements were back down to around $10 billion to $12 billion per year. In addition, U.S. and European arms exporters must contend with both the growing ambitions of several third world countries to produce arms indigenously and the fact that many developing countries are no longer content to simply buy weapons off the shelf. Instead, these countries are demanding industrial participation in arms production in the form of offset manufacturing arrangements, licensed production, and technology transfers.

Owing to this increasingly tight and competitive international arms market, foreign military sales are no panacea for defense enterprises seeking to overcome their economic problems at home. Globalization, on the other hand, offers a number of potential benefits to arms producers that extend beyond those that accompany mere arms exports:

1. Collaboration permits the economic rationalization of military research and development and the sharing of R&D costs and risks. As military R&D and manufacturing becomes costlier, few countries can afford to develop a major weapons systems autonomously. By cooperating on ad hoc codevelopment projects or by consolidating operations through multinational joint ventures, companies can spread the costs of design and development among several partners while simultaneously reducing duplicative R&D activities.

2. Producers can attain increased economies of scale through larger production runs of specific weaponry. By concentrating on the joint manufacture of common weapons systems, armaments production can be more efficient and less expensive than if a number of competing weapons were produced separately and in smaller numbers.

3. Efficiencies in armaments production also may be supplemented by moving certain elements of production offshore, particularly to the developing world, where labor costs may be lower. There are limits to such an approach, but certain componentry (particularly low-tech ones) have been produced successfully in the newly industrialized countries and sent to developed countries for final assembly.

4. Cooperation in military R&D can help a country gain access to innovative foreign technologies. Few countries are leaders in all

critical technologies, and technology sharing through defense industry globalization permits additional shortcuts to developing, producing, and acquiring more advanced weaponry.

5.   Globalization can aid in the penetration of foreign markets that might otherwise be closed to off-the-shelf arms sales. As already noted, fewer and fewer countries are willing to buy finished weapons systems and instead are insisting on having a role in the production or even the development of the armaments they are purchasing. Some form of local participation as a condition of an arms sales is increasingly the "price of admission," therefore, and by agreeing to licensed production, offsets, or codevelopment arrangements, arms suppliers can make offers more attractive to prospective buyers.

In certain respects the globalization of arms production can be viewed as *a transnational extension of the consolidation process taking place within the defense industry.* Defense enterprises see globalization as a way to make arms production more efficient and cost effective, while it also, they hope, increases defense work by expanding into new markets. Governments, in turn, hope to reap procurement savings and technology bonuses from this process.

Developments and Trends in Defense Industry Globalization

In a broader sense, the "globalization of arms production" is nothing particularly novel.[11] Military technology has flowed across borders for centuries. As the technology to build weapons became more advanced and therefore more esoteric and even protected through patent rights and corporate secrecy, governments and companies still continued to acquire the know-how to develop and manufacture foreign armaments, either through illegal (i.e., stealing or copying foreign designs) or legal means (i.e., paying royalties to foreign companies to produce their weapons). In such a manner, for example, did the then state of the art in military technology—breech-loading rifles, machine guns, and rapid-fire artillery—diffuse throughout the world during the nineteenth century. During the 1920s and 1930s the aviation industries in several countries benefited significantly from technology imports—including, ironically enough, Japan, which obtained much of its aircraft know-how from the United States.

Even during the early years of the Cold War (from approximately 1950 to the mid-1960s), both the United States and the Soviet Union relied heavily on *licensed production* arrangements to help their friends and allies rebuild or develop their indigenous defense industries. The United States, for example, licensed the manufacture of a number of weapon systems, such as the F-4 fighter jet (to Great Britain and Japan) and the Sidewinder missile (to Germany and Taiwan), while China and several Warsaw Pact countries established their own factories to produce Soviet-designed tanks, fighter jets, missiles, and other arms. Even up until the early 1980s, licensed production was the predominant form of international arms cooperation. (See Figures 12–1 and 12–2.)[12] On a lesser but nonetheless important scale, beginning in the early 1960s licensed production was increasingly supplemented by various *coproduction* initiatives, which entailed the joint production of a common weapon system, even if development of that weapon took place in only one country. One of the best examples of a fully integrated coproduction scheme was the transatlantic F-16 fighter program that took place during the 1970s and 1980s, in which the United States and four west European countries (Belgium, Denmark, the Netherlands, and Norway) shared out the production of parts and components for F-16s collectively purchased by all five countries. As a result, U.S. Air Force F-16s contained European-produced parts and subsystems, while F-16s also were assembled in Europe. In another type of coproduction activity—the *family-of-weapons* concept—several partnering countries individually developed several pieces of related military equipment and then jointly produced and procured all the systems; this approach was used successfully by Britain and France in the late 1960s with the Lynx/Puma/Gazelle family of utility helicopters.[13]

In terms of the overall number of program start-ups, the Cold War era certainly witnessed an unprecedented expansion in international arms collaboration. But what is more significant about the current trend in the globalization of arms production is not just its *quantitative* growth but its *qualitative* development as well. Beginning around the early 1960s but especially over the past decade or so, both governments and defense industries found it necessary to expand their transnational connections and to engage in more international codevelopment and coproduction programs in order to share risks and costs, gain access to foreign technologies and markets, and achieve economies of scale in arms production. More important, the process of international arms cooperation has become increasingly less ad hoc and "a one-way street" in terms of technology diffusion; instead it has developed into a more formal, integrative, and truly collaborative (i.e., involving back-and-forth technology flows) arrangement.

312

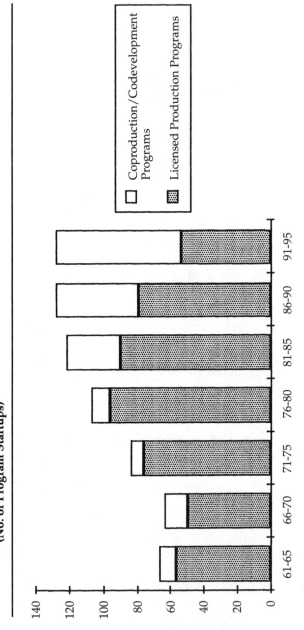

Figure 12–1 International Arms Cooperation, 1961–95
(No. of Program Startups)

Coproduction/Codevelopment Programs

Licensed Production Programs

Source: DBP Globalization Database.

Figure 12–2   International Arms Cooperation with the Developing World, 1961–95 (No. of Program Startups)

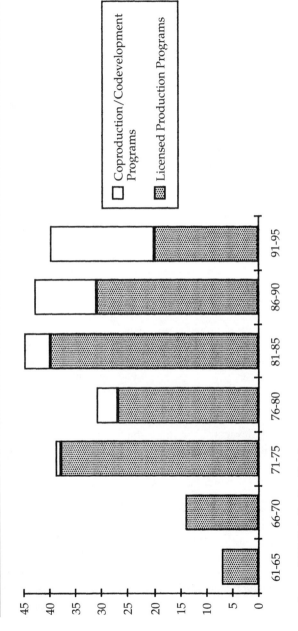

Source: DBP Globalization Database.

Table 12–1: The Globalization of Arms Production: A Typology

Term	Definition
Licensed Production:	The transnational sale or transfer of the rights to manufacture a weapons system in another country.
Coproduction:	The internationally share manufacturing of a weapons system originally evelope by one country.
Codevelopment:	The international esign, evelopment, an (usually) pro uction of a weapons system.
"Family of Weapons":	A international ivision of labor whereby a group of nations agree to un ertake the pro uction of several relate weapons systems (e.g., air-to-air missiles or helicopters), but with each in ivi ual weapon being evelope within a single country an then copro uce by all participating countries.
International Strategic Alliance:	A loose in ustrial arrangement between efense firms in two or more countries to share information or to stu y future possible copro uction or co evelopment.
Joint Venture:	An international subsi iary jointly owne an operate by efense firms in two or more countries for the purposes of co eveloping an copro ucing a particular weapon or class of weapons.
Transnational Mergers and Acquisitions:	The purchase of shares in a efense firm by a efense firm in another country, up to gaining majority control.

Since the late 1970s, a clear trend could be identified toward moving international arms collaboration further back to the beginning of the product cycle—a development reflected in the growing preference for multinational teaming on military R&D—*codevelopment*—over licensing and coproduction arrangements. This trend became particularly apparent by the early 1980s, and this decade was in some ways the "golden age" of international arms cooperation. During this period, for example, the West found itself awash in a slew of major codevelopment programs, including the Anglo-Italian-German Tornado fighter jet; the Franco-German HOT/Milan series of antitank weapons; the Anglo-American

AV-8B Harrier II jet; the Franco-Italian OTOMAT antiship cruise missile; and the Franco-Dutch-Belgian Tripartite-class minesweeper. In the West, this process culminated in the mid-1980s with the inauguration of the so-called Nunn programs, named for an amendment (sponsored by Georgia Senator Sam Nunn) that specifically authorized monies from the Department of Defense R&D budget to be spent on U.S.-allied weapons codevelopment. By the late 1980s, 28 collaborative weapons projects were being funded under the Nunn Amendment, and 26 memoranda of understanding had been signed between the United States and its allies. Major Nunn programs included the NATO Frigate Replacement-1990s (NFR-90), the Modular Standoff Weapon (MSOW), and the Autonomous Precision-Guided Munition (APGM).[14] Even in the 1990s, the ad hoc codevelopment of weapons systems remains a highly preferred form of international arms cooperation—witness, for example, the Anglo-German-Italian-Spanish Eurofighter-2000 fighter jet, the Franco-German Tigre antitank helicopter, and the U.S.-Japanese FSX/F-2 fighter.

In addition to the increasing frequency of international codevelopment programs surrounding major weapons systems, anecdotal evidence suggests that there is an increasing incidence of globalization taking place at the subsystems level as well. The growing use of *offsets* in arms deals—arrangements whereby, as a condition of a sale, the buyer manufactures some of the components or subsystems for the particular weapon it is purchasing—has become an important factor in the diffusion of military technology, especially to the developing world. An indicator of how common offsets have become, and how they may involve even the most advanced weapons systems, is illustrated in Table 12–2. The *international trade in defense-applicable subsystems and components*—especially those based on dual-use technologies or components, such as computers, electronics, and telecommunications—can be viewed as another, often undetected phenomenon in the globalization of arms production. U.S. combat aircraft, for example, are equipped with British head-up displays, while American precision-guided munitions may rely on Japanese computer chips and ceramic packages.[15] Another area of defense industrial globalization that may not involve the actual joint production of armaments includes *international cooperation in the area of basic or exploratory defense research and development,* such as the Rockwell/DASA X-31 experimental aircraft or cooperation between McDonnell Douglas and British Aerospace on advanced vertical takeoff technology.

Perhaps the most critical and noteworthy development in the process of the globalization of arms production, however, is that *since the late 1980s, industry, rather than the state, has increasingly taken the initiative in restructuring the international defense industrial base,* in particular by the

Table 12–2   Recent Major U.S. Arms Sales Involving Coproduction Offsets

Country	Offsets
Israel	
F-15 fighter	Aircraft components manufacture
	Aircraft engine components manufacture
F-16 fighter	Aircraft components/subcomponents manufacture
Canada	
F/A-18 fighter	Aircraft subcomponents manufacture
	Aircraft engine assembly
Spain	
F/A-18 fighter	Aircraft components/subcomponents manufacture
Korea	
F-16 (first buy)	Aircraft components/subcomponents manufacture
P-3 patrol aircraft	Aircraft components assembly
Singapore	
F-16 fighter	Aircraft subcomponents manufacture
Greece	
F-16 fighter	Aircraft components manufacture
Indonesia	
F-16 fighter	Aircraft subcomponents manufacture
Taiwan	
F-16 fighter	Aircraft components/subcomponents manufacture

Source: Robert H. Trice, "Transnational Industrial Cooperation in Defense Programs," in Ethan B. Kapstein, ed., *Global Arms Production: Policy Dilemmas for the 1990s* (Lanham, Md.: University Press of America, 1992), pp. 165–66.

establishment of new transnational, interfirm link ups that are intended to form the basis for future military R&D and production. While the more traditional government-run and ad hoc process of international arms collaboration may provide considerable benefits in terms of cost savings, R&D sharing, and economies of scale, it also has its costs, as one defense analyst has put it: "Bargaining between governments and bureaucracies can lead to inefficiencies through time-delays and administrative costs. Work is often allocated on the basis of equity inputs rather than efficiency and comparative advantage. Collaboration also involves high transaction costs reflected in the duplication of management structures and decision-making processes. The net effect is delays, cost overruns and high unit costs."[16] As a result of the defense firms themselves taking the lead (with government acquiescence), international arms production increasingly has involved ever more complex, integrated, and permanent crossborder industrial partnerships. These new industrial arrangements are recasting the shape and structure of international arms production dramatically.

In recent years, for example, the number of *strategic alliances* and *international joint venture companies* engaged in arms development and production has grown dramatically. One example of such a strategic alliance is an agreement between British Aerospace and France's Dassault on a joint design study for a future attack aircraft, while recent defense-industrial joint ventures include (1) Eurocopter (jointly owned by France's Aérospatiale and DASA of Germany, combining the helicopter production operations of both companies); (2) TDA Armaments, a venture formed by merging the munitions subsidiaries of Thomson Brandt (part of France's Thomson-CSF conglomerate) and DASA; (3) Thomson-Shorts Missile Systems, jointly owned and operated by Britain's Short Brothers and Thomson-CSF; (4) the creation of Matra Marconi Space, an Anglo-French subsidiary of Matra's and GEC-Marconi's space systems divisions; and (5) Matra-BAe Dynamics (MBD), joining the missile divisions of British Aerospace and Matra. In the case of MBD, this new joint venture company created almost overnight the largest missile-production operation in Europe. Finally, although it is not a defense enterprise per se, the various European companies that comprise Airbus Industries agreed in 1997 to transform this consortium from a risk-sharing partnership into a single corporate entity.

In many such joint venture companies, while current programs remain the province of the original firm, the partners agree to cooperate on the development and production of all future systems. For example, within Eurocopter, Aerospatiale and DASA continue to produce their own premerger lines of helicopters—although marketing now is done jointly—while working together to develop new products, such as the Tigre antitank helicopter. In addition, while politics often dictates that all partners have an equal say regardless of their share in the joint venture, workshares and revenues usually are parceled out according to the size of the parent company's investment in the venture and the value of the orders placed by the company's government.[17]

The *transnational mergers and acquisitions* (M&As) that have taken place within the worldwide defense industry, particularly in recent years, are an even more significant event in the globalization process. Major recent defense M&As include (1) the takeover of FN Herstal of Belgium by the French munitions manufacturer, GIAT; (2) Rolls-Royce's purchase of Allison, a U.S. builder of small turbofan engines; (3) Thomson-CSF's acquisition of the Dutch defense electronics firm, Hollandse Signaalapparat; (4) DASA's purchase of the now-defunct Dutch aerospace firm Fokker; (5) Bombardier of Canada's acquisition of Britain's Short Brothers; and (6) the joint purchase of Siemen's defense electronics division by British Aerospace and DASA. Cross-shareholding within the defense industry is also on the rise; the German missile producer BGT is 22 percent owned by Matra, Thomson-CSF holds a 20 percent share in Spain's Indra, and Sikorsky once owned a minority stake in Britain's Westland Helicopter Company. Defense industry mergers and acquisitions are a recent phenomenon, and, in fact, nearly all major crossborder M&As involving defense-related firms have occurred just since the mid-1980s.[18]

This process of industry-led defense globalization has been especially pronounced in western Europe, where overcapacity and redundancy in arms production is particularly dramatic. It is important to note, therefore, that *nearly all* recent major defense-related joint ventures or M&As have taken place within western Europe. (See Figures 12–3 and 12–4.) As a result, a *regionalized* arms production network increasingly is supplementing national defense industrial bases in Europe.

One final observation can be made of the current trend in the globalization of arms production: as this process has grown both in sheer numbers of incidents and in terms of more formal and integrated interfirm linkages, *the globalization process has expanded geographically* as well to include many countries in the developing world. Since the late 1970s, more than 20 developing countries on five continents have participated in hundreds of cooperative arms projects, including more than 50 current major programs. Such globalization activities have served as an important means by which many developing countries have been able to establish and nurture national defense industrial bases.

While the licensed production of western or Russian weapon systems remains the major mode of arms manufacture in most newly industrialized countries, codevelopment and coproduction programs between the developing and industrialized nations have shown a gradual but impressive expansion over the past two decades. (Figure 12–2). Examples of recent North-South arms collaboration include the Italian-Brazilian AMX attack jet, the U.S.-South Korean KTX-2 advanced trainer/lightweight fighter jet, and Taiwan's Indigenous Defensive Fighter (IDF), the result of close collaboration with several U.S. defense firms. As a result of such collaborative arms programs or foreign military-technological assistance, some newly industrialized countries have succeeded in reaching an impressive level of capability and even sophistication in a few selected areas of indigenous armaments production, such as light combat aircraft (Taiwan), primary trainer aircraft (Brazil), multiple rocket launchers (Brazil), long-range artillery (South Africa), main battle tanks and armored vehicles (Israel and Brazil), tactical missiles (Israel, Taiwan, South Africa, and South Korea), and systems upgrades and adaptations (South Africa, Singapore, and Israel).

**Figure 12–3   Defense Industry Joint Venture Companies, 1986–95:
Transatlantic vs. Intra-European**

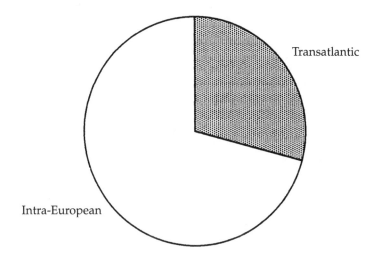

Transatlantic

Intra-European

Source: DBP Globalization Database.

**Figure 12–4   Defense Industry M&As, 1986–95:
Transatlantic vs. Intra-European**

U.S.>Europe

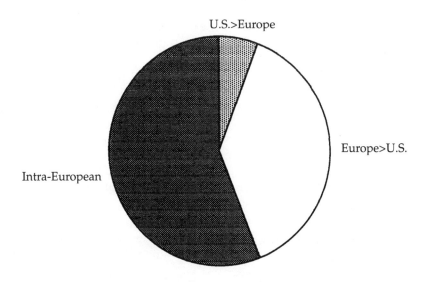

Europe>U.S.

Intra-European

Source: DBP Globalization Database.

To a limited extent, third world collaborative arms efforts *exclusive of the industrialized world* are also increasingly evident. Much of this cooperation is kept secret—especially since it frequently involves the illegal retransfer of western- or Russian-originated technology—but some details are known. Israel, for example, has licensed the production of its Gabriel antiship missiles to Taiwan and South Africa, while it is reportedly collaborating with China on a new combat aircraft (the F-10 fighter) based on the canceled Lavi fighter program.[19] China and Pakistan are cooperating in the development of several weapons systems, including the FC-1 fighter jet, the K-8 light trainer jet, and the Al-Khalid main battle tank. Brazil has licensed the production of its Tucano turboprop trainer aircraft to Egypt.[20] Partnerships involving defense technology transfers within the newly industrialized countries could have increasing potential over the long term—especially since nearly all arms sales to the developing world nowadays entail some form of offset production and industrial participation; therefore, as many of these countries attempt to peddle their wares on the international arms market, this phenomenon of joint third world weapons development and the diffusion of weapons technology from one developing country to another should continue to be monitored closely.

The emergence of a more transnational defense industry means that arms production no longer can be viewed in strictly national terms. Internationalized armaments development and manufacture, coupled with formalized and integrated interfirm linkages, blurs the concept of "indigenous" weapons systems. For example, Taiwan's new IDF fighter draws heavily on the United States for design expertise as well as for its licensed-produced engine and radar. This same blurring of national distinctions can be said increasingly of defense firms: Is Hollandse Signaal still a Dutch company now that it is wholly owned by France's Thomson? Is Matra Marconi Space a British company, a French company, or something else?

Finally, and perhaps most important, the global arms trade no longer can be defined as simply the export of finished weapons systems. Rather, the international arms market increasingly will be characterized by the international commerce in military technology, production know-how, and arms manufacturing.

Implications of Defense Industry Globalization

The increasing globalization of arms production has economic, political, and military implications for both industry and government. With the end of the Cold War, and in an era of shrinking military budgets and increasingly competitive defense markets, a growing number of governments regard transnational arms development and production as essential to preserving national defense industrial and technology bases. Internationalizing their arms industries is becoming a critical means by which some nations can maintain most cost effectively a "critical minimum" of military R&D and production capacity necessary to meet national defense requirements. In addition, globalization is increasingly a potentially important mechanism for technology flowbacks. Governments and defense firms that refuse to globalize their arms development and production activities eventually could find themselves closed off to critical overseas markets, technologies, and resources.

At the same time, the globalization of arms production capabilities raises considerable apprehensions about the continuing proliferation of conventional arms, military systems technologies, and other know-how pertaining to defense production and systems integration. As outright sales of weapons systems are increasingly supplemented or even supplanted by globalization activities, leading to more sophisticated arms production within the third world, the spread of advanced military technologies to the developing world is becoming both more complex and more difficult to arrest or slow.

A GROWING TRANSATLANTIC SPLIT?

The United States and western Europe—particularly during the Cold War and for reasons of promoting intra-NATO rationalization, standardization, interoperability—have long pursued an expanded transatlantic partnership when it comes to armaments cooperation. In the past decade, however, *intra*-European weapons collaboration and defense industry integration have expanded at a rate that far outstrips transatlantic cooperation. (See Figure 12–5.) In fact, this process of the regionalization of the European defense industrial base poses a potentially quite serious challenge to future U.S.-European arms collaboration, and could be the start of a much more competitive, rather than cooperative, relationship arising between the U.S. and west European arms industries.

More than anywhere else perhaps, western Europe's process of regionalizing arms production activities is an extension of the overall rationalization of the defense industrial base. The "tyranny of the market" has promoted further arms cooperation as a means of gaining greater economies of scale on a regional basis, while encouraging the west European defense industries to integrate or consolidate operations

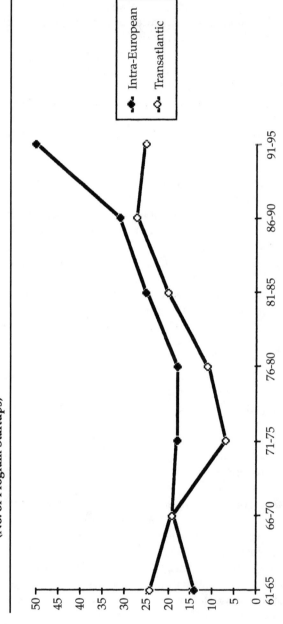

Figure 12–5 Transatlantic vs. Intra-European Arms Cooperation (Licensing, Coproduction, Codevelopment), 1961–95 (No. of Program Startups)

Source: DBF Globalization Database.

322

across national borders. Particularly for western Europe, wholly indigenous defense R&D and production have become especially difficult to maintain as technology and development costs for next-generation weapons systems have grown and production runs have been shortened.[21] Despite recent efforts at national consolidation—such as the creation of "national champions" (British Aerospace, DASA, the Swedish Celsius group, etc.)—western Europe still possesses considerable excess capacity and redundancy in many defense industrial sectors.[22] In 1993, for example, the west European defense industry was building 125 various types of major weapons systems, compared with just 53 in the United States; these included 16 types of armored combat vehicles (versus 3 in the United States), 7 types of fighter aircraft (compared to 5 in the United States), 7 different assault rifles (1 in the United States), and 11 different frigate (1 in the United States).[23]

Additional efficiencies within the European arms industry can be achieved only by rationalizing military R&D and production on a *transnational* scale.[24] Furthermore, the radical consolidation and downsizing in the U.S. defense industrial base that has taken place since the early 1990s—in particular, the creation of three U.S. mega-defense companies (Lockheed Martin, Boeing McDonnell Douglas, and Raytheon), each with annual revenues far in excess of most of their west European rivals—has put considerable pressure on west European arms manufacturers to copy the consolidation strategies of their U.S. counterparts in order to remain globally competitive.[25] For example, when in late 1997 the governments of Britain, France, and Germany referred to "international competition" in calling for the speedy integration of their defense and aerospace industries, they were almost certainly talking about the United States.[26]

As a result, many west Europeans increasingly see their local defense industrial bases as threatened by a larger and much more cost-efficient U.S. arms industry. Moreover, the United States has exacerbated these concerns by frequently turning out to be a very unreliable partner in international collaborative arms ventures, even with its closest allies. Congress and many segments of the executive branch never have been very enthusiastic about international arms programs that involve the export of advanced defense technology or that might create foreign dependencies for critical military systems. For their part, the U.S. armed forces often have been lukewarm in their support of collaborative arms programs, preferring specialized systems that are tailored to their specific requirements.[27]

Overall the United States has hardly been consistent about promoting, or participating in, intra-alliance arms collaboration. Therefore, many Europeans—especially the French but increasingly the Germans as well—have come to view transatlantic defense cooperation as, at best, a highly uncertain and unequal relationship, with their industry consigned to a perpetual junior partnership, receiving "second-best" technology and serving mainly as subcontractors to U.S. industry. Regional defense cooperation has come to be seen as a matter of basic survival, therefore, if Europe is to maintain a viable and independent defense industrial and technology base.[28] In western Europe, the effort to retain some degree of self-sufficiency in arms production has essentially moved from being a *national* to a *regional* concern—that is, "Europeanizing" the local defense industry.

Of course, the process of west European defense industrial integration has not been, in the words of one European analyst, a "simple story of unidirectional upwards progress."[29] Indeed, there have been many setbacks on the road toward creating a pan-European defense industrial base. The region's national arms markets are still plagued by a number of factors that hinder unfettered intra-European arms collaboration, including differing weapons requirements, differing corporate structures across western Europe (some defense firms are state owned, while others are private), the dearth of appropriate intra-European legal instruments to deal with such transnational defense enterprises, and simple protectionism on the part of governments when it comes to restricting foreign ownership in such "national assets" as defense industries (especially if they are state owned) and forcing militaries to "buy local" in order to limit further job losses in their own arms industries and prevent tax monies from leaving the country.[30] As a result, several proposed intra-European collaborative arms programs have broken down (e.g., the Franco-German APACHE, after DASA withdrew from the program) or have been stillborn (e.g., an initiative in the late 1980s to merge the missile operations of Aérospatiale and British Aerospace and, more recently, efforts by Britain, France, and Germany to merge British Aerospace, Aérospatiale, Dassault, and DASA into a European Aerospace and Defense Corporation).[31] At the same time, the lure of U.S. weaponry remains strong: several European countries recently have chosen U.S. weapon systems over locally available options. Britain and the Netherlands, for example, both purchased the AH-64 attack helicopter instead of the Franco-German Tigre, while the United Kingdom also has decided to procure C-130J transport planes instead of buying all-European.

A unitary European military-industrial complex is highly unlikely, therefore: "national champions" will be around for some time, and not every collaborative arms program will enter production successfully.

Nevertheless, there appears to be a growing belief on the part of many European defense industrialists and government officials that, over the longer run, there is little alternative to increased regional arms collaboration—especially in the face of growing competition from the U.S. defense industry.[32] Despite the aforementioned obstacles, therefore, the trend in Europe is definitely moving in the direction of further integrating regional arms production networks. British Aerospace and Matra recently have succeeded in joining their missile operations, and Britain will buy a version of the French APACHE cruise missile, which will be coproduced by this new joint venture. DASA has established several defense-related joint ventures with both Aérospatiale and Thomson-CSF in the past two years.[33] In fact, all-European joint-venture companies lead their transatlantic counterparts by a two-to-one margin; at the same time, intra-European defense-oriented mergers and acquisitions are much more likely to involve two major arms producers than are transatlantic M&As (which usually have entailed a larger defense firm absorbing a minor player).

Western Europe increasingly views the United States more as a competitor than a prospective partner when it comes to arms production. The emergence of a pan-European arms industry, especially if it comes at the expense of transatlantic arms collaboration, could have several possible consequences. First, if U.S. defense firms continue to treat their west European counterparts as junior partners in the globalization process, they could find themselves increasingly frozen out of much of the European arms market. The loss of doing business with such countries as Britain and Germany—which increasingly emphasize codevelopment and coproduction—could be particularly adverse. Second, the loss of shared development costs, technology synergies, and economies of scale in production that might have occurred through greater intra-Alliance rationalization of arms production likely will mean more expensive weapons on both sides of the Atlantic.

Finally, defense industry regionalism/protectionism within the Atlantic Alliance could be signaling the emergence of a much more polarized U.S.-European security relationship. The emergence of two distinct and competitive defense markets within the alliance is unlikely to lead to the collapse of NATO. On the other hand, the inability to secure a strong NATO commitment to improving transatlantic arms collaboration certainly will not enhance future alliance cooperation.

GLOBALIZATION: THE NEXT PROLIFERATION CHALLENGE?

The globalization process also raises several obvious proliferation concerns. The spread of arms production capabilities to the developing world, as a result of technology transfers, licensed production arrangements, and (increasingly) North-South military codevelopment programs, is a form of arms proliferation that, until quite recently, went almost unnoticed. A general preoccupation with overseas arms sales has caused many observers to overlook the emergence of an increasingly internationalized defense industry. Yet such international arms collaboration, involving as it does the diffusion of the resources, skills, and technology that underlie armaments production, is potentially more destabilizing than outright arms sales.

Despite some instances where countries in the developing world have begun to act as codevelopment or technology-sharing partners in international arms projects, it is too soon to tell if the third world ever will be more than a modest or sporadic player in collaborative arms efforts. Codevelopment arrangements involving the developing world remain few and intermittent. Most developing countries—and even many of the newly industrialized countries—still lack a sufficient indigenous military industrial and technological base to participate as full-fledged partners in collaborative arms projects with industrialized nations. Moreover, the rapid contraction in the global arms market has severely undermined many export-oriented third world arms producers, such as Israel and Brazil; for example, Engesa of Brazil—for a time the world's largest manufacturer of wheeled armored vehicles—was in the early 1990s forced to declare bankruptcy and lay off nearly its entire workforce. The financial crisis that struck Asia in late 1997 has had an especially devastating effect on some of the developing world's most advanced arms producers; South Korea and Indonesia in particular have been forced to scale back many of their ambitious plans for their local defense and aerospace industries.

Nevertheless, joint development and transfers of defense-related technology likely will increase in importance to these countries' efforts to develop their indigenous defense industrial bases. In particular, by collaborating with the industrialized nations, certain developing countries gradually are acquiring knowledge and expertise in working with advanced defense technologies, such as composites, electronics, sensors, and aerospace designs. In addition, offsets and licensed production likely will remain a critical component of third world arms production.

The globalization process has, in fact, already enabled some developing countries to build up their indigenous defense industries to the point where they have become exporters of arms to other developing nations. Together with the typically lower costs and ready availability of these weapons (countries such as China, South Africa, and Israel, for instance, generally have a "no-questions-asked" policy when it comes to arms sales), this raises the specter of new third world producers flooding certain sectors of the global arms market—particularly in the field of "mid-tech" weapons systems—possibly upsetting regional arms balances and accelerating local arms races.[34]

By contributing to conventional arms proliferation and technology diffusion, globalization eventually may prove threatening to the West, and particularly to the United States. In attempting to maintain its defense industrial base, the industrialized countries may be trading away short-term gains that eventually could lead to emergence of more technologically advanced military challengers in the developing world. Certain types of arms—such as tactical missiles or long-range artillery—conceivably could threaten western (and particularly U.S.) operations. Thus the West might find itself having to increase military spending and defense R&D efforts in order to maintain its current military-technological advantage.

Conclusion

The globalization of arms production appears to be increasing not only in terms of the sheer number of collaborative arms activities but also in terms of depth, as armaments cooperation reaches down to the level of technology and componentry; of sophistication, as defense firms around the world forge new, direct links with each other; and of geographic scope, as more countries in the developing world become involved in collaborative arms ventures. The defense industry, like many other high-tech manufacturing fields, has found the development of more integrated global linkages and operations to be increasingly critical. Declining military budgets, tightening defense markets, the rising costs of next-generation weaponry, and the continuing globalization of the world economy will put growing pressures on arms producers to accelerate and expand their globalization efforts.

This unfolding process poses a serious challenge to policymakers as they determine how best to support globalization's more positive economic features while ensuring at the same time that this process does not adversely affect international security interests. The globalization of arms production is to some extent inevitable, beneficial, and even desirable: globalization permits arms manufacturers to pool their financial and intellectual resources in order to be more competitive and cost-efficient in an increasingly tight global marketplace. For the industrialized countries, it may even serve as an alternative to exporting arms to the developing world, by rationalizing defense R&D and manufacturing, and therefore making arms production more cost efficient. At the same time, the growing incidence of armaments collaboration with the developing world may undermine international security by facilitating the diffusion of defense-related technologies and by promoting weapons proliferation.

Any decision to permit the export of defense-related technology or of arms-producing capabilities must carefully balance defense industrial base needs against other security concerns. The industrialized nations need to delineate clearly between "good" globalization and "bad" globalization. Those developed countries with large, mature defense industries might consider taking a two-track approach toward globalization, one that distinguishes between arms collaboration within the bloc of industrialized nations, where the benefits of globalization appear to outweigh the possible drawbacks, and armaments collaboration involving the developing world, where the risks of proliferation and of exacerbating regional tensions due to globalization activities are much greater. Admittedly, this will not be an easy task: U.S. defense-industrial assistance to South Korea or Turkey, for instance, would be very difficult to terminate for military reasons, while countries such as Russia are under very powerful domestic pressures to export arms (which usually entail some kind of offsets) in order to save jobs and factories at home; in addition, countries such as Israel have become very important niche suppliers of military technology to the West. Nevertheless, at the very least long-range proliferation concerns should be considered in any decision regarding the release of defense-related technology and arms production know-how to the developing world.

We all need to have a greater awareness of and appreciation for the globalization process as a critical trend in the international defense industry. The globalization of arms production should be seen as a phenomenon at least as important as the international trade in finished weapons systems. In fact, the globalization process could be an even more critical development, since it entails not only the proliferation of weapons but of the capability to build them as well.

With regard to controlling the growth of arms production in the developing world, it is important that the industrialized countries be aware of the tremendous leverage they still possess. Despite their considerable progress in recent years, defense industries in the developing countries remain highly dependent on the industrialized nations when it comes to design and development, systems integration, and even production technologies. It has been argued that in the absence of the foreign assistance, "the indigenous defense industrial capability of most of the developing nations would cease to expand and might even collapse."[35] If so, then restricting or cutting off military technologies is a potentially powerful arms control tool that the industrialized countries should consider using.

Most of all, the industrialized nations of North America and western Europe need to mend a growing transatlantic schism when it comes to armaments cooperation and defense industry globalization. Not only does this split threaten to distort the globalization process and hinder transatlantic arms collaboration, but the growing competition between these two centers of advanced arms production could greatly undermine efforts to control the spread of weapons and military technology to the developing world, as the United States and a more integrated European defense industry group both scramble to secure their share of the global arms market.

Notes

The analysis and conclusions expressed in this chapter are strictly those of the author and should not be interpreted as representing those of the U.S. government or any of its agencies or organizations.

1. Arms Control and Disarmament Agency (ACDA), *World Military Expenditures and Arms Transfers, 1993–1994* (Washington, D.C.: U.S. Government Printing Office, 1994).

2. Michael Brzoska, Peter Wilke, and Herbert Wulf, *The Changing Civil-Military Mix in Western Europe's Defense Industry,* Paper prepared for the Council on Foreign Relations Study Group on International Defense Downsizing, Arms Exports, and Conversion, October 1996, p. 5.

3. Ibid., table 1, pp. 4–5.

4. Bonn International Center for Conversion, *Conversion Survey 1996: Global Disarmament, Demilitarization, and Demobilization* (Oxford: Oxford University Press, 1996), p. 113. See also Herbert Wulf, "Arms Industry Limited: The Turning-Point in the 1990s," in Herbert Wulf, ed., *Arms Industry Limited* (Oxford: Oxford University Press, 1992), p. 18.

5. Brzoska, Wilke, and Wulf, *Changing Civil-Military Mix,* p. 8.

6. Steven Kosiak and Richard A. Bitzinger, *Potential Impact of Defense Spending Reductions on the Defense Related Labor Force by State* (Washington, D.C.: Defense Budget Project, May 1993), p. 3.

7. Michael Oden, *Cashing-in, Cashing-out, and Converting: Restructuring of the Defense Industrial Base in the 1990s,* Paper prepared for the Council on Foreign Relations Study Group on International Defense Downsizing, Arms Exports, and Conversion, February 1996.

8. See Brzoska, Wilke, and Wulf, *Changing Civil-Military* Mix; Richard A. Bitzinger, *Adjusting the Drawdown: The Transition in the Defense Industry* (Washington, D.C.: Defense Budget Project, April 1993); and James B. Steinberg, *The Transformation of the European Defense Industry* (Santa Monica, Calif.: RAND Corporation, 1992), pp. 65–67.

9. Federation of American Scientists, *Arms Sales Monitor* (February 1997): 6.

10. Arms Control and Disarmament Agency (ACDA), *World Military Expenditures and Arms Transfers 1995* (Washington, D.C.: U.S. Government Printing Office, April 1996), p. 9, 103; Stockholm International Peace Research Institute (hereafter SIPRI), *SIPRI Yearbook 1996* (Oxford: Oxford University Press, 1996), p. 463.

11. For recent studies of international armaments collaboration and the globalization of arms production, see: Richard A. Bitzinger, *The Globalization of Arms Production: Defense Markets in Transition* (Washington, D.C.: Defense Budget Project, December 1993); Pierre DeVestel, *Defense Markets and Industries in Europe: Time for Political Decisions?* (Paris: Western European Union, 1995); Ethan B. Kapstein, ed., *Global Arms Production: Policy Dilemmas for the 1990s* (Lanthan, Md.: University Press of America, 1992); U.S. Office of Technology Assessment (hereafter OTA), *Global Arms Trade* (Washington, D.C.: U.S. Government Printing Office, June 1991); OTA, *Arming Our Allies: Cooperation and Competition in Defense Technology* (Washington, D.C.: U.S. Government Printing Office, May 1990); Virginia C. Lopez and David H. Vadas, *The U.S. Aerospace Industry in the 1990s: A Global Perspective* (Washington, D.C.: Aerospace Industries Association of America, September 1991); Elisabeth Skoens, "Western Europe: The Internationalization of the Arms Industry," pp. 160–90 in Wulf, ed., *Arms Industry Limited;* Elizabeth Kirk, *U.S. and European Defense Industries: Changing Forces for Cooperation and Competition* (Washington, D.C.: American Association for the Advancement of Science, 1991); Andrew Moravcsik, "The European Armaments Industry at the Crossroads," *Survival* (January/February 1990): 65–85; Andrew Moravcsik, "Arms and Autarky in Modern European History," *Daedalus* (Fall 1991): 23–45; Frans Nauta, *Armaments Coproduction at a Crossroads: U.S. Policy Options After the Cold War* (Bethesda, Md.: Logistics Managements Institute, 1993); Judith Reppy, *Defense Industries in the US and Europe: Shrinking, Not Converting,* Paper presented to the International Studies Association, March 26, 1993; Judith Reppy, *Defense Companies' Strategies in a Declining Market: Implications for Government Policy* (Ithaca, N.Y.: Cornell University Peace Studies Program, December 1992); Mario Pianta and Sergio Andreis, "The Transformation of the Arms Industry in the European Community," in W. Thomas Wander and Eric H. Arnett, eds., *The Proliferation of Advanced Weaponry: Technology, Motivations, and Responses* (Washington, D.C.: American Association for the Advancement of Science, 1992); pp. 203–20 Willie E. Cole et al., *Europe 1992: Catalyst for Change in Defense Acquisition* (Washington, D.C.: Defense Systems Manage-

ment College, 1990); David Gold, "The Internationalization of Military Production," *Peace Economics, Peace Science, and Public Policy* 1, no. 3 (1994): 1–11 Martyn Bittleston, *Co-operation or Competition? Defense Procurement Options for the 1990s*, Adelphi Paper no. 250 (London: International Institute for Strategic Studies, May 1990); Ian Anthony, Agnes Courades Allebeck, and Herbert Wulf, *West European Arms Production: Structural Changes in the New Political Environment* (Stockholm: Stockholm International Peace Research Institute, 1990); William Walker and Philip Gummett, *Nationalism, Internationalism, and the European Defense Market* (Paris: Institute for Security Studies of Western European Union, September 1993); *From Shadows to Substance: An Action Plan for Transatlantic Defense Cooperation,* Conference Summary and Background Report of the CSIS Atlantic Partnership Project (Washington, D.C.: Center for Strategic and International Studies, 1995); and Simon Webb, *NATO and 1992: Defense Acquisition and Free Markets* (Santa Monica: RAND Corporation, 1989).

12. Much of this chapter's statistical analysis and findings are derived from the DBP Globalization Database, initiated by the author while working at the Defense Budget Project. This database contains information on over 1,000 major international cooperative arms activities since the early 1960s, including licensed-production arrangements, large military coproduction and codevelopment programs, and international cooperative activities initiated by defense firms, such as the creation of transnational joint ventures and crossborder mergers and acquisitions. The database mainly documents international collaboration on large weapons systems, such as aircraft, missiles, or armored vehicles, or on major components, such as radar systems or jet engines. It should be noted that the database does not track offset arrangements that may arise as the result of foreign arms sales or foreign subcontracting at the component or subsystem level, nor does it attempt to document the covert or "black-market" transfer of military technologies (which may not be possible on a systematic basis). Finally, owing to the lack of reliable information, the database can claim to have only partial coverage of armaments cooperation that took place within the communist bloc.

13. "Europe Does It the Second-Best Way," *The Economist,* June 21, 1986, pp. 21–23.

14. Nearly all of the Nunn Amendment programs eventually were canceled, however, because of budget cuts and conflicting requirements. In fact, the DBP Globalization Database reveals that major military codevelopment programs undertaken during the late 1980s involving the United States and western Europe suffered a nearly 50 percent cancellation rate. Overall, codevelopment consortia traditionally have suffered a relatively high failure rate. The database reveals that nearly one-fifth of all such arrangements collapsed before the manufacturing phase, a rate of failure much higher than other forms of arms collaboration. This dropout rate is most likely due to the fact that, while consortia are on the whole easier to start

up, they are also easier to exit. Particularly during their initiation phase, consortia tend to be rather tentative arrangements, and many members may reassess their participation as the demands of the program grow.

15. Masako Ikegami-Andersson, "Japan: A Latent but Large Supplier of Dual-Use Technology," in Wulf, ed., *Arms Industry Limited,*" p. 340; Moravscik, "European Armaments Industry," p. 78; see also U.S. Department of Commerce, *National Security Assessment of the Domestic and Foreign Subcontractor Base: A Study of Three U.S. Navy Weapons Systems* (Washington, D.C.: Bureau of Export Control, March 1992), p. 42.

16. Peter Batchelor, *Disarmament and Defense Industrial Adjustment: The Case of South Africa,* Paper prepared for the Council on Foreign Relations Study Group on Defense Industry Globalization, Conversion, the Arms Trade, January 1998, p. 43.

17. "A Eurogun Is a Tricky Thing," *Economist,* April 8, 1995, p. 54.

18. In 1969 the German aerospace firm VFW did attempt a merger with Fokker of the Netherlands, but this arrangement was later dissolved in the late 1970s. Lopez and Vadas, *U.S. Aerospace Industry,* p. 48.

19. See Bates Gill and Taeho Kim, *Chinese Arms Acquisitions from Abroad: A Quest for "Superb and Secret Weapons"* (Oxford: Oxford University Press, 1995), pp. 81–86.

20. In addition, in a rare turnabout in the usual direction of licensed production agreements, the United Kingdom is manufacturing the Brazilian-designed Tucano prop trainer for the Royal Air Force.

21. See Moravcsik, "Arms and Autarky in Modern European History"; and Moravcsik, "European Armaments Industry."

22. Herbert Wulf, "Western Europe: Facing Over-Capacities," in Wulf, ed., *Arms Industry Limited* pp. 143–59. See also Anthony et al., *West European Arms Production,* pp. 5–16.

23. European Institute for Research and Information on Peace and Security (GRIP), *European Armaments Industry: Research, Technological Development and Conversion, Final Report* (Luxembourg: European Parliament, Directorate-General for Research, November 1993), p. 14.

24. Richard W. Stevenson, "Europe Uniting in Building Arms," *New York Times,* August 14, 1994, pp. D1, D14; David Tirpak, "Next Stop: International Defense Consolidation," *Aviation Week & Space Technology,* October 24, 1994, p. 57; "A Eurogun Is a Tricky Thing," pp. 53–54.

25. Giovanni de Briganti, "European Leaders See Need for More Mergers," *Defense News* (December 8, 1997), p. 14; J. A. C. Lewis, "Euro Defense Groups Ordered to Rationalize," *Jane's Defense Weekly,* December 17, 1997, p. 17; J. A. C. Lewis and Barbara Starr, "A Landmark Year for Crucial Con-

solidation, *Jane's Defense Weekly*, December 17, 1997, pp. 20–22; Michael Peter and Friedrich Thelen, "The Last Screw," *Düsseldorf Wirtschaftswoche*, December 11, 1997, p. 22.

26. Nick Cook, "As Europe Seeks to Consolidate, the USA Pursues a Global Vision," *Jane's Defense Weekly*, December 17, 1997, p. 16.

27. Bitzinger, *Globalization of Arms Production*, pp. 17–31.

28. Carol Reed, "Technology: USA v. Europe: Industry Prepares for Battle," *Jane's Defense Weekly*, June 12, 1993, pp. 48–55; Jacques Isnard, "Cooperation: The Key to Independence," *Defence & Armament*, April 1984, p. 38.

29. John Lovering, *Which Way to Turn? The European Defense Industry After the Cold War*, Paper prepared for the Council on Foreign Relations Study Group on International Defense Downsizing, Arms Exports, and Conversion, September 1996, p. 13.

30. Brzoska, Wilke, and Wulf, *Changing Civil-Military Mix*, p. 14; Walker and Gummett, *Nationalism, Internationalism*; "A Eurogun Is a Tricky Thing"; Andrew Hull and David Markov, *The Changing Nature of the International Arms Market*, IDA Paper No. P-3122 (Alexandria, Va.: Institute for Defense Analyses, March 1996), p. 7.

31. Giovanni de Briganti, "European Restructuring Lags Behind U.S. Pace," *Defense News*, May 23, 1994, p. 16.

32. Stevenson, "Europe Uniting in Building Arms"; "Commentator Urges 'Quality Leap' in Defense Cooperation," *Il Sole-24* (Milan), February 25, 1997 (Foreign Broadcast Information Service Document # FTS19970626002067 translation); "European Weapons Industry Split on Strategy to Resist U.S.," Agence France-Presse (Paris), October 11, 1996; Giovanni de Briganti and Charles Miller, "Is Consolidation Salvation? European Industry Leaders Vow to Match U.S. Juggernauts," *Defense News*, September 9, 1996.

33. Elisabeth Skoens, "Arms Production," *SIPRI Yearbook 1996*, p. 426.

34. See Batchelor, *Disarmament and Defense Industrial Adjustment*.

35. OTA, *Global Arms Trade*, p. 26.

13

Which Way to Turn? The European Defense Industry After the Cold War

JOHN LOVERING

COMPARED TO events in the United States, the pace of change in the European defense industry since the end of the Cold War has been slow and the effects to date are unremarkable.[1] Europe spends around two-thirds as much as the United States on defense equipment but still has well over twice the number of contractors in many sectors.[2] While a few companies (notably in Britain) have reconstructed themselves as dynamic and competitive international players, others (notably in France and Italy) have only just begun to restructure. However, 1996 is set to become a landmark year in the post–Cold War history of the European defense industry. The first real transnational European defense company is being formed, and the radical restructuring experienced by the British defense industry since the mid-1980s is being echoed in the French and German industries.

The European defense industry as a whole is in transition, involving the rationalization of capacity on a national and continental basis, and the internationalization of the economic units of which the industry is composed. This does not, however, mean that the separate national defense industries of the post–World War II period are giving way to a unitary European military-industrial complex. Instead, piecemeal developments are leading to a uniquely complex and decentered system of economic governance in defense. In the closing years of the decade there were signs that the pace was quickening, and that the European defense industry might, after all, form a new integrated entity in the early years of the new century. However, the implications, in both industrial and military terms, are likely to be profoundly ambivalent.

Background: The West European Defense Industry in the Cold War

The construction of modern defense industries was a significant component of the economic reconstruction and "long boom" in western Europe.[3] A major share of U.S. assistance under Marshall Aid went to industries with military significance. Defense considerations also played a key role in the movement toward European economic integration. The formation of the European Coal and Steel Community in 1951, the first step toward economic integration, was justified explicitly in military terms. The Schuman Declaration noted that "the pooling of coal and steel production" would alter the destinies of "regions which have long been devoted to the manufacture of munitions of war."[4]

Despite U.S. State Department hopes, the emergent arms industry did not take a truly "European" form, with a rational division of labor among the different countries.[5] Thanks to the power of national political and industrial elites, it evolved instead into a set of national establishments, mostly state owned, and oriented to domestic armed service requirements. In the Big Three defense-spending countries—France, Britain, and Germany—the industry was able to design and manufacture weapons across the board, although the most advanced technologies, notably in nuclear weapons and missiles, were often dependent on the United States. Even as late as the 1980s the Big Three countries procured around 90 percent of their defense equipment domestically. Smaller European countries tended to import a larger proportion of their equipment, mostly from the United States. (See Table 13–6.)

Most of the leading national arms companies of the 1930s and World War II reemerged in the 1950s and became the bases of the Cold War arms industries: Vickers, Plessey, Dassault, Krupp, Messerschmidt, FIAT, and so on. Most gradually were absorbed into new corporate structures, often as a result of nationalization; this occurred with Daimler Benz, British Aerospace, Aérospatiale, and Alenia. A newer group of private-sector companies, especially in electronics and aerospace, joined to form the core of the national military-industrial apparatuses; these companies included Dassault, Matra, and English Electric-GEC. By the 1980s the European defense industry was dominated by a small number of large companies. These were supplied by an unknown number of smaller companies, including some specialists that became significant niche exporters in their own right.

EUROPEAN INTEGRATION AND THE "EXCEPTION" OF THE DEFENSE INDUSTRIES

The nationally based structure of the defense industry survived despite the process of European economic integration associated with the development of the European Economic Community (EC).[6] The "exceptional" status of the national defense industries was underwritten by article 223 of the 1958 Treaty of Rome (reproduced unaltered in the 1993 Treaty of European Union [EU]), which excluded the European Commission from jurisdiction in matters relating to defense. Article 223 lists 58 items of military significance, including nuclear arms, ammunition, torpedoes, guided missiles, tanks, warships, military aircraft, and military electronics, which are estimated to account for around two-thirds of total European Union defense procurement spending.[7] In practice, different governments choose to interpret the article differently. France and the United Kingdom traditionally have favored a wider conception of the list as "indicative," while Germany has proposed a revision of the list of items and the transformation of article 223 into a clear set of rules. The article has been described as more of a symbolic weapon than a practical tool. (It has been invoked formally only twice.)

It is nevertheless regarded as very important by smaller supply firms, countries with small or less developed defense industries such as Belgium and Italy, and the "developing defense industry" countries of Spain, Portugal, and Greece.[8] The spirit of the article is invoked to underpin the system of *juste retour* whereby work on collaborative projects is allocated to partners on the basis of the amount of equipment each county agrees to buy.[9] Similarly, it supports the system of "offset" arrangements guaranteeing local work to companies in countries buying major arms imports (generally from the United States). The article symbolizes the protectionism that has been fundamental to the European defense industry since the 1950s.

THE EUROPEAN DEFENSE INDUSTRY IN THE POST–COLD WAR ENVIRONMENT

In the closing years of the Cold War, the defense spending of west European countries (including Sweden) was a little over half that of the

United States, around the same as that of the Soviet Union or ten times that of Asia.[10] It was of the same order of magnitude as the gross domestic product (GDP) of Hungary.[11] Almost two-thirds of west European defense spending (and almost four-fifths of equipment spending) was accounted for by the Big Three of France, Britain, and Germany. (See Table 13–1.) These countries still dominate defense spending, but the total spent has fallen. The decline was first and largest in Britain, least and latest in France.[12] (See Tables 13–2 and 13–3.) German spending fell by 70 percent in three years. In countries on the periphery of the European Union, notably Turkey, Portugal, and Norway, defense spending continued to increase into the early 1990s, albeit from a very low base. Defense spending imposes the greatest burden on national GDP in Greece and Turkey. Per capita defense spending is highest in Norway, followed by France. (See Table 13–1.)

In real terms, total European defense spending fell by about one-twentieth between 1989 and 1994, just under half the U.S. decline. As a result total European spending rose to two-thirds of U.S. spending (See Table 13–4), and Europe had more men and women in uniform than the United States.[13] Despite the relatively modest fall in aggregate defense spending, major equipment purchases in Europe fell at around the same rate as they fell in the United States, a reduction of one-fifth between 1989 and 1992. (See Table 13–3.) In Germany the contraction in procurement following unification was particularly sharp, bottoming out in the mid-1990s.

Estimates of the total turnover of the European defense industry range from 65 becu (billion Ecu) in 1990 to around 50 becu in 1996.[14] The European share of the total world defense market appears to have fallen from one-third to one-quarter between the late 1980s and mid-1990s.[15] According to the European Commission, around 1 million jobs currently depend on the defense industry—two-thirds of these being "direct" employment. The employment of high-level scientists, engineers, and technologists is disproportionately concentrated in the larger defense companies. Defense industry jobs are also unevenly distributed geographically.[16]

The Restructuring of the European Defense Industries

The broad outlines of the restructuring of the defense industries of western Europe are fairly well known and have been described in innumerable press reports and studies.[17] The industry has been contracting in terms of employment and the number of companies involved. As in the United States, the responses of European defense companies can be grouped into

Table 13–1   Defense Spending in Europe, 1995 ($U.S. millions)

	Total	As % GDP	Per capita
France	47,735	3.1	820
Germany	41,060	1.7	509
United Kingdom	34,086	3.1	586
Italy	20,041	1.9	349
Spain	8,464	1.5	216
Netherlands	8,181	2.1	527
Turkey	6,015	3.9	97
Greece	5,059	4.6	481
Belgium	4,572	1.7	455
Norway	3,758	2.9	863
Denmark	3,152	1.8	600
Portugal	2,819	2.7	285
Luxembourg	141	0.9	365

Source: Statement on the Defence Estimates 1996 (HMSO), p. 50.

Table 13–2   Trends in Defense Spending in Western Europe (constant 1990 $U.S.)

	1985	1989	1994
France	39,918	42,793	41,235
United Kingdom	43,549	40,792	35,055
Germany	38,824	40,146	31,258
Italy	19,538	24,304	23,492
Spain	9,058	9,668	8,141
Netherlands	7,350	7,636	6,263
Turkey	4,011	4,398	6,173
Sweden	5,234	5,762	5,260
Greece	4,524	3,819	3,778
Belgium	4,789	4,732	3,549
Norway	3,339	3,369	3,523
Denmark	2,613	2,648	2,608
Portugal	1,336	1,824	1,948
Luxembourg	74	93	110
Europe Total	184,713	192,509	173,006
United States	313,307	320,427	252,358
Europe/U.S.A	59.0%	60.1%	68.6%

Source: Commission of the European Communities, *The Challenges Facing the European Defence-Related Industry: A Contribution for Action at European Level* (Brussels: CEC, 1996), (96)10 final.

Table 13–3   Changes in Defense Spending, 1985–94
             (% change in constant prices)

	1985–89	1989–94
France	7.2	–3.6
Unite King om	–6.3	–14.1
Germany	3.4	–22.1
Italy	24.4	–3.3
Spain	6.7	–15.7
Netherlan s	3.9	–18.0
Turkey	9.6	40.4
Swe en	10.1	–8.7
Greece	–15.6	–1.1
Belgium	–1.1	–25.0
Norway	0.9	4.6
Denmark	1.3	–1.5
Portugal	36.5	6.8
Luxembourg	25.7	18.3
Europe Total	4.2	–10.1
Unite States	2.3	–21.2

Source: CEC, 1996.

a small set of categories.[18] Some exited the defense market completely. The leading example is the Dutch firm Phillips, which has concentrated on becoming Europe's leading consumer electronics producer. Other companies moved the other way, entrenching into defense. The leading example is probably Thomson CSF, the defense electronics division of the half-state-owned French company Thomson SA. Thomson CSF bought up several former Phillips plants in France, Germany, Britain, and the Netherlands. British Aerospace moved first one way, then the other. In the late 1980s it diluted its defense dependence by acquiring property companies and the Rover car firm. But these were shed in the early 1990s, and the company explicitly—and profitably—refocused on defense. The Daimler Benz group also diversified into defense in the late 1980s as part of a strategy to become a comprehensive high-technology company and European champion, albeit mainly in civilian fields. In the mid-1990s, however, these ambitions were scaled down, and the defense component, while relatively modest, remained important.

It would be difficult to generalize about companies at different stages in the supply chain, since there is no comprehensive research evidence. However, it is clear that there have been several waves of closures and

Table 13–4   Changes in Total Defense Spending and Major Weapons
Purchase, United States and Europe

	Change 1989–1992 (%)	
	Europe	U.S.A
Total defense spending	−5.4	−11.3
Major weapons procurement	−23.9	−21.5

Source: CEC, 1996.

diversifications of former defense-dependent companies, alongside a considerable increase in corporate specialization and concentration. To date these trends have operated primarily at a national level. The major British companies began shedding jobs before the formal end of the Cold War, driven by changes in government procurement budgets and practices. German, French, and Italian defense companies began to shed jobs somewhat later, under similar influences.

The European Commission suggests that about a third of defense industry jobs have been lost in the decade to 1994, falling from 1.6 million to 1 million.[19] This may well be an underestimate of the decline. (See Table 13–5.) Job loss has uneven geographical implications.[20] These effects drew forth the European Commission's only (and reluctantly) funded involvement in the defense industry in the form of the KONVER program to compensate regions hit by job losses. KONVER, modeled on earlier European relief programs for steel and coal regions, was essentially a mopping-up provision intended to support local responses to job losses arising from defense industry restructuring. Officially, since European Community funds cannot be used to subsidize individual firms, KONVER did not directly address that restructuring. In reality, national practice varied widely, and some imaginative regional development agencies (such as Lancashire Enterprise in the United Kingdom) and national governments (Spain) were able to use the money to subsidize product development initiatives and other measures in small and medium-sized enterprises.

PRESSURES FOR FURTHER RESTRUCTURING:
COSTS AND OVERCAPACITY

National peak organizations for the defense industry, such as the Defence Manufacturers Association in Britain, regularly express great anxiety about the integrity of the national defense industrial base, especially among the smaller firms. These organizations tend to voice the concerns

Table 13–5 Employment in the European Defense Industry

	(1) mid-1980s	Employment as % of Industrial Employment	(2) 1990–92
China	5,000,000	10.0	3–5,000,000
U.S.S.R	4,400,000	11.6	. . .
United States	3,350,000	14.4	2,750,000
United Kingdom	620,000	9.8	(400,000)
France	400,000	7.5	255,000
West Germany	191,000	2.2	250,000
Italy	103,000	2.1	80,000
East Germany	66,000	2.7	41,000
Spain	66,000	2.6	100,000
Belgium	33,000	3.7	25,000
Netherlands	29,000	3.2	(20,000)
Sweden	28,000	2.7	(30,000)
Austria	16,000	1.8	. . .
Norway	15,000	3.7	10,000
Greece	9,000	1.2	14,000
Finland	5,000	0.8	10,000

Sources: CEC, *The Economic and Social Impact of Reductions in Defense Spending and Military Forces on the Regions of the Community Commission of the European Communities* (Brussels: Commission of European Communities, 1992); Michael Renner, *Economic Adjustments After the Cold War: Strategies for Conversion* (Dartmouth, New Hampshire: Dartmouth Publishing Company, 1992), pp. 15, 72; Herbert Wulf, ed., *Arms Industry Limited* (London, England: Oxford University Press, 1993), pp. 14–15.

of subassembly and component suppliers and manufacturers of less technology-intensive inputs, which have found themselves exposed to new and sometimes fierce competitive forces. At the other end of the corporate spectrum, a small core of companies has been consolidated as market leaders at the national level. Through acquisitions, mergers, and their command over key assets and major programs, these are the companies that most politicians have in mind when pressed to consider the defense industry. They in turn tend to have the greatest influence. Increasingly, the leading examples—BAe, DASA, and Thomson-CSF—are becoming specialists in systems integration, rather than in in-house manufacture. However, considerable duplication remains, and a further wave of rationalization and concentration across borders is widely regarded as inevitable. The industry has been substantially concentrated through mergers within national borders, and this strategy is now reaching its limits. It has been expected for some time that the next step will be concentration and rationalization on a crossborder basis.[21]

The fact that the pace of concentration and rationalization in the European defense industry in the 1990s has been far slower than in the

United States has been the source of much criticism. U.S. defense procurement is around five times that of each of the European Big Three, although the latter have many more contractors. In 1996 in Europe as a whole, there were 10 major aerospace companies, 10 armored vehicle producers, 11 missile manufacturers, and 14 shipyards, between two and three times the number in equivalent categories in the United States.[22] U.S. firms, correspondingly, are very much larger and able to enjoy greater economies of scale. A few European firms, notably BAe, have restructured themselves and now match their U.S. competitors in terms of output per employee. But many have yet to complete the measures of cost reduction, consolidation, and internationalization that are required before they can position themselves for the more competitive global arms market of the coming century, and above all confront or complement the U.S. competition.[23]

The restructuring of the European defense industry is far from being a simple pro rata adjustment of supply to changes in demands arising from objective changes in the security environment. It is inextricably bound up with the development of institutions, policy paradigms (in both the military and the industrial domains), business networks, and relationships between companies and governments. The details of the restructuring are in effect negotiated through a maze of formal and informal institutions. At the formal level, the key organizations are associated with the integration of the European Union on the one hand and the reconstruction of NATO on the other. But these are in some respects less important than the informal, and less visible, relationships among companies and between companies and governments. The restructuring is bound up with the unique and complex evolution of institutional, political, and industrial structures in Europe.

National Experiences in Europe: Convergence Toward the British Model

BRITAIN

Until the late 1980s, Britain spent more on defense than any other European country. (See Table 13–2.) The military establishment and defense industry remained large and influential throughout the Cold War era, and defense issues have been subject to a de facto consensus between the leaderships of the main political parties (although it was well known that this consensus disguised fundamentally opposed views within their memberships and electorates). The new course adopted by the government of Margaret Thatcher from the mid 1980s radically broke with tradition in several respects. Defense spending fell to a greater degree than under any previous postwar government. Established interests in the armed forces and Ministry of Defence, and in defense companies and workforces, found themselves facing unprecedented and largely unexpected challenges.[24] The radical change in government-industry relations in defense was the result of a generic economic strategy, based on the reduction of public spending commitments, rather than a rethinking of defense and defense-industry policies. From the mid-1980s defense procurement policies insisted on open competition wherever practicable, and the share of contracts let competitively rose. Cost pressures tended to forge a link between the Treasury and the armed forces in favor of off-the-shelf U.S. equipment, which also had the advantage of interoperability. Among defense managements and workforces, however, the governments of Thatcher and John Major became deeply unpopular.

Faced with declining domestic procurement the British defense industry turned increasingly to exports, with the energetic support of government (for both foreign policy and procurement cost reasons). Export promotion has arguably formed the core of government policy toward the defense industry in the Thatcher–John Major period.[25] Exports worth £5 billion to £7 billion per annum account for 145,000 jobs, a quarter of defense industry employment. This proportion is far higher than in any other advanced economy. Arms exports have become vital for individual firms. British Aerospace, Vosper Thorneycroft, and numerous smaller specialist suppliers sell more to foreign governments than to the British Ministry of Defence. (See Table 13–5.)

Although Britain is responsible for about 20 percent of world arms exports, the export base is narrow and is focused on a small set of controversial and potentially unstable regimes, notably Saudi Arabia, Indonesia, and Malaysia. The United States is a vital customer for some firms; Britain accounts for half of all U.S. arms imports. The Defence Export Services Organisation (DESO) of the Ministry of Defence has been revamped to intensify the export effort and raise the United Kingdom's share of the world export market further. DESO aims to improve the collective competitiveness of British arms exports by avoiding "destructive competition between British companies in overseas markets."[26]

As compared to France, British defense industry policy has been characterized by an emphasis on short-term financial constraints rather than long-term strategic capacities. This was symptomized by the fact that the end of the Cold War was followed not by a full-scale public defense review, but by a bureaucratic and secretive reappraisal of procedures relating primarily to costs (dignified for public relations purposes as "Options for Change"). Since 1991 "market testing" has become a key element in official policy for the reform of the armed forces and the defense industry, along with other parts of the public sector. The management and sometimes the ownership of a wide range of military activities, from catering and transport, to nuclear weapons facilities, has been transferred to private companies. Further marketization in defense was promised by the 1994 Defence Costs Study Front Line First. Defense spending is set to stabilize in cash terms, at just over £22,000 million. This would reduce its share of GDP from just over 4 percent in 1991 to just under 3 percent in 1998.

Through the late 1980s and early 1990s the British government stood out from its European partners in the degree to which it insisted on open competition in defense. The competitive emphasis succeeded in purging the British defense industry of the inefficient habits of the Cold War decades, not least in terms of employment. But by 1995–96 a consensus seemed to have emerged that the phase of severe competition had done its job. British defense companies, notably British Aerospace and GEC, were emerging leaner and meaner from a decade of downsizing and restructuring. The declining trend in their share prices had been reversed. BAe was now the largest European defense contractor, with 75 percent of its sales in defense. Employment at BAe fell from 140,000 in 1980 to 44,000 in 1996. BAe and GEC shed over 37,000 and 17,000 jobs, respectively, in five years. VSEL (the sole surviving submarine builder in the United Kingdom) cut employment from 16,000 to 4,000 in a decade. In the United Kingdom's defense industry as a whole, employment fell by almost a quarter of a million jobs between the late 1980s and mid-1990s. This was matched by equally dramatic changes in employment conditions and in trade union bargaining power.[27] From the perspective of the United Kingdom, the defense industries of the rest of Europe are overmanned as a result of "entrenched employment rights, and a political climate which opposes large-scale redundancies."[28] The leading British companies dramatically improved their competitiveness (especially compared to other European companies). By the late 1990s, they could argue that the priority could deepen this through a return to longer-term investment strategies. To this end they also were now abandoning the ruthless employment policies of the recent past and adopting a more participatory style of industrial relations aimed at increasing commitment and skill retention. Specialization rather than competition was the new watchword favored by industry.

Soon after coming to power, Labour set in motion a Strategic Defense Review, the first of its kind in two decades. Before waiting for the outcome of the review, however, it approved a substantial investment to support the British Aerospace bid with Lockheed for the JSF contract, and together with European partners gave the long-awaited go-ahead on the Eurofighter program (232 of the total of 620 aircraft would be purchased by the United Kingdom). In December of 1997, George Robertson, British minister of defense, issued a joint statement with the defense ministers of France and Germany calling on Europe's major defense companies to explain their plans for concentration and rationalization. Six months later the Strategic Defense Review was published. This proposed the adoption of a "Smart Procurement Initiative," modeled on American practice, with the aim of systematizing the early involvement of companies in defining future weapons programs. At the same time, the Ministry of Defense committed itself to a more active and positive engagement with European partners to develop European-wide procurement initiatives. In opposition Labour had announced that it would be in favor of Britain joining the Franco-German "Eurocorps" and the associate pan-national armaments agency, known from its French initials as OCCAR. By the fall of 1998 OCCAR was set to manage its first project, a collaborative armored vehicle development in which British companies were linked in a consortium with French and German companies. In the meantime the leading European aerospace companies had begun to respond to the collective ministerial call for a restructuring strategy. In October the press carried a report on the proposed merger of their military aircraft divisions of British Aerospace and Daimler-Benz. This turned out to be premature, and intended to encourage a more rapid response by potential French partners, but the writing was clearly on the wall. The arrival of "New Labour" had hastened the restructuring of the European defense industry, and fortified the intention of British companies to play a major role in this.

In the meantime, Labour published a White Paper on defense diversification. The new proposal to establish a Defense Diversification Agency (DDA) had a lengthy history. It originated in the 1980s in response to sustained pressure from the trade unions concerned to combat job losses by developing conversion projects at the plant and company level. By 1998, however, the radical elements had been shed, and the proposal had taken on a different hue. The original reference to "conversion" was replaced by "diversification." The term "conversion" was anathema to the Labour Party, because it was popularly associated with the Lucas Plan of the 1970s, with resonances of pacifism and powerful trade unions. The 1998 White Paper made clear that the new agency would be primarily concerned with maximizing the ability of U.K. defense companies to exploit available technologies, rather than to promote alternatives to defense production. Accordingly, the agency was to be placed within the main British defense research establishment Defence Evaluation and Research Agency (DERA).

The role of the Labour party in the British defense industry is not what might be expected. Labour has generally been more supportive of the industry than have the Conservatives. Britain's Cold War defense industry was initiated by the postwar Labour government, which decided in the later 1940s to develop an indigenous fleet of nuclear carrier aircraft, and an atom bomb "with a Union Jack on it," in response to American withdrawal of nuclear cooperation. Every Labour government has increased defense spending (with the one exception of the termination of the "East of Suez" commitments in 1967, and this for financial rather than military reasons). The Blair government sits firmly within this tradition. As a result, the process of integration and reconstruction in Europe's defense industry is likely to accelerate in the late 1990s and early 2000s, but the precise terms upon which this is done are likely to be shaped primarily by the companies themselves.

FRANCE

France is the largest military and military-industrial player in Europe, and the second- or third-largest military spending nation in the world (after the United States and possibly China). The enduring military emphasis in French politics, from Charles de Gaulle's "certain idea of France" in the 1950s through the presidency of Jacques Chirac has been reflected in a distinctive social consensus.[29] Defense strategy and defense industry questions were conspicuously absent in the debates leading up to the 1995 presidential election. Notwithstanding the radical changes in that strategy and policy in 1996, the French commitment to a strong defense remains exceptionally ambitious by European standards. This fact is reflected in the nation's diplomatic and operational postures. France responded rapidly to post–Cold War peacekeeping opportunities, notably in Rwanda and Bosnia, and adopted a distinctive position over the U.S. air strikes in Iraq in September 1996.

While French military aspirations remain ambitious, new economic pressures have made themselves felt. From the early 1990s the French government began to accept that it would need to reappraise its defense industry practices, and the Délégation Général d'Armements (DGA), responsible for defense research and the defense industry, was reorganized. A cost-saving initiative was launched with the aim of persuading equipment suppliers to cut costs by 2 percent a year (but without immediate success; in 1995 the aeroengine firm SNECMA went on strike in response). Future DGA contracts would increasingly be on a fixed price basis. In 1994 the first French White Paper on Defense in 22 years was published. This paper reasserted the commitment to a strong and integrated European defense in both operational and industrial terms, and emphasized the importance of a major French role within both. But it signaled a new French rapprochement with NATO. The close personal relationship between President François Mitterand and German Chancellor Helmut Kohl as the key drivers of European integration was manifested in the creation of Eurocorps, initially a Franco-German brigade that, it was claimed, would become the kernel of European defense cooperation. Closer operational collaboration is also being developed with Britain, notably through the creation of a joint air force command based at High Wycombe, under a French general. The White Paper also promised that France would continue to defend the homeland through its nuclear deterrent and upgraded air defenses, while also building up capacity for distant action. To this end new military satellites, especially HELIOS and a forthcoming radar satellite, would be developed along with new aircraft carriers (the *Charles de Gaulle*), and new transport aircraft (the collaborative Future Large Aircraft, or FLA).

The 1995 defense budget indicated that while defense spending was not to be cut (as it was in Britain), it would grow more slowly in the late 1990s. But a year later Chirac introduced an unexpectedly radical package of reforms, tackling not only security issues but also the corporatist structure of the defense industry, which his Socialist predecessor had not challenged. French armed forces were to be cut by a third and remolded around four elite units adapted for rapid deployment abroad. Land-based nuclear missiles were being phased out, and conscription would be replaced by an all-professional force along lines similar to Britain. The procurement budget would be cut by a fifth by the end of the decade. Even more unprecedented was the abandonment of France's old ideal of self-sufficiency in weapons; an attempt would be made to overhaul completely what *The Economist* has called "its cumbrous arms industry." Dassault and Aérospatiale were to merge within two years and Thomson CSF was to be privatized. Following the election of Jospin, many of these expectations were dashed and it appeared that the promised revolution in the French defense-industrial system would not happen after all. The Socialist government's thinking was shaped not only by the French military ambitions, but also by the street riots of 1996 in response to the threat of job losses arising from cuts in public spending. Accordingly, the future of the defense industry became unclear again. Between 1996 and 1999, the process of the privatization of Aérospatiale and its merger with Dassault was almost undetectably slow, yet it was increasingly clear that this outcome would arrive eventually. As noted above, other European companies, notably BAe and Daimler-Benz, began to play a more direct role in attempting to shake up the French system, if only threatening to leave French firms behind.

The reorientation of French defense industry policy echoes many of the pressures and responses adopted in Britain over the previous decade, allowing for the more emphatic French commitment to high spending and national champion firms. French arms exports fell following the end of the Gulf War, and (as in Britain) major efforts were made to break into the growth markets of Pacific Asia. Britain and France alternate as the world's second-largest suppliers of arms after the United States. As French exporters look to wider export markets, they face the need to reduce costs. The new procurement minister has been charged with reducing costs by 30 percent by the new century. The associated changes have shaken a number of collaborative programmes involving French firms. Several Franco-German ventures that depended critically on French public spending came under review.

As indicated in Table 13–4, the French defense industry has employed rather fewer people than the British, although different bases of calculation make accurate comparisons difficult.[30] Until recently employment fell less rapidly in France, but major job losses are now under way. Aérospatiale shed 1,100 jobs in 1993 and 2,000 in 1994. Until recently, an influential view throughout Europe has been that the French have the only real long-term strategy toward the defense industry. Nevertheless, it is widely expected that French companies will form a major component within the emergent European defense industry. One reason is that defense research and development spending has not fallen in France, unlike every other European country, especially Britain. The main obstacles in the way of a more rapid convergence of French defense firms with foreign partners are the former employment structures. French companies have much de-manning to do, compared especially with British firms, and are legally constrained as to how they do this (many being classified in effect as "civil service" employments). Foreign partners are unwilling to tie themselves too closely to French firms, so long as this might commit them to taking on the high costs of de-manning, especially when they have just completed the same adjustment themselves (again, the key example is British Aerospace). However, things began to change markedly in the closing years of the decade. The French defense-industrial "model" began to appear much less coherent and sustainable than in the past, while the modernized, slimmed-down, profitable, new corporate style represented by companies such as British Aerospace and Daimler-Benz (especially following the announcement of the latter's link on the civil side with Chrysler) appeared to be more in keeping with the new era of globalization.

GERMANY

In sharp contrast to France and Britain, defense spending and the defense industry in Germany have been beset by controversy ever since the 1950 accord between the U.S. and the Adenauer governments to promote German rearmament. On the left, Social Democratic and Green politicians and lobbies based on the trade unions and peace groups have sustained a critical opposition to prevailing defense and defense-industry policies. On the right there has been criticism of Germany's "subordinate" role in the NATO security architecture and dependence on imported (U.S.) weaponry. Nevertheless, from Konrad Adenauer and Franz Joseph Strauss through to Helmut Kohl, a number of powerful politicians have promoted the development of an indigenous defense industry. In the late 1980s this coalesced around Daimler-Benz. Through a series of acquisitions and mergers, eventually the company grew to account for about two-thirds of defense industry as its output, although civilian activities remained its predominant output. Many of the key programs have been international collaborations, mainly with France and Britain. Industrialists report that the French connection has been vital, because France (before Chirac) had been seen as the only European country really committed to sustained high defense spending and the development of a European defense industry.

Defense spending in West Germany contracted sharply following reunification, and in the East it collapsed. Aggregate real German defense spending fell by around 70 percent between 1990 and 1994. Defense spending bottomed out at 47.2 billion deutsche marks in 1994 and was set to remain roughly static in the late 1990s. But constraints on public spending arising from the unexpected costs of reunification, deepening recession, and the pressure to meet the Maastricht convergence criteria have refueled the controversy over defense spending. These arguments have been brought into sharp focus periodically in the debates over the necessity for the Eurofighter/Jager-90. The British decision to go ahead on the production phase put pressure on Germany to reach a similar decision, which was finalized in 1998.

The rapid reunification of 1989–90 prompted some within and without Germany to question whether it would remain a NATO member. Germany's commitment to the alliance has remained strong, and its defense strategy now centers on the protection of the home territory in collaboration with European allies within a broadened NATO.

In addition, following a controversial debate over the constitutionality of "out-of-area" roles, new flexible capacities are to be developed for crisis management and peacekeeping. Germany's citizen army is to be transformed into an all-professional "crisis reaction force" to be "55,000 strong and in trim by 1999."[31] Presumably new intelligence and transportation equipment and new weaponry will be required. Equipment spending was expected to rise from around 20 percent to around 30 percent of the budget by 2000 to 2005.

This increase is not likely to reverse the decline in defense industry employment, which fell in former West Germany from around 280,000 in 1989 to around 100,000 in the mid-1990s. German firms face greater problems in responding to failing domestic demand by boosting exports than do British or French companies. Exports of warlike equipment have been strictly regulated under the Kriegswaffenkontrollgesetz and limitations on trade with particular countries have been inscribed in the Aussenwirtschaftsgesetz. In the 1990s these restrictions have been weakened de facto, under pressure from companies to establish a more level playing field with French and British companies. Since 1995, for example, German engines can be exported to France for incorporation into Leclerc tanks for export to the United Arab Emirates. German contributions to the Eurofighter will no longer limit the aircraft's possible exports. The German defense industry is engaged in 27 collaborative programs with France. However, the oscillations in French defense industry policy have created new uncertainties, and many aerospace and other programs are under review "to reduce costs and solve major budget difficulties faced by both governments."[32] In 1993 DASA announced a radical restructuring plan involving the closure of six sites and loss of 10,300 jobs by the end of 1996 owing to market weakness in civil and military sectors. In the mid-1990s, DASA entered a phase of unprecedented difficulties that led it to a radical restructuring.

The Dutch Fokker subsidiary was closed in 1996 and in 1998 the link with Chrysler was announced. Soon afterwards, Daimler-Benz let it be known that it was thinking of merging its military aircraft business with British Aerospace.

Meanwhile other segments of the German defense industry were also undergoing restructuring, and in some cases this pointed to the development of powerful new industrial networks. If British strength is concentrated in military aircraft and avionics, and French in ships and missiles, the German defense industry is perhaps strongest in the field of armored vehicles. German companies secured the lion's share of the major transnational program for a new armored vehicle announced in 1998.

ITALY AND SMALLER COUNTRIES

Italian security and defense policy in the 1990s has been clouded by the far-reaching virtual collapse of the dominant political classes that followed, and was partly precipitated by, the end of the Cold War. Since World War II Italian defense has depended heavily on American financial, technical, and military cooperation, oriented to the threat from the East. But the relevance of traditional NATO conceptions of the importance of the central European theater as against a Mediterranean-centered security policy and military theater has been contested. These positions reflect differences in values and political sentiment that have never been manifested in a simple way at the electoral level. The left and elements of the Catholic Church long have strongly opposed both high defense spending and defense exports. Their efforts resulted in a major reduction in exports since the late 1980s, most of which went to small third world governments. The preoccupation of the "technical governments" of the 1990s with economic matters has meant that the defense debate has been muted. Future national defense demands remain particularly unclear. Meanwhile, the defense industry has been largely gathered together under the umbrella of a state holding company, Finmeccanica, which is attempting to encourage rationalization, international collaboration, and cost reductions. Meanwhile Fiat is one of the major actors in European defense and aerospace, not least through the Eurofighter program. This strategy bore fruit in 1998, when the British GEC corporation announced that it was to merge several businesses with the Finmeccanica subsidiary, Alenia Difesa, in a $3.4 billion partnership in defense systems and missiles. This was reported as if it was a response to the tripartite statement by European defense ministers calling for industry to respond to the American challenge.[33] But in fact, like most of the other large mergers and joint ventures announced in the wake of the ministerial declaration, it had been under development long before that declaration was written. Meanwhile Fiat is one of the major actors in European defense and aerospace, not least through the Eurofighter program.

Other, smaller European countries generally had only modest military capacities during the Cold War, met by high spending on imports. (See Table 13–6.) The ubiquitous emphasis in the 1990s on the need for peacekeeping capacity is fueling demand for new equipment in these countries too. In southern Europe, tensions between Greece and Turkey and uncertainties over the Mediterranean, including French policy toward North Africa, are fueling a sustained demand for defense equipment. Government policies vary from the extreme free-market bias of

Table 13–6   European Arms Imports as Percent of Total Defense Spending ($U.S. millions)

	Imports 1987–91	% of Defense Spending
United Kingdom	2,190	1.3
France	130	0.5
Germany	2,215	1.2
Italy	1,260	1.0
Spain	3,300	7.2
Netherlands	2,305	6.4
Greece	3,030	15.9
Belgium	1,110	4.8
Denmark	500	3.7
Portugal	1,030	24.6
Ireland	50	2.0
Luxembourg	65	12.0

Source: Derived from Happe and Wakeman-Linn, Table 7 (ACDA estimates).
Average imports 1987 to 1991; total spending 1991.

the Netherlands to highly protectionist strategies for building up new defense industries in Portugal, Greece, and Turkey, which are Developing Defense Industry (DDI) countries.

But the defense industries of countries other than the Big Three are, in general, small and dependent on orders arising as import offsets (usually of U.S. equipment). In many cases foreign ownership appears to be increasing, usually by one of the major European companies. In the early 1990s Thomson in particular extended its ownership of companies in other European counties. In Belgium, the defense industry essentially consists of small and medium-sized companies, most of which are linked formally or informally to larger foreign-owned companies.

Defense: The Exception in European Integration

Under the banner of European integration, most civilian markets within Europe have been opened substantially, a set of regulatory institutions has been put in place, and embryonic governmental organizations have emerged. The development of the European Union (EU) is, however, not a simple story of unidirectional upward progress.[34] The "European project" often has different meanings for different national governments and for different sections of industry. Nowhere are the tensions between these different interests and interpretations greater than in defense matters. This is not coincidental, for as sociologist Max

**Table 13–7   European Defense Companies Ranked by Value
of Defense Sales, 1993**

	Sales ($U.S millions)
BAe	5.86
Thomson-CSF	4.07
GEC	2.94
Aérospatiale	2.55
Alenia Difesa	1.72
Daimler-Benz Aerospace	1.64
Dassault Aviation	1.53
Rolls-Royce	1.47
GIAT	1.25
Celsius Group	0.99
Eurocopter	0.95
Matra	0.93

Source: SIPRI, *The Economist*, April 8, 1995, p. 84.

Weber noted, the legitimate control of organized violence is a defining characteristic of the state.

The ambivalence over whether "Europe" represents a move toward a new integrated political-economic entity, or whether it is instead a new framework within which the sovereignty of individual nation-states, is sustained is particularly significant in the defense sector.[35] In the mid-1990s the national and intergovernmental influences have been much stronger than the European or "federal."[36] In particular, European Union institutions have been sidelined by the reconstruction of the longer-established organs of "intergovernmental" cooperation associated with the NATO alliance. But even these have had only a faltering influence.

At the same time, conflicting approaches to European industrial and technology strategy also have had implications for the defense industry. The development of European industrial policy in general has been marked by tensions between the "strategic trade" approach associated with France (and Jacques Delors's presidency of the European Commission) and the "internal free market" emphasis associated with Britain.[37] The defense industry has focused these tensions.

THE RISE AND FALL OF A "STRATEGIC TRADE" APPROACH TO THE DEFENSE INDUSTRY IN THE EUROPEAN COMMISSION

For a brief period in the early 1990s, it seemed that Europe might adopt a "strategic trade" approach to the European defense industry.[38] Commissioners toured European defense-dependent localities promising that a major initiative would be forthcoming. It was suggested that the Maastricht Treaty had set in motion "the development of an integrated European defence equipment market" in parallel with the development of a common European defense policy.[39] In 1991–92 the European Commission took a close interest in the models of defense industrialization in countries such as Japan and Taiwan and the defense diversification initiatives of the new Clinton administration. The creation of the U.S. Office of Economic Security appears to have had a major impact, especially among German companies and within the Delors cabinet of the commission. Daimler-Benz, hearing of the initiative through its Washington office, delivered a series of presentations at conferences in Brussels and elsewhere extolling its virtues and the need for something similar in Europe, preferably promoted by the commission.

However, Euro-skepticism was on the rise, and national governments (especially Britain) emphasized those aspects of the Maastricht Treaty, including the preservation of article 223, that enabled them to resist commission efforts to play a role in defense-industrial matters. In 1992 the Council of Ministers rejected the commission's proposals to promote restructuring in the aerospace industry. Industry ministers meeting in Lisbon debated the arms industry but were unable to agree.[40] By 1994 the impetus to develop a strategic policy for the European defense industry from within the institutions of the European Union appeared to have been exhausted. With the end of the Delors era in 1995 the strategic line of thinking about the defense industry within the commission faded away.

In January 1996 the commission produced a new set of proposals for the European defense industry. These were characterized by a markedly "neoliberal" agenda. Four recommendations were set out to encourage rationalization, concentration, and internationalization among European defense companies. These included the application to defense of EU principles for opening generic public procurement, the redirection of public subsidies for defense companies to encourage cross-border integration and rationalization, increased use of common EU research resources for dual-use technologies (said to account for one-third of the current 12.3 billion Ecu Framework Four program), and greater commonalities in the export regulations of member states. The latter could be achieved first by greater governmental openness concerning export procedures, second by encouraging the use of prime contractors and allowing the export rules of the prime's country to apply to the whole collaborative product.[41]

The commission's return to defense industry policy questions has not drawn significant support from any member governments, and the British have been opposed. The emphasis on easing export restrictions appeals to German companies but offers little to British or French companies, which already enjoy lax regimes. The commission's desire to impose a common "enabling environment" is generally welcome in the industry, but the leaders are more interested in bringing about the supply-side measures that will equip them to take advantage of it. Companies like British Aerospace emphasize the desirability of creating true transnational companies, with all the autonomy that civilian companies enjoy. Such developments will involve national governments, and specific orders, rather than European institutions and generalized policies.

THE ROLE OF ALLIANCE INSTITUTIONS

Since the defense industry remains nominally outside the purview of the European Commission, responsibility for defense policy development formally lies solely with national governments, although their decisions naturally are influenced by membership of alliances. The NATO structure includes several fora intended to bring together decision-makers concerned with the defense industry. But the main focus for policy for the European defense industry until 1998 was formally the West European Armaments Group (WEAG), now part of the Western European Union (WEU).

The WEU was resuscitated at the Rome conference of 1984 as an instrument for strengthening the European arm of NATO and developing European armaments cooperation. In April 1989 William Van-Ekerlen, formerly Dutch defense minister, was appointed WEU secretary-general and became an advocate of a strategic trade approach to the European defense industry. Following the Maastricht Treaty the WEU was to become both "the defence arm of the EU" and the European pillar of NATO. This formulation left many questions open, and a joint WEU-EU working group was set up in 1994 to report to the EU Intergovernmental Conference (IGC) in 1996.[42] A new commission directorate (DG1) was also set up to deal with security and external affairs.

The WEU has a 115-member Parliamentary Assembly drawn from members of the intergovernmental Council of Europe, but it has no formal link to the European Parliament. Nor does it link coherently to the committees of national parliaments dealing with defense issues. This detachment makes it attractive to those, like the British, who wish to resist the development of a strong European policy actor in defense. It also helps to retain governmental, rather than parliamentary, control over defense matters.

The West European Armaments Group

The WEU apparatus includes the WEAG, which is the main organization concerned with the restructuring of the European defense industry as a whole. This organization began life in 1976 as the Independent European Programme Group (IEPG), spurred by U.S. demands that the Europeans should coordinate their defense-industrial policies and by the wish of European companies and governments to pressure the U.S. government to open up its domestic arms market, so creating a two-way street. In 1988 the IEPG action plan urged greater efforts to reduce excess capacity in the face of the impending reduction of military needs. In 1990 the nine IEPG member countries announced a commitment to further opening of defense contracts.[43] According to the *Financial Times*, this was "a grudging response to pre-empt EC effort to apply liberalisation measures in arms."[44] The WEAG is responsible for the European Cooperation for the Long Term in Defence (EUCLID) program for collaborative defense research and development. In 1995 the WEAG established a research cell based on EUCLID. This is intended to be transitional toward EUCLID's becoming a full agency with contractual powers.

The WEAG is tasked with identifying the possibilities for common procurement in Europe and one of its panels is examining equipment replacement schedules for the next 10 years to identify the scope for technical harmonization. It has been suggested that this body, now renamed the West European Armaments Organization (WEAO), might form the basis of a possible European Armaments Agency. However, it has a competitor.

THE FRANCO-GERMAN ARMAMENTS AGENCY

In the 1970s and 1980s proposals for a European Armaments Agency floundered on the resistance of national armed forces to use common equipment, and suspicions that the bulk of the benefits of closer transatlantic cooperation would go to the United States.[45] In the 1990s the prospect of a European Armaments Agency of some form or other was revived. Despite the new prominence of the WEU and WEAG, the most important development emanated from neither.

In 1992 the French and German governments proposed a European Armaments Agency to take over some of the activities of IEPG, such as

EUCLID. Following the creation of the Franco-German Eurocorps in November 1993, this mutated into a proposal for a Franco-German procurement agency. The British government stood its distance until it began to fear that its suppliers might lose out. In March 1995 France and Germany offered the United Kingdom a role in the proposed new agency, and the then defense procurement minister, Roger Freeman, responded positively.[46] In December France and Germany created a joint armaments agency with the power to award contracts. In early 1996 *The Economist* reported that "France and Britain do not want Britain to join the agency, they dislike its tendency to buy relatively cheap, American weapons off-the-shelf. But by June the British government was negotiating terms of entry."[47] OCCAR's precise role in future procurement and its relationship to the WEAO apparatus remained unclear. The WEU, which is in the habit of being very optimistic in public, argued that the existence of two separate bodies was less untidy than it first appeared, and insisted that OCCAR would eventually become a WEU subsidiary body, which would bring it under the same umbrella as WEAO. With the granting of the first contract to OCCAR (noted above) in 1998, the balance appeared to tip in favor of OCCAR as the basis of a new trans-European procurement system.

THE RELATIVE MARGINALITY OF THE FORMAL INSTITUTIONS

In 1994 the WEU declared that it was developing "an industrial armaments policy . . . an arms export policy; a joint European equipment procurement mechanism; and means for further opening the European market." It was also examining "how to establish a common European defense science and technology base."[48] In fact, the WEU has had virtually no impact on the defense industry other than to oblige it to send representatives to a maze of new organizations. The WEU and WEAG networks remain largely talking shops. Although the reinvented NATO alliance structures have claimed the security and defense high ground, they have had little impact on the industrial aspects of defense. As noted earlier, it now appears that OCCAR is likely to be the formal framework under which a collective European procurement structure will eventually be established. But for this to be successful, a cultural change is required.

Some industrialists complain that these bodies are staffed by "military kinds of people" who "don't understand business." As such these organizations are anachronistic. One of the most important effects of the wave of neoliberal thinking and attempts to reduce public spending has been the transformation of the defense firm into a commercial actor, rather than an agent of a Ministry of Defense.[49] The leading European defense companies no longer operate as passive executors of government instructions and behave much more like normal corporations with normal business practices and managements. They cannot wait until groups of politicians and military committees have formulated a grand plan. The advantage of OCCAR seems to be that it is proceeding case-by-case as collaborative procurement deals are announced, rather than waiting to formulate a comprehensive strategy for the European defense industry as a whole.

PRIVATIZATION AND "MARKETIZATION"

To varying degrees, every major European defense industry has been privatized or exposed to forms of "marketization." The process began in Britain with British Aerospace, Ferranti, Rolls-Royce, Shorts, and Royal Ordnance. Since the 1980s Daimler-Benz Aerospace—formerly DASA—has been taken out of Bavarian state ownership and private shareholding increased. In Italy the clustering of defense industries in Finmeccanica has been accompanied by a commitment to some privatization, although the details and time scales remain to be clarified. In France the privatization of Thomson CSF and forced merger of Dassault and Aérospatiale promise to liberalize almost a third of the European defense industry.[50]

Survival Strategies: Widening the Market

Given declining domestic defense budgets and increased import penetration (especially from the radically reorganized U.S. industry), European defense companies are under pressure to find new markets and to develop new ways of securing access to them. In the short to medium term, this has focused attention on export sales of existing products. In the longer term, it focuses attention on the possibility of constructing new transnational and intercompany partnerships for the development of new products and markets.

EXPORTS

It was noted in the country case studies that national governments have supported arms exports for both political and industrial reasons. But this playing field remains uneven. During the Gulf War, Belgian regulations prohibited sales of munitions to Britain since it intended to use them in the conflict. In the early 1990s France proposed to sell naval ships to Taiwan but was unable to incorporate Dutch-made systems/components as this would have violated Dutch export policies.

Companies and the European Commission have increasingly urged greater commonality in arms export regulations. Many companies expect that the main benefits from collective European policy developments in the foreseeable future will be limited to the gradual harmonization of arms export policies among EU members. In 1996 the commission claimed legal competence in arms exports, following a European Court of Justice ruling.[51] The commission's claims of legal competence over arms exports currently are falling on deaf ears, as national governments prefer to make their own decisions or operate bilaterally. Nevertheless, the European Commission has won recognition that dual-use products fall under its remit.[52]

Meanwhile, collaborative projects increasingly include provisions whereby one partner will not prevent another's exports of the joint product, implying a lowest-common-denominator principle. The extension of this approach is advocated by Martin Bangemann, the European industry commissioner who is particularly close to German companies.

"NEW MODEL" COLLABORATIONS

The market in mass-production weapons, like civilian products, is not one in which high-cost western companies can hope to compete against cheaper competitors. In the longer term, their competitive survival depends on their ability to incorporate technology to create unique products, and doing so requires long-term development projects. But such projects are technically risky, promise a low rate of return on investment in early years, and face uncertain final demand. Such problems were relatively unimportant when defense companies were effectively part of the state and could expect follow-on contracts stretching across decades. But, for commercially oriented companies, they are serious. The solution is to establish a degree of market closure, tying companies, funders, and potential customers together for a sustained period.

One route to market closure favored by most large and niche-specialist companies is international collaboration. A number of collaborative ventures are under way, several are under development, and many are being mooted. New developments should be distinguished from the older models represented by some legacies of the Cold War such as the Eurofighter and the Franco-German Tiger helicopter.[53] Newer projects tend to incorporate more commercial principles, breaking with the traditional model in which governments agree to the division of labor between the partners. New model collaborations such as the HORIZON air-defense frigate and the possible Future Large Aircraft (FLA) program aim to allow companies to choose how best to exploit their technological capacities and the skills of their workforces.

Many current and proposed ventures are tentative or even experimental. It takes some time to establish ending partnerships. Some are intended to result in mergers, potentially leading to new cross-national companies. Although several such mergers have been proposed in the 1990s, few have yet materialized. However, as noted earlier, by the late 1990s some substantial mergers seemed underway, notably the integration of GEC (Britain) with Alenia Difesa (Italy), plus the integration of Dassault and Aérospatiale and DAe and GEC-Marconi French companies. In addition it was likely GKN-Westlands (UK) and Agusta (Italy) would merge their helicopter businesses.[54]

POLITICAL RISK AS A MOTIVE FOR COLLABORATION

A major problem confronting both defense companies and armed services in Europe is the lack of public enthusiasm for defense spending. The political cycle is much shorter than the time scale required to develop new defense technologies of the type the armed services believe they need. In the post–Cold War environment, defense spending is widely unpopular. And the recession has put strains on public budgets. In Germany in particular the debate over defense spending, especially major programs such as Eurofighter, has been intense.[55] Nevertheless, Eurofighter development and production were eventually approved.

Collaborative programs are seen as a means to overcome what many defense industrialists regard as their primary problem: fickle national politicians anxious to please electorates in the short term and uneasy about defense spending in the absence of an agreed threat. It is said that technical problems are not the issue, the fundamental point is the unreliability of politicians. Collaboration provides protection against this political risk because it shores up long-term programs with both legal-technical formalities (subject to withdrawal penalties) and foreign policy commitments. (These are much harder for governments to cancel; the companies are very much aware that local politicians will not be able to alter it.)

A precedent was established in the early years of European integration. In 1958 Alfried Krupp chose to deal with the European Coal and Steel Community rather than the German government because "its supranational status meant that its decisions could not be questioned by any government."[56]

The construction of transnational networks does not only allow companies to achieve market closure.[57] Such networks also can be acceptable to governments since they promise to reduce costs.[58] For the customer armed services, networks also promise to ring-fence important projects. One industrialist commented that "the only security that the armed forces have is if projects become collaborative." In 1989 the British government Foreign Secretary Geoffrey Howe welcomed the fact that greater reliance on collaborative European armaments programmes implied "less and less political surveillance over defence production."[59] (See Table 13-8.)

The drive to establish cross-border collaborations also has implications for corporate restructuring. To avoid being subordinated by powerful partners, a company must have bargaining power arising from a distinctive technological advantage, financial resources, or a diverse product portfolio. Many European firms fear collaborating with U.S. companies because they perceive the closeness between U.S. companies and the government as a threat to outsiders. Such considerations reinforce the wish to form strong European companies as a precondition for American collaborations. The drive to collaboration is therefore reinforcing the general pressure to reduce costs, especially through removal of overmanning and the reform of pay agreements.[60]

THE LURE OF THE U.S. MARKET

For companies that have moved down this road, the U.S. market is seen as critically important. While BAe is collaborating with Dassault on the Future Offensive Aircraft, it is also collaborating with McDonnell Douglas on the potentially much larger new combat aircraft project.[61] Rolls-

Table 13–8 **Collaborative Defense Projects Involving the United Kingdom (1996)**

	In Production or in Service	Under Development	Study
Belgium	2	1	
Denmark	2	1	
France	8	6	11
Germany	9	7	6
Greece	1		
Italy	6	2	5
Netherlands	3	3	1
Norway	1	2	1
Portugal	1		
Spain	2	3	
Turkey	2		1
United States	6	4	9

Source: Statement on the Defence Estimates (London: HMSO, 1996).

Royce is probably even more committed to transatlantic links, since the United States is developing a new generation of vertical take-off aircraft to replace the Harrier. GEC teamed with Hughes to compete against a British Aerospace consortium with European companies to supply the Royal Air Force cruise missile. In October 1998 the prime contractorship for the U.S. Army and U.S. Marine Corps 155mm Howitzer programme was transferred from Textron to GEC, which had previously acquired the U.S. firm Tracor. The British government presents itself in the United States as a bulwark against European attempts to "exclude the U.S. from European markets."[62]

The U.S. Department of Defense (DoD) has undertaken a study comparing U.S. and European capabilities in 20 so-called critical technologies. It concluded that European firms do not "significantly lead" in any technology but that they are "capable of making major contributions" in seven sectors.[63] Meanwhile, U.S. firms are involved in most of the major weapons development programs in which European companies are involved. Different combinations of European and U.S. firms are bidding on several proposed programs, particularly for the United Kingdom and European and also U.S. companies.[64]

Virtually all European companies are also energetically promoting exports and developing collaborative arrangements in the regional growth market of Pacific Asia. Some (including BAe and Daimler) also are exploring possibilities in South Africa, which has good links to China and other potential customer countries. The development of various sorts of collaborative programs is now driving the internationalization of the defense industry, and not solely in Europe.[65] So long as defense demands remain so much larger in the United States, and continue to be buoyant in the Middle East, and in what was until 1998 the rapidly growing market in Pacific Asia, defense firms in Europe are bound to look beyond their immediate neighbors. Global market opportunities mean that the outcomes of the restructuring of the European defense industry will not be Eurocentric.

The growth of prime contractor arrangements, pioneered in Britain, and extension of collaboration not only entwines companies in new developments crossing national borders; it also allows the relocation of employment toward lower-cost labor. British defense companies already subcontract software work to India, and companies across Europe are extending their sourcing beyond their national boundaries. The increased need for offsets along with exports also results in some work being relocated abroad. European defense companies are playing an important role in the internationalization of arms production.

The other side of the coin of this internationalization is the contraction and fracturing of the former defense industries within Europe. At one pole a small core of major producers (and some niche specialists) is being consolidated as monopolists or oligopolists in the production of specialist high-technology defense equipment (and of dual-use products). These companies increasingly look to each other as allies and potential partners in collaborative development and production on both the European and the global scale. At the other end of the spectrum, smaller suppliers and manufacturers of less technology-intensive inputs are increasingly exposed to new competitive forces to which many are unable to adapt. While the large corporations energetically engage in informal politics through various channels in an attempt to construct market closure, smaller firms are left to follow market forces. The economic realpolitik of the defense market is reproducing trends familiar elsewhere in industry, including the polarization and concentration of industrial power and the polarization and relocation of employment.

"INDUSTRY IS DOING IT FOR ITSELF"

The gradual coalescing of Europe's major arms producers in the 1990s was seen by many as *too* gradual, especially when set against the rapid concentration of the U.S. defense industry. As noted earlier, the European Commission and WEAG issued a number of statements calling for greater haste, but without effect. In 1997, however, the pace quickened. In December of that year the defense ministers of Britain, France, and Germany issued a joint statement calling on companies to explain how they were going to merge and create a new European Defense Aerospace Company (christened by the press as "EuroCo"). It is worth noting how minimalist this initiative was when compared to the "Last Supper" meetings that precipitated the mergers in the United States. In summer 1998 the ministers, now joined by three other countries, reissued their demand for action. In practice, the main impact appears to have been to hasten developments that were already underway, such as the GEC-Alenia Difesa merger noted above. In mid-1996 British Aerospace and Daimler-Benz announced the possible merger of their military aircraft divisions. This turned out to be a "suggestion" rather than a firm plan, intended to encourage a more rapid response by French companies. It seems inevitable that the divisions between European defense companies will be overcome by the creation of major new corporate entities early in the new decade. But the role of European governments in this process remains distinctively at "arms-length."

While national governments, rather than Europe-wide organizations, continue to have the critical influence over the industry, this influence is increasingly of a new kind; rather than managing the industry, as was the case during the Cold War, governments are shifting toward an "enabling" stance. Government involvement is still essential, since the sharing of defense technologies raises defense and security questions. Government assistance through access to research resources is also important. Not least, home government orders provide an invaluable platform upon which to negotiate collaboration with others.

As a director in one leading European defense company put it: "Industry isn't waiting for these things. . . . The restructuring of the defense industry will be determined by/led by the industry itself rather than the politicians"(anonymous source interview).

One consequence is the development of a host of new links between companies and nonhost governments. Examples include Daimler-Benz and the French government via Eurocopter and mergers in satellites, missiles, and munitions, or BAe and the U.S. government (via stealth work, work on the FJSF bid, and vertical take-off).[66] Thomson is also developing links to a wide range of governments, especially by virtue of its unique position in naval radar technologies. BAe and DASA have busy Washington offices.

Among the more advanced companies there is a growing consensus that the long-term ideal is the transformation of provisional collaborative ventures into permanent entities: "a program organization [that] will become a company" as one industrialist put it. Many believe that the growth of such entities at the core of the European defense industry means that in 20 years, "it will be the same as European telecommunications is now."[67] The Anglo-French civilian power-generating company GEC-Alsthom has been cited as an example that "may serve as guide to the integration of European defence companies."[68] Other models that have been cited by insiders include Unilever and Royal-Dutch Shell, companies that are transnational and able to play in several national, and sectoral, markets.

But at present European defense collaborations are product specific, resulting in companies that are much more limited than their U.S. competitors. Different governments have different views as to the best way to go. The French bias is toward the creation of national champions before establishing cross-border companies; and this appears still to be the case despite the Chirac defense policy "revolution" of 1996. The British Ministry of Defence (MOD) resisted attempts to form a national champion out of BAe and GEC for two decades, but in 1999 this outcome became irresistible (as a result of company strategies and shareholder-value considerations, rather than government's strategies choices).

Conclusion

TOWARD A EUROPEAN DEFENSE INDUSTRY, OR GLOBAL DEFENSE COMPANIES WITH A EUROPEAN BASE?

One effect of the experimental and negotiated nature of restructuring in which companies are the key actors is that the net outcome may not be European in any strong sense. In the absence of a coherent and directive overall strategy and effective European defense-industrial organizations, the companies are under pressure to deepen their existing comparative advantage. Following their existing lines of specialization leads many to look outside of Europe rather than inside it. The European defense industry is not an integrated whole but a thing of parts, some of which are oriented to European markets, others to these and markets elsewhere.

While the West European Union, and to a lesser extent the European Union, slowly develop new formal structures for European procurement and defense research, the industry is getting on with business as best it can, with uneven assistance from national governments. It seems clear that the main contribution of the formal institutions and procedures will be to endorse post hoc the industrial realities that will have been forged incrementally and piecemeal by corporate collaborations. Based on present trends, the formal systems will provide a legal ratification for patterns that already will have been put in place, at the initiative of companies, with the assistance of governments operating bi- or multilaterally.

This is why the dismantling of Europe's national Cold War defense industries is unlikely to lead to the formation of a coherent new European military industrial complex.[69] Most of the existing or emergent collaborations do not embrace more than a few European supplier countries, and many are driven by the desire to become suitable allies or partners for firms outside Europe, particularly in the United States. No single European body, and no elected polity, has oversight of the restructuring process or the will and the instruments to shape it. The companies themselves, together with departments within national governments and the armed forces, are playing the key role in industrial change and thereby to some extent in the definition of security and defense problems and solutions.

The emerging pattern of economic governance in the European defense industry has not solved all its problems, especially those of smaller producers. At the same time, the marginal role played by formal

democratic structures, both within national states and at the collective
European level, reveals an important democratic deficit. In the background, but ever present, is the lure and threat of the enormous U.S.
defense market and industry.

Notes

This chapter draws on an Economic and Social Research Council–funded project, "The
Restructuring of the European Defence Industry and European Community-Policy,"
undertaken by the author and Louise Curran. Unacknowledged quotes are from managers of European defense companies interviewed from 1994 to 1996.

1. "Towards a Euro-mix," *The Economist,* March 11, 1995, pp. 30–31.

2. Commission of the European Communities (hereafter Commission), *The Challenges Facing the European Defence-Related Industry. A Contribution for Action at the European Level* (Brussels: COM(96), 10 final, 1996).

3. This chapter draws on an Economic and Social Research Council–funded project, "The Restructuring of the European Defence Industry," under-taken by the author and Louise Curran. Unacknowledged quotes are from managers of European defense companies interviewed from 1994 to 1996.

4. Robert Schuman, "The Schuman Declaration," in Brent F. Nelson and Alexander C.-G. Stubb, eds., *The European Union* (Boulder, Colo.: Lynne Rienner, 1952), pp. 1–12; Imanuel Wexler, *The Marshall Plan Revisited: The European Recovery*

5. *Program in Economic Perspective* (Westport, Connecticut and London: Greenwood Press, 1987).

6. The European Community officially became the European Union (EU) in 1993.

7. Keith Hartley and Andrew Cox, *The Costs of Non-Europe in Defence Pro-curement* (Brussels: European Commission, DG3, 1992).

8. David White, "Europe Takes First Step towards a More Open Weapons Market," *Financial Times,* February 22, 1990.

9. Trevor Taylor, *European Defence Co-operation* (London: Brassey's, 1984).

10. Mike Renner, *Economic Adjustments after the Cold War: Strategies for Conver-sion* (UNIDIR/Dartmouth: U.N. Institute for Disarmament Research, 1992).

11. There are no completely reliable, comprehensive, consistent estimates for defense industry output, turnover, and employment across all countries. All estimates cited here should be treated with caution.

12. Jean Paul Hérbert, *Production d'armement: mutation du systèmê français* (Paris: Etudes de la Documentation Francaise, 1995), p. 12; SDE, *State-ment on the Defence Estimates* (London: Her Majesty's Stationery Office, 1995).

13. Jacques Delors, "European Unification and European Security," *Adelphi Papers* 284 (1993).

14. Commission, *Challenges Facing the European Defense-Related Industry,* p. 4; Hans Feddersen and Armindo Silva, "The Single European Market and the Defence Industry," Nato's Sixteen Nations 2 (1992): 13–16; Hartley and Cox, *Costs of Non-Europe.*

15. Commission, *Challenges Facing the European Defence-Related Industry.*

16. Commission, *The Economic and Social Impact of Reductions in Defence Spending and Military Forces on the Regions of the Community Commission of the European Communities* (Brussels: Commission of European Communities, 1992). John Lovering, "After the Cold War: The Defence Industry and the New Europe," in P. Brown and R. Crompton, eds., *A New Europe? Economic Restructuring and Social Exclusion* (London: UCL Press, 1994), pp. 175-95.

17. See, for example, Bernard Adam, *Prospects for the Defence Industry and the Conversion of European Armaments Companies to Civil Production* (Brussels: European Institute for Research and Information on Peace and Security [GRIP]: 1992); Commission, *Economic and Social Impact of Reductions;* Hartley and Cox, *The Cost of Non-Europe;* Philip Gummett and Josephine Ann Stein, *European Defence Technology in Transition,* Science Policy Support Group, 22 Henrietta Street, London, 1995; Lovering, "After the Cold War"; John Lovering, *A Mixed Blessing: The Unmaking and Remaking of the British Arms Industry* in *The British Economy in Transition: From the Old to the New,* Royce Turner, ed. (Routledge: London, 1996), pp. 88–122; Scientific and Technological Options Assessment (STOA), *European Armaments Industry: Research, Technological Development, and Conversion* (Luxembourg: European Parliament Directorate General for Research/ STOA, 1993); Taylor and Hayward, *The UK Defence Industrial Base;* Brookes Tigner, "The Future of Europe's Defence Industry," Background report to conference entitled "The Future of Europe's Defence Industry," European Commission DG3, June 18, 1996; Bernard Udis and Simon Booth, *Restructuring and Conversion in the Defence Industry: A Review of Recent Literature* (Paris: Centre Européen de Resources sur les Reconversions et les Mutations, DG5, 1994); Pierre Vestel, "The European Defence Industry," *Chaillot Papers* (Western European Union), Institute for Security Studies, 1996; William Walker, "Defence," in C. Freeman, M. Sharp, and W. Walker, eds., *Technology and the Future of Europe* (London Pinter Publications/Science Policy Research Unit, 1992), pp. 365–82; Walker and Gummett, "Nationalism, Internationalism and the European Defence Market," *Chaillot Papers* 9 (Western European Union), Institute for Security Studies, 1993.

18. Ann Markusen, *"The Post-Cold War American Defense Industry: Options, Policies and Probable Outcomes,"* Working Paper no. 108, Project on Regional and Industrial Economics, Rutgers University, New Brunswick, N.J., 1996.

19. Commission, *Challenges Facing the European Defence-Related Industry.*

20. Commission, *Economic and Social Impact of Reductions.*

21. J. Paul Dunne and Ron Smith, "Thatcherism and the UK Defence Industry," in J. Michie, ed., *The Economic Legacy: 1979–1992* (London: Academic Press, 1992); "Towards a Euro-mix"; Walker and Gummett, "Nationalism, Internationalism."

22. Commission, *Challenges Facing the European Defence-Related Industry.*

23. Ibid.

24. Dunne and Smith, "Thatcherism and the UK Defence Industry"; Lovering, "Mixed Blessings."

25. Lovering, "Mixed Blessings"; Walker and Gummett, "Nationalism, Internationalism."

26. SDE, *Statement on the Defence Estimates* (London: Her Majesty's Stationer's Office, 1996).

27. Lovering, "After the Cold War."

28. Bernard Gray, "U.S. deal signed to develop military jets," *Financial Times,* April 20, 1995.

29. Herbert, *Production d'armement.*

30. Commission, *Economic and Social Impact.*

31. Ibid. Klaus Naumann, "German Security Policy and the Future Tasks of the Bundeswehr," *R.U.S.I Journal* (1994): 8–13.

32. "France and Germany Rethink Joint Defence Programmes," *Flight International,* June 12–18, 1996.

33. Beth and Taylor, 1998.

34. Keith Middlemass, *Orchestrating Europe: The Informal Politics of European Union 1973–1995* (London: Fontana Press/HarperCollins, 1995).

35. Alan S. Milward (with George Brennan and Federico Romero), *The European Rescue of the Nation State* (London: Routledge, 1992).

36. The term "federal" used in this context has a peculiarly negative connotation in political discourse in Britain. For background, see Middlemass, *Orchestrating Europe.*

37. Stephen George, "The European Union, 1992 and the Fear of 'Fortress Europe,'" in Andrew Gamble and Anthony Payne, *Regionalism and World Order* 1996. n.a. Middlemass, *Orchestrating Europe.*

38. M. Clarke and J. Sharp, "Defence and Security in the New Europe," in David Miliband, ed., *A More Perfect Union?—Britain and the New Europe* (London: Institute of Public Policy Research, 1992); Elisabeth Skoens, "Western Europe: Internationalization of the Arms Industry," in Herbert

Wulf, ed., *Arms Industry Limited* (London: Oxford University Press, 1993), pp. 160–90.

39. Feddersen and Silva, "The Single European Market and the Defence Industry," pp. 13–16.

40. Elisabeth Skoens, "Western Europe: Internationalization of the Arms Industry."

41. CEC, *The challenges facing the European defence-related industry: A contribution for action at European level.*

42. Laurence Martin and John Roper, eds., *Towards a Common Defence Policy* (Paris: European Strategy Group and the Institute for Security Studies of the Western European Union, 1995).

43. White, "Europe Takes First Step."

44. "Competition in Arms" (editorial), *Financial Times*, February 23, 1990.

45. Grosser.

46. Douglas Barrie, "A Minister for Europe," *Flight International*, March 15–21, 1995, pp. 28–29; and Bernard Gray, "Portillo plea to U.S. for two-way arms market." *Financial Times*, May 2, 1996.

47. "American Monsters, European Minnows," *Economist*, January 13, 1996, pp. 63. Commission, *Challenges Facing the European Defence-Related Industry*; "Towards a European Armament Agency," *Military Technology* 18, no. 6 (1994): 10–20.

48. Carol Reed, "European Minds Look to Meet on Mergers," *Jane's Defence Weekly* II, February 23–24, 1993.

49. Richard Cocker, *Thinking the Unthinkable: Think-tanks and the Economic Counterrevolution* (London: Fontana Press, HarperCollins, 1994); Dunne and Smith, "Thatcherism and the UK Defence Industry."

50. David Buchan, "Battle Plan for French Defence Industry," *Financial Times*, February 22, 1996, p. 2; "A French Projection," *Economist*, March 2, 1996, pp. 63.

51. Commission, *Challenges Facing the European Defence-Related Industry.*

52. Ibid.; Walker and Gummett, "Nationalism, Internationalism."

53. Keith Hayward, *European Aerospace Collaboration in Transition Royal*, Whitehall paper 2 (London: United Services Institute for Defence Studies, 1991).

54. David Buchan, "French Big Guns Look for Right Target," *Financial Times*, April 4, 1996, p. 3.

55. Ulrich Albrecht, Peter Lock, and Jonathan Cohen, "Germany—The Reluctant Eurofighter Partner," in Randall Forsberg, ed., *The Arms Production Dilemma—Contraction and Restraint in the World Combat Aircraft Industry* (Cambridge, Mass.: MIT Press, 1994), pp. 177–92.

56. Michael Joseph, *The Arms of Krupp 1587-1968* (London: William Manchester, 1969).

57. Alan Cawson et al., *Hostile Brothers: Competition and Closure in the European Electronics Industry.*

58. SDE, *Statement on the Defences Estimates 1996.*

59. Keith Haywood, *The West German Aerospace Industry and Its Contribution to Western Security,* Whitehall Paper 2 (London: Royal United Services Institute for Defence Studies, 1990), p. 39.

60. Hartley and Cox, *Costs of Non-Europe;* Lovering, "Mixed Blessings."

61. Bernard Gray, "U.S. deal signed to develop military jets."

62. Bernard Gray, "Portillo Plea to U.S. for Two-Way Arms Market." Bernard Gray, "Defence Policy Gives a Nod and a Wink to U.S.," *Financial Times,* May 7, 1996, pp. 6.

63. SDE, *Statement on the Defence Estimates 1996.*

64. Gray, "Defence Policy Gives a Nod"; Bernard Gray, "Eurofighter Programme Leads Defence Bonanza," *Financial Times,* June 24, 1996, p. 6.

65. David Gold, "The Internationalisation of Military Production," *Peace Economics, Peace Science, and Public Policy* 1, no. 3 (1994): 1–12; Richard Samuels, *Rich Nation, Strong Army: National Security and the Technological Transformation of Japan* (Ithaca and London: Cornell University Press, 1994).

66. "France Puts Pressure on Dutch to Pick Tiger," *Jane's Defence Weekly,* April 1, 1995, p. 5.

67. See also Alan Cawson et al., *Hostile Brothers: Competition and Closure in the European Electronics Industry* (Oxford: Clarendon Press, 1990).

68. Barrie, "Minister for Europe."

69. For an analysis of this concept, see Ben Fine, "The Military-Industrial Complex: An Analytic Assessment," *Cyprus Journal of Economics* 6 (1993): 26–51.

14

The Changing Civil-Military Production Mix in Western Europe's Defense Industry

MICHAEL BRZOSKA, PETER WILKE, AND HERBERT WULF

EVEN BEFORE the collapse of the Soviet Union, defense industries in western Europe had come under severe pressure to restructure. Established as predominantly national industries or heavily protected private industries, they had been allowed to become uncompetitive: too small measured by fixed costs for new projects, with too many employees and with high levels of bureaucracy. During the 1980s cost consciousness grew, beginning with the "Levene" reforms in Britain and spreading to other countries such as the Netherlands and Germany. During the 1980s national consolidation of industry was promoted especially by German and British governments, primarily for cost reasons. With the deepening of the European Common Market agreed upon, company managers became enthusiastic about breaking national barriers and creating a (west) European defense industry.

Pressure to change business practices increased at the end of the Cold War, when defense policies were reviewed and procurement budgets decreased. But the end of the Cold War also put some peculiar twists into the readjustment process. West European governments became less willing than before to further the internationalization, or rather Europeanization, of industries. Owing in part to the lobbying activities of industry, strategic insecurity, and the political problems of European integration, they became more inclined again to protect national assets. Governments sent a conflicting message: there would be less money, but the defense industry would be protected to maintain a "critical mass" defense industry or a core industrial defense base of high-technology companies.

Beyond that, governments (with the exception of France until 1996) generally put the planning for adjustments into the hands of company managers. With differing attitudes toward planning vs. markets, west European governments did not want to be burdened with this additional problem. They called on company managers to take the necessary steps. The market should be the criterion for success and failure.

However, claims about free markets in connection with the west European arms industry have to be taken with a grain of salt. Not only is the defense market itself well protected, there is also a dense structure of government support for all kinds of structural, regional, and industrial problems. Support has existed in western Europe for a long time and has become more and more (though far from exclusively) the prerogative of the European Union. In addition, the European Parliament (against the wishes of most governments in the Union) established a special program to help communities and companies to adjust to the defense drawdown: the KONVER program.

Even so, company managers became the most important actors for adjustment. Whatever plans there were—in governments, among unions, or in peace movements—for civil-military conversion remained irrelevant as they all envisaged an increased role for governments. Instead, whatever adjustments were needed to adapt business to the changing conditions, the managers had to initiate by themselves, although in an economic environment with a fair amount of subsidies and regulations.

This chapter sets out to demonstrate to what extent, under these conditions, companies choose to convert or to diversify into civilian markets and how successful they are. Increasing the nonmilitary component in the civilian-military mix is only one option open to company managers when adjusting to reductions in defense markets. This company strategy is selected here for special scrutiny because of its social aspects, above and beyond the narrower business considerations: it can help to cash in earlier investments in defense industry assets, stabilize employment in disadvantaged regions, help further industries that are considered important for future growth, and contribute to political goals, such as confidence building among former adversaries.

The chapter argues that, if stripped of some of its ideological connotations and overly high hopes, and considering some adverse circumstances of the early 1990s, civilian countermoves to defense downsizing have, thus far, been modestly successful in western Europe, albeit with differences among countries. In this process, conversion in the narrow sense of reusing all production factors within an existing plant has been an exception with minor employment effects. Partial reuse of resources, for instance, of persons employed or of technologies available has had more success. This occurred within strategies of diversification of production that changed the civil-military mix of production within corporations. In some cases diversification was the result of the acquisition of civilian business that made little use of the resources formerly used for military production (except equity capital and some management skills).

This partial success has been the result of neither government intervention nor support. It came about mainly because of preconditions in the defense industry itself and a concerted willingness within companies to try to change the civil-military mix. With fewer cuts in public budgets or in a more benign general economic climate, a better outcome may have been possible. It is unlikely that large-scale specific government support would have been more successful. Some specific additional support, though, could have provided arms-producing companies with more incentives for change. In addition, clearer government statements about future procurement decisions would have helped companies in making decisions.

The chapter first sets out the framework for the changes in civil-military production in western Europe in the early 1990s. It then looks into what governments have done to support such change, followed by a discussion of company strategies. The material in these sections then is summarized and generalized to arrive at lessons for future adjustment paths and conclusions on perspectives.

Framework for Civil-Military Mix of Production

With the end of the Cold War, governments in western Europe reconsidered their security and defense policies, beginning with Germany in 1990 (where the process has not yet been finalized) and ending with France in early 1996. All of these defense reviews were carried out within an atmosphere of enormous financial constraint. Some outcomes were uniform, such as drops in military spending, a reorientation toward creation of rapid reaction forces (including deployment to areas outside of the North Atlantic Treaty Organization [NATO]), reductions in the number of armed forces personnel, fewer major weapons systems, and fewer military bases. Other outcomes differed; for example, Belgium, the

Table 14–1   Expenditures on Procurement of Heavy Equipment
(In million 1993 $; figures rounded)

	Average 1985–89	Average 1990–94	1995
Belgium	630	330	250
Denmark	370	430	410
France	7,200	6,700	7,100
Germany, FRG	8,100	5,400	4,000
Greece	770	930	830
Italy	4,100	3,300	3,000
Luxembourg	3	4	5
Netherlands	1,500	1,100	1,000
Norway	640	800	820
Portugal	150	130	320
Spain	1,500	990	1,000
Turkey	720	1,480	2,200
United Kingdom	9,850	7,700	9,600
Sum NATO Europe	*35,600*	*29,300*	*30,500*
United States	89,400	76,500	74,500
Canada	2,100	1,900	2,000

Source: NATO gopher, except France, where estimate is based on NATO Europe average.

Netherlands, and France eliminated compulsory military service while
the German government was not prepared to take this step.

PROCUREMENT BUDGETS

Smaller military budgets translated into fewer orders for defense producers. Procurement budgets in western European countries went
down considerably in the early 1990s. (See Table 14–1.)

Between the late 1980s and the early 1990s, the reduction in spending
on heavy equipment as recorded by NATO was 18 percent. This compares to 14 percent for the United States. Initially, spending on procurement of heavy weapons went down faster than military spending in total.
The share of heavy equipment in total military expenditures dropped to
a low for west European NATO member countries of 15 percent in 1992,
from 16.6 percent for the period 1985 to 1990. But after 1993 the share
increased again to 17.3 percent in 1995. Although figures for 1995 are preliminary, they show a slight increase in procurement spending.

Reductions were far from uniform. They were the largest in Germany, followed by Italy and the Netherlands. Some countries, such as
Norway, increased procurement of heavy equipment. The United King-

Table 14–2 Exports of Newly Produced Major Weapons (SIPRI trend indicator expressed in 1990 $U.S. millions)

	Average 1985–89	Average 1990–94	1995
Austria	112	26	33
Belgium	5	6	161
Denmark	18	34	0
Finland	2	8	22
France	2,546	951	612
Germany, FRG	908	912	1,070
Greece	0	9	0
Italy	475	320	316
Luxembourg	0	0	0
Netherlands	281	202	211
Norway	0	6	0
Portugal	0	0	0
Spain	184	76	34
Sweden	189	74	220
Switzerland	132	206	132
Turkey	0	0	0
United Kingdom	1,497	925	769
Sum Western Europe	*6,348*	*3,758*	*3,580*
United States	8,553	7,948	6,743
Canada	127	127	290

Source: SIPRI database. Supplied by the SIPRI arms trade project for this chapter.

dom, the largest spender in western Europe, first reduced spending but slowly increased it again in the mid-1990s. For France, there was little change in the first half of the 1990s. It was not until spring of 1996 that President Jacques Chirac announced far-reaching changes in French defense policy, including major reductions in procurement spending.[1]

In the final analysis, these reductions in expenditures on heavy equipment, as defined by NATO, are smaller than many observers thought likely when the Cold War ended. Still, their effects should not be underestimated. Arms production is concentrated in sectors with fairly high productivity increases in the early 1990s. Just keeping production at constant capacity requires more than 3 percent annual growth in demand.

EXPORTS

Weapons exports from west European countries also have declined. In fact, the statistics in Table 14–2, based on figures for exports of newly produced major weapons (exports from surplus stocks of the armed forces are not included), suggest that downward trends for exports were even more pronounced than those for domestic procurement. National statistics give a somewhat different perspective—for instance, arms exports according to British statistics remained constant between 1990 and 1994; German and Dutch arms exports even increased during the 1990s as compared to earlier periods; a constant trend is reported by Sweden.[2] However, as has been emphasized, only a small fraction of exports were from orders for new weapons in the defense industry in some countries. For example, not a single major weapon system was exported by the German industry between 1992 and 1994.[3] Arms exports definitely have been sharply reduced in France and Sweden.[4] France, the most important western arms exporter in the late 1980s, has seen exports reduced to less than half, according to official statistics.[5] For Italy, reduction is on a similar scale.[6]

The figures in Table 14–2 suggest a share of exports in total production of about 15 percent for all of western Europe. National figures, which include deliveries of components, light weapons, and so on, suggest a substantially higher share. Still, it is obvious that the share of exports in total production generally has declined. While available statistics imply that the main reason is the general decline of the arms export markets, closer scrutiny reveals that west European producers have most likely lost market shares. If the fall in exports for the Soviet Union/Russia is discounted, since much of the Soviet exports were not paid for and thus given away for free, the share of producers for western Europe has decreased. Their markets have been picked up mostly by U.S. producers.

Because of higher research and development spending by the government, larger production runs, and more aggressive political marketing, U.S. producers have increasingly gained a competitive edge vis-à-vis their west European competitors. Unless the trend toward high spending on military research and development (R&D) in the United States is reversed, it is likely that west European producers will become even less competitive in the future.

LOSSES IN EMPLOYMENT

One measure of the reduction in defense production is the change in employment. Companies had to react to shrinking markets by downsizing capacities. In fact, employment downsizing was larger than the figures for demand reduction imply, owing to earlier overcapacities and the continuing productivity increases.[7]

According to our estimate (see table 14–3) employment in defense production went down from about 1.5 million in 1985 to just over 900,000 jobs in 1996. Approximately 590,000 jobs were lost between 1985 and 1995 in western Europe.[8] This reduction of about 40 percent of employment in the defense industry of western Europe is approximately the same proportion as in the United States and in Russia—although the total number of jobs lost in western Europe is much smaller.

MODELS OF DEFENSE PRODUCTION IN WESTERN EUROPE

The reduction in military demand, both domestic and external, occurred in industries not unfamiliar with such events. Many of the major arms producers have histories going back to the nineteenth or early twentieth century and have experienced drastic plunges in demand after both the first and second world wars as well as the resurgence of arms production in the 1930s and between the 1950s and 1980s. Even between 1950 and 1990 industry did not experience unchanging high growth rates. Although cyclical developments are not unfamiliar to the industry, scenarios for the short- and medium-term future do not allow for prediction of a return to previous levels of turnover.

This fact alone does not make companies in Europe distinct from companies in the United States. But the lessons learned, and the policies adopted, differ somewhat between the United States and western European states, with wide variation among the latter.[9] The following models can be distinguished[10]: (1) warfare and welfare and (2) the technology pool.

Warfare and Welfare

In France, governments have pursued a dual course of promoting military and civilian technology simultaneously, despite the fact that the sectors remain institutionally separated.[11] This occurred under strict government control from the early 1960s on. The strategy is closely linked to the Gaullist project of building strong, independent French industry and armed forces at the same time.[12] For example, military R&D is prioritized but is implemented in a manner that helps encourage strategic civilian industries. Both sectors, civil and military, are heavily protected and have to compete internally. Thus the high cost of developing an independent nuclear weapons force was matched with the development of a large nuclear power sector. Similarly, the aerospace sector was heavily subsidized in both the civilian and the military field. This was done with one company in the military field (Dassault)

Table 14-3 Employment in Arms Production in West European Countries[a]

	1985	1986	1987	1988	1989	1990	1991	1992	1993	1994	1995
United Kingdom	470	460	450	490	430	440	380	390	320	310	290
France	340	340	330	320	310	300	290	280	270	260	250
Germany	307	280	260	240	220	200	190	180	160	140	120
Italy	86	80	80	80	80	80	70	60	50	45	40
Spain	66	80	90	100	100	100	80	60	50	40	30
Sweden	35	35	35	30	30	30	30	30	30	30	30
Turkey	20	20	20	25	25	25	25	30	30	30	30
Switzerland	30	30	30	25	25	25	25	25	20	20	15
Netherlands	18	18	18	20	20	20	18	18	18	15	15
Greece	15	15	15	15	15	15	15	15	15	15	15
Belgium	35	35	30	30	25	25	20	15	15	12	10
Finland	10	10	10	10	10	10	10	10	10	10	10
Norway	15	15	15	10	10	10	10	10	10	10	10
Portugal	10	10	10	10	10	10	10	10	10	10	10
Denmark	6	6	6	6	7	7	6	6	5	5	5
Austria	8	8	6	6	5	5	5	4	4	3	3
W. Europe, in millions	1.47	1.44	1.41	1.42	1.32	1.30	1.18	1.14	1.02	0.96	0.88

[a] Estimate of direct and indirect employees, in 1,000s.

Source: Bonn International Center for Conversion, *Conversion Survey 1996* (Oxford: Oxford University Press, 1996), pp. 272–3.

and one in the civilian (Aérospatiale); they cross-fertilized each other through subcontractor work, employment of common suppliers, and technology transfer. The strategy was built on arms exports to finance a good part of the public investment.[13] It was successful in cases where the link between civilian and military activities was strong and encouraged competitiveness. However, the model ran into severe financial problems when exports decreased. In addition, in some sectors, such as shipbuilding and automobiles, the link between civilian and military production was never strong and deteriorated when these civilian industries entered severe crises in the 1970s. Moreover, it is not compatible with the general trend of economic liberalization that was discernible in France throughout the mid-1980s. But despite its problems, the different French governments have clung to this approach and thus had to make adaptations. Consolidation is now promoted in aerospace between Dassault and Aérospatiale, and the shipbuilding and automobile sectors have to be severely reduced.

Other governments following this approach, which is typical for an industrial latecomer with strong military-strategic aspirations, were the Spanish in the late 1970s and early 1980s and the Italian in the early 1980s.

Technology Pool
A completely different philosophy with a similar outcome was developed in Germany in the 1950s. With domestic arms production forbidden between 1945 and 1954, the industry was built mostly on the expertise found in existing civilian companies and military R&D personnel and entrepreneurs returning home with some of their exotic projects in Egypt, Argentina, India, Spain, and Portugal.[14] Many of the German companies had a military past but had successfully competed in civilian markets. Thus the first tank, the Leopard I, was designed by car manufacturers, Porsche and Daimler-Benz, and produced by a manufacturer of locomotives, Krauss-Maffei, using a wide range of components found in civilian markets, such as gearbox elements and suspensions. Submarines, the U-206 for the domestic market and the highly competitive U-209 for export markets, were designed by an old hand, U. Gabler, who had designed submarines for the Wehrmacht that were built at Germany's largest civilian shipyard, HDW. In aerospace, the process went even further. Large amounts of public money were spent on military R&D projects, most notably V/STOL aircraft, which never became operational. Still, the industry gained enough expertise to participate later in both civilian projects, such as Airbus, as well as military ones, such as Tornado and Eurofighter. One element in this strategy is *spin-in* of technology from the civilian to the military side; another is

flexibility in production. Companies were encouraged to engage in both civilian and military markets; in fact, the defense ministry tried to split projects and give parts of a program to a number of successful, predominantly civilian companies. A problem with this approach is that it produces competitive military products in only small sectors that benefit from expertise found in civilian sectors, such as tanks with emphasis on mobility and small ships. Since competitiveness is otherwise low, this approach requires a high level of protectionism.

Other countries where this model can be found include the Netherlands and Sweden.

Similarities in outcome between these two models include a high level of government protection of defense production as well as a low degree of separation between the military and the civilian sectors. This lack of a "firewall" between the two sectors is most noticeable in the "technology pool" model, but also marks the "welfare and warfare" model despite its institutional separations.[15] While there are military specifications, special security requirements, and the like, there is much less red tape. The lower degree of separation may be possible only when there is a fairly high degree of government confidence that industry will play by the rules. In the French model this is largely established through personal relations in an elite society and a constant exchange of personnel (the so-called armament engineers) between industry and the government procurement agency, DGA. In Germany the basis is a general corporatist spirit that permeates the industry.

The British defense industry is more difficult to categorize. Its initial phase, in the late 1930s and during World War II, was driven by an outright war economy, similar to that of the United States. But since World War II British industry, both civilian and military, has been in secular decline. Various governments have tried to stop this decline, with little success.[16] For the defense sector this has meant frequent fundamental changes—nationalization in the 1970s, comparatively free market in the 1980s, a return to more protectionism in the 1990s. Only the most robust organizations have survived. Typically these have been either highly specialized military producers, who had a competitive edge throughout, such as Vickers Shipbuilders and Vosper Thornycroft, or companies with a lot of flexibility and adaptability or a civilian-military mix of products. The government, in order to increase the competitiveness of what remained of the industry, has cut through much red tape, so that separation between military and civilian production is weaker than what is generally found in the United States, yet stronger than in other west European countries.

GENERAL BUSINESS SITUATION

Adaptation to reduced military demand occurred at a time when economic fundamentals were not favorable. Thus economic growth was slow in the early 1990s, decreasing from an annual growth rate of 3.0 to −0.5 percent in the European Union countries between 1990 and 1993, while improving in the United States from 1.3 to 2.2 percent during the same period.[17] Unemployment ran high and capacity utilization was low. Public sector demand did not expand much, with governments under heavy pressure to cut deficits. The early 1990s were not a good time for proposals of large-scale public investment, such as in mass transport, or solar energy. At the same time, globalization of production rose, increasing the level of competition.

Another factor that made any kind of change in the civil-military mix difficult in the early 1990s was the prevailing attitude among management consultants. Contrary to earlier times, companies were advised to stay in and expand their core business. There was also an emphasis on overhauling all administrative and production procedures through business reengineering. But generally this did not include any advice to try to find new markets.

CONVERSION AND DIVERSIFICATION

One more remark is in order here on the use of terms. The empirical emphasis in this chapter is on the changing civilian-military mix within corporations. This can, but must not, mean that the same people work first on military and then on civilian products with the same machinery under the same roof. In fact, this direct switch will seldom occur, not only when there is a shift from military to civilian production, but also when there is a shift from one product to another within civilian production. Competition today is such that almost-appropriate machinery and near-optimal production methods are not viable. Personnel are a somewhat different matter, at least in most countries of western Europe. People can be and are being retrained. There is no such "species" as a typical defense worker; most employees are trained in common professions (and have acquired skills) that are found in civilian branches of industry too.[18] The costs of retraining must be compared with the generally high costs of firing people in an ongoing business.

The situation is different at the middle level of management. Even without an administrative "firewall" between it, military and civilian production is so different that a change in the mix requires major changes, both in the way production is organized and in know-how of personnel. In the civilian sector marketing is different, costs are more important, there are generally more customers to take care of, and so on. Thus, very often, marketing and after-sales people have to be brought in even in companies that can produce competitively.

Beyond bringing in additional competence, it is not much of a step to bring in a whole company that is already marketing a civilian product. Sometimes this has an effect on existing resources (with the exception of equity capital). The exchange of experience between employees of the old and the acquired divisions often produces positive results.

In short, we are skeptical of the traditional approach to military-civilian defense downsizing that puts emphasis on a narrow concept of conversion as a complete reorientation of all resources available to a corporation to civilian production. This approach ignores the competitive pressure of today's market economy, which leads managers to seek for outlets of their products whether they are civilian or military, and which requires optimal production processes that cannot be achieved by clinging to existing production factors.[19] As long as some of the resources are reused in the transformation from military to civilian production, we are willing to speak of conversion, regardless of whether this takes place through buying in competence or companies.

Ultimately, therefore, for us the yardstick for successful conversion is the larger economy, not the corporation. The question in the end is whether labor released from defense production finds gainful employment, in the converted company or elsewhere, and whether skills and technology are usefully reused. Economic regions are most affected by employment or unemployment, while technology issues are a national and, increasingly, a European Union matter.

No west European government has had a specific industrial conversion support policy of more than marginal importance. Specific defense industry conversion policy instruments were mostly symbolic. At best, they provided seed funds for additional activities, but they were not effective economic tools in themselves. They were not capable of providing relief from the negative effects of defense industry downsizing. On the other hand, western Europe has a diversified public support infrastructure for depressed regions and sectors. Companies and regions affected by defense downsizing are able to draw on these funds on the same conditions that all companies and regions can.

Political Response: National and Supranational Support for Defense Industry Downsizing and Civilian Reorientation

The political and economic context for defense industries in western Europe is influenced by two factors, the end of the Cold War, which considerably reduced threats and threat perceptions, and international competition and limited defense budgets, which have forced all west European governments to reevaluate national concepts of independent defense industries. The existing fragmentation of defense markets in Europe offers no answer to the technological and economic challenges of the future.

The need for intensified cooperation by giving up the national focus, by avoiding duplication of projects, and by merging companies is not a new discovery of the 1990s; the subject is as old as NATO. Various bodies (Euro-centered or transatlantic) have made numerous rational and sensible proposals. The latest initiatives have been taken by the West European Union, to create the West European Armaments Group (WEAG), which eventually should function as a common defense procurement agency and by the Commission of the European Communities, strongly advocating once more the economic, technical, and political requirements to ensure the existence of a future defense industry in the European Union.[20]

Despite the continuity of such proposals, in practice they remained largely political rhetoric. The facts speak for themselves: in 1993 west European defense companies were engaged in four main battle tank programs (compared to one in the United States); 16 types of armored combat vehicles (three in the United States); seven types of diesel-powered submarines (none in the United States); and eight types of air-to-air missiles (four in the United States).[21] Similar lists circulated at least 10 years ago and underpinned calls to streamline west European procurement policy.[22] Although most of these programs are too small to flourish, they are too large to vanish as governments continue to insist on their national companies' share in development and production and as long as governments pay for the projects. The ability of defense companies to rationalize and consolidate their business, according to the commission of the European Union, is restricted by the following five factors: (1) lack of consent of governments to allow for cross-border restructuring; (2) considerable differences in the relation between companies and governments in the member countries; (3) lack of harmonized arms export policies; (4) difference in national requirements of defense equipment (including timing and strategic concepts); and (5) lack of transnational legal structures to recognize international partnerships as eligible for funding under national research budgets.[23]

A major obstacle to cooperative development, production, and procurement is now, as in the past, the overarching goal of maintaining, at the national level, the highly developed scientific, technological, and industrial capabilities for the full range of conventional weapons. Governments as well as academic proponents of a more effective and competitive west European defense industry do not recognize the contradiction in holding on to concepts of minimum national capacities in almost all areas of conventional weapons technology and at the same time calling for overcoming fragmented markets and duplication of projects.

Political and economic concepts for defense industries in post–Cold War western Europe aim at divergent goals:

1. To manage downsizing with the lowest possible economic pains and social disruption;

2. To restructure different nationally orientated defense producers in order to create a competitive common defense industrial base in Europe;

3. To maintain some defense technology capabilities, with the level depending on the available R&D and procurement funds;

4. To use prior investment in defense R&D and technologies in civilian markets (spin-off).

As far as conversion and downsizing are concerned, in most countries the shrinking of defense industrial capacities between 1989 and 1996 was managed without larger economic programs especially designed and used for the military sector. Although defense-related employment has fallen substantially, no single west European state has introduced an economic conversion program on a national level. The responses to defense industry downsizing have been different in all countries, but the practical outcomes were quite similar.[24] Examples will demonstrate this for France, Germany, Great Britain, and Italy. These four nations account for 90 percent of the defense equipment production in western Europe, estimated at $65 billion of total turnover, or about 3 percent of all industrial output.

Out of this group of four countries, reductions have been most severe in Germany and Great Britain. And even in these countries defense industry–related economic problems emerged only in some heavily defense-dependent regions and were small—compared, for example, to the general level of unemployment. This fact explains why the pressure for national programs was never very strong.

NATIONAL POLICIES

In Germany, the conservative government of Helmut Kohl always argued that conversion was not on his government's agenda. Defense-producing companies are privately owned, and the government has taken a hands-off approach. This argumentation is in line with the more general debate on economic policy and the role of the state in economic policy in Germany. However, the government supported the national restructuring of defense industrial capacities by favoring national champions with major procurement orders and also stepped in when single companies were in economic difficulty. The German participation in the Eurofighter combat aircraft program and part of the navy shipbuilding programs is an attempt to maintain a critical mass of a national defense industrial base and to secure jobs. The dominant role within the German defense industry of Daimler-Benz (with its subsidiary DASA in aircraft manufacturing) is due to coordinated action between politics in Bonn and business decisions in the Stuttgart company headquarters.

The German case is unique because shrinking of defense industrial capacities happened parallel to German unification and the de facto deindustrializing of east Germany. Compared to the loss of more than 80 percent of the industrial capacities in East Germany and the effects of unemployment of up to 50 percent in some regions, loss of about 100,000 jobs in defense production seemed less important, if not marginal. Unprecedented financial transactions with West-East transfer of more than $100 billion each year since 1990 are going into labor market programs, subsidies, and investments in public infrastructure in east Germany.

Defense industry conversion was of low priority on the political agenda. Most companies managed the process of downsizing capacities in a comparatively short time. More problematic and politically important were questions related to base closures and, in particular, reuse of military facilities. Some of the new German Länder introduced limited regional conversion programs. All of them are products of Social Democratic–led governments that felt more obliged to act (even if sometimes only symbolically) with public programs in a desperate labor market situation.

One rare example of a regional defense industry conversion program has been implemented in the state of Bremen. The government of Bremen initiated, in 1989, a small but ambitious regional conversion program (partly financed by the European Union) with a budget of only $11 million. Although the program is designed to offer incentives in strategically placed high-technology branches, the effects have been limited. The bankruptcy of one large company, the Bremen-based shipyard and machine tool company Bremer Vulkan in 1996, more than wiped out the positive effects of the conversion program. Bremer Vulkan was the largest company in both the civilian and the defense area in Bremen. While the defense part remained profitable and will be sold to the highest bidder, civilian shipbuilding incurred large losses and will be severely downsized.

In France, the defense industry is closely related to the state. In fact, the state still controls 80 percent of production of military equipment and supports companies with an active arms export policy. French ambitions in striving for maximum national autonomy and resistance against U.S. hegemony resulted after 1989 in a paradoxical situation in that in its arms industry policy, the government did not react to the changed security environment at the end of the Cold War. "France's defense industry, defense policy and armed forces suddenly found themselves out of step with strategic and economic realities. The most logical reaction would have been a rapid realigning and reduction of the defense effort (with force restructuring, a new estimation of requirements and reductions or abandoning of certain programs), but nothing of the sort happened."[25]

While proponents of a strong and independent French defense industrial base might have hoped to be able to hold on to existing capacities with the strong backing of public funds, financial constraints led to and facilitated the conservative government's radical and abrupt shift in policy in 1996. With a time lag of about five years, the French government has announced its intention to implement a policy of reduction and adjustment, deemphasizing the role of the defense industry.

The management scandal at GIAT, with losses of more than $1 billion in a deal to export Leclerq main battle tanks to the United Arab Emirates, probably will speed up a process of restructuring in the defense industry. This process is focused on creating larger players in key business areas (by merging the big companies in the aerospace and electronic sectors) at the expense of small and medium-sized companies. The defense industry and government policy of favoring the key defense technology producers in France has been described as "nuclear structure" with a heavy hard core and a barren periphery.[26]

As a consequence of this policy of delayed reduction, few incentives for conversion have been offered to French companies. The national conversion program is limited to about $50 million as a counterpart to the European Union's KONVER program.[27]

In the United Kingdom, the conservative government has pursued a systematic policy of privatization of defense enterprises and emphasized, in its so-called Levene reform, international competition to get the best products at competitive prices. Without regard for the interest of British arms producers, the government wanted to opt for the most competitive offer and tendered procurement orders internationally.[28] However, recently there has been a resumption of the practice of favoring British companies.

The example of British Aerospace shows that for the major industrial players, defense industry conversion at the factory level has not been an attractive alternative recently. British Aerospace's reaction to the Levene reform was to diversify into civilian markets. The most striking activity was its short-lived acquisition of the British car producer Rover. After running into severe problems both with Rover and in the civilian commuter aircraft market, British Aerospace sold nonprofitable civilian parts of the company and concentrated on its core profitable military business.[29]

Government-sponsored conversion efforts and programs exist in Great Britain, similar to those in Germany, but on a regional and local level.

In Italy, the post–Cold War decline in military expenditures has led to an increased interest in conversion by major Italian arms producers. But no consistent industrial, plant-level conversion strategy has been formulated. Instead, an increasing concentration at the main contractor level has taken place and the state is now, more than ever, in a position to control military-industrial activities. The number of defense-dependent companies and jobs has decreased from 300 companies with 65,000 jobs in 1979 to 26 companies with 30,000 jobs in 1996.[30] The main actor is the state-owned company Finmeccanica (part of the IRI group), which has integrated during the last three years a number of smaller, previously independent companies.

Fiat is the main private company still involved in military production. This is less the result of active conversion than the withdrawal of private firms from this market. Conversion programs exist on a local and regional level connected to the KONVER program of the European Union.[31]

The 1996 report entitled "The Challenges Facing the European Defence-Related Industry," published by the European Union Commissioner for Industrial Policy, Martin Bangemann, concludes:

Conversion of military into civilian-oriented production "at factory level" is not considered a feasible strategy by most companies. Apart from the huge investment costs and difficulties of access for newcomers to established civilian markets, conversion is hindered by the difference between, on the one side, production of defense goods which is driven by technology and government specifications and, on the other side, civilian markets which are mainly driven by price with marketing playing a major role. However, conversion in the sense of redeploying a company's R&D base from defense-oriented work to a technically related field has proved practicable for a number of companies with established non-defense activities.[32]

KONVER and the Structural Funds of the European Union

All European Union governments have a complex system of economic and labor market policies that can and also have been used to manage the effects of shrinking defense budgets for the military industry. These programs are larger and more important than the more experimental, regionally focused conversion funds. An often-mentioned argument against a conversion-specific program is that the regular programs are sufficiently flexible to tackle defense industry requirements too.

On the insistence of the European Parliament and with the backing of the commission, the resistance of national governments toward a special conversion fund was overcome and the KONVER program was put in place in 1994. This program, designed to assist regions in which defense-related activities are concentrated, is comparatively small, with about $800 million for the period 1993 to 1999. The program is aimed specifically at compensating for job losses due to both military base closures and defense industry downsizing.

> The purpose of KONVER is to provide support for economic diversification in areas heavily dependent on defense-related activities through the encouragement of commercially viable activities not related to defense.... The eligible areas are small geographic regions in which actual or announced defense-related job losses total 1000 or more since 1990.... A full range of conversion measures including the financing of both tangible and intangible investment in alternative economic activities, the modernization of infrastructure in relation to the economic regeneration strategy of the area concerned, and measures in favor of the environment and tourism can be financed through KONVER.[33]

By far most of the money spent within the KONVER program has gone into base closure projects and not into defense industry adjustments. Comparing the quantitative magnitudes of KONVER to other

European Union programs, priorities are quite obvious. KONVER's $800 million for a seven-year period is but a fraction of 1 percent of the structural funds. The European Union structural funds have a volume of Ecu 148 billion ($185 billion) for the period 1994 to 1999. Among those, two are particularly relevant for and can be taken advantage of by the defense industry: the European Regional Development Fund (ERDF) with Ecu 118 billion (almost $150 billion) and the European Social Fund (ESF), with Ecu 17 billion ($21 billion).

A specific labor market instrument, the Community Initiative ADAPT, is also available for defense industry adjustment. Assistance is available for measures that help workers threatened with unemployment due to industrial change to adapt. Emphasis is placed on improving qualifications and creating employment opportunities for affected employees. KONVER is mainly of interest in those regions that are not eligible for assistance under the structural funds instruments. For the larger industrial players in the defense industry, KONVER cannot offer much in the way of real incentives. To give an example from the civilian car industry in Germany: For the establishment of a new production facility in Saxony, Volkswagen received roughly $600 million between 1992 and 1996 as a subsidy funded from the European Regional Development Fund. This subsidy alone is more than the whole of what Germany is to receive from the KONVER program.

Although economic problems (especially unemployment) loom large in defense-dependent regions, from the perspective of the top companies and prime contractors, downsizing has been implemented fairly smoothly. The main burden of the drawdown has affected small and medium-sized companies, the second- and third-tier suppliers and subcontractors. Whether a large-scale, defense-industry-specific public support program would have resulted in more conversion at the factory level, would have facilitated the process of diversification into civil markets, or would have resulted in speeding up downsizing remains an open question and would have depended on the criteria of such support.

Company Reactions to the Demand Decline

Company strategies to cope with the decline in demand were not uniform; during the late 1980s and early 1990s management reacted with a variety of different strategies. Two basic approaches can be distinguished; companies either tried to stabilize (and in some rare cases expand) their market share or alternatively they tried to withdraw, partly or totally, from arms production.[34]

STABILIZATION STRATEGIES

National and International Mergers, Takeovers,
and the Formation of New Companies

Mergers on a national level and expansion through the acquisition of other companies within the arms industry are not new phenomena, but it seems that they have taken place recently at an accelerated rate. They continue to take place, especially in the European aircraft industry, which has evolved from dozens of companies to basically one or two major companies in each of the large west European countries. Compared to the large mergers in the defense sector in the United States, it seems that "Europe's defense industry suffers from too many companies, too much capacity and too many workers."[35] Cross-border mergers and international takeovers in the defense sector are relatively new trends that have intensified over the last few years and are a reaction to shrinking domestic markets. In terms of mergers, the largest producers—including GEC, Rolls-Royce, and British Aerospace (United Kingdom), Thomson, Matra and Aérospatiale (France), DASA and its subsidiaries (FRG)—have sought to form new international companies. In a number of cases, such cooperation resulted in the dominance of certain west European market sectors by individual companies. However, U.S.-style megamergers of the largest companies into new companies have not occurred yet.

Strategic Alliances and Industrial Cartels

Not all international cooperation leads to the formation of new companies or takeovers. So-called strategic alliances between companies may increase the probability of securing military contracts in an increasingly uncertain market, without sacrificing company autonomy. Major actors who once would have bid alone instead submit joint bids for contracts. This form of company behavior has a longer history than mergers between arms-producing companies—indeed, in major programs, such as the Eurofighter and in helicopter and missile development and production, collaboration has become a way of life and with the decision to spend more money on new airborne cruise missiles in the United Kingdom, two likely realignments are taking place: British Aerospace and Matra, part of France's Lagardère plan to merge their missile divisions into the largest European missile company. This move might affect DASA and Aérospatiale's plans for merger or alignment in missile development. This trend in the aerospace sector is absent in vehicle, artillery, or ship production, though.

Producing Weapons Not Affected by Arms Control and Budget Cuts
Not all programs are affected by arms control and budget cuts. Reductions in traditional areas of military budget, especially investments in weapons platforms, may be compensated for by high technology. Producers of military electronics, telecommunications, and data processing equipment—often key technologies in modernization programs—are less affected than companies making the platforms.

Increased Exports
While the export of major conventional weapons has been shrinking, some European companies nevertheless remained major exporters of weapons, partly at the expense of other companies. However, the overall export market cannot compensate for reduced domestic procurement. Thus compensating for lost business in the domestic market by intensifying exports is not a viable strategy for the whole industry.

ADJUSTMENT STRATEGIES

Layoffs and Shrinkage
Several of the strategies just mentioned involve reductions in employment. While the practice of "hire and fire" is more common in the United States, where tens of thousands of employees have been given notice, western Europe has experienced this, with a time lag, as well. Almost no major arms producer did not lay off large numbers of employees. As a result (as stated previously) about 40 percent of all defense jobs were lost during the last few years. GIAT in France is such an example of most recent employment reductions without much attempt to find civilian alternatives. GIAT has announced its intention to reduce its labor force from 12,400 to fewer than 9,700 employees in 1996 alone.

Sale of Production Facilities
In addition to layoffs, some companies have sold their arms production facilities (or subsidiaries thereof) or considered plant closures. The most prominent examples are the sale of the Dutch Philips arms production facilities, operating in several countries, to Thomson of France, and Krupp's divestment in defense production in Germany. In Great Britain, both Thorn EMI and Ferranti Signal were sold or dissolved and sold in units. Major sales in Italy included EFIM's defense activities (Agusta, Oto Melara) purchased by Finmeccanica within the IRI group. Other companies that want to remain in the defense business, such as Oerlikon Bührle of Switzerland or British Aerospace, have decided to

sell off arms production subsidiaries or have closed several plants to downsize defense production capacities.

Diversification or Conversion into Civil Production

Arms-producing firms are responding to the market situation with two types of diversification strategy. The first is to reduce dependence on arms contracts by acquiring civilian-oriented companies. A typical recent example is the German artillery producer, Rheinmetall, which acquired enterprises in the automobile sector. This diversification strategy is the opposite of the concentration on core business strategy.

The second concept attempts to convert production capacities from military to civilian production. Few companies actually have been able to convert arms production to nonmilitary production facilities. Naturally, there is no general rule for the effectiveness of such processes, and the record shows that both failures and successes have occurred. One of the most successful examples for a long-term conversion strategy in a large defense company is the German tank producer Krauss-Maffei. During the 1980s Krauss-Maffei was one of the most important producers of main battle tanks in Europe; it sold 7,000 tanks, among them Leopard 1, Leopard 2, and Gepard, in more than 12 nations. Out of 5,000 employees 3,500 worked on military contracts.

In reaction to decreasing defense orders, Krauss-Maffei decided in the mid-1980s to change priorities toward a diversification strategy into civilian markets. The military share in turnover decreased from 66 percent in 1986 to 20 percent in 1995. The company introduced a series of new technologies and products in the field of plastic forming machines and extruders and also has been successful in increasing business in automation technology and general metalworking machinery.[36] Employment in the Krauss-Maffei group remained more or less stable during this time. However, on a workplace level, there have been fluctuations in personnel. Part of the employment increase that compensated for jobs lost in defense production resulted from buying smaller civilian companies engaged in interesting market segments and with special technological know-how.

Disarmament-Related Diversification

Also of interest are areas that emerge as a result of arms control and disarmament. Dismantlement and destruction of weapons have become interesting and increasing markets for some defense firms. West European companies have worked not only in their own domestic markets but to a limited extent also have worked on disarmament-related international projects, such as munitions dismantlement or fissile material

Table 14-4 Performance of West European Arms-Producing Companies (comparison of performance from 1990 to 1994)

Number of Companies	Type of Performance	Defense Sales	Civilian Sales
15	"downsizers"	minus	minus
19	"converters"	minus	plus
8	"expanders"	plus	plus or na
6	"terminators"	nil	N/A

Note: na = not applicable.
Source: Based on tables A14.1–A14.4 in the appendix (SIPRI company data bank).

disposition, in Russia and other countries of the Commonwealth of Independent States. However, high-flying hopes for stable demand for disarmament technologies especially by smaller companies in East Germany have not materialized. After a short time in dismantling weapons of the former East German army, many of these companies are facing severe economic problems. Once again companies such as Buck Inpar Pinnow, Spreewerke Luebben or Mittenwalder Gerätebau must find new markets outside the area of weapons dismantlement.

A review of the largest companies in western Europe—those among the top 100 producers in the Organization for Economic Cooperation and Development (OECD) Countries and developing countries—illustrates that most companies have tried to apply a mixture of these eight strategies. The majority of companies have lost defense business. Table 14–4 illustrates that:

• Fifteen companies lost both in defense and civilian sales. The management downsized capacities and reduced employment substantially. Apparently this policy was profitable for the companies: only two of these companies recorded losses in 1994 while all other companies in this group made a profit.[37]

• Nineteen companies converted or diversified into civilian business. While their defense sales went down, they could increase their civilian turnover—not always on a large scale. Some of the companies in this group recorded high losses in 1994; among them were companies with a high defense dependency, such as Thomson and GIAT (France) and Eidgenössische Rüstungsbetriebe (Switzerland). Other companies with huge losses were the public enterprises INI (Spain) and IRI (Italy).

- Three large new defense conglomerates were formed between 1990 and 1994 by concentrating on defense production and purchasing defense subsidiaries: Celsius in Sweden, Lagardère in France, and Eurocopter, a French/German helicopter company. In addition to these companies, defense sales increased in five companies in the United Kingdom and in Germany.

- Six companies that were among the top 100 in the world in 1990 have disappeared or given up their defense production completely: EFIM in Italy: the defense production was taken over by Finmeccanica when the large public enterprise filed for bankruptcy; Hachette of France, which merged with Matra in 1992, sold its defense interest concentrated in Matra to Lagardère, Bofors/Nobel of Sweden, which was purchased by Celsius; Thorn EMI of the United Kingdom and Ferranti Signal of Italy—both sold in units; and Hawker Siddely, taken over by BTR.

Factors Shaping Success and Failure

Detailed studies of countries and individual companies indicate that a host of factors, almost universal and not west European–specific, can be considered responsible for the mixture of success and failure in finding more civilian business. We shall consider eight prominent factors.

GENERAL ECONOMIC ENVIRONMENT

Obviously it is easier to find more civilian business in a growing economy than when demand is going down or in an outright recession. Depending on the market reach of the relevant producers, the regional, national, or international economy may be the relevant category. Regional economic health often offers alternatives to company-based approaches in that resources, such as skilled labor, can be utilized in other companies.[38]

INDUSTRY

In some industrial branches barriers to entry are lower than in others. Also, differences between civilian and military "business cultures" and relations among R&D, production, and marketing are at least partially specific to industries.[39] In aerospace industry, for instance, civil-military interchange and synergies seem to be less rigid than in automobiles or electronics, where civilian markets are mostly mass markets.

ACTOR ACTIVITY

Case studies prove that, in many countries, the willingness of owners, managements, and workers (including their unions) to take often-unknown risks is the crucial factor. Conversion often requires extensive retraining, retooling, and reconsideration of management structures. While "business reengineering" through business reorganization is rather common, managements in defense companies especially are often reluctant to pursue this course. To owners, managers, and even those workers who still are employed, a smaller business in traditional defense markets may look more secure than a risky reorganization aimed at increasing civilian business.

PREVIOUS CIVIL-MILITARY MIX

Companies that already have had experience in civilian markets have fewer difficulties coping than those with a dominating defense culture. German companies, for instance, were privileged in this sense by the government's earlier decision to insist on a mix of civilian and defense production, while some French companies were hampered by their historic orientation toward or even exclusive focus on defense production.

DEGREE OF GOVERNMENT REGULATION

The degree of government regulation is closely related to the civil-military mix. Enterprises under strict government control, either because of being run as arsenals, or because of extensive regulation of arms production activities, have a harder time adjusting to civilian markets than companies already used to more competitive environments.

INSECURITY ABOUT DEFENSE MARKET DECLINE

Even now there is no general agreement about the midterm future of defense markets. Companies remain hopeful for a return of these markets. In western Europe, this insecurity is confounded by the insecurity about the development of a possible western European market, including more common rules on arms exports.

OWNERSHIP

Two-thirds of arms production in western Europe occurs in privately owned companies, although state ownership is still predominant in

France, Italy, and Spain.[40] Defense research and development facilities are predominantly government owned, especially in France and the United Kingdom, where large-scale nuclear research occurs, although most work is conducted in private companies in countries such as Sweden and Germany. Government-owned companies often face specific difficulties in expanding civilian business. Administrative regulations limit their access to civilian markets and require them to behave in certain ways. Specific company cultures behaving like government agencies have developed over time. Regularly, privatization therefore is considered as a necessary step before systematic commercialization.

GOVERNMENT SUPPORT

Government support is not negligible although often it is given too much weight. Government support for expansion of civilian business has been given mostly in the form of research and development subsidies. Although such subsidies have not been tailored to serve defense conversion, certain technology lines benefit defense industry conversion almost automatically, such as aerospace technologies, certain types of material technology, and certain types of electronics. In the field of R&D subsidies, the European Union is playing an ever more important role, with the Fourth Framework Program on Science and Technology running into the tens of billions of dollars, although national governments remain the largest spenders. Other types of government assistance benefiting defense conversion are regional and structural assistance programs, for instance, for regions with high rates of unemployment and for shipbuilding industries. Support here comes from both national governments and the European Union. Case studies, as of the regions of Bremen in Germany and Brest in France, demonstrate that integrated regional support often has been fairly effective.[41]

The Way Ahead

What are the prospects of the west European defense industry in the near and medium term to restructure or convert? How does the political and economic environment in western Europe influence these perspectives?

Despite substantial cutbacks in procurement, exports, and (as in most countries) employment, overcapacity in defense production remains a problem in western Europe, especially in France and the United Kingdom. Further reductions in capacity are unavoidable even if procurement and exports should stabilize at current levels. Productivity increases will continue to put pressure on downsizing.

In all likelihood, the budget squeeze is not over yet. Some of the ambitious—although already scaled down—large west European procurement projects are likely to be reduced further. The effects on companies will require further cuts of capacity.

Looking at the long history of political rhetoric directed at a unified, truly international west European defense industry and a common procurement policy, and at the failures to put such policies into practice, it is hard to believe that conditions for a fundamental change are ripe, although the economic pressures are stronger now than ever before. There is, however, a great gap between what is called for and what is achieved. Fragmentation of markets, not coordinated procurement; protectionist initiatives, not trade liberalization; favoring national champions, not international competition; exorbitant cost overruns in multilateral projects, not production by the most efficient producer are the prominent characteristics of the west European defense industry and weapons procurement programs.

A common west European or European Union foreign and security policy concept does not exist yet. Additionally, since time schedules for procurement of weapons systems are not synchronized among west European countries (not even among NATO member countries), and because of differing strategic and tactical doctrines, unilateral decisions are still likely in the future. These trends, in combination with the continued political will to favor national champions and to maintain a critical mass of a defense industrial base, likely will prevent the emergence of a more efficient and competitive west European defense industry and at the same time keep the national champions in business. As long as companies can hope for the next cycle in procurement, based on national favoritism, they need only to adjust to lower demand; managers do not need to convert fully.

There is perhaps no other industrial branch as dependent on government decision-making (for R&D contracts, procurement of weapons, export licenses) as the weapons-producing industry. Despite this fact, company managers were the most important actors for adjustment of the defense industry during the 1990s. They had to initiate their readjustment in a difficult economic environment, although with a fair amount of subsidies and regulations. Direct government conversion assistance or plans among unions or in peace movements for military-civil conversion remained marginal. With the current dominant political and economic notion of a reduced role for the state, company managers also will have to adapt their business to changing conditions.

Conversion at the factory level is generally too narrow a concept. Reusing all production factors, finding job alternatives for each and every employee within an existing plant, has been an exception. Partial reuse of resources, know-how, skilled labor, and technologies has had more success. This broader type of conversion occurred within strategies of diversification of production that changed the civil-military mix of production within corporations. The measure of success and failure of conversion cannot be a complete reorientation of all resources within a corporation to civilian production. Ultimately, the yardstick for successful conversion is the larger economy, not the corporation. In that sense, with still existing overcapacities in western Europe, more conversion is likely to occur in the medium term.

Adaptation will be most painful in the near future in France, where the government has protected the defense industry for a long time. Unlike Germany, Spain, Belgium, and the Netherlands, where substantial downsizing closely followed political changes in Europe, French governments and industrialists bided their time to downsize and lost this battle. The financial burden has become too large to reconcile with efforts to limit budget deficits. The United Kingdom and Italy are intermediate cases. There is little reason to think that future adaptation to shrinking defense markets will be much different from past muddling through. The mixture of strategies adopted by companies will not be different: some will try to increase defense business by capturing larger market shares, some will opt out, others will try to gain more civilian business.

It is unlikely that, in the future, downsizing will be more of an international enterprise than it has been in the past. Companies will look for global markets both in the civilian and the defense field. They will organize and join consortia, predominantly within western Europe, but also with U.S. companies and, in rare cases, Russian partners for weapons programs. Exchanges of equity capital will continue to be limited in the defense field and frequent on the civilian side.

Efforts to change the civil-military production mix will continue to be hampered by the general economic problems affecting manufacturing in western Europe. Deflationary budget and monetary policies are unlikely to change even after the introduction of a single currency in some countries of western Europe. Global competition in civilian markets is tougher than ever. While west European companies have done better than often is perceived, the barriers for market entry are generally high.

The west European defense industry has, in the final analysis, reacted to the crisis brought about by shrinking markets in a fairly timid way, at least as far as public relations go. The national parts of it have looked back to national governments for protection of cores and assets, clearly indicating that "west European defense industry" is probably a misnomer. Conversion has been denounced as total failure, although if measured in terms of increasing civilian business, it has been at least partly successful.

From a political and social perspective, in the end the question is whether labor released from defense production finds other income or gainful employment, in the converted company and elsewhere, and whether skills and technology are reused usefully. Considering that unemployment rates were at a historic peak in western Europe in the mid-1990s, not all jobs endangered in the defense industry can be compensated for in the future. It is not company managers, however, who are to blame, but rather politicians and national policies. In economic crisis, they became more national again. The Soviet threat has been partly replaced by the threat of "Brussels," at least in some quarters. This is the more surprising, as "Brussels" is in fact providing substantial economic aid to distressed regions and industries. Companies that tried to shift the civilian-military mix have benefited from this support in the same way that fully civilian ones have. A number of them have been quite successful in getting public money, although success depends mainly on the initiative of companies themselves. Certainly many hopes of economic gains from defense downsizing, conversion, and the peace dividend expressed in the early days after the end of the Cold War were overly optimistic. But the tendency to see it as a failure because it did not deliver according to such expectations is equally erroneous. Compared with changes occurring in industry in general, defense downsizing was and will remain a secondary matter. Like that larger change, it has its successes and failures, shaped by government policies, but even more so by the willingness and capabilities of company managers and workforces.

Notes

1. Jean Paul Hébert, "1994: une année charnière pour la restucturation d'armement en France," in European Institute for Research and Information on Peace and Security (hereafter, GRIP), *Memento Défense-Désarmement 1995–96* (Brussels: GRIP, 1996), pp. 327–52.

2. Stockholm International Peace Research Institute (hereafter, SIPRI), *SIPRI Yearbook 1996: World Armaments, Disarmament and International Security* (Oxford: Oxford University Press, 1996), p. 474.

3. Joachim Rohde, *Der Deutsche Rüstungsexport 1992–1994.* SWP-KA 2918. (Ebenhausen: Stiftung Wissenschaft und Politik, August 1995).

4. SIPRI, *SIPRI Yearbook 1996.*

5. Jean Paul Hébert, "Programmation militaire: l'urgent vs. l'important," *Le Débate Stratégique* 1, July 1996, p. 6.

6. Guilio Perani, "Conversion Experiences and Policies in Italy." Mimeo. Rome: Archivio Disarmo, 1996.

7. Herbert Wulf, ed., *Arms Industry Limited* (Oxford: Oxford University Press, 1993).

8. Bonn International Center for Conversion (hereafter BICC), *Conversion Survey 1996* (Oxford: Oxford University Press, 1996), pp. 272–73.

9. Michael Brzoska and Peter Lock, *Restructuring of Arms Production in Western Europe* (Oxford: Oxford University Press, 1992).

10. BICC, *Conversion Survey 1996*, chap. 2.

11. United States Congress, Office of Technology Assessment, *Assessing the Potential for Civil-Military Integration*, OTA-ISS-611 (Washington, D.C.: Government Printing Office, 1994).

12. François Chesnais and Claude Serfati, *L'Armement en France: Genèse, ampleur, et Coût d'une industrie* (Paris: CIRCA-Nathan, 1992).

13. Jean Paul Hébert, *Production d'armement: mutation du système français* (Paris: La Documentation Française, 1995); Edward Kolodziej, *The Making and Marketing of Arms* (Princeton, N.J.: Princeton University Press, 1987).

14. Ulrich Albrecht, *Der Handel mit Waffen* (Munich: Hanser Verlag, 1971).

15. Ann Markusen, "Defense Spending: A Successful Industrial Policy?" *International Journal of Urban and Regional Research* 10 (1986): 105–22.

16. Nicholas Hooper and Keith Hartley, *UK Defence Contractors: Adjusting to Change*, Research Monograph Series 3, Centre for Defence Economics (York: University of York, 1993).

17. International Monetary Fund, *World Economic Outlook.* (Washington, D.C.: IMF, 1996).

18. Klaus Schomacker, Peter Wilke, and Herbert Wulf, *Alternative Production statt Rüstung* (Cologne: Bund Verlag, 1987).

19. BICC, *Conversion Survey 1996*, pp. 16–22.

20. Commission of the European Communities (hereafter, Commission), *The Challenges Facing the European Defence-Related Industry: A Contribution for Action at the European Level* (Brussels: Commission of the European Communities, 1996); Pierre DeVestel, *Defence Markets and Industries in Europe: Time for Political Decisions?* Chaillot Paper 21 (Paris: Western European Union, November 1995).

21. Joachim Rohde, "Keine Zukunft für Eigenbrötler," *Frankfurter Allgemeine Zeitung*, September 16, 1996, p. 10.

22. Jan van Houwelingen, "The Independent European Program Group (IEPG): The Way Ahead," *NATO Review*, no. 4 (1984): 17.

23. Commission, *Challenges Facing the European Defence-Related Industry*, pp. 9–10.

24. GRIP, *Mememto Défense;* Keith Hartley, "Crise de l'índustrie de armement et reconversion au sein de l'Union Européene," *Penanros* (1995): 95–108;

Luc Mampaey, "Les données macro-économiques de la défense des pays occidentaux," in GRIP, *Mememto Défense*, 381–446; William Walker and Philip Gummett, *Nationalism, Internationalism, and the European Defence Market.* Chaillot Paper 9 (Paris: Western European Union, November 1995).

25. De Vestel, *Defence Markets and Industries*, p. 64.

26. Christian Muguet, *Die französische Rüstungsindustrie im Umbruch.* Arbeitspapiere 2911 (Ebenhausen: Stiftung für Wissenschaft und Politik, 1995).

27. Roland de Penanros, ed., *Reconversion des industries d'armament* (Paris: La Documentation Française, 1995).

28. Steven Schofield, "The Levene Reforms: An Assessment," *Defense Analysis* 11, no. 2 (1995): 147–74.

29. *Financial Times,* December 18, 19, 1995.

30. Perani, "Conversion Experiences."

31. Ibid.

32. Commission, *Challenges Facing the European Defence-Related Industry,* p. 5.

33. Ibid., p. 25.

34. Ian Anthony and Herbert Wulf, "The Economics of the West European Arms Industry," in Brzoska and Lock, *Restructuring of Arms Production,* pp. 17–35; Jörg Huffschmid and Werner Voss, *Militärische Beschaffungen, Waffenhandel, Rüstungskonversion in der EG.* Ansätze koordinierter Steuerung, PIW-Studien no. 7 (Bremen: Progress-Institut für Wirtschaftsforschung, 1991).

35. *The Economist,* August 10, 1996, p. 50.

36. Krauss-Maffei *Annual Report* (Munich: Krauss-Maffei, 1995).

37. The data used here do not distinguish between profits made in defense and the civilian division of the company; in most cases such disaggregated figures are not available.

38. Liba Paukert and Peter Richards, *Defence Expenditure, Industrial Conversion and Local Employment* (Geneva: International Labor Office, 1991); Wolfram Elsner, "Instruments and Institutions of Industrial Policy at the Regional Level in Germany: The Example of Industrial Defense Conversion," *Journal of Economic Issues,* Vol. 29, No. 2, 1995, pp. 503-16.

39. David B. Audretsch, *Innovation and Industry Evolution* (Boston: MIT Press, 1995); Martin Grundmann, et al., *Rüstungskonversion: Erfolg durch Wandel der Unter-neh-menskultur* (Münster/Hamburg: Lit Verlag, 1995).

40. DeVestel, *Defence Markets and Industries,* p. 64.

41. Wolfram Elsner, ibid; Marie-Noelle Le Nouail, Roland de Penanros, and Thierry Sauvin, "Activitiés militaires et expérience de diversification dans la région brestoise," Penanros, pp. 177–94.

Table A14-1   Performance of European Arms Producers: The "Expanders"
Increasing Defense Sales, Increasing Nondefense Sales, and Newly Formed Defense Units

Company[a]	Country	Defense sales in 1990 million $U.S.	Defense sales in 1994 million $U.S.	% of defense sales in 1994	% change of nondefense production 1990–94	Profits in 1994 million $U.S.
Celsius[a]	Sweden	180	1,190	67	–48	99
Lagardère[b]	France	na	950	10	na	111
Eurocopter[c]	France/Germany	na	860	52	na	–71
Hunting	United Kingdom	420	670	39	+0.03	22
GKN	United Kingdom	180	550	12	–6	141
HDW	Germany	190	410	52	45	53
Vosper Thorn.	United Kingdom	230	340	89	95	38
Wegmann	Germany	270	280	45	29	N/A

[a] takeover of Bofors.
[b] takeover of defense from Matra.
[c] newly formed by DASA and Aérospatiale.
na = not applicable.
N/A = not available.
Source: SIPRI company database. It is gratefully acknowledged that Elisabeth Sköns provided the data.

Table A14–2 Performance of European Arms Producers: The "Converters" Decreasing Defense and Increasing Nondefense Sales

Company	Country	Defense sales in 1990 million $U.S.	Defense sales in 1994 million $U.S.	% of defense sales in 1994	% change of nondefense production 1990–94	Profits in 1994 million $U.S.
Thomson	France	5,250	4,270	32	+7	–390
Daimler-Benz	Germany	4,020	3,200	5	+25	552
IRI	Italy	3,270	2,070	4	+0.4	–912
Aérospatiale	France	2,860	2,450	29	+75	–87
INI	Spain	1,560	1,020	5	+18	–602
GIAT	France	1,430	1,030	75	+803	–526
Oerlikon Bührle	Switzerland	1,340	750	27	+0.01	55
Bremer Vulcan	Germany	1,050	740	20	+125	35
Siemens	Germany	990	870	2	+34	1228
Diehl	Germany	860	740	43	+8	N/A
VSEL	United Kingdom	930	650	99	+133	100
Eidg. Rüstungs.	Switzerland	700	660	92	+61	–107
Rheinmetall	Germany	700	480	24	+39	N/A
SAGEM	France	570	540	67	+33	107
Dassault Electr.	France	530	490	67	+18	10
Devonport	United Kingdom	470	380	91	+27	17
Mannesmann	Germany	410	260	1	+28	210
SNPE	France	330	290	45	+24	26
Ericsson	Sweden	300	270	3	+41	512

N/A = not available.
Source: SIPRI company database. It is gratefully acknowledged that Elizabeth Sköns provided the data.

Table A14-3 Performance of European Arms Producers: The "Downsizers" Decreasing Defense and Nondefense Sales

Company	Country	Defense sales in 1990 million $U.S.	Defense sales in 1994 million $U.S.	% of defense sales in 1994	% change of nondefense production 1990–94	Profits in 1994 million $U.S.
British Aerosp.	United Kingdom	8,270	7030	64	–63	214
GEC	United Kingdom	4,280	3190	20	–0.1	864
DCN	France	3,740	2730	98	–24	N/A
Dassault Av.	France	2,260	1330	72	–58	47
Rolls-Royce	United Kingdom	1,830	1360	28	–26	124
SNECMA	France	1,490	1070	31	–15	–410
FIAT	Italy	1,180	660	2	–9	776
Thyssen	Germany	710	640	3	–4	427
Lucas Industries	United Kingdom	630	490	12	–2	–256
Dowty Group	United Kingdom	520	150	33	–64	46
Westland	United Kingdom	510	330	72	–42	29
FFV	Sweden	500	120	73	–92	22
Smith Industries	United Kingdom	490	470	40	–3	122
Racal Electron.	United Kingdom	480	450	31	–70	89
Saab Scania	Sweden	460	350	9	–16	322

N/A = not available.

Source: SIPRI company database. It is gratefully acknowledged that Elizabeth Sköns provided the data.

Table A14–4 Performance of European Arms Producers: The "Terminators" Companies Leaving the Defense Sector

Company	Country	Defense sales in 1990 million $U.S.	Defense sales in 1994 million $U.S.	% of defense sales in 1994
EFIM	Italy	1,710	na	transferred to Finmeccanica (IRI)
Matra	France	1,180	na	taken over by Lagadère
Bofors/Nobel	Sweden	930	0	bought by Celsius
Thorn EMI	United Kingdom	450	0	defense production sold
Ferranti Signal	United Kingdom	440	0	dissolved, sold in units
Hawker Siddely	United Kingdom	480	0	taken over by BTR

na = not applicable.
Source: SIPRI company database. It is gratefully acknowledged that Elizabeth Sköns provided the data.

VI

An Industry for the Future

15

Policy Choices in Arming the Future

ANN R. MARKUSEN AND SEAN S. COSTIGAN

I N THE 1990s the durable American military industrial complex meta-
morphosed. Post–Cold War defense spending cuts were deep and
rapid. Most analysts, industry watchers, and policymakers were
taken by surprise at the subsequent transformation in American
defense industrial capacity. Unprepared for the task of massive downsizing, the Bush and Clinton administrations brooded and waffled,
while the industry proved remarkably agile. Within five short years,
before the window of opportunity was closed by new leadership at the
Clinton Pentagon, the ranks of major American contractors imploded
from 15 to 4, compounding the Pentagon's perennial problem of
procuring top-quality equipment at affordable prices. And transnational mergers and partnerships could further alter the face of the
industry beyond recognition. How should our leaders guide the future
of the global defense industry in the years to come?

The central dilemma, balancing economic against security concerns,
is not new. The Pentagon devoted considerable staff time throughout
the Cold War period to industry oversight and regulation. Numerous
studies and initiatives, including the remarkable efforts by Robert
McNamara, sought to ensure that the nation would receive the highest-
quality weapons at a fair price: design and procurement competitions,
performance standards, accounting oversight, and often contorted
efforts to ensure that three or more competitors possessed the potential
to compete in each major weapons system. At times, the Pentagon
experimented with radically new arrangements, such as insisting, for

instance, that rival services cooperate on a single fighter (the TFX, the future Joint Strike Fighter) or that systems be purchased with fixed-price rather than cost-plus contracts. None of these experiments fully solved the procurement dilemma.

The dilemma is exacerbated by the fact that designing, making, and buying weapons engages a range of actors with differing, often incompatible goals. The armed forces are trying to match firepower and mobility to perceived threats. Civilian Pentagon managers are trying to deliver defense at a reasonable price to the citizenry, constrained by trade-offs with other claims on the same resources—other public services, public investment, private investment. Members of Congress represent the interests of their constituents, as both consumers of defense and civilian goods and as producers of military equipment and services. Contractors are trying to satisfy shareholders. Unions are trying to preserve members' jobs and incomes.

If this process was complex during the Cold War, it is even more so now for several reasons. First, the precipitous fall in the domestic and world arms market has pushed effective demand down below the level of minimum efficient scale for many existing weapons laboratories and production facilities. As a result, economic imperatives have entered even more forcefully and explicitly into the policy deliberation process in planning future weapons systems and in crafting export policy. Second, the arms market is becoming increasingly international as heightened competition and the slump in domestic demand drive firms to compete for export markets, supported in most cases by their governments. Third, the implosion in the number of firms competing in the U.S. market and their increasing attention to customers other than the United States shifts the power balance in the market away from the Pentagon and in favor of the contractors. And finally, fiscal austerity at home and abroad leaves very little room for new initiatives. Sizeable requests for additional funds for either modernization or beefed-up Pentagon oversight are apt to fall on deaf congressional ears, while low oil prices and the Asian financial crisis are reversing the growth in developing countries' arms purchases.

The authors of this book demonstrate that important decisions regarding defense conversion, mergers, and exports were made in the first post–Cold War decade. The result has been less conversion than was anticipated, markedly fewer firms competing in the systems integration end of the market, and a rise in American firms' domination of the arms export market, despite falling absolute export levels. By and large, the conversation about conversion is over, not the least because American defense budgets currently are stabilized at about $255 billion a year. But a number of new, knotty policy issues are emerging, captured in the following questions: What and how much should we buy? How should the Pentagon buy it? From whom to buy? Should the military and the Pentagon produce or buy their equipment and services? Who should be permitted to merge? What and how much should we export? Is globalization of the industry, formally or informally, a welcome development?

In this final chapter, we review each of these policy areas. We show that the contexts for many of them are not independent of decisions made in others. The international defense industry, we conclude, is still in formative stages. Its size, structure, location, national character, and performance are questions of national and international policy. We tailor our remarks here to the case of the United States, but much of what is said applies equally to our allies around the world.

What and How Much to Buy?

Weapons system procurement ought to be driven by military strategies developed to respond to current and potential threats. This exercise is more difficult in the post–Cold War period because the threats are more diffuse. As Gregory Bischak shows in Chapter 2, the budgetary consequences for different possible security scenarios vary by as much as $100 billion a year.

Even when guided by an official strategy (e.g., the Quadrennial Defense Review), deciding what to buy and how much is no longer a simple linear process from threat (demand) to equipment (supply) but a more flexible, interactive process. Contractors signal both the technological capabilities they think are developable and the cost of development of such systems vis-à-vis existing technologies. Pentagon planners and acquisition officers take these signals into account in drawing up longer-term plans and budgets. Since the cost is not independent of the number of units purchased, long-term domestic demand and export potential fit into the calculus as well. But as Lora Lumpe points out in Chapter 11, liberalized exports, especially of modern equipment, may alter the security threat assessment. To complicate matters, interservice rivalries and porkbarreling practices in Congress tend to distort procurement choices.

Although the initiative for procurement planning should remain the domain of military strategists, the economics of outfitting the military has become so pervasive that greater formal attention to these forces ought to be built into the planning process. For each existing and potential weapons system, an assessment of related economies of scale, potential to develop into a porkbarrel item, and the security effect of its diffusion to other nations should be built into the planning and evalua-tion process. Each of the following policy choices has consequences for this exercise.

How to Buy It?

Private sector–provided equipment and the services to install and oper-ationalize them consume a larger share of the military budget than before the 1980s buildup, reinforcing a secular trend toward the replacement of the soldier with remotely guided munitions. Thus the perennial quality and cost issues that have dogged this market since World War II are more compelling than ever.

As the reality of post–Cold War spending cuts set in, it was hoped that procurement reform and increasing civil-military integration would engender vigorous technological and price competition, enabling the mil-itary to get the most bang for the buck.[1] The dual-use policies of the Bush and Clinton administrations were designed to encourage such a trend. As Jay Stowsky in Chapter 4 and Paul Walker in Chapter 5 show, these were largely gutted by the 1994 Republican Congress. The Pentagon remains committed to procurement reform, meaning both the elimination of "red tape" and increased "off-the-shelf" purchases of components from a wider civilian market. But modest gains have lagged behind the rapid consolidation process in which the ranks of major systems integrators and R&D performers have shrunk to four giants.

A clear policy choice faces the Pentagon. With fewer competitors, it must either intensify its regulatory oversight or seek to expand the pool of competitors. The regulatory route is encumbered by many well-known problems and may be particularly difficult in a climate of anti-regulatory sentiment. Nevertheless, Harvey Sapolsky and Eugene Gholz in Chapter 6 as well as Erik Pages in Chapter 7 argue that to the extent that the Pentagon must buy from emerging "private arsenals," it has little choice. Many Pentagon watchers point out that considerable savings can be gained by eliminating anachronistic regulations while increasing oversight of contractor bids and performance.[2]

Alternatively, the Pentagon could seek to widen the pool of competi-tors in several ways while simultaneously discouraging further merg-ers. First, as Sapolsky and Gholz suggest, it could promote greater competition among the services in bidding for missions. Second, new domestic competitors might be found among the ranks of second-tier suppliers or by forcing divestiture from the largest firms. Third, bids could be accepted from foreign producers on equal par with domestic firms. An accurate assessment of economies of scale, as Kenneth Flamm demonstrates in Chapter 8, would be very helpful in deciding which of these paths to pursue and determining the net cost/benefits of cultivating greater competition.

From Whom to Buy?

Even if the number of competitors were to increase, the question of from whom to buy could not be answered simply. Accepting the lowest bid might bring adverse consequences—the failure of losing firms or dependence on foreign sources.

By announcing in 1994 that he expected to see fewer firms in the industry, Secretary of Defense William Perry signaled his unwillingness to continue decades of informal "follow-on" awards, where contractors often won a bid because they were deemed to need it the most or it was "their turn."[3] Nevertheless, it is unlikely that when making awards among even fewer competitors, the Pentagon will be able to ignore adverse economic consequences for the losers. In other words, current awards may be made with an eye toward the preservation of future competition. Ability to make such determinations requires a familiarity with corporate financial status as well as with technical competence.

The decision to award contracts to foreign firms would carry with it even weightier extraeconomic concerns. Many nations have relied on foreign purchases for military equipment. More recently, as John Lovering recounts in Chapter 13, the formerly self-sufficient Britain decided to award contracts to the lowest bidder, whether domestic or foreign, in an unambiguous initiative to procure the best at the lowest cost regardless of the consequences for domestic suppliers or defense dependency. The United States has "Buy America" practices, embodied in law, that limit the Pentagon's ability to import any item that might be considered critical and permit it to award contracts to higher-cost domestic firms if their bids do not exceed foreign bids by a certain margin. It may no longer be necessary to continue these practices for security reasons; indeed, the emergence of cooperative security arrangements may counsel greater interdependence among supplier countries. And as we note later, the issue of from whom to buy is closely tied to policies on international mergers and joint ventures and to those governing arms exports.

The Make or Buy Decision, or How Much to Privatize?

A related policy issue is the extent to which the Pentagon should continue to privatize functions that are now performed in the public sector, either by civilians in the Pentagon or its many regional offices or by the uniformed services on bases, depots, and laboratories. That is, should government "make" for itself, as it still does in hundreds of laboratories, arsenals, and depots, or should it buy these services on the market? Secretary Cohen, in 1997, stated his support for continued privatization as a cost-saving measure, and a number of industry groups are lobbying intensely for privatization, particularly the large defense contractors and the fast-growing large defense service firms, such as SAIC and BDM.

Privatization is supported by those who believe that government cannot perform work as efficiently as the public sector. Advocates point to lower wages in the private sector and the flexibility of firms that can use temporary workers on spot contracts to perform services such as maintenance and repairs or hardware and software installation. The contention is that considerable cost savings will follow privatization. Some savings have been realized in specific cases, although the overall evidence is not compelling.

There may indeed be areas where privatization will improve quality and reduce cost. However, critics of privatization raise several caveats. First, some point to the growing concentration in the market and worry that most such services will be performed by a handful of firms, with the same monopolistic distortions in cost and quality predicted by standard economic theory and observed consistently in the procurement process. Whether this occurs depends very much on whether the contracts go to diversified firms in highly competitive contests or end up being snapped up by beltway insiders.

Second, the evidence from the privatization of public services at the local level (for bus service, garbage collection, waste disposal, etc.) shows a pattern of initial competition followed by a lock-in by the winning contractor, often accompanied by graft, and thus higher costs in the longer run.[4] Third, the more that defense-related activity moves into the private sector, the greater the potential for porkbarreling behavior. Public sector employees and members of the armed services do lobby to retain their jobs, but they do not have large budgets to spend on lobbying Congress. Private firms, especially the large ones well positioned to win privatization contracts, can and do. William Burnett and Frederic Scherer found that public arsenals were disproportionally closed in favor of private sector firms during the Cold War because contractors were more politically influential than managers and employees of public facilities.[5]

Finally, military leaders are concerned that privatization will affect surge capacity and their ability to ensure supply lines and maintenance in the event of war. As more functions on bases and depots are privatized, the armed forces could find themselves with suppliers facing bankruptcy, preoccupied with hostile takeovers, driven to "plant" closings, or simply enjoying higher returns in other activities. The imperatives of the military mission, especially in war, could stand in stark contrast to the need to maximize shareholder value in the private sector. Just where the line should be drawn between operations that should continue to be performed by soldiers subject to military authority and those that might be privatized is currently a subject of much internal contention.

Who Should Merge/Collaborate with Whom?

Most commentators believe that the era of consolidation among the ranks of the large American defense contractors is over. However, two types of consolidation still may take place: mergers with smaller contractors, often suppliers, and mergers with foreign firms. Either could substantially change the way that arms are made and sold.

Mergers with subcontractors, or vertical integration, in economists' jargon, has lagged behind the "horizontal" or market extension mergers described by Michael Oden in Chapter 3. Vertical mergers could intensify price and quality problems by eliminating competition among suppliers who sell to the big-firm systems integrators. In 1996 the Pentagon asked its Defense Science Board to study the incidence and consequences of vertical mergers. The study found that although some vertical integration had taken place, it did not yet appear to be a systemic problem. The task force noted that the Department of Defense (DoD) "is not well postured in its ongoing acquisition management processes to recognize or address problems emerging as a result of vertical integration."[6] It recommended that the department's monitoring of vertical supply relationships be expanded. Further, it suggested strengthening the business and industry-related skills of DoD acquisition personnel. In July 1997, Pentagon Acquisition Chief Paul Kaminski announced a vertical integration "warning system" as a follow-on measure.

Academic research suggests that vertical integration is not apt to be as common as feared. Many large defense contractors have selectively vertically disintegrated, following a general corporate trend toward greater outsourcing of more routine functions.[7] Externalizing component design and production enables a firm to benefit from competition among suppliers and to pass the lumpy and cyclical nature of demand in this market on to subcontractors. Lockheed among others has been characterized as a corporation with considerable flexibility in both internal operations and in its ability to employ subcontractors.[8]

A greater challenge is presented by the prospect that defense-specialized firms may quicken the pace of international acquisitions, mergers, joint ventures, and strategic alliances, a trend Richard Bitzinger documents in Chapter 12. A mix of motivations—the desire to use excess capacity more efficiently, to gain access to markets, to increase, perhaps dominate, market share—is at work across borders as well as within nations. In a recent major policy speech, Vance Coffman, chief executive officer of Lockheed Martin, strongly opposed a Fortress America vs. Fortress Europe scenario, favoring transatlantic industrial partnerships.[9]

Considerable obstacles, however, stand in the way of globalization. European firms, which have much smaller markets and are thus in greater distress over the cuts in defense spending, have been the subject of considerable public debate and private intrigue over whether they will merge on a European basis or take on transatlantic partners. As John Lovering in Chapter 13 and as Michael Brzoska, Peter Wilke, and Herbert Wulf in Chapter 14 show, despite the pro-rationalization intentions in the Western European Union (WEU), the European Community's defense organization, little progress on pan-European consolidation has taken place, chiefly because individual governments fear the negative employment consequences of such mergers and because of real or imagined national security concerns.[10]

In addition, the WEU has been slow to adapt a joint security strategy and has been largely supplanted by an invigorated and expansionist North Atlantic Treaty Organization (NATO). As NATO interoperability proceeds, the Europeans fear that U.S. equipment will become the standard, further limiting their sales. Popular opposition to western European subsidies for arms exports to the new members of NATO may help to clear the way for American sales.

The key players on the European side in this drama are Britain, France, and Germany, all of whom have substantial defense industries and face continued retrenchment. Over the past decade, each has taken a somewhat different stance. The British government under Margaret Thatcher, placing quality and affordability above preserving a domestic industrial base, was more willing to buy abroad and to encourage firm partnerships with foreign firms. It permitted Raytheon, for instance, to purchase an important defense firm, and it has encouraged British Aerospace to team with Lockheed on future fighter craft. The French government has been least willing to permit international mergers and the slowest of the three to pursue state-owned firm privatization. Shifts in the ruling party have made negotiations more difficult, as pronounced policy changes followed the changeover from more conservative to more labor/social democratic parties in Britain and France in 1997.

Continued European government inaction and standoffishness actually may enhance informal American ties with European firms. Although formal mergers may be effectively discouraged, active American efforts to sell arms to Europe may result in partnerships in which European firms increasingly become suppliers of subsystems or components to American systems integrators. Demands for offsets on the part of European partners will more or less ensure that a substantial portion of the work associated with major weapons purchases will take place in Europe, requiring in turn a relaxation of "Buy America" provisions. Some loosening of these provisions already has occurred. Jacques Gansler, the newly appointed Pentagon acquisition chief, seeks increased purchasing from abroad, chiefly to engender competition.[11] But a more likely scenario is one in which the Pentagon will buy from American firms with European suppliers, instead of buying directly from European firms.

Such an outcome would present the U.S. government with a substantially new defense industrial base configuration. On one hand, it may indeed save on weapons costs by increasing the scale of output and thus lowering unit cost. On the other hand, it will result in many fewer jobs in the United States associated with defense production and lead inexorably to American defense industry dependence on foreign suppliers. Because some components may be considered critical, greater oversight will be required in the process—a virtue of "Buy America" practices was its simplicity.[12]

This scenario also suggests a waning of Pentagon power and a waxing of defense contractor power in a market that is already a bilateral oligopoly. If formal or informal internationalization of American defense companies takes place, the U.S. government will become a somewhat less important customer (although still dominant) to the American companies. At the same time and owing to the recent mergers, the number of competitors on the seller's side has diminished, unless the Pentagon is willing to permit major European firms to compete for large weapons contracts. The net result is an American market with fewer sellers but effective demand spread among more buyers, which will enhance the market position of the large defense contractors. The policy choices here are linked closely to those governing arms exports and imports, to which we now turn.

What to Export and to Whom?

In the 1990s the international arms market shrank by more than 30 percent, precisely at a time when domestic demand was declining rapidly in most countries. Despite a post–Gulf War sales boom, arms sales from the United States fell by more than 10 percent from the late 1980s. U.S. firms enhanced their share of the market, as David Gold shows in Chapter 9, chiefly at the expense of the former Soviet states. Declining demand and excess capacity have, our authors agree, heightened competition for international markets and helped to undermine progress toward conventional arms control agreements. U.S. arms export oversight has shifted to include explicitly industrial capacity concerns in decision-making. In the export area more than in any other area covered in this book, our authors stress the tension between economic and security drivers.

Although threats are more diffuse in the 1990s, Americans continue to face the possibility that conventional arms as well as weapons of mass destruction will proliferate. Surplus weapons have been marketed formally and on the black market to potentially unstable or aggressive regimes in problem regions of the world. Exports of new and sophisticated weapons are being sold to regions where they were long banned (e.g., Latin America). As Judith Reppy shows in Chapter 10, the tendency for weapons to embody more dual-use technologies, especially in their guidance and intelligence systems, raises concerns that more countries will develop the potential to design, use, and market them. Some have argued that the United States would do well to pursue an arms monopoly because, as the world's arms outfitter, the United States would possess intimate knowledge of any potential adversary's capabilities. However, in this case the United States also would be in the awkward position of engaging in an arms race with itself, as new weapons would have to be developed to counter the possibility of our own weapons being turned on American soldiers. The fact that the newest weapons systems, such as the Joint Strike Fighter, are being designed with an intention to sell abroad from the outset underscores this point.

The United States and other advanced weapons-producing countries all have security screens through which export proposals must pass. These screens have been relaxed to some extent since the end of the Cold War, in the American decision to begin exporting complete weapons systems to Latin America, for instance. At the same time, arms control advocates have worked to enhance export controls in a period where most countries have fewer security reasons for selling to others, as they did when the world was divided into two Cold War camps. Official negotiations have been directed disproportionately toward weapons of mass destruction—the Nuclear Nonproliferation Treaty (NPT), the Comprehensive Test Ban (CTB), the chemical and biological weapons treaties. Progress on conventional arms export controls, such as the multilateral Waasanar agreements, has been sluggish. In individual countries, code-of-conduct proposals to restrain trade in certain types of weapons and to certain types of regimes are being debated, and an international code of conduct has been drafted. The European Parliament has adopted a Code of Conduct, but to date these proposals have not received majority support in the American Congress, chiefly because of supply-side pressures.

The industrial restructuring currently taking place is apt to intensify the export imperative. Efforts to create a post–Cold War multilateral regime stumbled on individual countries' ambitions to export for economic reasons, as when President Bush decided to permit the sale of F-15s to Taiwan in the midst of the 1992 presidential election, announcing the sale at the MacDonnell Douglas plant in St. Louis; in response, China pulled out of the talks. Furthermore, if companies become more global, determining just what they are exporting may become more difficult. Firms desiring to escape restrictions in their home countries could use foreign branches or partners to design, produce, or sell weapons forbidden at home. Or a decision to deny an export license might be responded to by a threat to move production overseas. The jobs of officials trying to monitor and license arms exports will become more difficult. Chapters 10 and 11 document the security threat posed by an increasingly "leaky" domestic arsenal; their authors argue strongly for security priorities and active arms export restraint, both unilaterally and multilaterally.

As with the Pentagon posture toward defense firm mergers, no longer can arms export policy be detached from the larger nexus of issues around outfitting for war. Each of several different potential configurations for the arms industry carries with it implications for the volume and character of the arms trade. And each of several different foreign policy and military strategies bears a distinctive set of implications for both industry and trade. In our conclusion, we lay out three possible scenarios that might unfold. The remarkable variation among these demonstrates the need for presidential leadership and Pentagon defense industrial expertise.

Conclusion

What possible configurations might the defense industry assume in the future? What might each mean for Pentagon planning and procurement? We offer here three stylized possibilities.

First, imagine a future built on current trends. States still adhere to individual military strategies, à la the U.S. commitment to "go it alone" if necessary and the European states' reservation of the right to refrain from joining in an attack on Iraq in the winter of 1998. Weapons modernization—the continued investment in an even larger share of annual defense budgets in the design and development of new weapons—would serve as the centerpiece of defense planning. The United States would continue to dominate leading-edge weaponry and the international arms market, and would continue its de facto role as the world's policeman. In order to cover the escalating costs of developing new weapons systems, higher levels of arms exports would be planned from the outset. Large contractors would be encouraged implicitly to place all of their developmental eggs in one basket—the military's. To hedge against arms export limits and to respond to buyers' demand for offsets, American firms would find joint ventures, even outright purchase of foreign firms, an attractive alternative to arm's-length exporting. As American firms become more competitive, on both cost and quality bases, some European firms would be forced to exit the market, perhaps to be bought up in whole or in part by American firms. However, because American firms would then account for fewer U.S. jobs, their political clout might deteriorate, with salutary effects on weapons spending, priorities, and exports.

Alternatively, imagine the future as a security/industrial standoff between a Fortress America, Fortress Europe, and perhaps a newly configured Fortress Asia. Suppose that the European nations agree to a cooperative security arrangement outside of and perhaps superseding NATO, without the United States, and agree also to joint procurement, sharing orders around a set of firms rationalized on a European-wide basis. The result would be a European defense industry selling to European governments and attempting to export, competing with an American industry that is confident of its own home market and aggressively exporting. Trade across the Atlantic would be limited, and arms trade would move chiefly along a north/south axis. The result would resemble the contemporary civilian aircraft competition between Airbus and Boeing. (In the latter, airlines benefit from playing off one airplane maker against the other, with some benefit to consumers, but the transatlantic rivalry maintains pressures on governments to subsidize their home industries in various ways.) If a Fortress Europe results in a consolidated and robust European industry, the Pentagon might more easily entertain bids from European competitors to induce variety in design and ensure cost savings. However, under this scenario, a defense-specialized corporate sector would have greater stakes in porkbarreling, devoting considerable effort to pressing for higher defense budgets and more liberalized arms exporting arrangements. Their dependence on the American market would likely lock in American orders, even if the cost is higher and/or the quality lessened.

Finally, imagine a 21st century in which cooperative security and conflict resolution arrangements come to dominate over individual national strategies. In this world, aggressive actions on the part of any state would be responded to by joint forces comprised of the military services of many nations. As Chapter 2 suggests, a strategy of this sort likely would result in larger defense budget cuts and greater restraint in the development of new weapons systems. Under such conditions, defense contractors would be more apt to choose diversification into nondefense-related fields as their dominant business strategy. As part of the give-and-take of creating cooperative security structures, most states would demand that a share of procurement be devoted to purchases within their borders; those shares most likely would end up reflecting their purchasing power (i.e., they would be proportional to the extent to which they are committed to participating, supplying troops, and maintaining readiness). The industry would become more international: some nations would specialize in certain weapons systems and others in components, but these would be determined largely through negotiations on the part of the states participating, not at the initiative of individual corporations or via international mergers.[13]

Our own preference is for the third scenario. The current indeterminancy of future threats, relative stability in geopolitical matters, and global preoccupation with trade and growth offer us a window of opportunity to slow weapons innovation, arms exports, and transnational mergers, while building international organizational capability along the lines of a World Trade Organization, for managing international defense industrial capacity and sharply limiting conventional arms proliferation. The United States is the only nation with the credibility to lead in this direction, but it will require a markedly more coherent and pointed policy approach than has prevailed in the post–Cold War period to date.

None of the above scenarios, however, implies a less active Pentagon industrial oversight role. And the wide range of potential outcomes suggests just how much is at stake. Pentagon policy is crucial to the shaping up of the industry for the 21st century. The Pentagon plays a lead role in merger approval and arms export policy, even if formally these are lodged in the Commerce and State Departments, respectively. The shift from the Bush to the Clinton administrations brought a marked policy shift in favor of mergers and consolidation; in the second Clinton administration the changeover from DoD Secretary Perry to Cohen led to greater scrutiny of merger proposals and, ultimately, denial of approval for the merger of Lockheed Martin with Northrop Grumman. Likewise, a strong "no" from the Pentagon on particular arms sales will nix a deal thought to be desirable from an economic point of view. Pentagon purchasing policies, from the number and national origin of competitors allowed in major bids to success or failure in off-the-shelf procurement practices, can have a powerful impact on the configuration of competitors and the success of individual firms.

The Pentagon does not appear to have either adequate industrial base analytical capability or sufficient interagency channels to be able to chart a course in this uncertain world. An Office of Economic Security was established inside the Pentagon early in the Clinton administration to address the former gap, but it was more or less dismantled within two years. As Lovering says of Europe in Chapter 13, we are in danger, in the United States, of industry initiatives running ahead of governmental ones. In the future we could face a multinational defense industry whose influence is more coordinated and pervasive than that of our government or those of our allies. Even if competition were to survive among these giants, their influence over security strategy and military innovation would wax dangerously.

If we are to have an effective defense industry in the 21st century, the nation must have an independent industrial base assessment capability. This capability should be fostered both inside the Pentagon and externally, among researchers in think tanks and universities. A corpus of researchers and expertise of this sort, equivalent to what we have for the financial and agricultural sectors in the United States, would be able to help the president, the Pentagon, and Congress answer the following questions: How much capacity can the United States be expected to support? Where we cannot support more than one contractor, should that capacity remain, as Chapter 6 phrases it, a private arsenal? Where we cannot support even one contractor, should we consider partnership with our close and more industrially sophisticated allies? If so, what are the security and economic implications of real interdependency? Would pursuing dual-use strategies vigorously and curtailing those policies that encourage "pure play" defense industrial firms make defense outfitting more affordable? More innovative? Should we seek to sell to all reliable allies, or should we work actively to limit conventional arms proliferation with other major sellers (i.e., form an arms cartel)?

Gradually, the structure and habits of more than 40 years of Cold War are giving way to more expansive thinking about future security threats, the adequacy of current force structure, the role of competition among the services, and the appropriate public/private split in providing national defense. The defense industry is as important as ever, especially as its share of the defense budget continues to rise. Our authors have together produced a fine-grained record of what happened in the

1990s and a fairly coherent vision of what is both possible and likely in the future.

The defense industrial challenge for the United States is to achieve the following goals simultaneously: (1) maintain a sophisticated, flexible, and tried-and-true defense industrial base; (2) ensure cost and quality discipline using market forces where possible and effective oversight where not; (3) constrain the distorting effects of industry political influence; and (4) link procurement to the most appropriate defense strategy for the coming decades. Weighing the evidence, we conclude that a concerted international consortium among allies, led by the United States, to rationalize defense industrial capacity and slow the pace of arms innovation and diffusion is the most promising route, one that maximizes our security while economizing on defense preparedness and harnessing the industry to security ends, rather than vice versa. This path is also the one most likely to maximize prospects for world peace and restrain the development, possession, use, and potentially destabilizing effects of sophisticated weaponry.

Notes

1. Jacques Gansler, *Defense Conversion: Transforming the Arsenal of Democracy* (Cambridge, Mass.: MIT Press, 1995).

2. Gene Porter, "Issues in Acquisition Reform." In Gerald I. Susman and Sean O'Keefe eds., *The Defense Industry in the Post–Cold War Era: Corporate Strategies and Public Policy Perspectives* (Oxford: Elsevier Science, 1998), pp. 357–73.

3. James Kurth, "The Follow-on Imperative in American Weapons. Procurement, 1960–1990." In Jurgen Brauer and Manas Chatterji, eds., *Economic Issues of Disarmament* (New York: Macmillan, 1993), pp. 304–21.

4. Elliot Sclar, *The Privatization of Public Services: Lessons from Case Studies* (Washington, D.C.: Economic Policy Institute, 1997); Moshe Adler, Evaluating the Privatization Record: Lessons from New York, Lecture given at Rutgers University, Fall 1997.

5. William B. Burnett and Frederic M. Scherer, "The Weapons Industry." In Walter Adams, ed., *The Structure of American Industry* (New York: Macmillan, 1990), pp. 289–317.

6. Office of the Secretary of Defense, *Defense Science Board's Task Force on Vertical Integration and Supplier Decisions* (Washington, D.C.: Department of Defense, 1997).

7. Michael Oden, Ann Markusen, Dan Flaming, Jonathan Feldman, James Raffel, and Catherine Hill, *From Managing Growth to Reversing Decline: Aerospace and the Southern California Economy in the Post–Cold War Era* (New

Brunswick, N.J.: Rutgers University, Project on Regional and Industrial Economics, February, 1996).

8.   Anthony Velocci Jr., "'Virtual' Enterprise: A Plus for Lockheed Martin," *Aviation Week and Space Technology*, February 10, 1997, pp. 86–87.

9.   Vance Coffman, "The Future of Transatlantic Industrial Partnerships." Remarks delivered at the Wehrkunde Conference, Munich, Germany, February 7, 1998. Mimeo, Lockheed Martin Corporation.

10. Ann Markusen and Claude Serfati, "Remaking the Military Industrial Relationship: A French-American Comparison," *Defence and Peace Economics*, forthcoming, 1999.

11. Gansler, *Defense Conversion*.

12. Ann Markusen, "The Rise of World Weapons," *Foreign Policy*, Spring 1999.

13. Ibid.

Contributors

Greg Bischak is a Senior Economist for the Appalachian Regional Commission (ARC), where he conducts and directs research on the economic development needs and programs of the 13-state Appalachian region. Mr. Bischak was executive director of the National Commission for Economic Conversion and Disarmament, where he was responsible for administering the organization and developing public education and policy research on topics of economic conversion, defense employment impacts, disarmament, and industrial policy. Most recently, Mr. Bischak has written *U.S. Conversion after the Cold War, 1990–1997: Lessons for Forging a New Conversion Policy* (1997) and *Welfare-to-Work: The Challenges and Opportunities for Appalachia* (1998).

Richard A. Bitzinger is an employee of the U.S. government. He researched and wrote most of this paper while he was an independent defense analyst. Prior to his present position, he worked for the RAND Corporation and the Defense Budget Project. He is the author of several monographs, journal articles, and book chapters, including *Adjusting to the Drawdown: The Transition in the Defense Industry;* "The Globalization of Arms Production: The Next Proliferation Challenge," *International Security* (Fall 1994); and *Gearing Up for High-Tech Warfare? Chinese and Taiwanese Defense Modernization and Implications for Military Confrontation Across the Taiwan Strait* (coauthor, 1996).

Michael Brzoska is head of research at the Bonn International Center for Conversion (BICC). Earlier, Dr. Brzoska codirected the Arms Transfer and Production Project at the Stockholm International Peace Research Institute in Sweden. He has been a lecturer and a project leader at the Center for the Study of Wars, Armaments and Development at the Political Science Department at the University of Hamburg. Dr. Brzoska is in charge of producing the BICC Conversion series, including the latest book entitled *Conversion Survey 1998: Global Disarmament, Defense Industry Consolidation and Conversion* (1998).

Sean S. Costigan is the editor of Columbia International Affairs Online (www.ciaonet.org). He served as the research associate for science, technology, and industrial policy at the Council on Foreign Relations from 1995 to 1998, prior to which he worked for Harvard University's Center for International Affairs. His research interests include information technology, space policy, and the history of science. Most recently, he co-authored the report *Exporting U.S. High Tech* (1997).

Kenneth Flamm is Professor and Dean Rusk Chair in International Affairs at the Lyndon B. Johnson School of Public Affairs, University of Texas at Austin, and Senior Fellow in the Foreign Policy Studies Program at the Brookings Institution. He is a former principal deputy assistant secretary of defense (economic security) and special assistant to the deputy secretary of defense (dual-use technology policy). Dr. Flamm's research at Brookings has centered on international competition in high-technology industries. He is now finishing an analytical study of the post–Cold War defense industrial base.

Eugene Gholz teaches at George Mason University's Institute of Public Policy. He recently completed a fellowship at Harvard University's Olin Institute for Strategic Studies. He wrote his dissertation "Getting Subsidies Right: Government Support to High-Technology Industry," while at MIT. His current research concerns business-government relations in the defense industry, trade and regulation in the aerospace industry, and American foreign policy.

David Gold is a Senior Economic Affairs Officer at the United Nations Department of Economic and Social Affairs. Previously, he worked at the United Nations Centre on Transnational Corporations and the Council on Economic Priorities, and taught at Columbia University, the University of California, and the New School for Social Research. He has contributed to major United Nations reports, including the *World Economic and Social Survey* and the *World Investment Report* and has written on the economics of military spending, transnational corporations, and foreign direct investment for professional journals and newspapers and magazines.

John Lovering is a Professor of Urban Development and Governance, since 1995, in the Department of City and Regional Planning at the University of Cardiff in Wales. Previously, Dr. Lovering was a Professor of Geography at the University of Hull and a Senior Research Fellow at the University of Bristol School for Advanced Urban Studies. For the past ten years, Dr. Lovering's research has focused on the defense industry and regional development. His recent publications include "Opening Pandora's Box: De Facto Industrial Policy and the British Defence Industry" in *Manufacturing in Transition*, edited by R. Delbridge and J. Lowe (1998), "The New Regionalism" in *International Journal of Urban and Regional Studies 1999* (forthcoming), and a book on the defense industry titled *The Means of Destruction* (forthcoming).

Lora Lumpe is a Senior Research Fellow at the Peace Research Institute of Oslo, where she researches the global proliferation of infantry weapons. She founded, and for seven years directed, the Federation of American Scientists' Arms Sales Monitoring Project, which aims to promote restraint in U.S. and global conventional arms production and trade. Ms. Lumpe has authored articles on arms proliferation in *Scientific American, Bulletin of Atomic Scientists, Arms Control Today, Arms Control*, and numerous book chapters, reports, and op-eds. She recently published *The Arms Trade Revealed: A Guide for Investigators and Activists*.

Ann R. Markusen is a Senior Fellow for Industrial Policy at the Council on Foreign Relations. Dr. Markusen also serves as Director of the Project on Regional and Industrial Economics and State of New Jersey Professor of Urban Planning and Policy Development at Rutgers University. She has served as a Brookings Institution Economic Policy Fellow and a Fulbright in Brazil. Her present research is on the impact of military spending on American technology, industry, economic, and foreign policy, and a comparative study of post–Cold War defense downsizing among significant Cold War protagonists. She is co-author of *Dismantling the Cold War Economy* (1992), and *The Rise of the Gunbelt* (1991).

Michael Oden is an Assistant Professor in the Community and Regional Planning program of the University of Texas at Austin. He was formerly a Visiting Professor and Research Fellow at Rutgers University, and has worked for the State of Michigan and the Organization for Economic Cooperation and Development. Dr. Oden's research centers on industry and regional adjustment to defense downsizing, the development of high-technology regions, and evaluation of economic development policies. His recent publications on post–Cold War economic adjustment and local development policy include, *Coming in from the Cold: Arms Industry Restructuring and Economic Conversion Policies in the United States, 1989–1993*, for the International Labor Office; "Austin Sui Generis" in the *Texas Business Review*; and "Distinguishing Development Incentives from Developer Give-Aways," *Policy Studies Journal* (forthcoming).

Erik Pages serves as Vice President for Policy and Programs at Business Executives for National Security (BENS). He previously served as Director of the Office of Economic Conversion Information at the U.S. Department of Commerce. He has also served as Legislative Director for Representative Gus Yatron (D-Pa.), and as an official adviser to the White House Conference on Small Business. He is an Adjunct Professor in the National Security Studies Program at Georgetown University.

Judith Reppy is a Professor in the department of Science and Technology Studies and Associate Director of the Peace Studies Program at Cornell University. She serves as cochair of U.S. Pugwash and is a member of the Council on Foreign Relations, Committee on International Security Studies of the American Academy of Arts and Sciences, and the Advisory Board of Women in International Security (WIIS). Dr. Reppy is the author of *The R&D Program of the Department of Defense* (1976), a coeditor and contributing author of *The Genesis of New Weapons: Decision Making for Military R&D* (1980, with F.A. Long), *The Relations Between Defence and Civil Technologies* (1988, with Philip Gummett), and *Beyond Zero Tolerance: Discrimination in Military Culture* (1999, with Mary F. Katzenstein), as well as numerous articles and contributed chapters.

Harvey M. Sapolsky is Professor of Public Policy and Organization at the Massachusetts Institute of Technology, where he directs the Security Studies Program. Dr. Sapolsky studies bureaucratic and programmatic success in government, the role of science in policymaking, and patterns of competition and innovation in both public and private organizations. Specifically in defense, Dr. Sapolsky has studied interservice rivalry, weapons acquisition, nonlethal warfare, and university-based research.

Jay Stowsky is Associate Dean for School Affairs and Initiatives at the Haas School of Business and a Senior Research Fellow with the Berkeley Roundtable on the International Economy (BRIE), both at the University of California at Berkeley. He was formerly Director of Research Policy for the nine-campus University of California system. From 1993–1995, Dr. Stowsky served as Senior Economist for Science and Technology on the staff of President Clinton's White House Council of Economic Advisers (CEA); he also served for three months as the CEA's acting Chief of Staff. Dr. Stowsky has published several pieces on U.S. technology policy, including "Technology and Economic Growth," in *Investing in Innovation* (1998), and is co-author, with Wayne Sandholtz, John Zysman, et al., of *The Highest Stakes: The Economic Foundations of the Next Security System* (1992).

Paul Walker is Director of the Legacy Program of Global Green USA, an effort focusing on the remediation of military toxic waste and other legacies of the Cold War. Dr. Walker was formerly a Professional Staff Member of the Armed Services Committee in the United States House of Representatives, where he served as senior adviser to the chairman and full committee. Dr. Walker has lectured widely, both in the United States and abroad, and has published numerous books, articles, and op-eds on military and foreign policy. He is coauthor of *The Price of Defense:*

A New Strategy for Military Spending (1979); *The Nuclear Almanac: Confronting the Atom in War and Peace* (1984); and *Post-Reagan America* (1987).

Peter Wilke is the managing director of ISA Consult, a consultant company. He was a former researcher at the Institute for Peace Research and Security Policy in Hamburg and the Institute of Political Science at the University of Hamburg. In 1995, Dr. Wilke served as a guest researcher at the Monterey Institute of International Studies in California. Dr. Wilke's research focuses on the areas of defense conversion, regional policy, and labor market policy.

Herbert Wulf is the Director of the Bonn International Center for Conversion (BICC) and served as consultant to the U.N. Center for Disarmament Affairs and the Human Development Report of UNDP. Dr. Wulf was Deputy Director of the Institute for Development and Peace at the University of Duisburg, and Senior Researcher at the Stockholm International Peace Research Institute (SIPRI) and at the University of Hamburg. Dr. Wulf has published several books on arms trade, arms industry conversion, and development theory.

Index

A

Advanced Research Projects Agency
 (ARPA), 126–31, 135, 137–38,
 142, 144–45, 150, 153
Advanced Technology Program
 (ATP), 117–18, 126, 132, 135,
 153, 156
Aerospace Corporation, 64
Aerospace Industries Association, 125
Aérospatiale, 9, 317, 325, 358, 379,
 390; general sales data for, 403;
 and mergers, 347; ranked by value
 of defense sales, 365
Afghanistan, 171, 296
Africa, 252. *See also* South Africa
AIDS, 121
Airbus, 379
Air Force (United States), 173, 197,
 232
Alenia Difesa, 351, 353, 360, 363
Alliant Technosystems, 213
Allied Signal, 88–89, 146
Allison, 317
American Electronics Association
 (AEA), 118–19, 125
American League for Exports and
 Security Assistance (ALESA), 173
Anderson, Stanton, 119
Andrews, Tom, 174
Antiballistic Missile Defense (ABM)
 Treaty, 53–54, 167, 170
Argentina, 379
Argonne Laboratory, 61
Armed Services Committee, 19,
 158–59, 163, 168, 171–78, 182–83
Arms Export Control Act, 270
Arms Trade Register (United Nations),
 175
Armstrong, Michael, 94

Artificial Intelligence (AI), 114, 136,
 142
Aspin, Les, 158–62, 165–67, 173, 184
Atlantic Alliance, 325
Atomic Energy Defense Activities
 (AEDA), 64–65
Augustine, Norm, 87
Australia, 260
Austria, 341, 375, 378

B

BAe, 341–42, 344, 348, 361, 363–65
Bangemann, Martin, 359, 387–88
Base Force Review, 57
Base Realignment and Closure
 Commission (BRAC), 62–63, 162
Bath Iron Works, 180, 194
Battle Act, 270
BDM, 414
Belgium, 336–41, 358, 361; and
 civil-military production mixes,
 374–75, 378, 398; employment
 data for, 378; export of newly
 produced major weapons by, 375;
 general defense spending data for,
 338–39, 352; and globalization,
 317; heavy equipment expenditures
 for, 374; imports to, as a percent of
 total defense spending, 352
Berlin Wall, 26, 121, 208
Bingaman, Jeff, 122, 125
Blair, Tony, 346
Board on Arms Proliferation Policy,
 5
Boeing, 146, 252; contract awards
 data for, 7–9; and diversification,
 89; and mergers, 207, 217, 252,
 254, 308; and restructuring, 87;
 and tactical missiles, 239–40

Bonn International Center for
    Conversion (BICC), 307
Bosnia, 164, 171, 346
Bottom-Up Review (BUR), 19,
    39–43, 51–53, 57; Flamm on, 235;
    Oden on, 76, 78–79, 84, 101,
    101–2; Walker on, 160–67
Brazil, 318, 326
Britain, 9, 12, 25–27, 285, 334–62;
    arms exports data for, 10; and
    civil-military production mixes,
    371, 374–75, 380, 384, 387, 391;
    and cooperation on security strat-
    egy, 25–26; and dual-use technol-
    ogy, 272; and globalization, 311,
    315, 318, 323–25; and Thatcher,
    26, 342–43, 416
British Aerospace, 9, 258, 315,
    317–18, 416; and civil-military
    production mixes, 387, 390, 391;
    and the European defense industry,
    334, 339, 344–45, 348, 350, 354,
    357, 359, 361–62, 387, 390–91;
    sales data for, 404
Brookhaven Laboratory, 61
Brookings Institution, 15, 41–43, 102
Brown, Ron, 119
BTR, 394
Buck Inpar Pinnow, 393
Bulgaria, 257
Bureau of Labor Data, 209
Bush, George, 4, 78; business support
    for, 111; defense cuts under, 28; and
    domestic discretionary spending,
    121; and two-theater military
    strategy, 15. *See also* Bush admin-
    istration
Bush administration, 4, 7, 409; and
    arms trade economics, 255, 287;
    budgets under, 28, 38–41, 160;
    and dual-use technology, 117–18,
    120–23; and security doctrines,
    38–42. *See also* Bush, George
Business Executives for National
    Security (BENS), 115
Business Week, 151

Butler, General Lee, 181
Buyer, Steve, 164

C

CALSTART consortium, 146
Canada, 316, 317, 374–75
Carlyle Group, 83
Carroll, Eugene, 163
Carter, Ashton, 168, 170
Carter, Jimmy, 208, 255; budgets
    under, 160; Conventional Arms
    Talks initiated by, 175; and dual-
    use policy, 110–11, 114, 122–23;
    stagflation under, 110
Center for Defense Information
    (CDI), 163
Center for Naval Analyses, 244
Central Intelligence Agency (CIA),
    179, 212, 288
Cheney, Richard, 39–40, 121, 212
China, 9, 12–13, 28, 251, 256–57;
    arm shipments from, value of, 286;
    danger of renewed conflict with,
    78; defense employment reduction
    in, 13; and deterrence strategy, 76;
    and dual-use technology, 270; and
    the European defense industry,
    341; and globalization, 311, 320;
    sale of missile technology to, 171;
    and Taiwan, 4
Chirac, Jacques, 27, 346, 364, 375
Chrysler Corporation, 110, 350
Civil War, 74, 144
Cleveland, Glover, 111
Clinton, Bill, 15–16, 28, 30, 128–34,
    409; education and training initia-
    tives of, 134; governing coalition of,
    106–8, 124; and military deploy-
    ments, 183; and nuclear weapons
    laboratories, 62, 65–66; Presidential
    Advisory Board on Arms Prolifera-
    tion Policy initiated by, 5, 255,
    291, 295–96; Presidential Directive
    on Conventional Arms Transfer
    Policy (PDD-34) initiated by, 231,

254–55; and R&D recoupment
fees, 261; reelection of, 151; and
the sale of fighter jets to Taiwan, 4.
See also Clinton administration
Clinton administration, 7, 18–19,
78–79, 271–72, 276–77; and arms
trade economics, 252, 254–55,
261, 287–88, 291–93; budgets
under, 28, 37–40, 42–43, 158,
208; and dual-use technology,
106–8, 123–35, 137–38, 140–41,
144, 149, 151–57; and the European defense industry, 354; and
mergers, 208, 213; and the private-
arsenal problem, 196; and the redefinition of national defense, 158,
170, 183–84; and the redesign of
the defense industrial base, 225,
231, 235; and security doctrines,
37, 38–43, 46–47, 54, 61–62; and
two-theater military strategy, 15.
See also Clinton, Bill
Clipper Chip, 152
Coalition Force Enhancement
Program, 172
Code of Conduct on Arms Transfers
Act, 294
Coffman, Vance, 416
Cohen, William, 4, 180, 421
Commerce Department, 117, 153,
175, 255, 261; Advanced Technol-
ogy Program, 151; expanded role
of, 127, 132; study of weapons
export agreements by, 257
Commodity Control List, 271
Comprehensive Test Ban (CTB), 418
Computer Professionals for Social
Responsibility, 115
Computer Sciences Corporation, 87,
89, 95, 97
Computer Systems Policy Project,
125
Congressional Budget Office, 52
Congressional Research Service
(CRS), 39
Conventional Arms Talk (CAT), 175

Convention on Conventional
Weapons, 295
Coolidge, Calvin, 111
Coordinating Committee for Multi-
lateral Export Controls
(COCOM), 24, 171, 270–72
Costello, Robert B., 117–18
Council of Economic Advisors, 144
Council of Europe, 355
Council on Competitiveness, 125
Council on Foreign Relations Study
Group on Defense Consolidation,
Downsizing, and Conversion in the
U.S. Military Industrial Base, 13
Cuban Missile Crisis, 52–53
Cunningham, Randy, 164
Curtiss-Wright, 195, 209

D

Daimler-Benz Aerospace, 9, 339,
345, 348–50, 353, 358, 363; and
civil-military production mixes,
379, 385, 403; general sales data
for, 403; ranked by value of defense sales, 353
DASA, 325, 341, 350, 358, 364; and
civil-military production mixes,
385, 390; and Eurocopter, 317;
purchase of Fokker by, 318
Dassault, 317, 379, 403–5; and
mergers, 335, 347, 358, 361; general sales data for, 403–4; ranked
by value of defense sales, 353
Davis, Lynn, 293
Defense Advanced Research Projects
Agency (DARPA), 109, 115–18,
120, 122–24, 126, 150–51, 215.
See also ARPA
Defense Authorization bill, 175–76,
182
Defense Budget Project (DBP), 163
Defense Diversification Agency
(DDA), 345
Defense Evaluation and Research
Agency (DERA), 346

Defense Export Services Organisation (DESO), 343
Defense News, 86
Defense Science and Technology Strategy, 51–52
Defense Science Board (DSB), 116–17, 213, 415
Defense Technology Conversion Council, 135, 150
Defense Technology Plan, 51
Dellums, Ronald V., 158–59, 162–71, 173, 175, 177
Denmark, 338–39; employment data for, 378; exports of newly produced major weapons by, 375; heavy equipment expenditures of, 374; imports to, as a percent of total defense spending, 352
Desert Shield, 42. *See also* Gulf War
Desert Storm, 39, 42, 241. *See also* Gulf War
Deutch, John, 131, 169, 212
Developing Defense Industry (DDI) countries, 352
Direct-TV, 91, 94
Direction des Constructions Navales, 9
Discriminate Deterrence, 50–51
Dornan, Robert, 164
Dowdy, John, 16
Dynamic random access memories (DRAMs), 142

E

Economist, The, 347, 357
Egypt, 12, 320, 379
Eisenhower, Dwight D., 6
Electroluminescent (EL) panels, 142
Electronics Industry Association of Japan (EIAJ), 119
Elrod, Marilyn, 167
Energy Department, 60–62, 135, 177
Engesa, 326
Environmental Protection Agency (EPA), 149

E-Systems, 8–9, 83, 308
Eurocopter, 317, 353, 402
Eurocorps, 347, 356–57
European Airbus, 131
European Armaments Agency, 356
European Armaments Group, 227
European Coal and Steel Community, 335, 260
European Commission, 336, 340, 353–54, 358, 363
European Common Market, 371
European Cooperation for the Long Term in Defence (EUCLID) program, 356
European Defense Aerospace Company (EuroCo), 363
European Economic Community, 336
European Parliament, 27, 355, 372
European Regional Development Fund (ERDF), 389
European Union, 3, 25–27; and civil-military production mixes, 382, 383–88; development of, 352–55; and the European defense industry, 336, 342, 352–55, 364–66; Intergovernmental Conference (IGC), 355; KONVER program, 27, 340, 372, 386–89; and the Maastricht Treaty, 252, 349, 354–55
Evans, Lane, 174
Export Control Act, 271
Export Administration Regulations (EAR), 271

F

Fairchild, 195
Federal Acquisitions Regulations (FAR), 219
Federally Funded Research and Development Facilities (FFRDCs), 60, 63–64
Federal Trade Commission (FTC), 213
Feingold, Russell, 258
Feldman, Jonathan, 99

Ferranti Signal, 317, 391, 394, 405
FIAT, 335, 404
Fields, Craig, 118, 120–22, 126
Financial Times, 356
Finland, 341, 378
Finnmeccanica, 9, 351, 387, 391
Fish, Howard M., 173
FMC Corporation, 88, 93, 95, 97, 209
FN Herstal, 317
Fokker, 317, 350
Ford Motor Corporation, 82
Forsberg, Randall, 15, 45–47
Forsberg proposal, 15, 40, 45–47, 54–56, 59, 70–71
Fowler, Tillie, 164
France, 9–13, 25–26, 174, 416; and arms trade economics, 252, 261, 263, 285; and civil-military production mixes, 373–79, 384, 386, 390, 394; defense spending data for, 338–39; employment data for, 378; and the European defense industry, 334–59, 362, 365; and the excess capacity problem, 27; exports from, 10, 25, 227, 286, 375; and globalization, 311, 315, 317, 320, 323, 325; heavy equipment expenditures of, 374; imports to, as a percent of total defense spending, 352
Freeman, Roger, 356
Furse, Elizabeth, 174
Future Years Defense Program (FYDP), 58, 161, 165, 243–44

G

Galvin Commission, 65
Gansler, Jacques, 4
Gaulle, Charles de, 346, 377
Gazelle Microcircuits, 121
GEC, 4, 9, 344, 351, 353, 360–64; and civil-military production mixes, 390; ranked by value of defense sales, 353

General Accounting Office (GAO), 28, 81, 165
General Agreement on Tariffs and Trade (GATT), 131–33
General Dynamics, 81, 163, 193–95, 202, 258; contract awards data for, 8–9; and diversification, 92, 95, 97; and mergers, 82–83, 207; and restructuring, 16, 86, 88; and tactical missiles, 243
General Electric, 9, 82, 86–87, 195, 207
General Motors, 94, 117, 130, 146, 207
Germany, 9, 12–13, 25–27, 272, 416; and civil-military production mixes, 371–76, 384–94, 398; employment data for, 378; and the European defense industry, 334–50, 352, 358, 361, 371–76, 384–94, 398; exports from, 227, 286, 375; general defense spending data for, 338–39; and globalization, 323; heavy equipment expenditures for, 374; imports to, as a percent of total defense spending, 352; post–Cold War reconstruction in, 108; reunification of, 349
GIAT, 317, 386, 391, 393; general sales data for, 403; ranked by value of defense sales, 353
Gingrich, Newt, 175
GKN-Westlands, 359
Glenn, John, 179
Global Positioning Satellite (GPS) system, 269, 276
Government-Owned Contractor-Operated (GOCO) program, 260
Gore, Albert, Jr., 114, 123, 125, 137
Gramm, Phil, 121
Great Society programs, 111
Greece, 292, 336–39, 341, 351–52; employment data for, 378; exports of newly produced major weapons by, 375; general defense spending data for, 338–39; and globalization, 316; heavy equipment expen-

ditures of, 374; imports to, as a percent of total defense spending, 352

Gross domestic product (GDP), 337, 344

Grumman, 8–9, 16, 88–90; and diversification, 89, 90, 93; and mergers, 82, 207, 209, 308, 421

GTE, 86, 88–89

Gulf War, 39, 51, 78, 182, 285; and arms trade economics, 251, 259, 263; and the Bottom-Up Review, 162; and the European defense industry, 348; export regulations during, 358; short-lived optimism after, 122; and tactical missiles, 241; and two-theater military strategy, 15; use of bombers during, 288; use of fuel air explosives during, 296

H

Haiti, 171, 182
Hamre, John, 165
Harman, Jane, 164, 171
Harsco, 209
Hawker Siddely, 394
High-definition television (HDTV), 116–21, 140, 259
Hollandse Signaalapparat, 318, 320
Hollings, Ernest, 117
Honeywell, 88
House Armed Services Committee, 19, 158–59, 163, 168, 171–78, 182–83
House National Security Committee Defense Authorization Bill Report, 64
Hughes, 16, 81, 174, 252; and diversification, 91–95, 97, 98; and dual-use policy, 130, 146; and mergers, 82–83, 308; and restructuring, 88; and tactical missiles, 240, 242, 243
Hungary, 337
Hussein, Saddam, 122

I

Idaho National Laboratory, 61
Independent European Programme Group (IEPG), 356–57
Independent Research and Development (IR&D) program, 260
India, 379
Indonesia, 316
Indra, 318
Industrial College of the Armed Forces, 237
Institute for Defense Analysis (IDA), 237
Institute of Defense and Disarmament Studies, 15, 45
Interagency Review of Federal Laboratories, 62
International Business Machines (IBM), 82, 93
International Institute for Strategic Studies, 226, 228
International Monetary Fund (IMF), 28, 252
International Trade in Arms Regulations (ITAR), 271
Iran, 272, 293
Iraq, 51, 251, 263, 419; and dual-use technology, 171, 279; status of, as a rogue regime, 293; U.S. air strikes in (1996), 346. *See also* Gulf War
Ireland, 352
Israel, 256–57, 307, 316, 326
Italy, 336, 340–41, 351–52, 360; arm shipments from, value of, 286; and civil-military production mixes, 374–75, 378, 384, 391, 393–94, 398; employment data for, 378; exports of newly produced major weapons by, 375; general defense spending data for, 338–39; and globalization, 318; heavy equipment expenditures of, 374; imports to, as a percent of total defense spending, 352
ITT Industries, 9, 86, 87, 89

J

Jackson, Andrew, 160
Japan, 226–27, 251, 256, 260, 263;
  and Air Force computer technology, 232; and dual-use policy,
  118–21, 123, 131, 140–41, 270,
  272; and the European defense industry, 353; and globalization,
  315; and high-definition television,
  118–21, 140–41; Ministry of International Trade and Industry
  (MITI), 118, 123, 227; and World
  War II, 199
Jefferson, Thomas, 160
Jones, Anita, 63

K

Kaminski, Paul, 415
Kasich, John, 171, 174
Kaufmann, William, 15, 41–42, 102
Kelley, Maryellen, 275, 278
Kennedy, John F., 52
Key Technologies Plan for 1992, 51
Keynesian macroeconomics, 110
Kohl, Helmut, 347, 349, 385
KONVER program, 27, 340, 372,
  386–89
Korb, Lawrence, 102
Korea. *See also* Korean War; North
  Korea; South Korea
Korean War, 192, 208
Kovacic, William E., 217
Krauss-Maffei, 379, 392
Krupp, Alfried, 335, 360
Kurds, 294
Kurth, James, 21, 194

L

Labor Department, 128, 153
Lagardere Group, 9
Lake, Anthony, 168
Latin America, 24, 252, 418
Lawrence-Berkeley Laboratory, 61

Lawrence Livermore Laboratory, 61
Lean Aircraft Initiative, 197
Libya, 293
Lincoln, Abraham, 160
Lincoln Laboratory, 61, 64
Litton Industries, 9, 83, 88, 93, 95,
  97
Lockheed Martin, 8–9, 174, 252,
  258, 416; and diversification,
  95–97; and dual-use policy, 146;
  and the European defense industry,
  345; F-22 contract secured by, 59,
  102; lobbying of Congress by, 288;
  and mergers, 4, 82–83, 207, 217,
  421; and the private-arsenal problem, 193–94; and restructuring,
  16, 86–89; and tactical missiles,
  239–40; and welfare systems, 20
Logistics Management Institute, 237
Loral, 82, 193; contract awards data
  for, 8–9; and diversification, 93,
  95–97; and mergers, 82–83; and
  restructuring, 86–89; and tactical
  missiles, 240, 242
Los Alamos Laboratory, 61
LTV, 4, 82
Luxembourg, 338–39, 352, 374–75

M

Maastricht Treaty, 252, 349, 354–55
McDonnell Douglas, 287, 361, 419;
  contract awards data for, 8–9; and
  diversification, 88–90, 95, 97; and
  globalization, 315; and mergers,
  207, 252, 254, 308; and restructuring, 86–87; shedding of labor
  and capital assets by, 80; and
  tactical missiles, 239–40, 244
McHale, Paul, 164, 174
McKinney, Cynthia, 294–95
McNamara, Robert, 409
Major, John, 343
Major Regional Conflicts (MRCs),
  164
Manatt, Charles, 119

Manufacturing Extension Partnership (MEP), 144
Marathon Oil, 111
Marine Corps (United States), 47, 166–67, 217, 362
Marshall Aid, 335
Martin Marietta, 193, 195; contract awards data for, 8–9; and diversification, 89; and globalization, 308; and mergers, 82–83, 207, 308, 421; and restructuring, 86–89; and tactical missiles, 240, 242
Massachusetts Institute of Technology (MIT), 44, 61, 275
Matra Marconi Space, 317–18, 320; and civil-military production mixes, 390, 394, 405; general sales data for, 405; ranked by value of defense sales, 353
Messerschmidt, 335
Microelectronics and Computer Consortium (MCC), 118
Middle East, 23–24, 174, 251–52, 262, 287; and the European defense industry, 361; peace process, 293. See also specific countries
Ministry of International Trade and Industry (MITI), 118, 123, 227
Minnich, Richard, 17
Missile Technology Control Regime (MTCR), 296
MITRE Corporation, 61, 63–64
Mitsubishi Heavy Industries, 9
Morrison, Philip, 44–45
Mosbacher, Robert, 117, 119, 120

N

National Academy of Sciences, 52, 53
National Aeronautics and Space Administration (NASA), 62–63, 135, 149
National Association of Manufacturers, 125
National Center for Manufacturing Sciences (NCMS), 118
National Defense University, 237

National Economic Council (NEC), 126, 132, 144
National Flat Panel Display Initiative, 140, 144
National Guard, 193
National Ignition Facility (NIF), 181
National Institute of Standards and Technology (NIST), 117–18, 126–27, 135, 144, 153
National Renewable Energy Laboratory, 61
National Science and Technology Council (NSTC), 126–27
National Steel and Shipbuilding Company, 194
Netherlands, 324–25, 341, 398; and civil-military production mixes, 374–78, 380; employment data for, 378; and the European defense industry, 374–78, 380, 398; exports of newly produced major weapons by, 375; general defense spending data for, 338–39; heavy equipment expenditures of, 374; imports to, as a percent of total defense spending, 352
Neustadt, Richard, 160
Nevada Nuclear Test Site, 65
New Deal, 112–13, 160
New Forum, 279
New Zealand, 260
Nixon, Richard, 119, 254
Nixon Doctrine, 254
North American Free Trade Agreement (NAFTA), 133
North Atlantic Treaty Organization (NATO), 43, 161, 226–28, 234; and arms trade economics, 250, 252, 260, 262; and civil-military production mixes, 373–75, 383, 397; and dual-use technology, 270–272; enlargement of, 184; and the European defense industry, 342, 347–57, 373–75, 383, 397; and globalization, 307, 315, 321, 325–26; possible supersession of, 420; procurement, distribution of

(1994), 226; R&D spending, 227–28; and Turkish-Greek relations, 292; and the WEU, 416

North Korea, 257, 291, 293

Northrop Grumman, 4, 85–87, 193, 209; contract awards data for, 8–9; and diversification, 93, 95, 97; and mergers, 82–83, 308, 421; and restructuring, 86, 87; and tactical missiles, 240

Norway, 174, 337–41; and civil-military production mixes, 374–75, 378; employment data for, 378; exports of newly produced major weapons by, 375; heavy equipment expenditures of, 374

Nuclear Energy Panel, 165

Nuclear Non-Proliferation Act, 271

Nuclear Non-Proliferation Treaty (NPT), 54, 65–66, 181, 271, 418

Nuclear Posture Review (NPR), 19, 53, 167–71, 181

Nunn, Sam, 161, 180, 315

O

Oak Ridge Laboratory, 61

Office of Economic Security, 422

Office of Science and Technology, 132, 144

Office of Technology Assessment (OTA), 67, 125, 219–20

Office of the Special Trade Representative (OSTR), 117

O'Hanlon, Michael, 42–43

O'Hanlon proposal, 40–44, 54–56, 59–60, 66, 70

Olin Corporation, 213

Operation Restore Jobs, 128

Operations and Maintenance (O&M) spending, 101

Organization for Economic Cooperation and Development (OECD), 393

P

Pacific Northwest Laboratory, 61

Pakistan, 320

Payment of Restructuring Costs under Defense Contracts (Department of Defense), 84

Perle, Richard, 271

Perot, H. Ross, 123–24

Perry, William, 4, 126, 137, 169, 413; on the Bottom-Up Review, 164; changeover from, to Cohen, 421; and mergers, 212, 214, 218

Persian Gulf War. *See* Gulf War.

Phillips, 339

Pitofsky, Robert, 213

Plessey, 335

Porsche, 379

Portugal, 336–39, 365, 374–75, 378 79; employment data for, 378; exports of newly produced major weapons by, 375; heavy equipment expenditures of, 374; imports to, as a percent of total defense spending, 352

Prabhakar, Arati, 126

Presidential Advisory Board on Arms Proliferation Policy, 5, 255, 291, 295–96

Presidential Directive on Conventional Arms Transfer Policy (PDD-34), 231, 254–55

President's Commission on Industrial Competitiveness, 116

Price, Don K., 192

Program on Regional and Industrial Economics (PRIE), 99, 101, 275, 276

Q

Quadrennial Defense Review (QDR), 15, 183–84, 235, 292

Quayle, Dan, 120

R

RAND Corporation, 61, 99, 232, 235–37

Raytheon, 7–9, 174, 416; and diversification, 90; and mergers, 83, 207, 308; and restructuring, 88; and tactical missiles, 240, 242

Reagan, Ronald, 160, 167, 208, 255; defense buildup under, 158, 192, 196–97, 200, 208; and dual-use policy, 111–17, 123–24

Regional Technology Alliances Assistance program, 143–45

Reich, Robert, 132, 134

Robertson, George, 345

Rockwell International, 16, 195; contract awards data for, 8–9; and diversification, 91, 102; and globalization, 315; and mergers, 207, 209; and tactical missiles, 239–40, 242

Roles and Missions Commission, 43

Rolls-Royce, 317, 358, 361–62, 404; and civil-military production mixes, 376–77, 390; ranked by value of defense sales, 353

Roosevelt, Franklin D., 160

Royal-Dutch Shell, 364

Russia, 4, 28, 196; arm shipments from, value of, 286; and arms trade economics, 250–51, 254–57, 264, 285–87, 289; danger of renewed conflict with, 78; and dual-use technology, 272, 280; and globalization, 306, 328; and the redefinition of national defense, 158–59, 169, 178, 180–81. *See also* Soviet Union; START treaties

Rutgers University, 275

Rwanda, 346

S

Samuels, Richard, 76

Sandia Laboratory, 61

Saudi Arabia, 251, 287–88, 293–94

Schenk, Lynn, 202

Scherer, F. M., 229

Schroeder, Pat, 159, 176

Semiconductor Equipment Manufacturing and Technology Consortium (SEMATECH), 117–18

Senate Armed Services Subcommittee on Defense Industry and Technology, 122

Senate Commerce Committee, 119

Siemens, 318, 403

Silicon Valley, 144

Singapore, 316

Sisky, Norman, 166

Sitenbrunger, 102

Skaggs, James, 214

Skelton, Ike, 164

Small Business Innovation Research (SBIR), 130–31

Smallwood, Dennis E., 217

Smith, Harold, 169

SNECMA, 346–47, 404

Somalia, 171

South Africa, 320, 361. *See also* Africa

South Korea, 256, 263, 289, 291, 326, 328; and dual-use policy, 119, 141–43; economic data for, 200; and globalization, 316, 318

Soviet Union, 9, 12–13, 26, 161, 250–51, 296; and civil-military production mixes, 371, 376, 398; collapse of, 38, 50, 102, 195, 285, 371; conflict with Afghanistan, 296; and the Cuban Missile Crisis, 52–53; and deterrence doctrine, 50–53, 76; and dual-use technology, 272, 276, 279; and the European defense industry, 337, 341, 371, 376, 398; and globalization, 307; and security doctrines, 47–48. *See also* Russia; START treaties

Spain, 316, 318, 374–79, 393, 398; employment data for, 378; and the European defense industry, 336, 338–39, 341, 352; exports of newly produced major weapons by, 375; general defense spending data for, 338–39; heavy equipment expenditures of, 374; imports to, as a percent of total defense spending, 352

Spense, Floyd, 159, 174
Spratt, John, 165
Spreewerke Luebben, 393
Sprey, Pierre, 163
Standard Industrial Classification (SIC) groups, 99
START treaties, 39, 43, 52–54, 65, 168–69, 181
State Department, 132, 255, 261, 294, 335
Steinbruner, John, 15, 41–42
Stockpile Stewardship plan, 65
Strategic Computing Program (SCP), 114, 136, 142, 148
Strategic Defense Initiative (SDI), 114–15, 161, 165
Strauss, Franz Joseph, 349
Strauss, Robert, 119
Study Group on Defense Consolidation, Downsizing, and Conversion in the U.S. Military Industrial Base (Council on Foreign Relations), 13
Sununu, John, 120
Sweden, 341, 376, 378, 380, 394
Switzerland, 174, 378, 391, 393

T

Taiwan, 256, 307, 320; and the European defense industry, 353; and high-definition television, 119; sale of fighter jets to, 4, 316, 318, 320
Taylor, Gene, 164, 166
Technology Reinvestment Program (TRP), 16–17, 140, 150–51, 272, 276; and battles over agendas and perceptions, 128; and defense conversion versus civil-military integration, 129; and diversification, 91, 94–95, 97, 98, 101; and mergers, 215; Regional Technology Alliances Assistance program, 143–45; Stowsky on, 106–10, 122, 128–57; and technology policy versus trade policy, 131–33
Teledyne, 83

Tenneco, 9, 87
Texas Instruments, 8–9, 16; and diversification, 94, 95, 97, 98, 102; and mergers, 308; and restructuring, 87, 89; and tactical missiles, 240, 242
Textron, 82, 88–89, 94, 362
Thatcher, Margaret, 26, 342–43, 416
Thomson-CSF, 4, 9, 317–18, 320, 325; and civil-military production mixes, 390, 393, 403; and the European defense industry, 339, 341, 347, 358, 390, 393, 403; general sales data for, 403; and globalization, 317–18; and privatization, 347, 358; ranked by value of defense sales, 353; as a specialist in systems integration, 341
Thorn EMI, 391, 394
Torkildsen, Peter, 164
Tracor, 4, 214
Transportation Department, 135, 149
Treasury Department, 132
TRW, 9, 16; and diversification, 91, 94–95, 97, 98, 102; and restructuring, 87, 89
Tsipis, Kosta, 44–45
Tsongas, Paul, 122, 124
Turkey, 292, 294, 328, 351–52; defense spending data for, 337–39; employment data for, 378; exports of newly produced major weapons by, 375; heavy equipment expenditures of, 374
Tyson, Laura, 132

U

Unilever, 363
Unisys, 83, 88
United Arab Emirates, 386
United Defense, 209
United Kingdom, 218, 252, 256–57, 258; arm shipments from, value of, 286; and civil military production mixes, 374–75, 378, 387, 390,

394, 398; employment data for, 378; and the European defense industry, 336–41, 343–46, 352, 357, 360–61, 374–75, 378, 387, 390, 394, 398; exports of newly produced major weapons by, 375; general defense spending data for, 338–39; and globalization, 325; heavy equipment expenditures of, 374. *See also* specific countries
United Nations, 43, 175; embargos, 293; Register of Conventional Arms, 292, 294; Security Council, 46, 293; and security proposals, 45–46, 56. *See also* Britain
United Technologies, 9, 93, 207
U.S. Arms Control and Disarmament Agency, 309
U.S. Steel, 111

V

Van Ekerlen, William, 355
Very High Speed Integrated Circuit (VHSIC) program, 114, 136, 148
Vickers, 335, 380
Vietnam War, 154, 159, 192, 200, 209, 296
Vitek, 90
Volkswagen, 389
Vosper Thornycroft, 380

W

Warner, Edward L., 163–64
Warsaw Pact, 78, 158–59, 161, 311

Warsaw Treaty Organization, 272
Washington, George, 160
Wassenaar Arrangement, 42, 272, 279–80, 418–19
Watertown Arsenal, 192
Watkins, Todd, 275, 278
Weber, Max, 353
Weir, Gary, 199
Western European Armaments Group (WEAG), 355–58, 362, 383
Western European Union (WEU), 25, 355–57, 364, 416
Westinghouse, 8–9, 83, 87, 128, 209
Westland Helicopter Company, 318
Wiesner, Jerome, 44–45, 52
Wisener Proposal, 40, 44–45, 52
World Bank, 28, 252
World Court, 181
World Policy Institute, 261
World Trade Organization (WTO), 250, 421
World War I, 74, 199
World War II, 28, 74, 163, 335, 351; and the British defense industry, 380; defense budgets during, 200, 208–9; the European defense industry after, 335–36; fleet boats of, 199; the Italian defense industry since, 351; and the private-arsenal problem, 191–92, 199

Z

Zenith, 119